Oahu Revealed

The Ultimate Guide to Honolulu, Waikiki & Beyond

Andrew Doughty & Harriett Friedman

WIZARD
PUBLICATIONS
INC

Oahu Revealed
The Ultimate Guide to Honolulu, Waikiki & Beyond

Published by Wizard Publications, Inc.
Post Office Box 991
Lihu'e, Hawai'i 96766–0991

ISBN 0–9717279–2–9   2094
Library of Congress Control Number 2004092191
Printed in China

Cataloging-in-Publication Data
Doughty, Andrew
    Oahu revealed : the ultimate guide to Honolulu, Waikiki and beyond / Andrew
Doughty and Harriett Friedman. – 1st ed. Lihue, HI : Wizard Publications, Inc., 2005
    302 p. : col. illus., col. photos, col. maps ; 21 cm.
    Includes index.
    Summary: A complete traveler's guide to the Hawaiian island of Oahu, with full
color illustrations, maps, directions and candid advice by authors who reside in Hawaii.
    ISBN 0-9717279-2-9
    LCCN 2004092191

        1. Oahu (Hawaii) – Guidebooks. 2. Oahu (Hawaii) – Description and travel.
    I. Friedman, Harriett   II. Title

    DU628.03   919.69'3_dc22

All photographs (except the cover) taken by Andrew Doughty. (And he *wishes* he
    had been able to take that one.)
Cover imagery courtesy of NASA.
Cartography by Andrew Doughty.
All artwork and illustrations by Andrew Doughty, Harriett Friedman and Lisa Pollak.

Pages 2–3: A kayaker loses herself in the beauty of the 1,000-acre sunken island
    in Kane'ohe Bay.

We welcome any comments, questions, criticisms or contributions you may have,
and will incorporated some of your suggestions into future editions. Please send to
the address above or e-mail us at **aloha@wizardpub.com**.

Check out our Web site at **www.wizardpub.com** for up-to-the-minute changes.

Although the authors and publisher have made every effort to ensure that the information was correct at press time, the authors and publisher do not assume and here-
by disclaim any liability to any party for any loss or damage caused by errors or omissions, whether such errors or omissions result from negligence, accident or any other
cause. Information has been obtained from sources believed to be reliable, but its
accuracy and completeness, and the opinions based thereon, are not guaranteed.

Dedicated to the wizard that exists in all of us...

CONTENTS

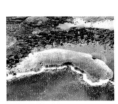

CONTENTS

WAI'ANAE & CENTRAL OAHU SIGHTS
95

BEACHES
123

ACTIVITIES
159

ATTRACTIONS
109

ADVENTURES
213

WHERE TO STAY
260

ISLAND DINING
222

INDEX
297

O'ahu: land of myths. We're not talking about ancient Hawaiian myths. We're talking about the myths that exist about this island, both from visitors and those who live on neighbor islands (including us before we moved here to do this book). The biggest myth is that O'ahu is Waikiki and Waikiki is O'ahu. *Nothing* could be further from the truth. O'ahu has all the wonder, adventure and discovery that a person could ever ask for—and far more.

We've had to deviate from our usual way of doing things for this O'ahu book. Put simply, this island is so vast, so dense and so full of choices that it's impossible to be fully comprehensive. If we were, you'd never be able to lift this book. So instead, we've chosen to show you those things that we think make O'ahu special. Lots of businesses, attractions and places had to be left out, lest we overwhelm you the way *we* were overwhelmed.

We first came to the islands as visitors and decided we could never live anywhere else. We now make our home here and divide our time between the islands. Most travel publishers send a writer or writers to a given location for a few weeks to become "experts" and to compile information for guidebooks. To our knowledge, we are the only guidebook writers who actually *live* our books.

We hike the trails, ride the boats, eat in the restaurants, explore the reefs and do the things we write about. It takes us two *years*, full time, to do a first edition book, and we visit places *anonymously*. We marvel at writers who can do it all in a couple weeks staying in a hotel. Wow, they must be *really* fast. Our method, though it takes much longer, gives us the ability to tell it like it is in a way no one else can. We put in many long hours, and doing all these activities is a burdensome grind. But we do it all for you—only for you. (Feel free to gag at this point.)

Longtime locals have been surprised at some of the items described in our book. We have found many special places that people born and raised here didn't even know about because that's *all we do*—explore the island. Visitors will find the book as valuable as having a friend living on the island.

We recognize the effort people go through to visit Hawai'i, and our goal is to expose you to as many options as possible so you can decide what you want to see and do. We took great pains to structure this book so that it will be fun, easy to read and loaded with useful information. This book is not a bland regurgitation of the facts arranged in textbook fashion.

If you are here on vacation, your time is extremely precious. You don't want to spend all your time flipping through a book looking for what you want. You need to be able to locate *what* you want, *when* you want it. You want to be able to access a comprehensive index, a thorough table of contents and refer to high-quality maps that were designed with you in mind. You want to know which helicopter, SCUBA, boat tour or lu'au is the best on the island. You want to find special hidden gems most people overlook. You want to be shown those things that will make this vacation the best of your life.

A quick look at this book will reveal features never before used in other guidebooks. Let's start with the maps. They are more detailed than other maps you will find, and yet they omit extraneous information that can sometimes make a chore out of reading a map. We know that people in unfamiliar territory sometimes have a hard time determining where they are on a map, so we include landmarks.

Neighbor islands have mile markers on the highways to indicate where you are, and we've used them in other books, but O'ahu's are mostly missing or facing the wrong way. So in more remote areas where it's hard to determine where you are, we've included random addresses and other landmarks to make sure you'll never wonder where you are on the map. We've also used a technique to highlight only the roads we think are relevant to you, and left the countless ancillary roads faint, but still visible, so you'll know they're there but you won't be overwhelmed when you read the maps. Where needed, we've drawn legal public beach access in yellow, so you'll *know* when you're legally entitled to cross someone's land. Most guidebooks have the infuriating habit of mentioning a particular place or sight but then fail to mention how to get there! You won't find that in our book. We tell you exactly how to find the hidden gems and use our own special maps to guide you.

One of the things unique to this book is the acceptance of change. We produce brand new editions of our books every two years, but in the intervening time we are constantly incorporating changes into the text nearly every time we do a new printing. We also post many of these changes on our Web site. This allows us to make some modifications throughout the life of each edition. We don't have the luxury of making every change that happens on a weekly basis, but it does give us more flexibility than if we only acknowledged changes every two years.

As you read this book, you will also notice that we are very candid in assessing businesses. Unlike some other guidebooks that send out questionnaires asking a business if they are any good (gee, they *all* say they're good), we've had personal contact with the businesses listed in this book. One of the dirty little secrets about guidebook writers is that they sometimes make cozy little deals for good reviews. Well, you won't find that here. We accept no payment for our reviews, we make no deals with businesses for saying nice things, and there are no advertisements in our book. What we've seen and experienced is what you get. If we gush over a certain company, it comes from personal experience. If we rail against a business, it is for the same reason. All businesses mentioned in this book are here by *our* choosing. None have had any input into what we say, and we have not received *a single cent* from any of them for their inclusion. (In fact, there are some that would probably pay to be left out, given our comments.) We review businesses as anonymous visitors to ensure that we are treated the same as you. (Amazingly, most travel writers *announce* themselves.) What you get is our opinion on how they operate. Nothing more, nothing less.

Sometimes our candor gets us into trouble. More than once we've had our books pulled from shelves because our comments hit a little too close to home. That's OK, because we don't work for the people who *sell* the book, we work for the people who *read* the book.

O'ahu Revealed is intended to bring you independence in exploring O'ahu. We don't want to waste any of your valuable time by giving you bad advice or bad directions. We want you to experience the best that the island has to offer. Our objective in writing this book is to give you the tools and information necessary to have the greatest Hawaiian experience possible.

We hope we succeeded.

Andrew Doughty
Harriett Friedman
Kailua, O'ahu

Four million years ago, before the dawn of man, the island of O'ahu emerged from a warm, frothing sea.

HOW IT BEGAN

Sometime around 70 million years ago an event of unimaginable violence occurred in the Earth's mantle, deep below the ocean floor. A hot spot of liquid rock blasted through the Pacific plate like a giant cutting torch, forcing liquid rock to the surface off the coast of Russia, forming the Emperor Seamounts. As the tectonic plate moved slowly over the hot spot, this torch cut a long scar along the plate, piling up mountains of rock, producing island after island. The oldest of these islands to have survived is Kure. Once a massive island with its own unique ecosystem, only its ghost remains in the form of a fringing coral reef, called an atoll.

As soon as the islands were born, a conspiracy of elements proceeded to dismantle them. Ocean waves unmercifully battered the fragile and fractured rock. Abundant rain, especially on the northeastern sides of the mountains, easily carved up the rock surface, seeking faults in the rock and forming rivers and streams. In forming these channels, the water carried away the rock and soil, robbing the islands of their very essence. Additionally, the weight of the islands ensured their doom. Lava flows on top of other lava, and the union of these flows is always weak. This lava also contains countless air pockets and is criss-crossed with hollow lava tubes, making it inherently unstable. As these massive amounts of rock accumulated, their bases were crushed under the weight of subsequent lava flows, causing their summits to sink back into the sea.

What we call the Hawaiian Islands are simply the latest creation from this island-making machine. Kaua'i and Ni'ihau are the oldest of the eight major islands. Lush and deeply eroded, the last of Kaua'i's fires died with its volcano a million years ago. O'ahu, Moloka'i, Lana'i, Kaho'olawe—their growing days are over, as well. Maui is in its twilight days as a growing island. After growing vigorously, Hawaiian volcanoes usually go to sleep for a million years or so before sputtering back to life for one last fling. Maui's volcano, Haleakala, awakened from its long sleep and is in its final eruptive stage. It last erupted around 1790 and will continue with sporadic eruptions

for a (geologically) short time before drifting into eternal sleep.

The latest and newest star in this island chain is the Big Island of Hawai'i. Born less than a million years ago, this youngster is still vigorously growing. Though none of its five volcanic mountains is considered truly dead, these days Mauna Loa and Kilauea are doing most of the work of making the Big Island bigger. Mauna Loa, the most massive mountain on Earth, consists of 10,000 *cubic miles* of rock. Quieter of the two active volcanoes, it last erupted in 1984. Kilauea is the most boisterous of the volcanoes and is the most active volcano on the planet. Kilauea's most recent eruption began in 1983 and was still going strong as we went to press. Up and coming onto the world stage is Lo'ihi. This new volcano is still 3,200 feet below the ocean's surface, 20 miles off the southeastern coast of the island. Yet in a geologic heartbeat, the Hawaiian islands will be richer with its ascension,

Ancient forests dripping with life still abound on O'ahu.

sometime in the next 100,000 years.

These virgin islands were barren at birth. Consisting only of volcanic rock, the first life forms to appreciate these new islands were marine creatures. Fish, mammals and microscopic animals discovered this new underwater haven and made homes for themselves. Coral polyps attached themselves to the lava and succeeding generations built upon these, creating what would become coral reefs.

Meanwhile, on land, seeds carried by the winds were struggling to colonize the rocky land, eking out a living and breaking down the lava rock. Storms brought the occasional bird, hopelessly blown off course. The lucky ones found the islands. The even luckier ones arrived with mates or were pregnant when they got here. Other animals, stranded on a piece of floating debris, washed ashore against all odds and went on to colonize the islands. These introductions of new species were rare events. It took an extraordinary set of circumstances for a new species to actually make it to the islands. Single specimens were destined to live out their lives in lonely solitude. On average, a new species was successfully deposited here only once every 20,000 years.

As with people, islands have a life cycle. After their violent birth, islands grow to their maximum size, get carved up by the elements, collapse in parts, and finally sink back into the sea. Someday, all the Hawaiian islands will be nothing more than geologic footnotes in the Earth's turbulent history. When a volcanic island is old, it is a sandy sliver called an atoll, devoid of mountains, merely a shadow of its former glory. When it's middle-aged, it can be a lush wonderland, a haven for anything green, like Kaua'i and O'ahu. And when it is young, it is dynamic and unpredictable,

Hawai'i's First Tour Guide?

Given the remoteness of the Hawaiian Islands relative to the rest of Polynesia (or anywhere else for that matter), you'll be forgiven for wondering how the first settlers found these islands in the first place. Many scientists think it might have been this little guy here. Called the kolea, or golden plover, this tiny bird flies over 2,500 miles

Before they leave for Alaska.

nonstop to Alaska every year for the summer, returning to Hawai'i after mating. Some of these birds continue past Hawai'i and fly another 2,500 miles to Samoa and other South Pacific islands. The early Polynesians surely must have noticed this commute and concluded that there must be land in the direction that the bird was heading. They never would have dreamed that the birds leaving the South Pacific were head-

When they return.

ing to a land 5,000 miles away, and that Hawai'i was merely a stop in between, where the lazier birds wintered.

INTRODUCTION

like the Big Island of Hawai'i, but lacking the scars of experience from its short battle with the elements. The first people to occupy these islands were blessed with riches beyond their wildest dreams.

THE FIRST SETTLERS

Sometime around the fourth or fifth century A.D. a large double-hulled voyaging canoe, held together with flexible sennit lashings and propelled by sails made of woven pandanus, slid onto the sand on the Big Island of Hawai'i. These first intrepid adventurers, only a few dozen or so, encountered an island chain of unimaginable beauty.

They had left their home in the Marquesas Islands, 2,500 miles away, for reasons we will never know. Some say it was because of war, overpopulation, drought or just a sense of adventure. Whatever their reasons, these initial settlers took a big chance and surely must have been highly motivated. They left their homes and searched for a new world to colonize. Doubtless most of the first groups perished at sea. The Hawaiian Islands are the most isolated island chain in the world, and there was no way for them to know that there were islands in these waters. (Though some speculate that they were led here by the golden plover—see box on previous page.)

Those settlers who did arrive brought with them food staples from home: taro, breadfruit, pigs, dogs and several types of fowl. This was a pivotal decision. These first settlers found a land that contained almost no edible plants. With no land mammals other than the Hawaiian bat, the first settlers subsisted on fish until their crops matured. From then on, they lived on fish and taro. Although we associate throw-net fishing with Hawai'i, this practice was introduced by Japanese immigrants much later. The ancient Hawaiians used fishhooks and spears, for the most

The Last Battle for Supremacy

One of the more popular lookouts on O'ahu is the Pali Lookout on Hwy 61. The view from this precipice is simply glorious. As you soak in the beauty of the lookout, it's difficult to believe that this was the scene of one of O'ahu's bloodiest battles.

King Kamehameha was sweeping across the islands on his way to becoming the first man to conquer them all. When his fleet landed at Waikiki he steadily drove the O'ahu army farther and farther up Nu'uanu Valley. Once they got to what is now the Pali Lookout, they had nowhere to go but down the cliffs. With the help of western arms and sailors (whom he had captured and then cunningly made into advisors) Kamehameha's army was turning the battle into a route. Once at this location some of the enemy tried to scale down the cliffs. Around 400 others were driven off, their bodies smashing onto the rocks below. This would be the last major battle for conquest in Hawai'i. Kaua'i would eventually surrender, and Kamehameha would at last have his kingdom.

It's hard to imagine, but fifty generations of Hawaiian royalty were born at these sacred rocks in central O'ahu.

part, or drove fish into a net already placed in the water. They also had domesticated animals, which were used as ritual foods or reserved for chiefs.

Little is known about the initial culture. Archeologists speculate that a second wave of colonists, probably from Tahiti, may have subdued these initial inhabitants around 1,000 A.D. Some may have resisted and fled into the forest, creating the legend of the Menehune.

Today Menehune are always thought of as being small in stature. Initially referring to their social stature, the legend evolved to mean that they were physically short and lived in the woods away from the Hawaiians. (The Hawaiians avoided the woods when possible, fearing that they held evil spirits, and instead stayed on the coastal plains.) The Menehune were purported to build fabulous struc-

tures, always in one night. Their numbers were said to be vast, as many as 500,000. It is interesting to note that in a census taken of Kaua'i around 1800, some 65 people from a remote valley identified themselves as Menehune.

The second wave of settlers probably swept over the islands from the south, pushing the first inhabitants ever-north. On a tiny island north of Kaua'i archeologists have found carvings, clearly not Hawaiian, that closely resembling Marquesan carvings, probably left by the doomed exiles.

This second culture was far more aggressive and developed into a highly class-conscious culture. The society was

INTRODUCTION

If ancient Hawaiian legend is correct, this rock near Ka'ena Point called Leina-a-ka-'uhane—the leaping place for souls—is the last earthly sight that a Hawaiian soul will see before he joins his ancestors.

governed by chiefs, called ali'i, who established a long list of taboos called kapu. These kapu were designed to keep order, and the penalty for breaking one was usually death by strangulation, club or fire. If the violation was serious enough, the guilty party's family might also be killed. It was kapu, for instance, for your shadow to fall across the shadow of the ali'i. It was kapu to interrupt the chief if he was speaking. It was kapu to prepare men's food in the same container used for women's food. It was kapu for women to eat pork or bananas. It was kapu for men and women to eat together. It was kapu not to observe the days designated for the gods. Certain areas were kapu for fishing if they became depleted, allowing the area to replenish itself.

While harsh by our standards today, this system kept the order. Most ali'i were sensitive to the disturbance their presence

caused and often ventured outside only at night, or a scout was sent ahead to warn people that an ali'i was on his way. All commoners were required to pay tribute to the ali'i in the form of food and other items. Human sacrifices were common and war among rival chiefs the norm.

By the 1700s, the Hawaiians had lost all contact with Tahiti, and the Tahitians had lost all memory of Hawai'i. Hawaiian canoes had evolved into fishing and inter-island canoes and were no longer capable of long ocean voyages. The Hawaiians had forgotten how to explore the world.

OUTSIDE WORLD DISCOVERS HAWAI'I

In January 1778 an event occurred that would forever change Hawai'i. Captain James Cook, who usually had a genius for predicting where to find islands, stumbled upon Hawai'i. He had not expected the islands to be here. He was on his way to Alaska on his third great voyage of discovery, this time to search for the Northwest Passage linking the Atlantic and Pacific oceans. Cook approached the shores of Waimea, Kaua'i, at night on January 19, 1778.

The next morning Kaua'i's inhabitants awoke to a wondrous sight and thought they were being visited by gods. Rushing aboard to greet their visitors, the Kauaians were fascinated by what they saw: pointy-headed beings (the British wore tricornered hats) breathing fire (smoking pipes) and possessing a death-dealing instrument identified as a water squirter (guns). The amount of iron on the ship was incredible. (They had seen iron before in the form of nails on driftwood but never knew where it originated.)

Cook left Kaua'i and briefly explored Ni'ihau before heading north for his mission on February 2, 1778. When Cook returned to the islands in November after failing to find the Northwest Passage, he visited the Big Island of Hawai'i.

The Hawaiians had probably seen white men before. Local legend indicates that strange white people washed ashore on the Big Island sometime around the 1520s and integrated into society. This coincides with Spanish records of two ships lost in this part of the world in 1528. But a few weird-looking stragglers couldn't compare to the arrival of Cook's great ships and instruments.

Despite some recent rewriting of history, all evidence indicates that Cook, unlike some other exploring sea captains of his era, was a thoroughly decent man. Individuals need to be evaluated in the context of their time. Cook knew that his mere presence would have a profound impact on the cultures he encountered,

but he also knew that change for these cultures was inevitable, with or without him. He tried, unsuccessfully, to keep the men known to be infected with venereal diseases from mixing with local women, and he frequently flogged infected men who tried to sneak ashore at night. He was greatly distressed when a party he sent to Ni'ihau was forced to stay overnight due to high surf, knowing that his men might transmit diseases to the women (which they did).

Cook arrived on the Big Island at a time of much upheaval. The mo'i, or king, of the Big Island had been militarily spanked during an earlier attempt to invade Maui and was now looting and raising hell throughout the islands as retribution. Cook's arrival and his physical appearance (at 6-feet-4 he couldn't even stand up straight in his own quarters) almost guaranteed that the Hawaiians would think he was the god Lono, who was responsible for land fertility. Every year the ruling chiefs and their war god Ku went into abeyance, removing their power so that Lono could return to the land and make it fertile again, bringing back the spring rains. During this time all public works stopped, and the land was left alone. At the end of this *makahiki,* mankind would again seize the land from Lono so he could grow crops and otherwise make a living upon it. Cook arrived at the beginning of the makahiki, and the Hawaiians naturally thought *he* was the god Lono coming to make the land fertile. Cook even sailed into the exact bay where the legend predicted Lono would arrive.

The Hawaiians went to great lengths to please their "god." All manner of supplies were made available. Eventually they became suspicious of the visitors. If they were gods, why did they accept the Hawaiian women? And if they were gods, why did one of them die?

Cook left at the right time. The British had used up the Hawaiians' hospitality (not to mention their supplies). But shortly after leaving the Big Island, the ship broke a mast, making it necessary to return to Kealakekua Bay for repairs. As they sailed back into the bay, the Hawaiians were nowhere to be seen. A chief had declared the area kapu to help replenish it. When Cook finally found the Hawaiians, they were polite but wary. Why are you back? Didn't we please you enough already? What do you want now?

As repair of the mast continued, things began to get tense. Eventually the Hawaiians stole a British rowboat (for the nails), and the normally calm Cook blew his cork. On the morning of February 14, 1779, he went ashore to trick the chief into coming aboard his ship where he would detain him until the rowboat was returned. As Cook and the chief were heading to the water, the chief's wife begged the chief not to go.

By now tens of thousands of Hawaiians were crowding around Cook, and he ordered a retreat. A shot was heard from the other side of the bay, and someone shouted that the Englishmen had killed an important chief. A shielded warrior with a dagger came at Cook, who fired his pistol (loaded with small shot). The shield stopped the small shot, and the Hawaiians were emboldened. Other shots were fired. Standing in knee-deep water, Cook turned to call for a cease-fire and was struck in the head from behind with a club, then stabbed. Dozens of other Hawaiians pounced on him, stabbing his body repeatedly. The greatest explorer the world had ever known was dead at age 50 in a petty skirmish over a stolen rowboat.

KAMEHAMEHA THE GREAT

The most powerful and influential king in Hawaiian history lived during the time of Captain Cook and was born on the Big Island around 1758. Until his rule, the Hawaiian chain had never been ruled by a single person. He was the first to "unite" (i.e., conquer) all the islands.

Kamehameha was an extraordinary man by any standard. He possessed herculean strength, a brilliant mind and boundless ambition. He was marked for death before he was even born. When Kamehameha's mother was pregnant with him, she developed a strange and overpowering craving—she wanted to *eat* the eyeball of a chief. The king of the Big Island, mindful of the rumor that the unborn child's real father was his bitter enemy, the king of Maui, asked his advisers to interpret. Their conclusion was unanimous: The child would grow to be a rebel, a killer of chiefs. The king decided that the child must die as soon as he was born, but the baby was instead whisked away to a remote valley to be raised.

In Hawaiian society, your role in life was governed by what class you were born into. The Hawaiians believed that breeding among family members produced superior offspring (except for the genetic misfortunes who were killed at birth), and the highest chiefs came from brother/sister combinations. Kamehameha was not of the highest class (his parents were merely cousins), so his future as a chief would not come easily.

As a young man Kamehameha was impressed by his experience with Captain Cook. He was among the small group that stayed overnight on Cook's ship during Cook's first pass of Maui.

(Kamehameha was on Maui valiantly fighting a battle in which his side was getting badly whupped.) Kamehameha recognized that his world had forever changed, and he shrewdly used the knowledge and technology of westerners to his advantage.

Kamehameha participated in numerous battles. His side lost many of the early ones, but he learned from his mistakes and developed into a cunning tactician. When he finally consolidated his rule over the Big Island (by luring his enemy to be the inaugural sacrifice of a new temple), he fixed his sights on the entire chain. In the 1790s his large company of troops, armed with some western armaments and advisers, swept across Maui, Moloka'i, Lana'i and O'ahu. After some delays with the last of the holdouts, Kaua'i, their king finally acquiesced to the inevitable, and Kamehameha became the first ruler of all the islands. He spent his final years governing the islands peacefully from his Big Island capital and died in 1819.

MODERN HAWAI'I

During the 19th century, Hawai'i's character changed dramatically. Businessmen from all over the world came here to exploit Hawai'i's sandalwood, whales, land and people. Hawai'i's leaders, for their part, actively participated in these ventures and took a piece of much of the action for themselves. Workers were brought from many parts of the world, changing the racial makeup of the islands. Government corruption became

O'ahu is blessed with more offshore islets than all the other Hawaiian islands combined.

the order of the day, and everyone seemed to be profiting, except the Hawaiian commoners. By the time Queen Lili'uokalani lost her throne to a group of American businessmen in 1893, Hawai'i had become directionless. It barely resembled the Hawai'i Captain Cook had encountered the previous century. The kapu system had been abolished by the Hawaiians shortly after the death of Kamehameha the Great. The "Great Mahele," begun in 1848, had changed the relationship Hawaiians had with the land. Large tracts of land were sold by the Hawaiian government to royalty, government officials, commoners and foreigners, effectively stripping many Hawaiians of land they had lived on for generations.

The United States recognized the Republic of Hawai'i in 1894 with Sanford Dole as its president. It was annexed in 1898 and became an official territory in 1900. During the 19th and 20th centuries, sugar established itself as king. Pineapple was also heavily grown in the islands, with the island of Lana'i purchased in its entirety for the purpose of growing pineapples.

As the 20th century rolled on, Hawaiian sugar and pineapple workers found themselves in a lofty position—they became the highest paid workers for these crops in the world. As land prices rose and competition from other parts of the world increased, sugar and pineapple became less and less profitable. Today, these crops no longer hold the position they once had. The "pineapple island" of Lana'i has shifted away from pineapple growing and is focused on tourism. The sugar industry is now dead on the Big Island and O'ahu, leaving only Maui and Kaua'i to grow it commercially.

The story of Hawai'i is not a story of good versus evil. Nearly everyone shares in the blame of what happened to the Hawaiian people and their culture. Westerners certainly saw Hawai'i as a potential bonanza and easily exploitable. They knew what buttons to push and pushed them well. But the Hawaiians, for their part, were in a state of flux. The mere existence of westerners seemed to bring to the surface a discontent, or at least a weakness, with their system that had been lingering just below the surface.

In fact, in 1794, a mere 16 years after first encountering westerners and under no military duress from the West, Kamehameha the Great volunteered to cede his island over to Great Britain. He was hungry for western arms so he could defeat his neighbor island opponents. He even declared that as of that day, they were no longer people of Hawai'i, but rather people of Britain. (Britain declined the offer.) And in 1819, immediately after the death of the strong-willed Kamehameha, the Hawaiians, on their own accord, overthrew their own religion, dumped the kapu system and denied their gods. This was before any western missionaries ever came to Hawai'i.

Nonetheless, Hawai'i today is once again seeking guidance from her heritage. The echoes of the past seem to be getting louder with time, rather than diminishing. Interest in the Hawaiian language and culture is at a level not seen in many decades. All of us who live here are very aware of the issues and the complexities involved, but there is little agreement about where it will lead. As a result, you will be exposed to a more "Hawaiian" Hawai'i than those who might have visited the state a decade ago. This is an interesting time in Hawai'i. Enjoy it as observers, and savor the flavor of the islands.

A surfer struggles with his technique.

GETTING HERE

In order to get to Hawai'i, you've got to fly here. While this may sound painfully obvious, many people spend time trying to find an ocean cruise to the Islands. Don't waste your time. There are no regular cruises between Hawai'i and the mainland.

When planning your trip, a travel agent can be helpful. Their commission has been paid directly by the travel industry, though that may change in the future. The Internet is a great source for companies selling travel packages. If you don't want to or can't go through these sources, there are several large wholesalers that can get you airfare, hotel and a rental car, often cheaper than you can get airfare on your own. **Pleasant Hawaiian Holidays** (800–242–9244) and **Suntrips** (800–786–8747) are reputable providers of complete package tours. They are renowned for their impossibly low rates. We've always been amazed that you can sometimes get round trip airfare from the mainland, a hotel and car for a week for as low as $700 per person, depending on where you fly from and where you stay. That's a small price to pay for your little piece of paradise. **Cheap Tickets** (800–377–1000) usually lives up to its name.

If you arrange airline tickets and hotel reservations yourself, you can often count on paying top dollar for each facet of your trip. The prices listed in the WHERE TO STAY section reflect the RACK rates, meaning the price you and I pay if we book direct. Rates can be significantly lower if you go through a wholesaler.

When you pick your travel source, shop around—the differences can be dramatic. A good package can make the difference between affording a *one-week* vacation and *two-week* vacation. Also, look in the Sunday travel section of your local newspaper—the bigger the paper, the better.

All passengers arriving on Oʻahu land at Honolulu Airport. When flying to Oʻahu from the mainland, try to sit on the left side coming in, the right going home. If you're going to any of the neighbor islands, inter-island flights are done by **Aloha** (800–367–5250) and **Hawaiian** (800–367–5320).

Even when they're crashing right in front of you, it's hard to appreciate the size of waves when no one's in the water to provide scale. This is what a four-story high wave looks like at Waimea Bay.

WHAT TO BRING

This list may assist you in planning what to bring. Obviously you won't bring everything on the list, but it might make you think of a few things you may otherwise overlook.

- Waterproof sunblock (SPF 15 or higher)
- Two bathing suits
- Shoes—thongs, trashable sneakers, reef shoes, hiking shoes
- Mask, snorkel and fins
- Camera with lots of film or a digital
- Junk clothes for bikes, hiking, etc.
- Light rain jacket
- Mosquito repellent for some hikes. (*Lotions*—not liquids—with DEET seem to work the longest.)
- Large insulated water jug; keep in car
- Shorts and other cool cotton clothing
- Fanny pack—also called waist pack,

to carry all your various vacation accouterments; waterproof ones are convenient for snorkeling
- Cheap, simple backpack—handy even if you're not backpacking
- Hat or cap for sun protection

GETTING AROUND
Rental Cars

Rental car prices in Hawai'i *can be* (but aren't always) cheaper than almost anywhere else in the country, and the competition is ferocious. O'ahu is the only major Hawaiian island where a sizeable number of visitors stay here *without* renting a car. (Waikiki is small and walkable, and many activity companies will shuttle you to their location.) While it's true that you *might* not need one if you don't plan to leave Waikiki or intend to let activity companies shuttle you to their offerings, we think it's a big mistake if you don't have a rental car for at least *part* of your stay. Even if you're planning to take tour buses or the county bus, many of the glorious sights described in the driving tours will be unavailable to you. If you're trying to save money and spend much of your trip in Waikiki, get a rental car for at least some *part* of your trip. You won't regret it.

Avis, Hertz, National, Dollar and Budget are the most convenient rental car companies due to their return locations. Other companies aren't at the airport. There's a gas station at the airport right before the car rental return, and they charge the usual confiscatory prices.

Many hotels, condos and rental agents offer excellent room/car packages. Find out from your hotel or travel agent if one is available.

If you're wondering why you can't get any radio stations, it's usually because the rental car companies push the antenna down to wash the car. So when you get *da car,* pull *da buggah* out!

Here's a list of rental car companies. All the big companies have desks at the airport and in Waikiki.

The Big Guys
Alamo (800) 327–9633
Avis (800) 321–3712
Budget (800) 527–0700
Dollar (800) 800–4000
Enterprise (800) 736–8222
Hertz (800) 654–3131
National (800) 227–7368
Thrifty (800) 367–5238

The Little Guys
JN Rentals (808) 831–2726
Tradewinds (808) 834–1465
VIP (808) 922–4605

4-Wheel Drive

On Kaua'i and especially the Big Island we've strongly recommended getting a 4WD vehicle, but it isn't as important on O'ahu. There aren't many off-road opportunities, and there are few places where access will require one. The dirt road leading part of the way to Ka'ena Point on the north shore is just about the only area where it's good to have 4WD, but it's hard to justify the increased price just for that. Consider skipping the 4WD. If you want to splurge, spring for a convertible instead. They can be fun.

Taxis & Shuttles

If you don't want a rental car (or will be renting one in Waikiki later during your stay), there are plenty of taxi companies around the island. Their meter rates are set. They charge around $27 from the airport to Waikiki. If you call them in advance (instead of hailing them) you can usually get a cheaper rate.

For instance, O'ahu Airport Shuttle (681–8181) charges about $20 to get you into Waikiki, as does Akamai Cab Company (377–1379). Tabi Trans (216–8006) *sometimes* charges as little as $5.

Once in Waikiki, cabs can easily be hailed.

Motorcycles & Scooters

If you think riding a HOG is something you do at a lu'au, you may want to skip this section. There's something about Harleys. Maybe it's the sound, or maybe the looks. But riding a Harley-Davidson around O'ahu is a blast. If you want to rent one to experience things on your own (freedom, after all, is what HOGs are all about), you can get them, and other motorcycles from:

Big Kahuna (924–2736) at 407 Seaside rents motorcycles for $80–$150 per day. Mopeds are $25 per day. Bicycles are $15 a day.

Hawaiian Island (382–3227) at 2025 Kalakaua rents Harleys from $75–$165, depending on the model and how much of the day you want it.

Paradise Motorcycle Rentals (924–7777) has several locations around Waikiki, and they have lots of bikes from $79–$179.

Adventure on Two Wheels (944–3131) at 1946 Ala Moana has mopeds for all different prices. Hourly rates available for $7 per hour, 2-hour minimum.

Check out the bike first. We've seen some pretty bald tires and snotty attitudes at some of these places.

You can also rent Segway Scooters in Waikiki. See page 47 for more.

Exotic Cars

O'ahu has lots of opportunities to rent a flashy ride. Ferraris, Vipers, 'Vettes, Porsches and other sexy autos can be had—for the right price. You're looking at around $400 for a Viper, $650–$950 for a Ferrari, etc. That's *per day!* Bear in mind that there are no good opportunities to open them up—we have no empty straightaways to throttle these puppies—but if you just want to experience the thrill of driving a fantasy car and you have a wad burning a hole in your pocket, give it a shot. (If you're also heading to Maui, consider renting your dream car there—it's cheaper.)

Paradise Rent-a-Car (946–7777) has four locations in Waikiki to rent heart-pounding cars. They require hefty credit card deposits. If you're 21–25 years old, it'll cost you more. Ferrari Rentals (942–8725) at 2025 Kalakaua Ave. in Waikiki has lots of grown-up car toys to rent. They'll simply take a credit card imprint instead of reserving space. At Ferrari Rentals if you're 18–21, bring cash if you want a car—your credit card won't impress them.

Driving Around O'ahu

O'ahu has some of the most confusing roads and highways you'll find anywhere in the U.S. Roads change names randomly and with no warning, leaving you confused as to where you actually are. Let's use an example. Kamehameha Hwy (a major island highway) is also called Hwy 99...until it changes its name to Hwy 80 where Hwy 99 changes to Wilikina Drive, then Kamahanui Road. Then Kamehameha Hwy (also called Kam Hwy) becomes Hwy 99 again, then Hwy 83, then Hwy 830 (*if* you remember to turn left at the Hygienic Store in Kahalu'u), then Hwy 83 again. All this for *one* highway. Or consider Farrington Hwy. Look on a map, and Farrington Hwy wraps around the western tip. Oh, except for the 6 miles around the tip where it doesn't actually exist. You'll have to go around via Hwy 99...or is it Kamehameha Hwy?

Plus when you're on our freeways, you'll find it maddening when you discover that you can often get *off* a freeway...but not back *on* it. Or maybe you can only get on it going the opposite direction you want to go.

While making our maps, we've repeatedly driven the roads with the computer files literally in our laps and tried to mark things as you're likely to see them, not necessarily by their official names. At times we've left off confusing and conflicting names. Nonetheless, though we've gone to considerable effort to make the maps as easy as possible, you *will* get confused and lost if you drive around long enough. Hey,

don't blame us. We just make the maps; we didn't devise this embarrassing road system.

Remember, Honolulu is a big city and you *won't* be the only one trying to get somewhere. Although traffic can be bad anywhere at any time, the **basic traffic pattern** is this: *into* Waikiki and Honolulu from all points in the morning, and *away* from Waikiki and Honolulu to all points in the afternoon. H-1 is backed up pretty often, especially eastbound where H-1 and Hwy 78 meet (called the *Middle Street Merge*).

If you're heading west on H-1, locals call that being *'Ewa-bound*. If you're heading east, it's *Koko Head-bound*.

Seat belt and **child restraint** use is required by law, and the police will pull you over for this alone. Open roads and frequently changing speed limits make it

Some of the things that we consider quintessential Hawaiian, like coconut trees, were actually imported by Hawai'i's first settlers.

easy to accidentally speed here. Sobriety checkpoints are not an uncommon police tactic on Oʻahu.

It's best not to leave anything valuable in your car. **Car break-ins** can be a problem here. Thieving scum looking for anything of value regularly hit rental cars. When we park at a beach, hiking trail or any other place frequented by visitors, we take all valuables with us, leave the windows up, and leave the doors *unlocked*. (Just in case someone is curious enough about the inside to smash a window.) There are plenty of stories about people walking 100 feet to a beach, coming back to their car, and finding that their brand new video camera has walked away. And don't be gullible enough to think that trunks are safe. Someone who sees you put something in your trunk can probably get at it faster than you can with your key.

If you are between the ages of 21 and 25, **Alamo**, **Dollar** and **Enterprise** are your best bets. You'll pay about $15–$20 extra for the crime of being young and reckless, but at least you won't have to take the bus. If you're under 21—rent a bicycle or scooter, or take the bus.

Buses

Oʻahu is the only Hawaiian island with a truly great bus system, cleverly called **The Bus** (848–4444). About 30% of visitors use the bus system, according to the state. You'll find bus schedules sprinkled in kiosks all around Waikiki. It's $2 for a one-way fare (transfers are free), $40 for monthly pass. Bus #8 is the one that circles Waikiki and Ala Moana Shopping Center (there's one every 10 minutes), and we've shown the route on the Waikiki map. Even if you have a rental car, it might be tempting to jump on the old #8 bus to take you to

the other end of Waikiki instead of worrying about parking.

Carry-on baggage is allowed, but "Baggage or carry-on items that will not be admitted on the bus shall include any large, bulky, dangerous or offensive article that may cause harm or discomfort to any passenger." *So there.*

The **Waikiki Trolley** (926–7604) on the other hand, is ridiculously overpriced. It's $25 per person per day or $45 for a 4-day pass. Its primary customer base seems to be Japanese tour groups.

GETTING MARRIED ON OʻAHU

Hawaiʻi, with its exotic beauty and nearly perfect weather, is one of the most popular wedding and honeymoon destinations in the world. And sunsets along the leeward side can provide a breathtaking backdrop for your ceremony.

License requirements in Hawaii are simple. You both must apply in person with photo ID and pay the $60 fee in cash. Your license will be good for 30 days.

All of the major resorts can provide planners to assist you with the details. They have the facilities and sites on their properties along with experienced staffs to make the day go smoothly. The resorts can provide chapels, gazebos, waterfalls and lush gardens for your ceremony. Some of more popular resorts in Waikiki are the Hilton Hawaiian Village, the Halekulani, the Royal Hawaiian and the Sheraton Moana. If you prefer a resort outside of Waikiki, consider the Kahala Mandarin, Turtle Bay or the JW Marriott ʻIhilani at Ko Olina.

There are also many independent coordinators with years of experience helping couples with their wedding plans. Be sure you and you planner are clear about your budgetary limits and

Rainfall Map

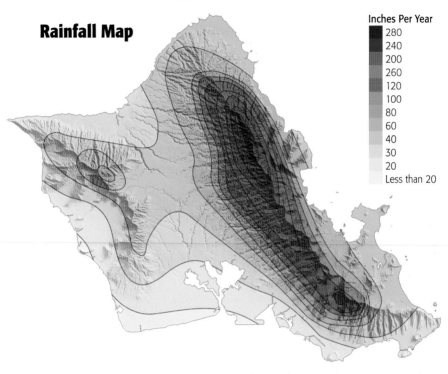

Inches Per Year	
	280
	240
	200
	260
	120
	100
	80
	60
	40
	30
	20
	Less than 20

what you want during your wedding day. Also be certain about the amount of assistance you will receive before the ceremony, so you can relax and enjoy your wedding day.

Be aware of holidays, the popularity of Valentine's Day and the month of June for weddings. By booking far enough in advance, you should be able to arrange a wedding during one of these busy times.

Always be sure there is a backup plan in case it rains. Beaches are public, so you will have other beachgoers present during your ceremony. If you're considering using a state or county park, be sure you have met their permit requirements.

Looking for a different but very Hawaiian reception? Consider holding it on one of the dinner cruises or joining in

with one of the island's lu'aus (remember that the Polynesian Cultural Center luau does not permit alcohol).

WEATHER

One of the biggest worries people have when planning their trip to the tropics is the weather. Will it rain? It it going to be too hot? What about hurricanes? Let's deal with the last one first. There have been only three recorded hurricanes in Hawai'i in the past two hundred years. One in the '50s, one in the '80s and one on September 11, 1992, clobbering Kaua'i. None have hit O'ahu, so you should probably spend your precious worry energy elsewhere.

As for rain, it works like this: The prevailing winds (called trade winds) come from the northeast, bringing their moisture with them. As the air hits the

Koʻolau mountains, it rises, cools and condenses into clouds and rain. So the mountains and shoreline facing the northeast, called the **windward side**, get the lion's share of the rain. Look at the rain graphic, and it will make more sense. Often by mid-morning the rising, cooling air causes clouds to form in the mountains, giving them an exotic, mystical look.

Once the air has had the moisture wrung out, it sinks and warms on the southwest side (called the **leeward side**) and often has minimal rain potential. So areas like Waikiki get little rain. The exception is when we get winds from the south or southwest—called Kona winds—where the rain pattern is reversed. These kona winds only happen about 5%–10% of the time, most often in the winter.

In the tropics, beautiful weather doesn't always mean sunny skies.

Waikiki has an embarrassingly equitable climate. The average high is 84°, and it has *never* gotten above 95° since thermometers have been in the islands. Waikiki gets only 20 inches of rain per year, and when it does rain, it's often in the form of short, intense showers.

Average **humidity** ranges from 65%–75%. And **ocean temperatures** go from 75° in February to about 80° in September.

GEOGRAPHY

The different Hawaiian islands have different geographic infrastructures. Kauaʻi is made up of one giant extinct volcano. Maui has two (one of them still barely alive). The Big Island lives up to its name, consisting of a staggering 5 volcanoes, only one of which is extinct (though only two of them are active enough for us to see them in our lifetime). On Oʻahu, it took two now-extinct volcanos to create this paradise. (The second one is *proba-*

bly extinct. See page 60 for more.) Wai'anae in the west poked above the water 2.2 million years ago, followed a million years later by its younger sibling, Ko'olau, in the east. Ko'olau (called the Ko'olau Mountains locally, even though it's really only one long mountain) is shorter—peaking at 3,150 feet, but it's over 30 miles long. What's most impressive is that it's only half the original mountain. The other half has been erased by ceaseless erosion. The top of the older volcano, Wai'anae, is called Mount Ka'ala and towers 4,025 feet above the ocean.

HAZARDS
The Sun

The hazard that by far affects the most people (excluding the accommodations tax) is the sun. O'ahu, at 21° latitude, receives sunlight more directly than anywhere on the mainland. (The more overhead the sunlight, the less atmosphere it filters through.) If you want to enjoy your *entire* vacation, make sure that you wear a strong sunblock. We recommend a waterproof sunblock with at least an SPF of 15. We use lotions when hiking, and the gel types like Bullfrog when going in the water (because they stay on better). Many visitors who get burned do so while snorkeling. You won't feel it coming because of the water. We *strongly* suggest you wear a T-shirt while snorkeling, or you may get a nasty surprise.

Try to avoid the sun between 11 a.m. and 2 p.m. when the sun's rays are particularly strong. If you are fair-skinned or unaccustomed to the sun and want to soak up some rays, 15–20 minutes per side is all you should consider the first day. You can increase it a bit each day. *Beware of the fact that our breezes will hide the symptoms of a burn until it's too late.* You might find that trying to get

your tan as golden as possible isn't worth it. Tropical suntans are notoriously short-lived, whereas you are sure to remember a bad burn far longer. If, after all our warnings, you *still* get burned, aloe vera gel works well to relieve the pain. Some come with lidocaine in them. Some of the resorts even have aloe plants on the grounds. Peel the skin off a section and make several crisscross cuts in the meat, then rub the plant on your skin. *Oooo, it'll feel so good!*

Water Hazards

The most serious water hazard is the surf. Though more calm in the summer and on the leeward side, high surf can be found anywhere on the island at any time of the year. The sad fact is that more people drown in Hawai'i each year than anywhere else in the country. This isn't said to keep you from enjoying the ocean, but rather to instill in you a healthy respect for Hawaiian waters. See BEACHES for more information on this.

Ocean Critters

Hawaiian marine life, for the most part, is quite friendly. There are, however, a few notable exceptions. Below is a list of some critters that you should be aware of. This is not mentioned to frighten you out of the water. The odds are overwhelming that you won't have any trouble with any of the beasties listed below. But should you encounter one, this information should be of some help.

Sharks—Hawai'i does have sharks. Most are the essentially harmless white-tipped reef sharks, plus the occasional hammerhead or tiger shark. Contrary to what most people think, sharks are in every ocean and don't pose the level of danger people attribute to them. In the past 25 years there have been only a handful of documented shark attacks off O'ahu, mostly tigers attacking surfers. Considering the number of people who swam in our waters during that time, you are statistically more likely to get mauled by a hungry timeshare salesman than be bitten by a shark. If you do happen to come upon a shark, however, swim away slowly. This kind of movement doesn't interest them. *Don't* splash about rapidly. By doing this you are imitating a fish in distress, and you don't want to do that. The one kind of water you want to avoid is murky water, such as that found in river mouths. Most shark attacks occur in murky water at dawn or dusk since sharks are basically cowards who like to sneak up on their prey. In general, don't go around worrying about sharks. *Any* animal can be threatening.

Portuguese Man-of-War—These are related to jellyfish but are unable to

swim. They are instead propelled by a small sail and are at the mercy of the wind. Though small, they are capable of inflicting a painful sting. This occurs when the long, trailing tentacles are touched, triggering hundreds of thousands of spring-loaded stingers, called nematocysts, which inject venom. The resulting burning sensation is usually very unpleasant but not fatal. Fortunately, the Portuguese Man-of-War is not a common visitor to most island beaches. When they *do* come ashore, however,

they usually do so in large numbers, jostled by a strong onshore wind usually at northeast-facing beaches. If you see them on the beach, don't go in the water. If you do get stung, immediately remove the tentacles with a gloved hand, stick or whatever is handy. Rinse thoroughly with salt or fresh water to remove any adhering nematocysts. Then apply ice for pain control. If the condition worsens, see a doctor. The old treatments of vinegar or baking soda are no longer recommended. The folk cure is urine, but you might look pretty silly applying it.

Box Jellyfish—O'ahu is the only island in the chain where these guys are a problem. Once a month, nine or ten days after the full moon, box jellyfish approach the shoreline, especially at leeward beaches, such as Ala Moana, Waikiki and Hanauma Bay, and will sting anything that comes in contact with them. These are *not* the same notorious box jellyfish that kill people in Australia. Although you're certainly *allowed* to swim during that time, personally we choose not to and suggest you do the same. Sting treatments are similar to Man-of-Wars, but vinegar *is* recommended for box jellyfish stings.

Sea Urchins—These are like living pin cushions. If you step on one or accidentally grab one, remove as much of the spine as possible with tweezers. See a physician if necessary.

Coral—Coral skeletons are very sharp and, since the skeleton is overlaid by millions of living coral polyps, a scrape can leave proteinaceous matter in the wound, causing infection. This is why coral cuts are frustratingly slow to heal. Immediate cleaning and disinfecting of coral cuts should speed up healing time. We don't have fire coral around Hawai'i.

Sea Anemones—Related to the jelly-fish, these also have stingers and are usually found attached to rocks or coral. It's best not to touch them with your bare hands. Treatment for a sting is similar to that of a Portuguese Man-of-War.

Bugs

Though we're devoid of the myriad hideous buggies found in other parts of the world, there are a few evil critters brought here from elsewhere that you should know about. The worst are **centipedes**. They can get to be six or more inches long and are aggressive predators. They shouldn't be messed with. You'll probably never see one, but if you get stung, even by a baby, the pain can range from a bad bee sting to a moderate gunshot blast. Some local doctors say the only cure is to stay drunk for three days. Others say to use meat tenderizer instead of a brain tenderizer.

Cane spiders are big, dark and look horrifying, but they're not poisonous. (But they seem to *think* they are. I've had *them* chase *me* across the room when *I* had the broom in my hand.) We *don't* have no-see-ums, those irritating sand fleas common in the South Pacific and Caribbean.

Mosquitoes were unknown in the islands until the first stowaways arrived on Maui on the *Wellington* in 1826. Since then they have thrived. A good mosquito repellent containing DEET will come in handy, especially if you plan to go hiking. *Lotions* (not thin liquids) with DEET seem to work and stick best. Forget the guidebooks that tell you to take vitamin B12 to keep mosquitoes away; it just gives the little critters a healthier diet. If you find one dive bombing you at night in your room and you have an overhead fan, turn it on to help keep them away. Local residents and some hotels often rely on genetically engineered plants such as Citrosa, which irritate mosquitoes as much as they irritate us.

Bees and wasps are more common on the drier leeward sides of the island. Usually, the only way you'll get stung is if you run *into* or step *onto* one. If you rent a motorcycle, beware; one of us received his first bee sting while singing *Come Sail Away* on a motorcycle. A bee sting in the mouth can definitely ruin one of your precious vacation days.

Regarding **cockroaches**, there's good news and bad news. The bad news is that here, some are bigger than your thumb and can fly. The good news is that you probably won't see one. One of their predators is the **gecko**. This small, lizard-like creature makes a surprisingly loud chirp at night. They are cute and considered good luck in the Islands (probably 'cause they eat mosquitoes and roaches).

There are no snakes in Hawai'i (other than some reporters). There is concern that the brown tree snake *might* have made its way onto the islands from Guam. Although mostly harmless to humans, these snakes can spell extinction to native birds. Government officials aren't allowed to tell you this, but we will: If you *ever* see one anywhere in Hawai'i, please *kill it* and contact the Pest Hotline at 586–7378. At the very least, call them immediately. The entire bird population of Hawai'i will be grateful.

Swimming in Streams

There are opportunities on O'ahu to swim in streams and under waterfalls. It's a fulfillment of a fantasy for many people. But there are several hazards you need to know about.

Leptospirosis is a bacteria that is found in some of Hawai'i's freshwater. It is transmitted from animal urine and can enter the body through open cuts, eyes and by drinking. Around 100 people a year in Hawai'i are diagnosed with the bacteria, which is treated with antibiotics if caught relatively early. You should avoid swimming in streams if you have open cuts, and treat all water found in nature with treatment pills before drinking. (Many filters are ineffective for lepto.)

While swimming in freshwater streams, try to use your arms as much as possible. Kicking an unseen rock is easier than you think. Also, consider wearing reef shoes while in streams. These water-friendly wonders are available all over O'ahu and allow you to walk in water while still protecting your feet.

Though rare, **flash floods** can occur in any freshwater stream anywhere in the world, even paradise. Be alert for them.

Lastly, remember while lingering under waterfalls that not everything that comes over the top will be as soft as water. Rocks coming down from above could definitely shatter the moment—among other things.

Dehydration

Bring and drink lots of water when you are out and about, especially when you are hiking. Dehydration sneaks up on people. By the time you are thirsty, you're already dehydrated. It's a good idea to take an insulated water jug with you in the car or one of those 1½ liter bottles of water. Our weather is almost certainly different than what you left behind, and you will probably find yourself thirstier than usual. Just fill it before you leave in the morning and *suck 'em up* (as we say here) all day.

Traffic

Oh, yeah. Traffic can be a *big* problem here, especially in Honolulu. See Driving Around O'ahu on page 24 for more.

Grocery Stores

A decided hazard. Restaurants are expensive, but don't think you'll get off cheap in grocery stores. Though you'll certainly save money cooking your own food if your room has cooking facilities, a trip to the store here can be startling. Phrases like *they charge how much for milk?* echo throughout the stores. Even items such as pineapples—*grown on this island!*—may cost more here than the ones jetted to you on the mainland. Go

figure. If you're stocking up, consider buying groceries at Costco (422–6955) west of Waikiki on Alakawa Street between Dillingham Boulevard. and Nimitz Hwy, or the massive 300,000 square foot Wal-Mart/Sam's Club just outside of Waikiki on Keeaumoku Street near Ala Moana Shopping Center.

TRAVELING WITH CHILDREN (KEIKIS)

Should we have put this under HAZARDS? If you're coming to Hawai'i and bringing the keikis (kids), O'ahu has more kid-oriented activities than any of the Hawaiian islands—Some of 'em cheap, some of 'em at *hurt-me* prices.

Hawai'i Children's Discovery Museum (524–5437) is at 111 Ohe St. It's $8 per adult, $6.75 for kids 2–17. Basically, kids up to about 9 will love the interactive exhibits rich with costumes, international cultures, various occupations and science. Kids 10 and up might get antsy. They have an unusually good gift shop.

The ATTRACTIONS chapter is the best place to check for keiki-friendly places. **Hawaiian Waters Adventure Park** at 674–9283 ($23 for kids, $34 for adults) is a pretty good water park. **Sea Life**

From the air, Kane'ohe Bay's odd-looking reefs appear to be more like giant amoebas than coral.

Park at 259–7933 is like a mini Sea World ($13 for kids, $26 for adults). The Waikiki Aquarium at 923–9741 ($7 for adults, 12 and under are free) and Honolulu Zoo at 971–7171 ($1 for kids, $6 for adults), both in Waikiki, get mixed reviews, as does the Maritime Center at 536–6373 ($4.50 for kids, $7.50 for adults).

If you're looking for a place for lunch, the Oceanarium Restaurant at 921–6111 (see DINING on page 230) has a quarter million gallon aquarium next to their tables, and at noon and 1 p.m. they send in the SCUBA divers to feed the fish. Always a hit with kids.

The Dole Plantation (621–8408) has a 100,000-square-foot hedge maze that keeps kids occupied for $3 ($5 for adults). See page 97 for more.

We're pretty sure that ice skating wasn't your primary reason for coming to Hawai'i. Nonetheless, if that's what floats your child's boat, the Ice Palace (487–9921) at 4510 Salt Lake Blvd. (call for directions) is available.

In the ADVENTURES chapter we have swimming with dolphins—the kind of adventure kids *dream* of.

Kids who want to try something more involved than snorkeling may want to try SNUBA. See page 206.

The accommodations reviews describe the resorts with good keiki programs. By the way, if your objective was to get *away* from the kids, then maybe these resorts won't be at the top of *your* list.

Lastly, you should know that it's a big fine plus a mandatory safety class if your keiki isn't buckled up.

THE PEOPLE

There's no doubt about it—people really *are* friendlier in Hawai'i, even in urban Honolulu. You will notice that people are quick to smile and wave at you here. (Those of us who live in Hawai'i have to remember to pack our "mainland face" when we journey there. Otherwise, we get undesired responses when we smile or wave at complete strangers.) It probably comes down to a matter of happiness. People are happy here, and happy people are friendly people.

Some Terms

A person of Hawaiian blood is Hawaiian. Only people of this race are called by this term. They are also called Kanaka Maoli, but only another Hawaiian can use this term. Anybody who was born here, regardless of race (except whites), is called a local. If you were born elsewhere but have lived here a while, you are called a kama'aina. If you are white, you are a haole. It doesn't matter if you have been here a day or your family has been here for over a century, you will always be a haole. The term comes from the time when westerners first encountered these islands. Its precise meaning has been lost, but it is thought to refer to people with no background (since westerners could not chant kanaenae—praise—of their ancestors).

The continental United States is called the mainland. If you are here and are returning, you are not "going back to the states" (we *are* a state). When somebody leaves the island, they are off-island.

Hawaiian Time

One aspect of Hawaiian culture you may have heard of is Hawaiian Time. The stereotype is that everyone in Hawai'i moves just a little bit slower than on the mainland. Supposedly, we are more laid-back and don't let things get to us as easily as people on the mainland. This is the

Ala Moana Beach Park is a hit with keikis (kids) of all ages.

stereotype... OK, it's *not* a stereotype. It's real. Hopefully, during your visit, you will notice that this feeling infects *you,* as well. You may find yourself letting another driver cut in front of you in circumstances that would incur your wrath back home. You may find yourself willing to wait for a red light without feeling like you're going to explode. The whole reason for coming to Hawai'i is to experience beauty and a sense of peace, so let it happen. If someone else is moving a bit slower than you want, just go with it.

Shaka

One symbol you will see often—and should not be offended by—is the *shaka* sign. This is done by extending the pinkie and thumb while curling up the three middle fingers. Sometimes visitors think it is some kind of local gesture indicating *up yours* or some similarly unfriendly message. Actually, it is a friendly act used as a sign of greeting, thanks or just to say, *Hey.* Its origin is thought to date back to the 1930s. A guard at the Kahuku Sugar Plantation used to patrol the plantation railroad to keep local kids from stealing cane from the slow moving trains. This guard had lost his middle fingers in an accident, and his manner of waving off the youths became well known. Kids began to warn other kids that he was around by waving their hands in a way that looked like the guard's, and the custom took off.

THE HAWAIIAN LANGUAGE

The Hawaiian language is a beautiful, gentle and melodic language that flows smoothly off the tongue. Just the sounds of the words conjure up trees gently blowing in the breeze and the sound of the surf. Most Polynesian languages share the same roots, and many have common words. Today, Hawaiian is spoken *as an everyday language* only on the privately owned island of Ni'ihau. Visitors are often intimidated by Hawaiian. With a few ground rules you will come to realize that pronunciation is not as hard as you might think.

When missionaries discovered that the Hawaiians had no written language, they sat down and created an alphabet. This Hawaiian alphabet has only 12 letters. Five vowels: A, E, I, O and U, as well as seven consonants, H, K, L, M, N, P and W. The consonants are pronounced just as they are in English, with the exception of W. It is often pronounced as a V if it is in the middle of a word and comes after an E or I. Vowels are pronounced as follows:

A—pronounced as in *Ah* if stressed, or *above* if not stressed.
E—pronounced as in *say* if stressed, or *dent* if not stressed.
I—pronounced as in *bee*.
O—pronounced as in *nose*.
U—pronounced as in *stew*.

If you examine long Hawaiian words, you will see that most have repeating syllables, making them easier to remember and pronounce.

One thing you will notice in this book are glottal stops. These are represented by an upside-down apostrophe ' and are meant to convey a hard stop in the pronunciation. So if we are talking about the type of lava called a'a, it is pronounced as two separate As.

Another feature you will encounter are diphthongs, where two letters glide together. They are ae, ai, ao, au, ei, eu, oi and ou. Unlike many English diph-thongs, the second vowel is always pronounced. One word you will read in this book, referring to Hawaiian temples, is *heiau* (hey-ee-ow). The e and i flow together as a single sound, then the a and u flow together as a single sound. The ee sound binds the two sounds, making the whole word flow together.

Let's take a word that might seem impossible to pronounce. When you see how easy this word is, the rest will seem like a snap. The Hawaiian state fish used to be the humuhumunukunukuapua'a. At first glance it seems like a nightmare. But if you read the word slowly, it is pronounced just like it looks and isn't nearly as horrifying as it appears. Try it. Humu (hoo-moo) is pronounced twice. Nuku (noo-koo) is pronounced twice. A (ah) is pronounced once. Pu is pronounced once. A'a (ah-ah) is the ah sound pronounced twice, the glottal stop indicating a hard stop between sounds. Now, you can try to pronounce it again. Humuhumunukunukuapua'a. Now, wasn't that easy? OK, so it's not easy, but it's not impossible either.

Below are some words that you might hear during your visit:

'Aina (EYE-nah)—Land.
Akamai (ah-kah-MY)—Wise or shrewd.
Ali'i (ah-LEE-ee)—A Hawaiian chief; a member of the chiefly class.
Aloha (ah-LOW-ha)—Hello, goodbye, or a feeling or the spirit of love, affection or kindness.
Hala (hah-la)—Pandanus tree.
Hale (hah-leh)—House or building.
Hana (ha-nah)—Work.
Hana hou (ha-nah-HO)—To do again.
Haole (how-leh)—Originally foreigner, now means Caucasian.
Heiau (hey-ee-ow)—Hawaiian temple.
Hula (hoo-lah)—The storytelling dance of Hawai'i.

Imu (ee-moo)—An underground oven.

ʻIniki (ee-nee-key)—Sharp and piercing wind (as in Hurricane ʻIniki).

Kahuna (kah-HOO-na)—A priest or minister; someone who is an expert in a profession.

Kai (kigh)—The sea.

Kalua (KAH-loo-ah)—Cooking food underground.

Kamaʻaina (kah-ma-EYE-na)—Long-time Hawaiʻi resident.

Kane (KAH-nay)—Boy or man.

Kapu (kah-poo)—Forbidden, taboo; keep out.

Keiki (kay-key)—Child or children.

Kokua (KOH-koo-ah)—Help.

Kona (koh-nah)—Leeward side of the island; wind blowing from the south, southwest direction.

Kuleana (koo-lay-ah-nah)—Concern, responsibility or jurisdiction.

Lanai (LAH-nigh)—Porch, veranda, patio.

Lani (lah-nee)—Sky or heaven.

Lei (lay)—Necklace of flowers, shells or feathers.

Lilikoʻi (lee-lee-koy)—Passion fruit.

Limu (lee-moo)—Edible seaweed.

Lomi (low-mee)—To rub or massage; lomi salmon is raw salmon rubbed with salt and spices.

Luʻau (LOO-ow)—Hawaiian feast; literally means taro leaves.

Mahalo (mah-hah-low)—Thank you.

Makai (mah-kigh)—Toward the sea.

Malihini (mah-lee-hee-nee)—A newcomer, visitor or guest.

Mauka (mow-ka)—Toward the mountain.

Moana (moh-ah-nah)—Ocean.

Moʻo (moh-oh)—Lizard.

Nani (nah-nee)—Beautiful, pretty.

Once endangered, green sea turtles are now much more common on Oʻahu than they used to be.

Nui (new-ee)—Big, important, great.
ʻOhana (oh-hah-nah)—Family.
ʻOkole (OH-koh-leh)—Derrière.
ʻOno (oh-no)—Delicious, the best.
Pakalolo (pah-kah-low-low)—Marijuana.
Pali (pah-lee)—A cliff.
Paniolo (pah-nee-oh-low)—Hawaiian cowboy.
Pau (pow)—Finish, end; i.e., pau hana means quitting time from work.
Poi (poy)—Pounded kalo (taro) root that forms a paste.
Pono (poh-no)—Goodness, excellence, correct, proper.
Pua (poo-ah)—Flower.
Puka (poo-ka)—Hole.
Pupu (poo-poo)—Appetizer, snacks or finger food.
Wahine (vah-hee-neh)—Woman.
Wai (why)—Fresh water.

Wikiwiki (wee-kee-wee-kee)—To hurry up, very quick.

Quick Pidgin Lesson

Hawaiian pidgin is fun to listen to. It's like ear candy. It's colorful, rhythmic and sways in the wind. Below is a list of some of the words and phrases you might hear on your visit. It's tempting to read some of these and try to use them. If you do, the odds are you will simply look foolish. These words and phrases are used in certain ways and with certain inflections. People who have spent years living in the islands still feel uncomfortable using them. Thick pidgin can be incomprehensible to the untrained ear (that's the idea). If you are someplace and hear two people engaged in a discussion in pidgin, stop and eavesdrop a bit. You won't forget it.

When you want to get away, but not too far away, how about visiting an offshore island?

Pidgin Words & Phrases

An' den—And then? So?

Any kine—Anything; any kind.

Ass right—That's right.

Ass wy—That's why.

Beef—Fight.

Brah—Bruddah; friend; brother.

Brok' da mouf—Delicious.

Buggah—That's the one; it is difficult.

Bus laugh—To laugh out loud.

Bus nose—How one reacts to bad smell.

Chicken skin kine—Something that gives you goose bumps.

Choke—Plenty; lots.

Cockaroach—Steal; rip off.

Da kine—A noun or verb used in place of whatever the speaker wishes. Heard constantly.

Fo Days—Plenty; "He got hair fo days."

Geevum—Go for it! Give 'em hell!

Grind—To eat.

Grinds—Food.

Hold ass—A close call when driving your new car.

How you figga?—How do you figure that? It makes no sense.

Howzit?—How is it going? How are you? Also, Howzit o wot?

I owe you money or wot?—What to say when someone is staring at you.

Make house—Make yourself at home.

Make plate—Grab some food.

Mek ass—Make a fool of yourself.

Mo' bettah—This is better.

Moke—A large, tough local male. (Don't say it unless you *like beef*.)

No can—Cannot; I cannot do it.

No make li dat—Stop doing that.

No, yeah?—No, or is "no" correct?

'Okole squeezer—Something that suddenly frightens you ('okole meaning derrière).

O wot?—Or what?

Pau hana—Quit work. (A time of daily, intense celebration in the islands.)

Poi dog—A mutt.

Shahkbait—Shark bait, meaning pale, untanned people.

Shaka—Great! All right!

Shredding—Riding a gnarly wave.

Sleepahs—Flip flops, thongs, zoris.

Stink eye—Dirty looks; facial expression denoting displeasure.

Suck rocks—Buzz off, or pound sand.

Talk stink—Speak bad about somebody.

Talk story—Shooting the breeze; to rap.

Tanks eh?—Thank you.

Tita—A female moke. Same *beef* results.

Yeah?—Used at the end of sentences.

THE HULA

The hula evolved as a means of worship, later becoming a forum for telling a story with chants (called mele), hands and body movement. It can be fascinating to watch. When most people think of the hula, they picture a woman in a grass skirt swinging her hips to the beat of an 'ukulele. But in reality there are two types of hula. The modern hula, or hula 'auana, uses musical instruments and vocals to augment the dancer. It came about after westerners first encountered the Islands. Missionaries found the hula distasteful, and the old style was driven underground. The modern type came about as a form of entertainment and was practiced in places where missionaries had no influence. Ancient Hawaiians didn't even use grass skirts. They were later brought by Gilbert Islanders.

The old style of hula is called hula 'olapa or hula kahiko. It consists of chants and is accompanied by percussion only and takes years of training. It can be exciting to watch as performers work together in a synchronous harmony. Both men and women participate, with women's hula being softer (though no less disciplined) and men's hula being more active. This type of hula is physically demanding, requiring strong concentration. Keiki (children's) hula can be charming to watch, as well.

BOOKS & MUSIC

There is an astonishing variety of books available about Hawai'i and O'ahu. Everything from history, legends, geology, children's stories and just plain ol' novels. Barnes & Noble (737–3323) in Kahala Mall has a great selection. Walk in and lose yourself in Hawai'i's richness. Borders Books (591–8995) in Ward Centre at 1200 Ala Moana Blvd. also has an excellent selection. Others include Borders Express (922–4154) at the Waikiki Shopping Plaza across from the Royal Hawaiian Shopping Center and Bestsellers Books and Music (953–2378) in the Hilton Hawaiian Village.

Hawaiian music is far more diverse than most people think. Many people picture Hawaiian music as someone twanging away on an 'ukulele with his voice slipping and sliding all over the place like he has an ice cube down his back. In reality, the music here can be outstanding. There is the melodic sound of the more traditional music. There are young local bands putting out modern music with a Hawaiian beat. There is even Hawaiian reggae. Hawaiian Style Band, the late Israel Kamakawiwo'ole (known locally as Bruddah Iz) and Willie K are excellent examples of the local sound. Even if you don't always agree with the all the messages in the songs, there's no denying the talent of these entertainers.

THE INTERNET

Our Web site, www.wizardpub.com has recent changes, links to cool sites, the latest satellite weather shots, calendar of events and more. We also show our own aerial photos of most places to stay on O'ahu, so you'll know if oceanfront *really* means oceanfront. It has links to every company listed in the book that has a site—both those we like and those we don't recommend. For the record we don't charge a cent for links (it would be a conflict of interest), and there are *no advertisements* on the site. (Well...except for our own books, of course.) We've been asked why we don't list Web sites and e-mail addresses in the book. Linking from the site makes more sense. Nothing is more mind-numbing than seeing URL addresses in print.

If you're on-island and need Web access (to check your mail, etc.), most of the big resorts have business services available for around $20 an hour, and Internet cafés or kiosks aren't hard to find. Among the cafés are Fishbowl Café (922–7565) in the Kuhio Village Resort Hotel at 2436 Kuhio Ave., Caffé Giovannini (979–2299) at 1888 Kalakaua, #C106 and the Sand Bar (922–4744) at Waikiki Sand Villas at 2375 Ala Wai Blvd.

If you brought your own computer, then shame on you—you're on vacation. Nonetheless nearly all of the hotel rooms have data ports on their phone. If you don't have an 800 number to call from your Internet account at home Lava.net (888–545–5282) can arrange unlimited local Web access for $12.50 for two weeks plus a $10 set-up fee. We also have a link to them. Pixi.com (888–722–4636) has $12 per week access and a $15 set up fee (which they waive if you set up by phone). Both of these are good on all the islands.

SHOPPING

Most of us long to return home with a smile, tan and gifts from Hawai'i for

Meet O'ahu's number one cash crop—after tourists, of course.

friends and family. Besides locally grown coffee, chocolate macadamia nuts, T-shirts, aloha wear and other reminders of your visit, there are some one-of-a-kind finds at nearby **Ala Moana Shopping Center**. Perhaps the million-dollar necklace from Cartier or the $200,000 ring from Tiffany will wow them back home. Or consider the $75,000 Hermes handbag or the $12,000 Montblanc pen for your boss. It's all there for you to choose from, and prices might even include a free gift box. (If the above shopping list seems reasonable to you, your humble authors could use one of those Montblanc pens.) Ala Moana is the largest shopping center in Hawai'i and draws neighbor island residents to its doors, as well.

In Waikiki, **Kalakaua Avenue** has a multitude of shops from the very expensive to the affordable. The **International Marketplace**, due to undergo a major renovation in a few years, is well known as a bargain hunter's paradise.

Looking for a taste of local foods? The Saturday morning **farmers market** in the parking lot of Kapiolani Community Col-

The waterfall at Waimea Valley Audubon Center is one of the few on the island that you can swim under.

lege (just east of Waikiki at the entrance to Diamond Head) is a popular event. It runs from 8 a.m. to noon.

The **Aloha Stadium Swap Meet** on Wednesdays, Saturdays and Sundays starts early and runs until 3 p.m. A good stop after visiting Pearl Harbor. It's where H-1, H-3, Hwy 78 and Hwy 99 converge.

Plan to spend some time browsing in **Hale'iwa**. There are a number of shops filled with artwork, clothing and other unique items. The surfing theme is everywhere.

Another good stop is **Hilo Hattie**. Their main store is on 700 Nimitz Hwy (at Pacific Street), accessible by shuttle from Waikiki. They also have a smaller store at Ala Moana Shopping Center.

Plan on spending a half day browsing the shops in **Chinatown** and grabbing lunch there. This is a good place to purchase a beautiful lei, some fresh produce or a one-of-a-kind gift.

Finally, if you're out on the west side, there's the **Waikele Premium Outlet** stores and several restaurants.

MISCELLANEOUS INFORMATION

Travelers checks are usually accepted, but you should be aware that some merchants might look at you like you just tried to offer them Mongolian money. You should also know that Discover Cards seem to be less welcome here than other destinations. *Many* places will not accept them.

It is customary here for *everyone* to remove their shoes upon entering someone's house (sometimes their office).

If you are going to spend any time at the beach, woven bamboo beach mats can be found all over the island for about $2. Some roll up; some can be folded. The sand comes off these more easily than it comes off towels.

It's a good idea to get your **photos** developed here. That's because developers are more familiar with the colors. (Just try to get a black or red sand beach to look right from a mainland developer; and you'll see what we mean.) If you don't want to pay retail-retail, try Longs, Costco or Wal-Mart. Most have cheap one-hour service and are surprisingly good. Most will redo the photos to make the color right. Also, if you're looking to dump your digital images onto a CD (so you can keep using your memory card) most of the photo shops in Waikiki can accommodate you.

The **area code** for all of Hawai'i is (808).

Around the island you'll see signs saying VISITOR INFORMATION or something similar. Allow me to translate: That's usually code for WE WANT TO SELL YOU SOMETHING.

If you want to arrange a lei greeting for you or your honey when you disembark the airplane at the airport, **Ali'i Leis** (800) 563–4449, **Greeters of Hawai'i** (800) 366–8559 and **Honolulu Lei Greetings** (800) 665–7959 can make the arrangements for around $20 and up. Nice way to kick off a romantic trip, huh?

A WORD ABOUT DRIVING TOURS

For directions, locals usually describe things as being on the *mauka* (MOW-kah) side of the road—toward the mountains—or *makai* (mah-KIGH)—toward the ocean.

Beaches, activities, attractions and adventures are mentioned briefly, but described in detail in their own sections.

GETTING INTO & OUT OF WAIKIKI

Though Waikiki is the main place that visitors stay, there is no dedicated on-ramp or off-ramp for it from the main highway, H-1. Leaving the airport, the most efficient way to Waikiki is H-1 East. Though the signs *won't* direct you this way, the quickest route is to drive past what they *call* the Waikiki exits, take exit 24A (Bingham), right on Farrington, right on Beretania, left on McCully, which will take you into Waikiki. (See map on page 48.) Taking the so-called Waikiki exits (exits 22 and 23) is a less direct route. Most visitors erroneously take the Nimitz Hwy from the airport and are greeted by heavy traffic most of the way.

Leaving Waikiki to get onto H-1, take Ala Wai Boulevard to McCully, and follow the signs if you're heading west (toward the airport), or take McCully, right on Kapiolani and follow the signs if you're heading east on H-1.

The ultimate swimming pool slide in Kane'ohe Bay.

A NOTE ON PERSONAL RESPONSIBILITY

Although this is our first edition of *O'ahu Revealed*, in our neighbor island books we've had the sad task of removing places that you can no longer visit. The reason, universally cited, is liability. Although Hawai'i has statutes immunizing private and government landowners, the mere threat is often enough to get something closed. Because we, more than any other publication, have exposed heretofore unknown attractions, we feel the need to pass this along.

Please remember, this isn't Disneyland. Mother nature is hard, slippery, sharp and unpredictable. In addition, *every single* rock and patch of dirt that makes up Hawai'i will fall into the sea. Not one rock will survive the process. The islands are being slowly erased by the ocean. *That's* why they're so beautiful. If you happen to get in the way of that process…then it just wasn't your day.

If the more crowded part of Waikiki gets you down, Fort DeRussy Beach is the widest part of Waikiki and there are usually far fewer people.

Honolulu is the central hub of the Hawaiian Islands, and Waikiki is the center of tourism. Lots of people work, live and play in this part of the state, and odds are overwhelming that this is where *you'll* be staying. That's because there are around 100 resorts on the island of O'ahu, and all but four of them are in Waikiki. At any one time, 44% of visitors *in the entire state of Hawai'i* are spending their night in Waikiki.

WAIKIKI

Imagine an area of less than one square mile that had over 60,000 hotel rooms. Imagine that this area was blessed with one of the most user-friendly beaches in the world. Where just about anyone could take a surf lesson and ride their first wave. A place with more restaurants than most decent-sized towns. A place with limitless shopping. Well, this place actually exists. Waikiki is the essence of carefree. Visitors here tend to feel safe, warm and happy.

Waikiki is about walking and gawking, eating and shopping, surfing and soaking up the sun. You don't come to Waikiki to get away from the action; you come here to get a *piece* of the action. This is the place where you and 4 million of your closest friends each year embrace the tropics and each other. If you're looking for a quiet, out-of-the-way destination, look elsewhere. Waikiki is a humming, happening visitor mecca.

There is almost nothing natural about Waikiki. A century ago the land behind

The electric energy that you'll find at Waikiki doesn't end when the sun goes down.

the beach was a swampy sponge. Three rivers emptied into the ocean here, and the beach, though still a great place to swim, was hardly a must-see destination. Then in 1921 they started draining the swamp. People often wonder, *how do drain a swamp?* Simple—you dig a canal to cut off the source of water and let nature dry it out. This they did by creating the Ala Wai Canal. And the rest is history. Waikiki, now backed by land suitable for development, was ready to take off. Throughout the 20th century, resort after resort sprung up, and visitors began coming here in droves.

Early evening is our favorite time to experience Waikiki, when the intensity of the sun is replaced by the joy of people-watching. Stroll along the sidewalks

of Kalakaua Avenue, shop, snack and enjoy the warm, secure feeling that dusk in the tropics provides. Incidentally, the main street, Kalakaua, has surprisingly few signs verifying that's the street you're on.

If you want to stroll along the beach, you can walk from the Hilton at one end of Waikiki all the way to Kapiolani Park at the other. Those few areas that lack sand have other means of traversing the shoreline that will keep you dry. A sunset walk along Waikiki Beach is always a dreamy experience as you listen to music often spilling from the various resorts. If you walk from the Diamond Head side toward Honolulu, you'll be walking toward the sun. During part of the summer the sun doesn't set over the ocean from most of Waikiki.

Though less than a square mile, it's one of those ironies of modern life that the smaller a place is, the more walking you're apt to do. *Forget the car, honey, we'll walk it.* That's the phrase you'll hear and say throughout your stay. Many people who come to O'ahu never even rent a car (which we think is a mistake—see BASICS on page 23). But for getting around this square mile of activity, odds are you'll either walk, take the bus, take a shuttle or rent a scooter. Driving your car around Waikiki can be a pain because parking is such a problem.

The bus costs $2 one way, or you can get monthly pass for $40. Route 8 is the main Waikiki route, so we've shown that one on our Waikiki map. The other bus, called the Waikiki Shuttle, is a rip-off at $20 *per person per day* to use. Scooters cost around $25. You can also rent small electric cars, but you'll have the same parking problems as regular cars. If you don't want to walk around Waikiki, there are Segways (394–5433) for rent. (Those are those self-balanced, self-propelled electric scooters.) It's *expensive*—$35 an hour or $45 for a guided tour. We suspect that the price won't stay that high for long. You'll find them on the corner of Kalakaua and Beachwalk.

One activity that has been going on in Waikiki for over a century is outrigger canoe rides. Aloha Beach Services (922–3111, ext. 2341) has rides for $10 (you get to ride two different waves) or you can charter the whole 8-passenger outrigger canoe (includes paddlers) for $225 per hour.

Picking where to stay in Waikiki is daunting. Price is presumably a factor, and generally the closer you get to the water, the higher the price. Distance to the heart of Waikiki also a consideration. If you don't want to walk great distances whenever you want to experience what

Waikiki has to offer, the best location is on the ocean side of Kalakaua between Saratoga Avenue and the Waikiki Beach Center. The area around the Royal Hawaiian and the Moana Surfrider is usually considered to be the center of Waikiki life.

Waikiki Beach

Although we have a dedicated chapter on beaches, we wanted to describe the beaches of Waikiki here instead of the BEACHES section because it's where nearly everyone stays on O'ahu, and it's likely you'll stroll along them at various time throughout your stay.

A REAL GEM

Waikiki is a swimming and surfing beach, not a snorkeling site, and there

48

WAIKIKI RESORTS

1 Ala Moana Hotel A3
2 Aloha Punawai F4
3 Ambassador Hotel of Waikiki E2
4 Aqua Marina Hotel B4
5 Aston Aloha Surf H2
6 Aston Coconut Plaza F2
7 Aston Waikiki Beach Hotel J4
8 Aston Waikiki Beachside I4
9 Bamboo (Aqua) I3
10 Breakers F4
11 Cabana at Waikiki J4
12 Continental Surf Hotel I2
13 Coral Reef Hotel (Aston) G2
14 Diamond Head Beach Hotel (Marc) ..N9
15 DoubleTree Alana Hotel D2
16 Ewa Hotel Waikiki J4
17 Hale Koa D6
18 Halekulani F5
19 Hawaii Polo Inn B4
20 Hawaii Prince Hotel Waikiki B5
21 Hawaiian King.....................G2
22 Hawaiian Monarch Hotel C1
23 Hawaiiana Hotel F4
24 Hilton Hawaiian Village C5
25 Hokondo Waikiki Beachside Hostel ...J4
26 Holiday Inn Waikiki C4
27 Holiday Surf G1
28 Honolulu Prince (Aston) H2
29 Hostelling International H3
30 Hyatt Regency Waikiki H3
31 Ilima Hotel G1
32 Imperial Hawaii Resort F5
33 Island Colony G1
34 Kai Aloha Hotel F4
35 Kuhio Village Resort (Aqua) I3
36 Marc Suites Waikiki F2
37 Marc Waikiki Royal Suites F4
38 Marine Surf Waikiki Hotel G2
39 Marriott Waikiki Beach Resort J4
40 Miramar at Waikiki H3
41 New Otani Kaimana Beach Hotel M8
42 Ocean Resort Hotel Waikiki J3
43 Ohana East H3
44 Ohana Islander Waikiki F4
45 Ohana Maile Sky Court E2
46 Ohana Reef Lanai F5
47 Ohana Royal Islander F5
48 Ohana (Waikiki) Malia F2
49 Ohana Waikiki Surf F2
50 Ohana Waikiki Surf East F2
51 Ohana Waikiki Tower F5
52 Ohana Waikiki Village F4
53 Ohana (Waikiki) West H2
54 Outrigger Luana Waikiki E3
55 Outrigger Reef on the Beach F6
56 Outrigger Waikiki on the Beach H4
57 Pacific Beach Hotel I4
58 Pacific Monarch (Aston) I3
59 Park Shore Waikiki J5
60 Queen Kapiolani Hotel K4
61 Radisson (Waikiki) Prince Kuhio J2
62 Renaissance Ilikai Waikiki Hotel B5
63 Royal Garden at Waikiki E2
64 Royal Grove Hotel I3
65 Royal Hawaiian (Sheraton) G5
66 Sheraton Moana Surfrider H4
67 Sheraton Princess Kaiulani H3
68 Sheraton Waikiki G5
69 W Honolulu Diamond Head M8
70 Waikiki Banyan (Aston) J3
71 Waikiki Beach Tower (Aston) I3
72 Waikiki Beachcomber G3
73 Waikiki Circle (Aston) I4
74 Waikiki Gateway E3
75 Waikiki Grand J4
76 Waikiki Joy Hotel (Aston) F3
77 Waikiki Parc Hotel F5
78 Waikiki Prince Hotel I3
79 Waikiki Resort Hotel I3
80 Waikiki Sand Villa H1
81 Waikiki Shore F6
82 Waikiki Sunset (Aston) J2

Honolulu

Tantalus Dr

To Manoa Falls

Mott-Smith

Round Top

Makiki Heights

University

Nehoa

Wahiolimu

Metcalf

Makiki

Wilder

Wilder

Exit 24A

Alexander

Dole

H-1

Isenberg

Exit 24A

Farrington

To H-1 West out of Waikiki

Piikoi

Exit 23 (Punahou) to Waikiki

Punahou

S. King

Kalakaua

Waikiki map on page 48

S. Beretania

McCully

Honolulu Academy of Arts

Pensacola

Piikoi

Rycroft

Keeaumoku

Sam's Club/ Wal-Mart

Makaloa

Century Center

Kapiolani

Hawai'i Convention Center

Kalākaua

Ena

Waikiki

Lipeepee

Hobron

Kapiolani

Ala Moana

Ward Village Shops

Piikoi

Ala Moana Shopping Center

92

Hobron

Kaioo

Kalia

Queen

Kamakee

Ala Moana Blvd

Ala Wai Yacht Harbor

Bishop Museum (mini)

d Gateway Center

Queen St.

Ward Centre

Ala Moana Blvd

Auahi

arehouse

Ala Moana Beach Park

Kahanamoku Beach portion of Waikiki

Pier

walo asin

Magic Island

A peaceful morning on Waikiki Beach.

are no great snorkeling conditions any-where along here. If you're insistent, the best conditions are off the tip of the Kapahulu Groin and the tip of the wall at the south end of Queen's Beach (both of these *only* if there are no surfers or boo-gie boarders in the area—they have little patience for snorkelers) and, ironically, offshore of the Waikiki Aquarium.

Also remember that although Waikiki Beach is very sandy, the nearshore waters often have lots of rocks and reef that conspire to attack your feet. Smart beachgoers wear reef or water shoes. The sandiest patches are off Waikiki Beach Center (for a little ways), in front of the ultra-pink Royal Hawaiian tower building (although the water there tends to be cloudy) and at the eastern (Dia-mond Head) side of Kahanamoku Beach up to the pier in front of the Hilton.

The entire beach is known as Waikiki Beach, but different stretches have differ-ent names. Starting in front of the mas-sive Hilton Hawaiian Village, Kahana-moku Beach (named after Hawai'i's favorite son, surfing legend Duke Ka-hanamoku) is usually very crowded. It's considered a very safe swimming beach

due to its protection from a breakwater on one side, a reef offshore and a jetty on the Diamond Head side. There's an easy-to-walk concrete beach path that runs from the Hilton to the far end of Fort DeRussy Beach. If you're looking for a snack, soda or adult beverage, grab one at the Hau Tree Beach Bar behind the beach, or, better yet, use the unexpect-edly cheap snack bar at the Hale Koa. It's a military hotel, not normally open to the public, but a little-known loophole allows

you to wander in from the beach and eat there. See DINING on page 228 for more.

Fort DeRussy Beach is the *widest* part of Waikiki Beach. The southeast end occasionally gets balls of seaweed washing ashore, and the water along the wall—especially on the left side—has cold basal springs that drop the water temperature. But this is a fantastic part of Waikiki and is a bit less crowded compared to other parts of the beach.

Gray's Beach is the one part of Waiki-

ki that has mostly washed away. Waikiki has been enhanced many times over the years with importations of sand. In recent years officials have been hesitant to bring in more sand, fearing that they'd alter the shape of Waikiki's famous waves. But being bureaucrats, they're also fearful of making making a wrong decision, so little has been done in recent years to stop the erosion of sand. As a result, Waikiki is thin in areas like Gray's Beach. It's also much less padded in the nearshore waters than it used to be, so water or reef shoes are recommended in most parts of the beach.

At Royal-Moana Beach, the beach is at its sandiest, and beach use tends to be high. You won't find a lot of vacant sand here.

Next door is the Waikiki Beach Center. This is the spot for surf lessons and outrigger canoe rides. There are no resorts lining this part of the beach, and Kalakaua Avenue is right next to the park.

Past here is Kuhio Beach, also known as The Ponds. Kuhio has concrete walls

A slightly less peaceful afternoon.

forming two separate ponds—perfect for kids and those skittish about swimming in the open ocean.

When you leave Kuhio Beach, you leave the resort towers of Waikiki behind. The Kapahulu Groin is the jetty extending into the sea where Kalakaua Avenue meets Kapahulu Avenue. This is our favorite place to be in Waikiki when the surf's up—usually in the summer. It extends out into the waves, so you'll feel like you're part of the action. Boogie boarders and body surfers cruise right up to you, then past you. You'll quickly gain a perspective of the waves that's not possible from the shore. Boogie boarders often surf right up to the shore, hop on the groin, run to the end and jump off to start over again. (By the way, *we* always thought a groin was something you pulled playing football. Actually, it's a wall that runs perpendicular to the beach to stop sand migration.)

Though the north end of the groin is usually swimming pool-calm, the south end sometimes provides some of the nicest and longest boogie board rides in South O'ahu. Queen's Beach is named after a long-gone restaurant by that name. It's also a good place to stretch a towel and is usually less crowded than the beaches in front of the resorts. Queen's Beach (AKA Queen's Surf Beach) is also where Sunset on the Beach takes place every other Saturday and Sunday. Picture a 30-foot screen on the beach, food concessionaires selling the expected junk food, and movies equivalent to recent DVD releases being shown for free. It's lots of fun (although crowded). Call 523–2489 for listings, or simply walk by and look at the sign.

The sand beach ends here. Behind you, Kapiolani Park is a giant, triangular-shaped lawn where people play soc-

Part of Waikiki Beach at Kuhio Beach Park is ultra-protected by a breakwater for effortless swimming.

Meet the only royal residence in the United States—'Iolani Palace.

cer, fly kites, walk their dogs and jog to their hearts' content. Diamond Head seems to tower over this park. The north end is where you'll find the Waikiki Shell, a seashell-shaped outdoor amphitheater where live performances are occasionally held.

Kapiolani Park is also where you'll find the Natatorium and the Waikiki Aquarium. (Before you get too worked up over the aquarium, read the ATTRACTIONS chapter to see if it's for you.)

The Natatorium is a WWI memorial built in 1927 to honor Hawai'i's casualties from the "great war." Its 100-meter pool was used by generations of residents for swim meets and recreation. The Natatorium fell into disrepair and was closed by the Department of Health in 1979. It's been partially renovated but no longer used for swimming and has been stuck in political quicksand for years. It's now merely a convenient place to park and used for its bathrooms by swimmers at Sans Souci Beach next door. At press time there were plans to return it to its former glory, but in the meantime, it's sort of a white elephant that Hawai'i residents, out of embarrassment, kind of hope you don't see.

Sans Souci Beach is a nice but small beach on the south end of the Natatorium. It's semi-protected by one wall of the Natatorium, has showers, restrooms (at the Natatorium) and life-guards. The sand is fairly coarse that brushes off more easily than the fine stuff, and it extends far enough into the ocean to provide a cushion for your feet. Park at the Natatorium on Kalakaua Avenue.

International Marketplace

The International Marketplace is a 125,000-square-foot brick-lined tropical bazaar with countless stalls of venders and bartering customers, sprawling banyan trees and a hissing waterfall. Though the shops gravitate toward the cheap knickknack, the atmosphere is too alluring not to be experienced at least once. Shop for pearls still in the oyster, tons of inexpensive jewelry, clothing, a surf shop, wood tikis and a billion things that you can put on your desk back home. Located between Kalakaua and Kuhio next to Duke's Lane.

Cocktails in Waikiki

It's been our observation that adult beverages in Waikiki that are served next to the beach tend to be a bit weak, especially when served by big resorts like the Hilton, and no amount of coaching seems to make a difference. Perhaps they're counting multiple purchases. For the record, it's illegal to consume alcohol on the beach in Hawai'i. This rule would come as a complete surprise to anyone visiting since restaurants and barefoot bars next to the beach often serve their drinks in plastic cups and sort of wink and nod while they tell you about the law when you ask for a drink to go. The law seems to be little enforced on Waikiki Beach, and a visit to nearly any beach on the weekend will reveal locals with giant ice chests full of beer.

HONOLULU

Honolulu is overrepresented when it comes to attractions you may want to visit. It's got so many, in fact, that we have a dedicated ATTRACTIONS chapter you should read. Check out places like 'Iolani Palace, Punchbowl National Cemetery, Chinatown, Bishop Museum, Doris Duke's Shangri La and garden tours.

Driving around Honolulu and Waikiki can be maddening, and no matter how much effort we put into our maps, they can't cover up the fact that our road system was created by...well, morons. (Sorry, but it's true.) Having a navigator who's good at reading maps on the fly can help, but you should count on getting lost, irritated and driving in the vicinity of something you're trying to get to only to curse in rage that you can't find it or maneuver to it. Hey...it's O'ahu. After a week or so you'll learn some of its tricks and shortcuts, but the learning curve can be steep. Even living here, we get frustrated at the unintuitive layout. And getting on and off H-1 freeway can be a joke. We still find it incredible that the primary place where visitors stay—Waikiki—doesn't have a dedicated on-ramp to get back onto H-1 west. From McCully, you're directed though a neighborhood until you wander onto an on-ramp. It's embarrassing, but it's part of our charm, right?

Tantalus

Regardless of how long you stay in Honolulu, at some point you should take a drive along Tantalus and Round Top. This 10-mile long road wiggles and winds up the mountains through a pretty forest above

NOT TO BE MISSED!

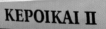

Cruisin' up to the beach at Waikiki.

Fifteen minutes from the asphalt jungle of Honolulu lies a different kind of jungle off Tantalus Road.

Honolulu to the 1,610-foot level, and in the process you'll gain an appreciation of Honolulu's beauty you never really expected.

As a loop road you'll start at one end and finish at another. Take Ala Wai Boulevard, then right on Kalakaua out of Waikiki, left onto Kapiolani, right onto Keeaumoku, up and over H-1, right on Wilder, left on Makiki. When you get to Makiki Heights Drive, take a left onto it (if it's the afternoon) and right when it dead ends onto Tantalus to do the loop. If it's the morning, stay on Makiki and go past Makiki Heights Drive and then turn left onto Round Top to complete the loop, turning left onto Makiki Heights when

you're done. (This routing takes best advantage of the lighting.) See maps on pages 50 and 68, which ought to help.

This is a great road to drive in a convertible. Leadfoots may be tempted to take the winding road fast, but you'll actually want to drive this road slowly, or it'll be over too soon and you'll miss some of the scenery. Keep an eye out for pullouts along the way. Several have fantastic views of the leeward side of O'ahu below you. No view, however, can compare to the pure majesty of the view from Pu'u Ualaka'a State Wayside. When you pull into this park, stay left at the intersections till it ends, then walk out a hundred feet to the point. From one corner of the island at Barbers Point all the way past Diamond Head to Kahala, a giant 25-mile swath of O'ahu presents itself. We're only sorry that we

Bishop Estate Kamehameha Schools

Everyone in who lives in Hawai'i knows what the Bishop Estate is. It is feared, admired, detested and loved. It is synonymous with absolute power—and absolute corruption. And it owns 9% of all the land in these islands.

The last descendant of King Kamehameha the Great was Princess Bernice Pauahi. She married an American named Charles Bishop and, when she died of cancer in 1884, left most of her assets—meaning 431,000 acres of Hawai'i—to a trust set up "to erect and maintain in the Hawaiian Islands two schools, each for boarding and day scholars, one for boys and one for girls, to be known as, and called, the Kamehameha Schools."

The will stipulated that trustees were to be chosen by the Hawai'i Supreme Court, and over the years, becoming a trustee became the ultimate political plum job. Hawai'i's old boy political machine took care of its own. Trustees paid themselves almost $1 million a year each, even during years of mind-boggling losses of a hundred million dollars or more, and sweetheart deals were rampant and only minimally covered up. Some of the land was sold, but with so much land and power remaining, the trust grew to be worth over $10 billion. All this to pay for a central school that houses around 3,200 students, some preschools and two small neighbor island campuses. (Despite the will's language, the trustees created a single co-ed O'ahu school in 1965.) Corruption, arrogance and mismanagement became the face that residents associated with Bishop Estate, but it was so intertwined with the political establishment that few challenged it. Finally in the late 1990s, the stench of corruption reached such unbearable levels that the state and federal governments stepped in. (The spark that started it all was an op-ed piece in the local newspaper written by five very respected members of the local community.) Smelling blood from the heretofore untouchable estate, newspapers, prominent leaders and government agencies converged on the Bishop Estate from every direction. All the trustees resigned or were removed. Indictments, convictions, prison and even suicide resulted from this reckoning, and the IRS came perilously close to revoking the estate's tax-exempt status since so few dollars were being spent on the supposed object of the charity—the school.

Today Kamehameha Schools/Bishop Estate tries to keep a lower political profile in Hawai'i. Trustees are now chosen by a probate judge, not the Supreme Court, and trustee fees are less, though still generous. They're still the largest private landowner in the state, but they've come down a notch or two in the eyes of most residents.

don't have a camera lens wide enough to show it all to you. You'll have to see for yourself.

Ala Moana Area

Just outside Waikiki is Ala Moana. If you'd been visiting Honolulu in the early 1900s, you'd never want to visit the Ala Moana area. It was a nasty, swampy and smelly area of mud flats that also housed the almost con-

A REAL GEM

tinuously burning Honolulu garbage dump. Everyone avoided the area except duck pond owners. Then in 1912 a dredging company owner named Dillingham bought this worthless land. His friends thought he was nuts, but Dillingham was looking for a place to dispose of all of his dredged earth. In the 1950s a mile of sand was dumped at this park, creating the perfect swimming spot you see today. And in 1959, the year Hawai'i became a state, the island's most prestigious shopping center was built across the street, the 50-acre Ala Moana Shopping Center. Ala Moana went from uninviting wasteland to a beautiful and treasured beach park backed by the largest open-air shopping center in the world in less than 50 years.

WAIKIKI & HONOLULU BEST BETS

Best Former Swamp—Waikiki Beach
Best Sunset Walk—From the Hilton to Kapiolani Park
Best Transportation on Two Wheels—Segway Scooters
Best Place to View the Most O'ahu Real Estate—From Pu'u Ualaka'a State Wayside
Best View at Night—From the Hanohano Room above the Waikiki Sheraton
Best Place to See How Royalty Lived—'Iolani Palace
Best Winding Road—Tantalus
Best Dining Deal on Waikiki Beach—Hale Koa Military Hotel
Best Place to Watch Boogie Boarders Close-up—Kapahulu Groin
Best Shopping Bazaar—International Marketplace

When Did the Last Eruption Take Place on O'ahu?

Surprisingly, nobody knows. Ask any geologist, and you might be told with complete confidence that it was 320,000 years ago...or over 100,000 years ago...or maybe as recently as 5,000 years ago. What we do know is that the most recent eruptions have been near the shoreline, from Diamond Head to Kaupo Beach Park. They were explosive eruptions where seawater mixed with underground magma and burst to form the hills and craters so prominent along here. The wicked snorkeling at Hanauma Bay, the popular hike up Diamond Head and the massive Koko Crater we all owe to O'ahu's last gasp at island-making. The rejuvenated phase of a volcano can have very long gaps, and technically the island could still be in its final phase of lava flows, though most geologists consider it highly improbable that there will be another eruption here.

Part of Highway 72 was carved out of the cemented ash of Koko Crater.

Talk about an embarrassment of riches. You have several ways to get to Kailua on the windward side, all of them pretty. Odds are you'll want to take the coastal highway (72) because there are a number of not-to-be-missed sights along the way. But even if you take the coastal road this time, you should definitely find the time during your stay to take one of the highways that punch though the Ko'olau mountains—the best being H-3, which is arguably the most beautiful stretch of freeway in the world.

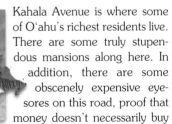

THE COASTAL ROUTE TO KAILUA

Leave Waikiki behind by taking Kalakaua to Diamond Head Road to Kahala Avenue—more scenic than getting on H1 East right away. You'll pass the lower part of Diamond Head where some pretty scenic lookouts await.

Kahala Avenue is where some of O'ahu's richest residents live. There are some truly stupendous mansions along here. In addition, there are some obscenely expensive eyesores on this road, proof that money doesn't necessarily buy good taste. Even the birds live better here. (Look at the birdhouse above the white gate at the ocean side of Kahala Avenue where it meets Elepioa Street at 4401 Kohala Avenue.)

Turn left on Pueo, right on Kilauea, right on Waialae, which'll turn into H-1 East. H-1 will become Hwy 72, known locally as the Kalanianaole Hwy. (Don't try to pronounce that seven syllable word, you might strain your tongue.)

The beaches along this lower leeward stretch aren't very good, thanks to runoff from Hawai'i Kai, a giant housing subdivision. Don't worry—the beaches will get *much* nicer.

When an island like O'ahu is nearing the twilight of its volcanic life, the volcanoes usually go to sleep for up to a million years, then sputter back awake for a short time, often creating explosive eruptions near the shoreline instead of the typical drooling type that characterize most of its eruptive life. Hawaiian volcanoes get hot-tempered in their old age. The results of the volcano's last gasp are often cone-shaped mountains of cemented ash called *tuff*, created when seawater seeps into the underground magma, flashing into steam and causing monstrous pressures that eventually explode. Diamond Head and the two giant hills in front of you—called **Koko Crater** (to your left) and **Koko Head** (to your right)—are examples of the volcano's final temper tantrums.

The populated section of Koko Head can be reached by taking Portlock Road or Lunalilo Home Road toward the ocean. If you drive to the end of Lumahai Road (see map), there's a little-known hidden gem near a hard-to-see public access corridor that requires a 2-minute walk down a steep path to an unnervingly-con-

stant sloping bluff. But, ahh, what a sight. The **spitting cave of Portlock** is below a

A REAL GEM

gorgeous layered shoreline. Even without the cave, the shoreline itself is mesmerizing. Each layer represents a different volcanic explosion

and the waters here are exceptionally clear and blue. The spitting cave is where the ocean is chiseling its way inland, attempting to break the point in two. As the waves drive into the cave, they're repelled by the backside, causing the ground to tremble beneath your feet and water and mist to explode out the cave if the surf is right. Summer generally brings higher surf to south-facing shores, but even smaller winter waves can cause the effect. Standing right over the cave creates the best tremble; standing to the right or left of the cave gives the best views. For generations locals have come here on weekends to jump off the 65-foot cliff in front of the cave during calm seas, but the injury and death toll from this has been particularly high, and you'll probably want to refrain from it.

Back on Hwy 72 you'll start climbing Koko Head and come to one of the

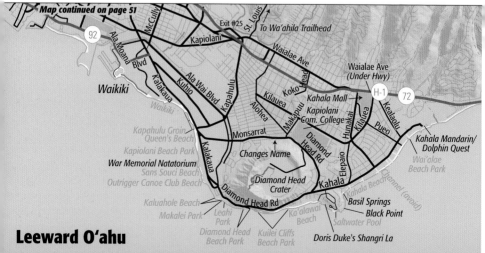

Map continued on page 51

Leeward O'ahu

island's biggest attractions. If you've heard *anything* about O'ahu, you've heard about the snorkeling at Hanauma Bay. It's one of the most popular activities on the island.

A REAL GEM

A lot of hype and misconceptions exist about this bay. Let's dispel some of them.

Hanauma Bay Nature Preserve (396–4229) is a crescent-shaped bay that's partially protected from the open ocean. In the past people fed the fish, which actually resulted fewer varieties of fish. (Bolder species did well, driving out meeker types.) Feeding is no longer allowed.

It's full of crystal clear water with tons of coral, right? 'Fraid not. The water tends to be a bit cloudy, and much of the reef is actually made from coralline algae, which *looks* like dead coral, but it's actually a stony material created by plants. It's *supposed* to look like that. And some of the real coral has been damaged over the years.

But what you *should* expect are fish...lots and lots of fish of many varieties that are so tame and used to peo-

ple, they'll hang out near you. This is the perfect place to spend some quality bonding time with the little (and not so little) buggers. You should also expect crowds, because you'll definitely get them here. Hanauma Bay is *not* a well-kept secret.

Hanauma Bay is safe most of the time. There are lifeguards, and the inner bay is pretty protected. That said, some years this is the drowning capital of O'ahu. After all, it *is* the ocean and anything can happen. Besides, if you invite over a million people a year to use *your bathtub*, odds are you'll lose one of two of them. Just remember not to go in the water 9–10 days after a full moon. (See box jellies under HAZARDS.)

The bay is open from 6 a.m. to 6 p.m., closed Tuesdays. (It's open till 10 p.m. on Saturdays for night snorkeling, and crowds at that time are non-existent—usually about 100 people at most show up, almost all of them locals. See ADVENTURES on page 218.)

It'll cost $1 per car and $5 per person to get in. You'll have to watch a 7-minute conservation video before you're allowed to walk down to the bay 150 feet below you. They also have a tram to

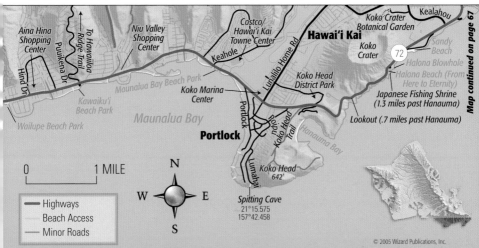

Map continued on page 67

© 2005 Wizard Publications, Inc.

Nearly everyone we've heard at the Lana'i Lookout speculates about which islands they're seeing. And nearly everyone gets it wrong. Here the islands are labeled as we saw them on this wickedly clear morning. Note that although Haleakala is twice as tall as East Moloka'i, it seems shorter due to its distance (100 miles). That's 1/250 of the circumference of the earth, so its bottom portion is below the planet's curvature.

East Moloka'i   *West Moloka'i*   *Maui's Haleakala*

the bottom for a couple of bucks. Good for hill-haters or those with lots of beach stuff or SCUBA gear. There's a food concession at the top and showers at the bottom. A $16 million "education center" is also at the top. (Though nice, it's hard to see how they spent *that* much on it.)

Snorkel gear is available for rent at the bottom—convenient, though it's overpriced at $6–$9 for cheap-o gear.

The parking lot is often full by 9:30 a.m. As groups of cars leave, the park will let small groups of cars in, but basically you'll want to arrive by 9 a.m. if you want to make sure you get a parking spot.

An alternative is **Hawaiian Ocean Promotions** at 396–9199. They have a shop at nearby Koko Marina where you can park. They'll drive you to Hanauma and pick you up for $5. For another $5 they'll get you snorkel gear. **Tommy's Tours** (373–5060) has a similar service. They'll pick you up at your Waikiki hotel and include the snorkel gear for $15 per person, reservations required.

For the most part, Hanauma Bay lives up to its promise. It's a great place to spend the morning or afternoon, whether you're a novice or an experienced snorkeler.

Continuing on Hwy 72, there's a turnout ¾ mile past the entrance to Hanauma Bay. This is the **Lana'i Lookout**, which is oddly named because if you see an island offshore, odds are it *ain't* Lana'i, it's Moloka'i. (See photo caption for an explanation.)

About 1³⁄₁₀ mile past the Hanauma Bay entrance is a very narrow pullout. There's a Japanese fishing shrine here with a carving of a Japanese guardian god that was said to preside over dangerous waterways. Originally, there was a stone statue installed by a Japanese fishing club, but during WWII it was demolished, and this carving took its place. Walk past the shrine along the ridge for a hundred feet or so, and you're treated to wonderful view of the **Halona Beach** below and Halona Blowhole. Though more distant, in some ways this vantage point is even better than the dedicated blowhole lookout 500 feet up the road. This perspective shows the size of the blowhole eruptions in relation to the people at the lookout platform above. Locals still call this beach *From Here to Eternity Beach* since they filmed what was then (in the '50s) a steamy love scene with the actors kissing and rolling around in the surf.

Lana'i

Just past the shrine is the parking lot for the **Halona Blowhole**. This is where the ocean has undercut the lava and drilled a hole through to the top. It's fairly reliable, but if the surf is not high enough, it won't

NOT TO BE MISSED!

be erupting. High tide is best. The lookout from above has a nice view of the blowhole, and you'll notice that the lower portion is closed off to dissuade you from walking down to the blowhole itself. (Give yourself a pat on the back if you guessed that *liability* was the reason.) Of course, it's perfectly legal to walk down to Halona Beach on your right and walk along the lava bench for a few minutes if you really want to visit the blowhole from below. If you do, be very cautious of the ocean, and never get between the ocean and the blowhole. Those who do and have been knocked in the hole are nearly always killed. Frankly, when we have visitors, we usually take them to see the blowhole from below. But we never do it when the ocean's raging, and we're always aware that our safety depends on the ocean being in a good mood.

Sandy Beach is your first good beach along this stretch. That giant lawn is

Snorkelers rejoice—the pool is open at Hanauma Bay.

It's impossible to resist stopping at the overlook above Makapu'u Beach backed by its offshore islands.

where hang gliders and paragliders land after soaring the cliffs of Makapu'u. It's not uncommon to have a hang glider pilot come up to you and ask you to drive him and his vehicle to the top of Makapu'u and return his car to Sandy Beach. (You can't drive up there on your own because permits are needed.) Sandy Beach is also where **ultralights** are launched. The aerial photos in this book and the aerials of the resorts were taken from our ultralight launched from here. Although the air along the windward coast tends to be smooth, the mountain toward the east causes nasty turbulence right over Sandy Beach, and ultralights landings here tend to look pretty ugly.

As you round the easternmost part of the island, giant **Makapu'u** defines the eastern tip. That abandoned road snaking to the 647-foot summit is hugely popular with locals who do their morning walks there. Sunrises are particularly nice from up top if you can motivate yourself to get up that early. During whale season the beasties tend to come pretty close to the point and are amazingly visible from up there. If you're looking for a series of blowholes that puts Halona Blowhole to shame and don't mind hiking, check out the **Dragon's Nostrils** under ACTIVITIES on page 179.

Make sure you stop at the overlook above **Makapu'u Beach**. The vantage point is excellent. Although this beach is popular with locals who bodysurf here and at Sandy Beach, novice bodysurfers need to be leery since the shorebreak at these beaches tends to be pounding, which can drill you into the sand like a fence post. Behind Makapu'u is **Sea Life Park**, east O'ahu's version of Sea World. See ATTRACTIONS on page 116 for more.

Those islands you see off Makapu'u were probably where the last eruptions took place on the island. The shorter island, called **Kaohi-ka-ipu** was made from a traditional lava flow when the ocean level was lower and the land there high and dry. It looks dark and burnt, a tribute to its relative youth. **Manana Island** behind it is a tuff cone like Diamond Head made from a steam explosion. Locals usually refer to it as **Rabbit Island** because a local resident used to raise rabbits there in the 1880s. They *say* that there are still rabbits there, but we've never seen any, only the thousands of seabirds that make their home there.

After Makapu'u you're driving through **Hawaiian Homelands** and the town of **Waimanalo**. In 1920 the government set aside over 200,000 acres of land to be used only by people of Hawaiian descent. Waimanalo is such a place.

The shoreline along here is almost uninterrupted sand beach consisting of Kaiona Beach, Waimanalo Beach, Bellows Beach and Waimanalo Bay State Rec Area. The latter is backed by a thick forest of ironwood trees. To this day locals refer to this area as **Sherwood Forest**. That's because during the '60s the forest became a hot place to strip cars and rob beachgoers. The gang that was responsible called themselves Robin Hood and the Merry Men because they took from the rich and gave to…well, *themselves*, actually.

Though the leeward side's Wai'anae Range is taller, the **Ko'olau Range** on the windward side *looks* taller and much

A REAL GEM

more dramatic. The sheer, fluted cliffs carpeted with every shade of green are among the most wondrous sights on the island and never fail to impress. The tallest peaks of the Ko'olaus, just south (to the left) of the Pali tunnel and peaking at 3,150 and 3,105 feet, are called **Konahua-nui**, literally translated as the *big, fat testicles*. Hey, we don't make up the legends, we just report 'em. (Perhaps they're named in honor of the first Hawaiian who had enough guts to climb them?)

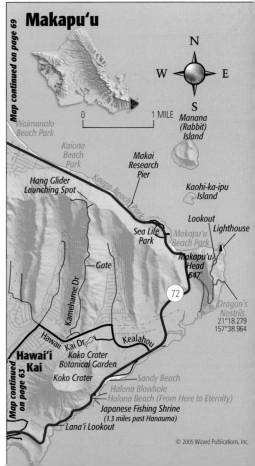

Makapu'u

Map continued on page 69

N
W E
S

0   1 MILE

Waimanalo Beach Park

Kaiona Beach Park

Hang Glider Launching Spot

Sea Life Park

Gate

Kamehame Dr

Kaupo Beach Park

Makai Research Pier

Manana (Rabbit) Island

Kaohi-ka-ipu Island

Lookout   Lighthouse
Makapu'u Beach Park

Makapu'u Head 647'

72

Dragon's Nostrils
21°18.279
157°38.964

Hawaii Kai Dr   Kealahou

Hawai'i Kai   Koko Crater Botanical Garden

Map continued on page 63

Koko Crater

Sandy Beach
Halona Blowhole
Halona Beach (From Here to Eternity)
Japanese Fishing Shrine
(1.3 miles past Hanauma)
Lana'i Lookout

© 2005 Wizard Publications, Inc.

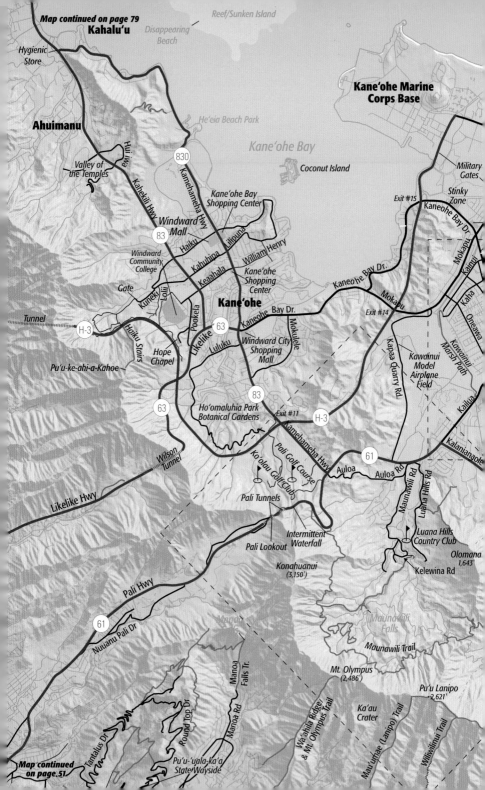

Kahalu'u

Disappearing Beach

Reef/Sunken Island

Hygienic
Store

Ahuimanu

*Valley of
the Temples*

Hui 'Iwa

Kahekili Hwy

Kamehameha Hwy

830

He'eia Beach Park

Kane'ohe Bay

Coconut Island

**Kane'ohe Marine
Corps Base**

Military
Gates

Stinky
Zone

Exit #15

Kaneohe Bay Dr.

Mokapu

Kainui

Kaha

Oneawa

Kane'ohe Bay
Shopping Center

Windward
Mall

83

Haiku

Kahuhipa

Keaahala

Lilipuna

William Henry

Kane'ohe
Shopping
Center

Kane'ohe Bay Dr.

Mokapu

Exit #14

Windward
Community
College

Kuneki

Lolii

Gate

Kane'ohe Bay Dr.

Kaneohe

Mokulele

Pookela

63

Tunnel

H-3

Haiku Stairs

Pu'u-ke-ahi-a-Kahoe

Hope
Chapel

Likelike

Luluku

*Windward City
Shopping Mall*

Kapaa Quarry Rd.

*Kawainui
Model
Airplane
Field*

Kawainui
Marsh Path

Kailua

Kalaniana'ole

63

83

*Ho'omaluhia Park
Botanical Gardens*

Exit #11

H-3

Kamehameha Hwy

61

Auloa

Auloa Rd

Maunawili Rd

Luana Hills Rd

Wilson
Tunnel

Ko'olau Golf Club

Pali Golf Course

*Luana Hills
Country Club*

Likelike Hwy

Pali Tunnels

Pali Lookout

Intermittent
Waterfall

Kelewina Rd

Olomana
1,643'

Pali Hwy

61

Nuuanu Pali Dr

Konahuanui
(3,150')

*Maunawili
Falls*

Maunawili Trail

Mt. Olympus
(2,486')

Pu'u Lanipo
2,621'

Tantalus Dr

Round Top Dr

Manoa Rd

Manoa
Falls Tr.

Pu'u-'uala-ka-'a
State Wayside

Wa'ahila Ridge/
& Mt Olympus Trail

*Ka'au
Crater*

Mauʻumae (Lanipo) Trail

Wiliwilinui Trail

Map continued
on page 51

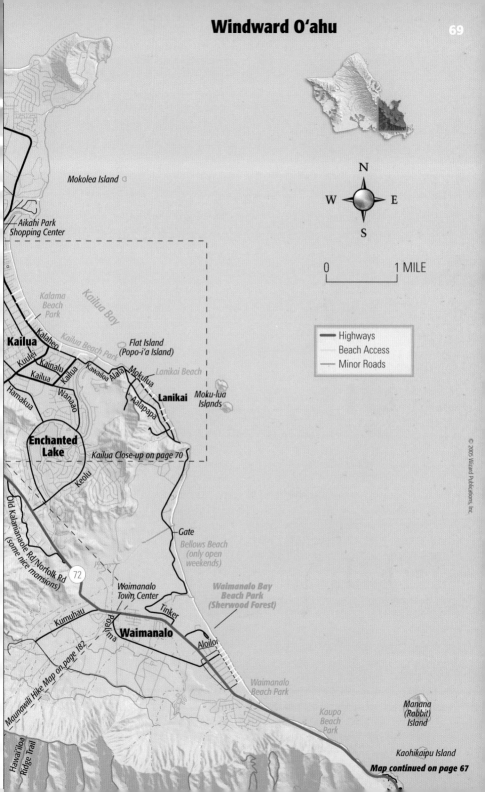

Mokolea Island

Aikahi Park
Shopping Center

Kalama
Beach
Park

Kailua

Kalaheo

Kuulei

Kainalu

Kailua

Kailua

Kawailoa

Alala

Mokulua

Kailua Bay

Kailua Beach Park

Flat Island
(Popo-i'a Island)

Lanikai Beach

Lanikai

Moku-lua
Islands

Hamakua

Wanao

Aalapapa

**Enchanted
Lake**

Keolu

Kailua Close-up on page 70

Old Kalanianaole Rd/Norfolk Rd
(some nice mansions)

72

Gate

Bellows Beach
(only open
weekends)

Waimanalo
Town Center

Waimanalo Bay
Beach Park
(Sherwood Forest)

Kumuhau

Tinker

Pohakupu

Waimanalo

Aloilo

Waimanalo
Beach Park

Kaupo
Beach
Park

Manana
(Rabbit)
Island

Maunawili Hike Map on page 182

Hawaii Loa
Ridge Trail

Kaohikaipu Island

Map continued on page 67

Legend
- Highways
- Beach Access
- Minor Roads

N W E S

0   1 MILE

© 2005 Wizard Publications, Inc.

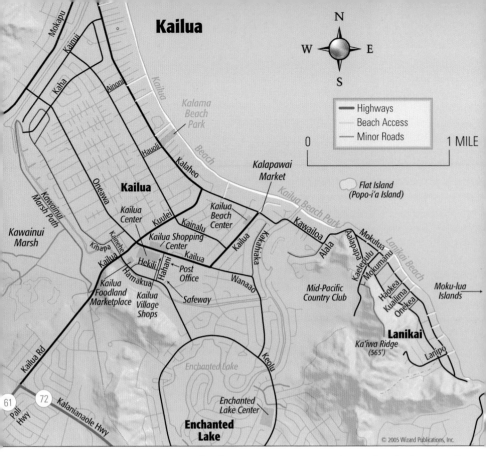

As you gaze at the splendid cliffs of the Koʻolaus, consider this. In old Hawaiʻi, when a particularly beloved chief died, it was customary to sacrifice several of his trusted servants, as well. (And you though *you* sacrificed a lot for your boss.) When the servant heard about his chief's death, he would kiss his wife and children goodbye and, without telling them why, leave to become a *moepuʻu,* or companion in death. He would then enter the hut where the chief's body was being kept and lie down between the dead man's legs. The only way his life could be spared was if one of the heirs to the kingdom so decided. If none of the dead chief's servants came forward to sacrifice themselves, one of his officers or relatives might be called upon to do so. This is why the chief's health was *always* a topic of interest to

those closest to him. They had a vested interest in keeping him healthy.

When it came time to bury the chief, the funeral procession often hiked to the top of the Koʻolaus from the leeward side. The chief's bones, having been separated from the valueless flesh, were lowered by rope along with a digger. Once the digger gouged out a cavity in the cliffs, the bones were placed inside and the digger would tug on the rope. Then the men at the top cut the rope, and the digger plunged to his death, taking with him the secret to where the chief's bones lay. In this way the sacred bones, which Hawaiians believed contained their *mana,* or spiritual power, could never be found and desecrated. And it was actually considered an *honor* to be the doomed digger.

KAILUA

Kailua is your classic beach town and, in our minds, one of the nicest places to stay if you're not going to stay in Waikiki. Though only 30 minutes from Honolulu via the Pali Hwy, it's a world away from the big city life. There are no resorts here, but vacation rentals and B&Bs are plentiful. Two of the finest beaches on the island bless this community, the kayaking in Kailua Bay to offshore islands is fantastic, and there are some excellent restaurants. If you're looking for a dreamy beach scene backed by offshore islands, **Lanikai** is a must. If you want a long, delicious beach to stroll along or want to kayak these waters to a nearby island, you gotta check out **Kailua Beach**. See BEACHES for more on these.

In addition to the beaches, scattered around Kailua are some things to keep an eye out for:

On Kapaa Quarry Road across from the *lovely* Kailua Dump is the **Kawainui Model Airplane Field** where people fly some surprisingly sophisticated model airplanes and helicopters. Well-used on weekends and less-so during the week. If you're already near the local dump, behind the green waste turn-off, ¼ mile from the entrance behind and to the right of a pool and spa place is a treasure trove of world-class wood furniture called **King and Zelko** (261–7239). They import all sorts of items, but the real masterpieces are the koa and mango furniture they manufacture right there. You'd never know this place was there, but it has some of the best koa we've seen anywhere.

Acting as an acid bath, the ocean is slowing dissolving the sand-stone that makes up Flat Island off Kailua Beach, creating a Swiss cheese landscape in the process. Here you can see a hole in the island and the morning light seeping in from underneath.

The Pali Lookout is one of the better reasons to take the Pali Hwy to Kailua...

On Hwy 61 (Kailua Road) between Hwy 72 and Hamakua Road across from the Tesoro Gas Station, there's a short path leading to the **Ulupo Heiau**, which, at press time, was little more than a pile of rocks. They were restoring this former Hawaiian temple—*slooowly.*

At a dirt turnout mauka (toward the mountain) of Kailua town is an access for a very nice walking path through the otherwise water-logged **Kawainui Marsh**.

The Direct Highways to Kailua

There are three highways that drill through the Koʻolaus directly to the windward side, ending up in Kailua or Kaneʻohe. Pali and Likelike are highways, not freeways, with traffic lights and intersections part of the way. H-3 is a classic elevated freeway.

Of all your non-coastal routes, **H-3** is the most rewarding, especially going from Kailua to Honolulu. H-3 is an interstate highway. *Hey, wait a minute. Hawaiʻi's a bunch of islands. How can it be an interstate highway?* Simple. If we'd called it a *state* highway, *we'd* have to pay for it. I believe I speak for all Hawaiʻi residents when I say, thank you for your generous federal tax dollars.

A REAL GEM

Anyway, this 16-mile road cost almost $100 million *per mile* to build and took a mere *37 years* to complete. They spent *20 years* of that time doing environmental impact study after environmental impact study. But the results are incredible. If you saw it in a movie, you'd dismiss it out of hand as too beautiful to believe. Elevated high above the ground while cruising toward and next to the fluted cliffs of the Ko'olaus, this is the next best thing to taking a helicopter ride along the mountains.

You'll often notice that as you pass through the H-3 tunnel, the weather might be different on each side. Weather on O'ahu is strongly affected by the mountains. Moist air from the northeast encounters the Ko'olau mountain range, rising and cooling. Cooler air can't hold as much moisture as warmer air, so the moister condenses—in other words, forms a cloud. If it has more moisture than this now-cooler air can hold, it rains. With the air-deflecting mountain behind it, the traveling air sinks and gets warmer. Having already wrung out the moisture over the mountains, this drier air tends to be less prone to cloudiness. Hence, the leeward side's sunny days.

By the way, shortly before the H-3 tunnel (if you're coming from the windward side), look for a metal staircase on the side of the mountain on your left.

It'll be winding it's way up into the clouds. That's the **Haiku Stairs**, also called the **Stairway to Heaven**, and it's an awesome adventure mentioned on page 214.

As an alternate to H-3, you can also take the **Pali Highway** (61) from Honolulu. It heads straight into downtown Kailua. Until the old Pali Road was built, leeward residents who wanted to visit friends and relatives on the windward side had to take a winding trail up Nu'uanu Valley, where it terminated at a sheer cliff. From there a nerve-wracking portion slithered down the cliffs to the plains below. With the completion of the Pali Road (later replaced by the Pali Highway) this place of fear became a place of wondrous beauty. Kane'ohe Bay, Mokapu Peninsula, the cliffs of Ko'olau and even Chinaman's Hat island off in the distance create a glorious expansive panorama at the

...and this is the reason to take H-3.

Pali Lookout. The last major Hawaiian battle took place here, and the results changed the political landscape. (See page 14.)

A REAL GEM

Bring the warmest clothes in your suitcase for the Pali Lookout. Yeah, sure, this is the tropics and the elevation is only 1,200 feet. But you're at a slit in a mountain that funnels the now-cooler trade winds piling up against the larger mountain, and you'll freeze your 'okole off here if you're not prepared. (Of course, maybe we're just wimps who have lived here in Hawai'i too long.) To the right are the remains of the old Pali Road, now a hike listed on page 179.

Got any bacon with you? Local custom says that if you take the Pali Hwy with any pork in your car, bad things will happen to you. This is because this area was said to be the home of Kamapua'a, a demigod who was half man, half pig. If you have any pork with you it's an in-your-face gesture that Kamapua'a will take offense with—and perhaps respond to.

The third highway poking through the mountain, **Likelike Hwy** (63) is the least attractive of the trans-Ko'olau highways and should be your last choice. By the way, if someone asks, it's pronounced LEE-KAY-LEE-KAY, not LIKE LIKE.

KANE'OHE

If you're heading north, Kane'ohe is your next town, and there are different ways to get there. Orient yourself with the map on page 68. The most important landmark in Kane'ohe is the **Kane'ohe Marine Corps Base**. Forget your visions of row upon row of barracks with privates running around as their sergeants bark out orders. This is a charming, self-contained city with all the comforts of

The serene setting of the Byodo-In Temple exudes peacefulness.

home, sort of an island within an island. It has restaurants, a movie theater, gas stations, neighborhoods of beautiful houses, schools and school buses, car rental companies, stellar beaches and a very nice golf course called Klipper. Everything a growing marine and his/her family could want. The only thing you won't find here is...*you*. As a marine base, access is restricted.

The prominent **Ulu-pa'u Head** at Kane'ohe Base is the result of steam explosions offshore that formed a separate island. The world was warmer then and the sea level higher. As the world cooled, the sea level dropped, connecting the land via a peninsula.

Ironically, Kane'ohe Base's destiny as an island apart from the rest of O'ahu is assured, both politically and geologically. It's *barely* attached to the main island by a nearly flooded plain. With naturally rising sea levels (which have risen 180 feet over the past 12,000 years), it almost certainly will be cut off from O'ahu within a hundred years or so without human intervention.

By the way, contrary to popular belief, Pearl Harbor was not the first place attacked on December 7, 1941. Kane'ohe was, since there was an airfield here that the Japanese wanted to neutralize before they went after the fleet on the other side of the island.

Driving along, if you've been lusting after the Ko'olau mountains and want to drive a bit closer to them, you can take a detour to a free botanical garden that backs up to them. On Hwy 83 just north of its intersection with H-3 is Luluku Road. Up this road is the **Ho'omaluhia Park Botanical Garden** (233-7323). The drive through the gardens gets you more intimate with the mountains. If you're interested in touring the gardens, see ATTRACTIONS on page 121.

The only thing more beautiful than the Ko'olaus on a clear morning is on those afternoons when the invisible trade winds cause the soft clouds to dance along the jagged summit in a scene that will surely cause you to think, *This must be what heaven looks like.*

If you take the Kahekili Hwy (83) through Kane'ohe (which is faster due to less traffic than Kamehameha Hwy 830), north of Kane'ohe town is the

A REAL GEM

Valley of the Temples. This is simply a large cemetery. Well, maybe not so simple. It's $2 per person to get in, and there are various temples scattered around the area. In the back is the greatest temple of them all. The **Byodo-In** is a grand replica of a 950-year-old Buddhist temple from Uji, Japan. Built in the 1960s to commemorate the 100th anniversary of the arrival of Japanese immigrant workers to Hawai'i, the temple is the absolute essence of serenity. It's like taking a mini-trip to Japan. Backed by the gorgeous Ko'olau mountain range and fronted by a large pond filled with koi fish and curious swans, it's impossible not to feel peaceful here. (The only distraction is the seemingly-constant sound of gas-powered weed whackers. Of course, it's those same personnel who keep the grounds so flawlessly sculpted.) This temple is still used today by worshippers. If you visit, it's customary to ring the richly-toned bell before entering. Morning light is best here.

In **Kane'ohe Bay**, Moku-o-Lo'e (usually called Coconut Island) was formally owned by a Fleishman yeast heir. (Ironically enough, the island actually did "rise" while this yeast guy owned it. He doubled its size by dredging and planted the coconut trees). The island went through a series of owners and is used today by the Hawaii Institute of Marine Biology. It's barely recognizable from the time it was filmed to represent *Gilligan's Island* in the '60s.

Kane'ohe Bay's reputation among long-time locals is less-than-pristine. For 25 years the military base and the local community discharged untreated sewage into the south part of the bay, and the bay became known as the *last* place you'd want to go into the water. Although the practice stopped in 1978 (treated water is piped to a trench *way* offshore where currents carry it away), many locals from the leeward side still connect Kane'ohe Bay with bad water and avoid it, which pleases windward residents who get it all to themselves.

In fact, one of our favorite kayak trips on the island is in Kane'ohe Bay. It visits a 1,000-acre sunken island and two beaches that appear and disappear twice each day. See KAYAKING on page 192.

After driving through the town of Kane'ohe heading north, you're committed to the shoreline route that you'll be hugging for the next 40 miles.

EAST O'AHU BEST BETS

Best Sunrise—From the top of Makapu'u for the motivated

Best Beach Stroll—Kailua Beach

Best Place to Get Drilled Into the Sand—Bodysurfing at Sandy Beach or Makapu'u Beach

Best Place to See Water Fly Out of a Cave—Spitting Cave of Portlock

Best Place to Lose Your Hat—A tie between the Pali Lookout and the top of Diamond Head

What could be more magical than greeting a new day from Kailua Beach?

Yeah, now that's what we call a highway.

The North Shore is the prettiest drive on the entire island. Forget the big city and its multi-lane highways. This is a place with only a few traffic lights and a two-lane road that hugs the shoreline, embracing the Hawai'i of yesteryear. Along the way you'll find yourself constantly drooling over the beaches and mountain scenery.

We've marked the map in terms of miles and time (without stops or traffic) from Windward Mall in Kane'ohe. You'll usually know when you've gone from one town to the next.

This is a long chapter because once you've driven past Kane'ohe, you're committed to the drive to Hale'iwa. So although part of windward O'ahu is on this tour, we're sticking with the term NORTH SHORE SIGHTS. (NORTH SHORE AND THE NORTHERN PART OF WINDWARD SHORE SIGHTS would look pretty annoying in that heading.)

KUALOA

As you approach the northern part of Kane'ohe Bay, the Kualoa Nursery and Gardens is a mac nut farm with a very pretty garden area and gorgeous monkeypod trees providing shade. They're very generous with the flavored mac nut samples. (They can afford to be at these prices.) Watch out for the two hazards here: wasps flying around the sampling area and tour buses flying around the parking lot.

Kualoa Park is at the very edge of Kane'ohe Bay. This gigantic beach park has an endless lawn, a long ribbon of sand fringing it and an *oh-so-tempting* offshore island called **Chinaman's Hat**. This uninhabited island can be yours to rule. See ADVENTURES on page 220.

Past the park, **Kualoa Ranch** is a huge, breathtakingly beautiful windward ranch. It's also a giant visitor processing machine that in some areas does a good job, but their prices are high. Many of their customers are tour groups from Japan. Some of their activities seem a bit over-hyped to us. For instance, they have a "secret island kayak tour." (Chinaman's Hat is the *least* secret island you'll find on O'ahu.) And the "private beach" that they'll take you to is a sandbar that anyone could walk to from the adjacent Kualoa Beach. But they also have horseback rides (nose-to-tail walks, but the mountain scenery is very pretty) and ATV tours (same description). See ACTIVITIES for more.

That old concrete chimney on the side of the road past Kualoa Park is all that remains of a short-lived, Civil War-era **sugar mill**.

Soon the highway starts cozying up to the ocean in a dramatic way. It's heavenly to drive along so close to the sand and the breakers. At the north end of the town of **Ka'a'awa** (pronounced as if you were coughing up a furball) after the 27 mile marker is the **Crouching Lion Inn**. Lava rocks on the mountain form a silhouette of a lion. Most people mistakenly look at the most obvious rocks near the road and think that's the lion. Actually, you'd have to be in the private driveway *before* (to the left of) the Crouching Lion Inn and look up past the cement driveway to see it from its best view. There you'll find the little bugger with his mouth slightly open facing partially away from you. By the way, don't believe any stories about a Hawaiian legend of a crouching lion around here. The ancient Hawaiians would have had

What's not to love about the northern end of Kane'ohe Bay and its uninhabited island, Chinaman's Hat?

as much familiarity with lions as they would have with chain saws. Lions ain't native to Hawai'i.

KAHANA BAY

After the tongue-twisting Ka'a'awa is the easier-to-pronounce Kahana Bay. Although the bay's waters are never ultra-clear thanks to runoff from the Kahana River, the beach setting is picturesque, and it's rare to find more than a few people here during the week. One of the easier kayak trips is up the jungly-looking river. (See KAYAKING on page 194 for more.) The state park behind the bay is the Ahupua'a O Kahana State Park. There are some hiking trails at the end of the road, but conditions tend to be unusually muddy in this valley, and mosquitoes are exceptionally aggressive here.

A REAL GEM

Your drive along the north shore won't be exactly *filled* with dining options (including the very avoidable Punalu'u Restaurant). Forget what you may have heard about eating lunch at the Crouching Lion—it's a disappointing visitor processing machine. Your best bet is to eat at one of the shrimp vendors ahead in Kahuku, wait until you get to the north shore around Sunset Beach or Sharks Cove, or hit Hale'iwa, which has a good restaurant selection.

In the town of Hau'ula, Sacred Falls Park *was* one of the most popular waterfall hikes on the island. A fatal landslide on Mother's Day in 1999 and subsequent lawsuits prompted its closure. The state has since passed a law immunizing itself from future lawsuits (isn't it cool to be able to pass a law immunizing yourself?), but at press time the falls and 1,300-acre park were still

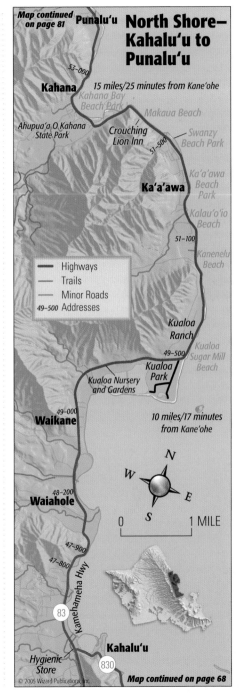

Map continued on page 81

Punalu'u

North Shore– Kahalu'u to Punalu'u

53–000

Kahana

15 miles/25 minutes from Kane'ohe

Kahana Bay Beach Park

Makaua Beach

Ahupua'a O Kahana State Park

Crouching Lion Inn

51–500

Swanzy Beach Park

Ka'a'awa Beach Park

Ka'a'awa

Kalau'o'io Beach

51–100

Kanenelu Beach

Highways
Trails
Minor Roads
49–500 Addresses

Kualoa Ranch

49–500

Kualoa Sugar Mill Beach

Kualoa Park

Kualoa Nursery and Gardens

10 miles/17 minutes from Kane'ohe

49–000

Waikane

N
W   E
S

48–200

Waiahole

0   1 MILE

47–900

47–800

Kamehameha Hwy

83

Kahalu'u

Hygienic Store

830

© 2005 Wizard Publications, Inc.

Map continued on page 68

Sometimes nature patiently chips away at things, and sometimes she's in a hurry. This sea arch off La'ie Point was created in one day when Mother Nature was in a foul mood.

closed as bureaucrats pondered its future. They only thing they've been able agree on is to change the name of this closed park to Kaluanui State Park. By the way, Kaluanui means *the big pit*.

LA'IE

The biggest town along this part of the island is La'ie. In terms of driving time, there is probably no place on the island that takes longer to get to from Waikiki than La'ie. It's also light years away in terms of the culture. La'ie is a town heavily dominated by the Mormon Church. Their university, Brigham Young University, has a campus and there's a beau-

tiful temple here. The only grocery store is closed on Sunday and refuses to sell any alcohol. The Chinese restaurant in La'ie doesn't serve tea unless you ask for it. And some of the businesses do things a bit differently in La'ie. (The local McDonald's has karaoke.)

One of the biggest attractions in all Hawai'i, the Polynesian Cultural Center, is in La'ie. This sprawling center was created to attract visitors who help subsidize Brigham Young students from all over the Pacific. They do a particularly good job re-creating island life from around Polynesia. See ATTRACTIONS on page 109 for more.

Take a right at the stoplight at Anemoku, then right on Maupaka. This leads to La'ie Point. Oh, what a beautiful sight! This point is made up entirely of sandstone with several small islands offshore. The closest one is 432 feet off-shore (looks closer, doesn't it?). It has a natural arch carved dead center that was created on April Fool's Day in 1946 when a

NOT TO BE MISSED!

tsunami literally punched a hole through the island. To the right are more islands, along with O'ahu itself. The 360° vantage from this point is grand, and if the surf is up, the symphony of crashing waves is a delight to listen to.

Past the center of town, La'ie Beach is also known as Hukilau Beach. A hukilau is a fishing event where non-fisher-men are able to catch fish. A net is laid out in a horseshoe shape with the open end toward the shore. While some people splash around, driving fish into the net, people on the shore slowly pull the net onto the land. After WWII the Mormon Church performed a monthly hukilau here to help raise funds for the church. It got so popular that a state agency, the Hawaii Visitor's Bureau, asked them to continue performing it and promoted it to visitors. So why doesn't the church still do hukilaus there anymore? Because *another* state agency saw its popularity as a way to get money. The Hawai'i government decided they wanted to tax the event in 1970, so the Mormons simply stopped doing it. Incidentally, as with other things in La'ie, Hukilau Beach is closed on Sundays.

After La'ie is a large state beach park called Malaekahana. If you're looking for a beach that takes a bit more to get to than simply walking up and falling into the sand, Moku'auia Island (also called Goat Island) is

A REAL GEM

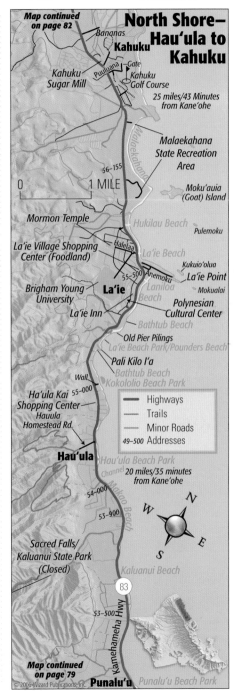

Map continued on page 82

North Shore— Hau'ula to Kahuku

Bananas

Kahuku

Kahuku Sugar Mill

Puuluana

Gate

Kahuku Golf Course

25 miles/43 Minutes from Kane'ohe

56–155

Malaekahana State Recreation Area

0 1 MILE

Moku'auia (Goat) Island

Mormon Temple

Hukilau Beach

Pulemoku

La'ie Village Shopping Center (Foodland)

Halelaa

La'ie Beach

Kukuio'olua

55–500 Anemoku

La'ie Point

Brigham Young University

La'ie

Laniloa Beach

Mokualai

La'ie Inn

Polynesian Cultural Center

Bathtub Beach

Old Pier Pilings

La'ie Beach Park/Pounders Beach

Pali Kilo I'a

Bathtub Beach

Wall

Kokololio Beach Park

Ha'ula Kai 55–000 Shopping Center

Hauula Homestead Rd.

Highways

Trails

Minor Roads

49–500 Addresses

Hau'ula

Hau'ula Beach Park

Channel

20 miles/35 minutes from Kane'ohe

54–000

Makao Beach

53–900

N W E S

Sacred Falls/ Kaluanui State Park (Closed)

Kaluanui Beach

83

53–500

Kamehameha Hwy

Map continued on page 79

© 2005 Wizard Publications, Inc.

Punalu'u

Punalu'u Beach Park

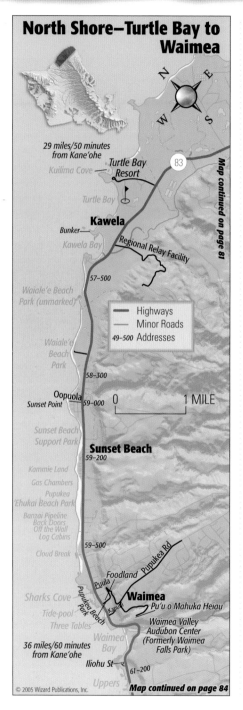

North Shore–Turtle Bay to Waimea

29 miles/50 minutes
from Kane'ohe
Kuilima Cove — Turtle Bay
Resort
83
Map continued on page 81

Turtle Bay

Kawela
Bunker —
Kawela Bay
Regional Relay Facility

57–500

Waiale'e Beach
Park (unmarked)

▬	Highways
—	Minor Roads
49–500	Addresses

Waiale'e
Beach
Park

58–300

Oopuola
Sunset Point 59–000   0   1 MILE

Sunset Beach
Support Park

Sunset Beach
59–200

Kammie Land
Gas Chambers
Pupukea
'Ehukai Beach Park
Banzai Pipeline
Back Doors
Off the Wall
Log Cabins

59–500

Cloud Break

Foodland   Pupukea Rd
Puula
Sharks Cove — **Waimea**
Tide-pool —   Pu'u o Mahuka Heiau
Three Tables
Waimea   Waimea Valley
36 miles/60 minutes   Bay   Audubon Center
from Kane'ohe   (Formerly Waimea
Iliohu St   Falls Park)

61–200

Uppers

© 2005 Wizard Publications, Inc.   **Map continued on page 84**

240 yards offshore from the park. You can usually wade to it, and those who put in the effort are rewarded with a picture-perfect crescent sand beach often deserted in the morning.

The other great thing about Malaekahana is the cabins for rent. They're old private beach houses taken over by the state when this area was converted into a park. Although less-than-pristine, they can be yours if you make arrangements in advance. See CAMPING on page 162 for more.

KAHUKU

Kahuku is famous for its shrimp trucks and shacks. Although shrimp is commercially grown nearby, only one of the businesses (Romy's) gets their shrimp there. (The others get them from off-island sources.) It's easy to look at businesses like these "sleepy little shrimp trucks" and assume that they're struggling little mom and pop enterprises. Sometimes they're much more. Giovanni's Aloha Shrimp Wagon is a case in point.

The current owner bought the business for $120,000. Four years later, in 2001, the previous owner said she wanted it back. Apparently, she *really* wanted it back. According to prosecutors, she met with the owner and demanded he sell her the business back for the price he paid. He replied that it was now worth much more— $700,000, to be precise. (If you've ever seen the long lines at Giovanni's during lunch, that sounds reasonable.) When he refused to sign a contract for $120,000, two large gunmen walked in, threatened his family on the mainland, stuck a gun in his left eye and politely asked him to sign the contract (which he did). He later went to police, and the woman was convicted of robbery, extortion and kidnapping. Sleepy little businesses, indeed.

You're nearing the northernmost part of the island. Past the shrimp vendors, there's a vast area on your right belonging to the James Campbell Estate. Although they occasionally offer tours when it's not nesting season, don't bother. Except for the wild, windy shoreline (for which we have a hike listed on page 185), the land you're not seeing is probably the ugliest part of the island. The land looks stressed, beaten up and tired. Every region has to have an ugly side, and this is Oʻahu's, in our opinion. So don't be concerned that you're missing something special. The $2 billion estate will be broken up in 2007 and distributed among its three dozen heirs.

After Kahuku is a store on the ocean side called S. Tanaka Store Antique & Bottles. This place sure lives up to its name. It's positively *packed* with very old bottles from early Hawaiian bottlers, endless Coca-Cola antiques, Japanese glass fishing floats and more. Worth stopping for if you like antiques.

TURTLE BAY

Oʻahu has been amazingly successful at containing resorts in a single area. Outside of Waikiki there are only four resorts. Turtle Bay is one of them.

As an aside, we always include aerial photos of all the resorts in our WHERE TO STAY section. This resort and beach are always the hardest to photograph. Their location at the end of the Koʻolau Mountains is where different types of winds converge, and the air above this resort is almost always turbulent to the point of being violent. Trying to hold the camera steady and flying the pitching aircraft while screaming and crying for mama is a bit awkward, so if our aerial shots of

this area are a bit blurry, you'll understand why.

THE NORTH SHORE

When surfers talk about the North Shore, they generally mean the seven miles of surf breaks from Sunset Point to Puaʻena Point near Haleʻiwa town. Other islanders consider the North Shore to be everything from Sunset Point all the way out to the westernmost tip of the island at Kaʻena Point.

The population of the North Shore doubles during the winter surf season, and traffic sometimes backs up near beaches visible from the road as rubbernecking drivers find wave-watching irresistible. (Residents are the *worst* offenders.) During those times when the waves don't materialize during the winter, you'll see them *bumming hard core, brah*. The pulse rate of the North Shore slows considerably when the surfing season dies down in the spring. Laid back and casual become the order of the day.

Just before Sunset Beach you'll see Ted's Bakery on the left. You should know that their chocolate/haupia (made from coconut) pie is legendary on the island. Frankly, to us it tastes pretty unremarkable, but some island residents get downright teary-eyed over it. If you try it, please let us know if we're off the mark on this one.

The Sunset Beach area was known to ancient Hawaiians as Pau-malu. According to lore, there was once a local woman renowned for her ability to catch octopus. One day as she was preparing to go hunting here, an old man stopped her and told her to limit her catch to a certain number. She agreed but, while hunting, she got carried away and caught more than the allotment. Just then a giant shark came and bit off both

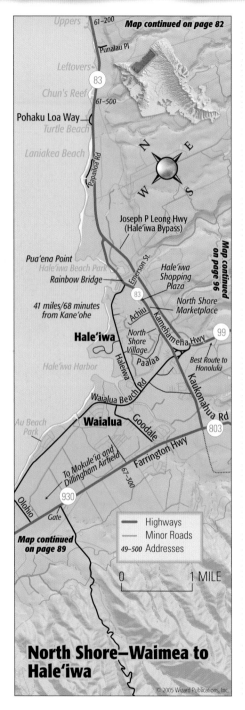

Map continued on page 82

Uppers
61-200
Punalau Pl
Leftovers
83
Chun's Reef
61-500
Pohaku Loa Way
Turtle Beach
Laniakea Beach

Joseph P Leong Hwy
(Hale'iwa Bypass)

Map continued on page 96

Pua'ena Point
Hale'iwa Beach Park
Rainbow Bridge
Emerson St.
Hale'iwa Shopping Plaza
83
North Shore Marketplace
41 miles/68 minutes from Kane'ohe
Achiu
Hale'iwa
North Shore Village
Kamehameha Hwy
99
Paalaa
Best Route to Honolulu
Hale'iwa Harbor
Halewa
Waialua Beach Rd
Au Beach Park
Waialua
Goodale
Kalukonahua Rd
803
To Mokule'ia and Dillingham Airfield
Farrington Hwy
67-300
930
Olohio
Gate

Map continued on page 89

Highways
Minor Roads
49-500 Addresses

0   1 MILE

North Shore—Waimea to Hale'iwa

© 2005 Wizard Publications, Inc.

her legs. Locals concluded that she had angered the shark god that watched over the reef and named the area Pau-malu, meaning *taken by surprise*.

Today Sunset Beach is a dreamy beach that brings fantastic waves in the winter and placid, warm waters in the summer.

Imagine owning a beachfront house along here. Then imagine this: The stretch of shoreline from Sunset Point almost to Sharks Cove is all sandy beach. In 1919 a developer broke the entire 2 miles into individual parcels for beachfront homes. He sold them all in less than two months and pocketed—are you ready for this?—a whopping $46,000 *for all the parcels combined*. Today it would cost 20 times that amount for a *single* parcel.

Surf sites vary in their fame. But in all Hawai'i there is no more famous surf

A REAL GEM

break than the Banzai Pipeline. During large (but not giant) surf, swells coming from the northwest form perfect barrels at this site. It's hard to find prettier waves anywhere in the world than a good day at the pipe. Yet there are no signs telling you where it is, and there's no beach named after it. So here's how to find it. Banzai Pipeline is 100 yards to the left of 'Ehukai Beach Park and 185 yards offshore. From the road you'll know if it's going off. Not because you can see the waves (which you can't), but because the small parking lot at 'Ehukai will be *filled* with local cars. (During calm summer months the amount of sand at the beach increases exponentially when truckloads of sand are transported here by the ocean.

Past 'Ehukai is Sharks Cove. During summer months (May to September or

The jumping rock at Waimea Bay...and the sound of a belly-flop heard round the world.

Who the Heck is Eddie…and Why Would He Go?

Drive around O'ahu and you'll see bumper stickers that say, "Eddie Would Go." The biggest big-wave surf contest in the world is the Quicksilver in Memory of Eddie Aikau contest. It's held every few years—only when waves on the North Shore are 20 feet high or more. (A 20-foot wave, measured from the back as many Hawaiian surfers do, has a 40-foot face!)

So who's this Eddie guy?

Eddie Aikau was a pure-blood Hawaiian big-wave surfer from O'ahu who, as a lifeguard at Waimea Bay, literally saved hundreds of people's lives by braving monster winter surf to rescue people who'd gotten into trouble. Long-time locals have memories of Eddie charging into waves three or four stories high to pull helpless visitors back in. Often a helicopter would be called to raise the swimmer in a basket. Then Eddie would swim back though the surf to the shore.

In the '70s a voyaging canoe called the Hokule'a was built to prove that Polynesians had navigated to and from Hawai'i using only the stars. For the first trip to Tahiti, the crew brought along a navigator from Micronesia to teach them how to navigate using only the heavens. But tensions were so high that the navigator refused to return to Hawai'i on the boat after fistfights erupted. The Hawaiian crew resented the rules and regulations set by the science-minded white leaders, and the white leaders resented the Hawaiians who only seemed to want to smoke their pakalolo (marijuana) and listen to their taped music.

In 1978 a second voyage was planned to Tahiti, and Eddie was accepted as a volunteer crewman. On March 16th a crowd of 10,000 gathered at Magic Island to see them off. Even though the weather was turning foul, the great turnout created pressure to leave anyway. That night, after some hatches had been improperly shut, the hulls filled with water and the canoe capsized. Their radio was flooded and their emergency beacon was lost. Almost immediately Eddie volunteered to take his surfboard through the 15-foot swells and 35 mph winds to Lana'i. The captain refused. Cold, wet and scared, the crew spent the dark night calling to each other to make sure no one washed away. The next day Eddie again asked to go. Although Lana'i was now 20 miles away through angry seas, the captain and his officers reluctantly agreed. "Eddie was godlike," one of his crewmembers said. If anybody could do it, it was Eddie.

The crew gathered around to say a prayer, and then Eddie started paddling his 12-foot surfboard. When he was 50 feet from the boat he took off his life jacket (so he could paddle better) and continued on his way. Eddie Aikau was never seen again. Later that evening the crew shot a flare in to the air as the last inter-island flight flew by and, miraculously, the pilot saw and responded to the flare. The remaining crew were rescued by a Coast Guard helicopter.

Today the name Eddie is synonymous in Hawai'i with trying…going for it…risking it all for your friends. Hey, brah, Eddie would go.

October) this is one one of the best places on the island to snorkel. Clear water, lots of fish and a fair number of turtles make this an inviting body of water. To the left of the

A REAL GEM

cove is a giant tide pool that kids love splashing in. See BEACHES on page 153 for more on Sharks Cove.

Just past Sharks Cove at the Foodland is Pupukea Road. About ⅔ mile up this road, turn right and drive another ¾ miles (over 10 speed bumps) to come to the Pu'u o Mahuka Heiau. These remnants of a Hawaiian temple, perched 250 above Waimea Bay on a ridge, possess a peaceful and serene view from the top of Mt. Ka'ala all the way out to Ka'ena Point. It's worth the detour for the view alone. One of the plaques says they could communicate with Wailua on Kaua'i by fire, but that's probably a Hawaiian wives' tale since Wailua is 86 miles away. (It's doubtful even a monstrously large fire could be seen that far away, even on a crystal clear day.) All that remains of this heiau is a lava stone foundation. While it's tempting to think of a temple as a spiritual place, this was a *luakini* heiau, where human sacrifices took place. Countless Hawaiians and possibly even some westerners were murdered here to feed the hungry gods. When the Hawaiians overthrew their religious kapu system in 1819 (by their

Innocent swimmers minding their own business when this rude turtle just cuts them off. Some turtles at Turtle Beach simply don't have any manners.

own hand and with no outside intervention or pressure—this was *before* any missionaries ever came to the island), few Hawaiians of that day shed a tear that this particular temple was being dismantled. Although the ali'i (chiefs) revered it, to the common man of that time, *luakini* heiaus were a place of oppression and fear.

WAIMEA BAY

Waimea Bay is the place to be when the winter surf it *really* high—say 20-foot waves and higher. Surf of this height causes other beaches to blow out and simply look messy and frothy. (See page 208 to learn more about waves and what surfers look for.)

A REAL GEM

Most people observe big surf from the beach, but finding a parking spot at Waimea Bay Beach Park can be difficult. We prefer a spot from the left side of the bay. There's a dedicated public access from the end of Iliohu Place, though at press time locals were parking at the end of Iliohu *Way* and taking a short trail through the brush. Either way it leads to a wicked vantage point.

Behind Waimea Bay is the entrance to Waimea Valley Audubon Center. If you've read about Waimea Falls Park and are jonesin' for some of the adventure activities there, you're in for a disappointment. It's been converted to a low-key botanical garden that also happens to have a waterfall you can swim to when it's flowing. See GARDEN TOURS under ATTRACTIONS on page 120 for more.

In 1792 George Vancouver (as in Vancouver, Canada), was visiting the islands. He had been on Captain Cook's fatal voyage to Hawai'i 13 years earlier. Vancouver was exceptionally skilled at diplomacy and was well-regarded by Hawaiian chiefs. While he was on Kaua'i, his sister ship stopped here at Waimea to secure water. The armed captain of that other ship and crewmembers were directed by the Hawaiians to travel farther up the stream (to avoid the saltier brackish water at the mouth). Then the Hawaiians further enticed the captain, the astronomer and two crewmen to come see some hogs and bananas they wanted to sell them. Once the men were away from their party, the Hawaiians stoned then stabbed them to death (one crewman escaped) and took their arms. In the 1800s the renowned Hawaiian historian *Kamakau* inter-

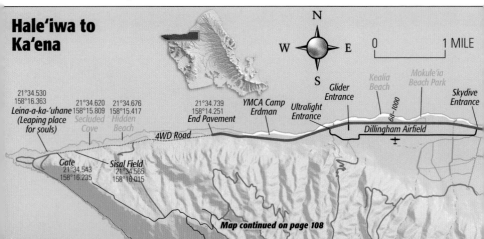

Hale'iwa to Ka'ena

N
W E
S
0   1 MILE

21°34.530
158°16.363
Leina-a-ka-'uhane
(Leaping place for souls)

21°34.620
158°15.809
Secluded Cove

21°34.676
158°15.417
Hidden Beach

4WD Road

21°34.739
158°14.251
End Pavement

YMCA Camp Erdman

Ultralight Entrance

Glider Entrance

Kealia Beach

Mokule'ia Beach Park

68-1000

Dillingham Airfield

Skydive Entrance

Gate
21°34.543
158°16.235

Sisal Field
21°34.565
158°16.015

Map continued on page 108

The simple life on a north shore beach...

viewed one of the aging killers, who told him, "We killed the men to get the guns," and that chiefs had ordered that "if a ship came in to the area, they were to kill the foreigners and get the guns" (which had that magical power to kill a man from a distance).

Unfortunately, this would be only one example of Hawaiians killing westerners and vice versa in the early years of western contact.

Halfway between Waimea Bay and Hale'iwa town (and at the south end of a loop road called Pohaku Loa Way) is a

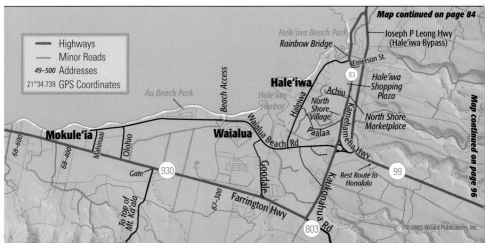

Legend:
- Highways
- Minor Roads
- 49–500 Addresses
- 21°34.739 GPS Coordinates

Map continued on page 84

Hale'iwa Beach Park
Rainbow Bridge
Joseph P Leong Hwy (Hale'iwa Bypass)
Emerson St.
Au Beach Park
Beach Access
Hale'iwa
83
Hale'iwa Shopping Plaza
Achiu
Hale'iwa Harbor
Haleiwa
North Shore Village
North Shore Marketplace
Paalaa
Mokule'ia
Mahinaai
Olohio
Waialua Beach Rd
Waialua
Kamehameha Hwy
68–600
68–400
Gate
930
Goodale
Best Route to Honolulu
99
Kaukonahua Rd
To top of Mt. Ka'ala
67–300
Farrington Hwy
803

Map continued on page 96

small beach known locally as Turtle Beach. This is the only place in Hawai'i where the turtles are so gregarious, we've seen them actually swim after beachgoers

NOT TO BE MISSED!

that have gotten bored from turtle-watching. (We suspect that some nearby resident might be secretly feeding them to get this kind of behavior.) Anyway, they're not *always* there, but when they are, it's a joy to see turtles so close to the shore (sometimes *on* the shore) and so accepting of people nearby. Remember that it's illegal to touch or handle them, and beware that, right at the shoreline, waves might send them crashing into your shin. (Got the scar to prove it.)

SURFING LIFE

There are two seasons on the North Shore—surfing season (during winter months) and the agonizing waiting season when the fickle waves pound the southern hemisphere. Winter waves usually start rolling in around November, and North Shore towns such as Hale'iwa and Waimea instantly transform themselves from sleepy summer towns to jam-packed surfing meccas.

Strewn along this stretch of the island are numerous surfing houses, many with notorious names known to surfers throughout the country. Each night during surfing season, throngs of surfers and those attracted to the lifestyle gather in these houses where BBQS are smoking, someone is always lifting weights, beer is being consumed *at all times*, surfing videos or surfing video games are being played, and talk is about waves and those who ride them. Some have outside jobs, some don't. All share a passion for waves that non-surfers find baf-

fling. You can listen to surfers talk for hours about how the waves are breaking and how they did or would respond. It's more than a lifestyle; it's closer to a religion.

Though O'ahu's North Shore is known around the world as home of the planet's best surfing, it's surprising to learn that until the 1950s nobody surfed any of the sites here. Waves were considered too big and too powerful, so Makaha in West O'ahu was the home to serious surfing. The first few hardy pioneers to surf the North Shore's waves got ground into dust by the breakers, but by the 1960s word got out, and North Shore was "discovered" by the outside world. The big change occurred when the old heavy redwood boards were replaced by new, lightweight (and more maneuverable) balsa wood boards, and a radical invention allowed surfers to tackle taller waves that would have turned their boards sideways. The invention? The surfboard fin. Now surfers had a chance. By the time fiberglass boards came along, North Shore waves were being shredded by riders lured from all over the world.

HALE'IWA

Hale'iwa is the biggest town on the North Shore. It's a quaint town that centers around surfing in the winter. (Summers are pretty mellow.) There aren't any resorts up here, but B&Bs aren't hard to find. Several good restaurants and some pretty good shopping are available. If you're looking for a treat, consider the shave ice at Aoki's or Matsumoto's on Kamehameha Highway. (The latter often has unjustifiably long lines so don't hesitate to go to Aoki's.) Chocolate lovers will go ape over the deadly chocolate at North Shore Chocolate Company at

What could possibly motivate you to walk a mile and a quarter from your car? How about Hidden Beach?

Kamehameha and Paalaa Road. It's in a shop that sells woodworks, but their chocolate business is the reason to stop by.

If you drive west on Hwy 930 (Farrington Hwy), there are stretches of sand beach past **Mokule'ia Beach Park** that are usually deserted. See BEACHES on page 157 for more.

PAST THE PAVEMENT

Although we generally don't recommend 4WDs on O'ahu the way we do on Kaua'i or the Big Island, this is the *one* occasion when you'll wish you had one, because the last 2¼ miles are an unpaved JEEP road, and there are a couple of sights worth seeing—enough so that you might want to walk to them.

At 1¾ miles into the dirt road (and 1,200 feet past the last of the roadside telephone poles) is a secluded cove that we're cleverly calling...secluded cove. (It has no actual name.) You can see it from the dirt road, and there's an old rusted pole in the ground nearby. The wind is almost always blowing in this area, and the seas are nearly always choppy. This cove is a wonderful exception. Except when the seas are very heavy, it's usually protected and calm with great swimming and a ruggedly beautiful, contoured shoreline patiently chiseled out of solid sandstone by the relentless sea.

The snorkeling is the best you'll find along the Mokule'ia shoreline. (Granted, this isn't an area renowned for its snorkeling.) Though the visibility is a bit cloudy, there's a nice variety of little fish. (Local fishermen tend to snag their bigger family members.) Until around 2 p.m. on weekdays this area tends to be unoccupied. Late afternoons sometime bring 4WD-equipped local fishermen.

To the right of the cove is a Jacuzzi-sized pool in the reef that makes a great swimming hole when the seas cooperate. You can't see it—or its occupants—from the shoreline; you have to know it's there.

Now that you've gone 2¼ miles on the unpaved road, there's a second gate, and even 4WD vehicles have to stop here. Less than a five-minute walk past the gate at end of the 4WD road is a layered sandstone rock on the ocean side of the path.

A REAL GEM

This rock was absolutely sacred to the ancient Hawaiians. The word "sacred" can be overused, but in this case it can't be overstated. This area is called *Leina-a-ka-'uhane*—the

About 1¼ miles into the dirt road, 15 telephone poles past the metal gate you went around and across from pole #196, is a hidden beach. You can't really see it well from the dirt road. Imagine having a small, sandy cove to yourself. Might happen, might not. But you've got a chance here. There's even a little snorkeling when the ocean's not pounding too hard.

leaping place for souls. The ancients believed that while you were on your deathbed, your soul left your body and wandered about. For those Hawaiians who lived on O'ahu, the soul eventually ended up here where it would climb this sandstone rock, face toward the ocean and leap into the company of its ancestors—and at that exact moment, the person died. If a soul had no ancestors who cared enough to greet it, the soul fell into the *po pau 'ole o milu,* the endless night, or they wandered about the island for eternity as a ghost, known in the islands as a night marcher.

AIN'T TECHNOLOGY GRAND?

Above Ka'ena Point is a satellite tracking station. That title implies that it was built to track satellites, but space technology wasn't always so advanced. Throughout the '60s, until 1972, a supersecret "black" group called the *Corona Project* carried out one of America's most important reconnaissance tasks.

Spy satellites launched about once a month took photographs of America's enemies during that part of the Cold War. But the images were just that… *photographs…on film*. The resolution of film was so much greater than beamable television cameras of that era that they had to take film-based snapshots. So how did they get the photos from the satellites to the spies who needed them? As strange as it sounds, canisters full of film were jettisoned from the satellites, small rockets guided the capsules to the appropriate drop zone 600 miles from O'ahu and parachutes were deployed to slow the film's descent. Air Force cargo planes were guided to the parachutes from Ka'ena Point Tracking Station and they snagged the parachutes, *in mid-air*. The films were then taken back and analyzed.

Imagine how hard it would be to fly a bulky cargo plane just *barely* over the top of a rapidly sinking parachute and snag it with a loop dragged behind you. If the plane missed, the capsules landed in the ocean and were designed to float for 1–3 days before sinking. That's long enough for a U.S. ship to locate it, but not long enough to fall into the wrong hands if lost. They accomplished this time-critical float with a method that would make Betty Crocker proud—they simply drilled a hole in the capsule and plugged it with compacted brown sugar that would dissolve in the seawater at a known rate.

Of all the U.S. space programs, this one had by far, the highest failure rate. Of the first 25 satellites launched, *only three* returned usable photos. But they learned from their mistakes, ultimately launching 145 satellites and discovering that the dreaded '60s "missile gap" with the Soviet Union was a hollow bluff on the part of their leader, Nikita Khrushchev.

NORTH SHORE BEST BETS

Best Shoreline Drive—From Kualoa Beach Park to Hale'iwa

Best Place to Watch Turtles—Turtle Beach

Best Snorkeling—Sharks Cove (when it's calm)

Best Beach That You Can't Drive a Car to—Hidden Beach

Best Place to Stay Out of the Water—Anywhere on the North Shore when the surf's up

Best Photo Op of You Under a Waterfall—Waimea Valley Audubon Center

Best Surf Spot That's Not Marked—Banzai Pipeline

Best Treat—North Shore Chocolate Co.

Best Use of a Cargo Plane—Snaring parachutes containing spy film

What a shame that few visitors will ever see some of the fantastic sights that Wai'anae has to offer, like Makua Beach.

Wai'anae in the west and Central O'ahu are the least visited parts of the island. Central O'ahu is dominated by vast fields of pineapple while Wai'anae is dominated by exceptionally clear water and an outdated reputation among island residents.

If you're heading out to Wai'anae, skip to page 104.

CENTRAL O'AHU

This may be a little disorienting, but we're going to describe Central O'ahu from the north to the south. That's because we're assuming that most people will first see it *after* having driving around the North Shore, and they're on their way back toward Waikiki.

Taking Hwy 99 leaving Hale'iwa, you'll notice that this entire area is dominated by one crop—pineapple. James Dole started planting the fruit here in 1900 and then bought the entire island of Lana'i in 1922, converting it to a gigantic pineapple farm. (They stopped growing it commercially on Lana'i in 1990 in favor of a more profitable crop—*visitors*.)

Pineapple likes to be warm during the day and cool at night. This plateau is at 1,000 feet and cooler than the shoreline. Dole Pineapple has 11,500 acres under cultivation. At 27,000–33,000 low-to-the-ground pineapple plants per acre, there could be as many as *350 million* plants out here. It takes 20 months to mature the first time they plant it.

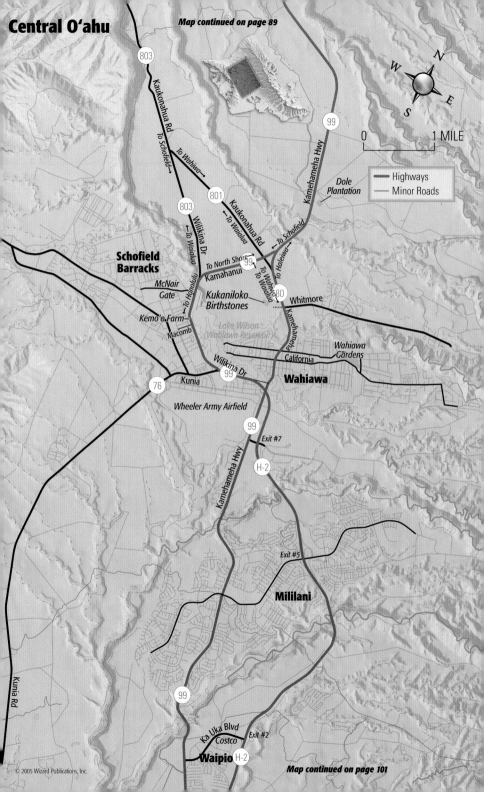

Central O'ahu

Map continued on page 89

803

Kaukonahua Rd

To Schofield→

To Wahiwa→

801

803

Kaukonahua Rd

To Waialua

99

Kamehameha Hwy

Dole Plantation

0   1 MILE

—— Highways

—— Minor Roads

Wilikina Dr

To Waialua

Schofield Barracks

To North Shore

99

To Wahiawa

To Waialua

To Haleiwa

To Schofield

Kamahanui

McNair Gate

Kukaniloko Birthstones

80

Whitmore

To Honolulu

Kemo'o Farm

Lake Wilson (Wahiawa Reservoir)

Macomb

Kamehameha

Wahiawa Gardens

Wilikina Dr

California

76

Kunia

99

Wahiawa

Wheeler Army Airfield

99

Exit #7

H-2

Kamehameha Hwy

Exit #5

Mililani

99

Kunia Rd

Ka Uka Blvd

Costco

Exit #2

Waipio H-2

Map continued on page 101

© 2005 Wizard Publications, Inc.

When they harvest the fruit, they twist the top off and replant it where it'll make more pineapples in a little more than a year. You might notice that the area is littered with tattered black plastic. They put it down during planting to reduce the amount of water and pesticides needed. (Kind of ironic, isn't it? The area is littered with black plastic *to protect the environment*.)

The shape of the individual fields is no accident. They're laid out so that the arm of the harvesting machine can reach out exactly halfway across the field while pineapple workers walk behind picking the fruit. It's tough, hot work, and walking through a pineapple field is a horrible affair. If you're curious what it's like, try practicing at home by walking through a giant pile of razor blades—same effect.

By the way, you'll hear lots of wives tales regarding how to check a pineapple for ripeness and sweetness. Pulling leaves from the crown, measuring the buds on the skin, looking for golden color, looking for smooth, and flattened eyes—there are plenty of ways, and everyone seems to swear by their method. Living in Hawai'i and having purchased countless pineapples, we can say authoritatively that the secret to getting a sweet pineapple is...pure luck. None of those tricks seem to work for us. And despite Dole's contention that "they're all picked ripe," we've certainly gotten some pretty sour pineapples over the years. One thing that does seem to help is to put it in the fridge for a day upside down to let the sugar even out instead of pooling at the bottom. (Otherwise, the bottom's sweet and the top is sour.)

As an aside, excessive consumption of pineapple cores can cause "fiber balls" to form in your digestive tract. (You'll need

instructions from your cat on how to cough them up.) And old-timers use pineapple juice to clean machetes and knife blades and will mix it with sand to clean boat decks.

On Hwy 99 just north of Hwy 80 and Wahiawa town is **Dole Plantation** (621–8408). While undeniably your classic "tourist trap," there are a couple of reasons some might want to stop here. They have a hedge maze that's 100,000 square feet—the largest in the world, according to the *Guinness Book of World Records*. The idea is to wander through the maze and locate six hidden stations before exiting. It'll take between 6 minutes (their record) to an hour and costs $5. The hedge is 8 feet tall. (If you want to take a photo of it, the only way we could do it was to put the camera on timer and hoist it up on a stick.) They also have a 3-acre garden that's $3.50 (and possibly overpriced at that unless you're a certified garden junkie) and a train ride tour for $7.50 ($5.50 for kids). A pineapple field is not exactly the most thrilling place to take a 20-minute tour, but kids seem to like riding the train. (Adults get antsy in about 5 minutes.) You'll learn everything you ever wanted to know about pineapple...but were afraid to ask.

Dole also has a gift shop with food in the form of hot dogs, chili and all things pineapple including flavors of frozen Dole whip. (We'll boldly predict that "pineapple" with be featured as their "flavor of the day.") You can drop a lot of money quickly at Dole, but the gift shop's not bad.

You'll have a choice of taking Hwy 99 through Schofield or Hwy 80 through Wahiawa. Wahiawa's technically shorter, but traffic usually makes the journey longer. Go through Wahiawa if you need gas or you want to see the birthing stones (below). Schofield is faster, and if you're hungry, check out Jimmy's Lakeside Cafe (see DINING) for their pizza, baked goods and killer view of the otherwise-hard-to-see Lake Wilson.

Just before Wahiawa on Hwy 80 you'll come upon a short dirt road on the right at the intersection of Hwy 80 and Whitmore. In the middle of a pineapple field is one of O'ahu's less-visited yet oddly peaceful sites. The **Kukaniloko birthing stones** are where royalty of yesteryear came to give birth to future rulers. The rocks in this area are strangely weathered and look out of place, yet legend states that the patterns are natural, not manmade.

Royal birthing procedures were different than what commoners went through. When the time came, the woman would arrive at what was then a secret spot, and in the presence of 36 male chiefs she would position herself at certain stones and in certain ways to give birth. Within minutes the child was taken away, and the mother would not see her child again until it was grown. This was to insure that the child would not be murdered. Infanticide in high-ranking families was common by rival chiefs.

The sign indicating the sacredness of this site to Hawaiians is real. We've seen entire Hawaiian families making pilgrimages to this site, chanting and praying for hours.

In ancient Hawai'i, parenting was a much different affair than what we're used to. The rights of the grandparents superseded the rights of the parents. Parents could not raise their own child without the consent of the grandparents. First-born children were whisked away from the mother at birth and raised by the husband's relatives if it was a boy, the mother's relatives if it was a girl. And every boy, first-born or not, was taken from the woman's hut when old enough to be weaned and raised in the men's hut. Never again in his lifetime would the male be allowed to eat with women, even his mother or his wife. The punishment for any male caught eating with women was death.

Some children were designated at birth never to do any kind of physical labor their entire lives. This extended to feeding themselves. Poi or fish would be dropped into their mouths and water poured directly into them. These people were required to sit around all day long on tapa mats being attended to and brought laziness to a fine art. The 17th century Hawaiian historian Kamakau referred to them as "human pets." (Today we simply call them *teenagers*.)

Youths raised by kahuna professionals, such as omen readers, deep sea fishermen, tapa cloth makers or star readers, were consecrated at birth, and everything associated with them was kapu—off limits to others. Their food calabash, their clothes, their houses—even their hair couldn't be touched or trimmed and grew tangled and snarled. Only when their training was complete were the kapus lifted and could they live a more normal and less sacred life.

WAHIAWA

Wahiawa, along with Wai'anae, often has the cheapest gas on the island after Costco, so gas up there.

In Wahiawa there's a garden called **Wahiawa Gardens** off California Street, but it's pretty pathetic. See ATTRACTIONS on page 122 if you're interested. (You won't be.)

After Wahiawa or Schofield you'll take H-2 south to H-1.

A visitor getting lost in the world's biggest maze at the Dole Plantation.

Of course, there's more to this area than meets the eye. There are large military bases out here, which you can only glimpse from the road. What you *won't* see, however, can be more interesting. There are miles and miles of tunnels carved underground. There's also a massive underground complex called the KUNIA REGIONAL SIGNALS INTELLIGENCE OPERATIONS CENTER buried near the pineapple fields. This is where intercepted messages from around the world are decrypted and analyzed.

MT. KA'ALA

Wai'anae and Central O'ahu are separated by the tallest mountain on the island. The top, called Mt. Ka'ala, is a flat plateau of swampy ground dominated by mosses and lichen. At 4,025 feet, it's usually cloud-covered, and trees at the top are stunted. Fully grown 'ohi'a trees—normally growing to over 20 feet tall—top out at only 2–3 feet, a natural bonsai garden. Unlike the similarly-soggy summit of Wai'ale'ale on Kaua'i, which the Hawaiians considered sacred, Ka'ala was held in slightly less regard by the Hawaiians of yesteryear. Nearly every recorded chant referring to Mt. Ka'ala, seems to focus on the "cold dews of Ka'ala," and little affection for the place percolated down to the common man.

At the summit today are radar towers that your Hawai'i-bound pilot communi-

Pearl Harbor

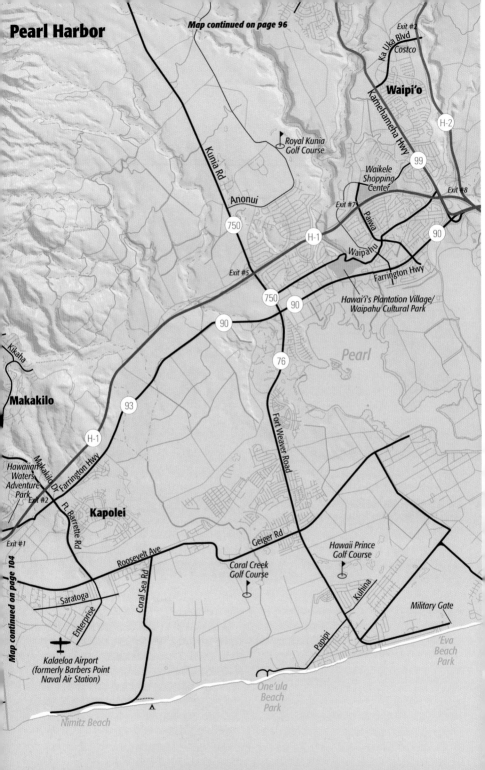

Map continued on page 96

Exit #2
Ka Uka Blvd
Costco

Waipi'o

Kamehameha Hwy

H-2

99

Royal Kunia
Golf Course

Waikele
Shopping
Center

Exit #8

Kunia Rd

Anonui

Exit #7

Paiwa

90

750

H-1

Waipahu

Exit #5

Farrington Hwy

750   90

Hawai'i's Plantation Village/
Waipahu Cultural Park

90

Pearl

76

Kikaha

Makakilo

93

Fort Weaver Road

H-1

Hawaiian
Waters
Adventure
Park

Makakilo Dr

Farrington Hwy

Exit #2

Ft. Barrette Rd

Kapolei

Geiger Rd

Hawaii Prince
Golf Course

Exit #1

Map continued on page 104

Roosevelt Ave

Coral Creek
Golf Course

Coral Sea Rd

Kuhina

Military Gate

Saratoga

Enterprise

Papipi

'Eva
Beach
Park

Kalaeloa Airport
(formerly Barbers Point
Naval Air Station)

One'ula
Beach
Park

Nimitz Beach

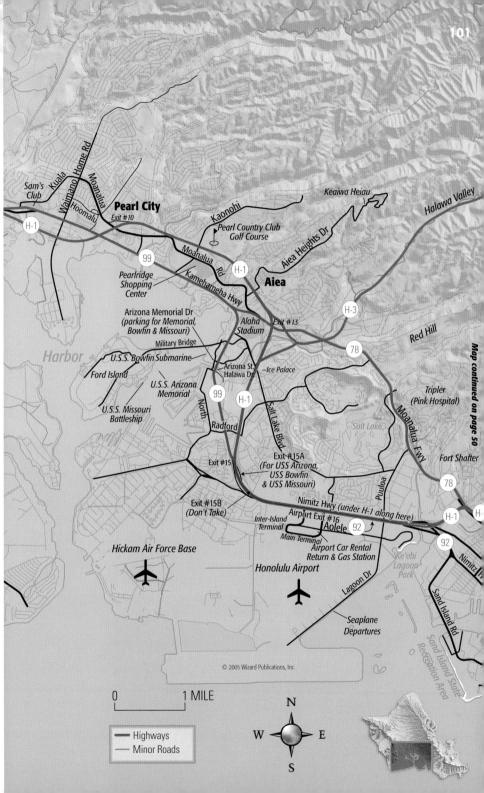

Sam's Club

Kuala

Waimano Home Rd

Hoomalu

Moanalua

Pearl City

Exit #10

H-1

Kaonohi

Keaiwa Heiau

Pearl Country Club Golf Course

Aiea Heights Dr

Halawa Valley

99

Moanalua Rd

H-1

Pearlridge Shopping Center

Kamehameha Hwy

Aiea

H-3

Arizona Memorial Dr (parking for Memorial, Bowfin & Missouri)

Aloha Stadium

Exit #13

Red Hill

Military Bridge

78

Harbor

U.S.S. Bowfin Submarine

Arizona St. Halawa Dr

Ice Palace

Ford Island

U.S.S. Arizona Memorial

99

H-1

Tripler (Pink Hospital)

Map continued on page 50

U.S.S. Missouri Battleship

North

Salt Lake

Moanalua Fwy

Fort Shafter

Radford

Salt Lake Blvd

Exit #15

Exit #15A (For USS Arizona, USS Bowfin & USS Missouri)

Puuloa

78

Exit #15B (Don't Take)

Nimitz Hwy (under H-1 along here)

H-1

H

Inter-Island Terminal

Airport Exit #16

Aolele

92

92

Main Terminal

Nimitz

Hickam Air Force Base

Airport Car Rental Return & Gas Station

Ke'ehi Lagoon Park

Sand Island Rd

Honolulu Airport

Lagoon Dr

Sand Island State Recreation Area

Seaplane Departures

© 2005 Wizard Publications, Inc.

0   1 MILE

Highways
Minor Roads

N
W   E
S

cated with when you got within 200 miles of Hawai'i. Although there is a paved road to the top, it's gated and you're not very welcome up there. There's a separate trail to the top, but it's insanely difficult and not particularly rewarding in the views department. While not as tall, the top of the Ko'olaus presents better views.

While it's tempting to assume the top of the mountain must have been the summit of the volcano that created the mountain, it's not. The actual summit was to the west. The peak of Mt. Ka'ala is simply the only remaining remnant of the original gently-sloping shield volcano that was once here. The rest has worn away from erosion, leaving this unusually hardened lava relic of the volcano's youth.

PEARL HARBOR

Pearl Harbor is named after the many pipi (Hawaiian oysters) that used to live here. Visiting ships from the late 1700s described abundant pearls from this harbor. A visitor in 1810 wrote that the king had discovered their value to the outside world and employed numerous divers to pluck the oysters from their shallow bed. By the end of the 1800s overharvesting and runoff from nearby cattle operations had virtually eliminated the pearl oysters, but the name Pearl Harbor lives on, and its Hawaiian name, Pu'u-loa (long hill), is scarcely known, even among Hawaiians.

The large island inside the harbor is called **Ford Island**. It is owned by the U.S. military and houses some of the officers and crewmen stationed at Pearl Harbor.

In ancient times, Ford Island had an entirely different purpose. It was called Moku-'ume'ume, meaning *island of the sexual game*. In those days, if a com-

moner couple had trouble conceiving a child, they came here. Large groups gathered around a fire, couples sitting apart. A master of ceremonies would go up to a man, tap him with a maile wand, then tap a randomly selected woman, and together they went off into the darkness to share the night. If a child was conceived, it was regarded as the offspring of the husband, not the biological

father. If no child was conceived, they'd head back to this island to give it a whirl again.

You can't do a driving tour of Pearl Harbor—it's still an active Navy base, and access is restricted. You can't even overfly it due to flight restrictions put in place after 9/11. But the most popular visitor attractions on the island—the **USS Arizona Memorial** and the **Battleship Missouri** are available for touring. See ATTRACTIONS on page 117.

With the USS Arizona Memorial in the distance, symbolizing the day America was caught by surprise, sailors on the USS Nimitz aircraft carrier stand guard with machine guns ready, ensuring that a surprise won't happen again on their watch.

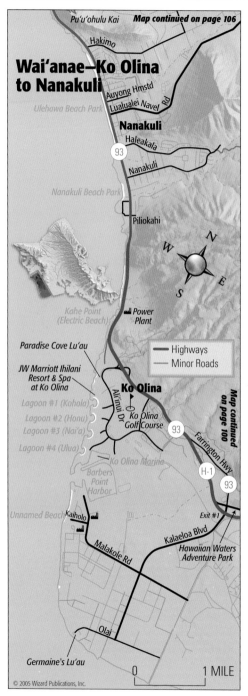

Wai'anae–Ko Olina to Nanakuli

Map continued on page 106

Pu'u'ohulu Kai
Hakimo
Auyong Hmstd
Lualualei Navel Rd
Ulehawa Beach Park
Nanakuli
Haleakala
93
Nanakuli
Nanakuli Beach Park
Piliokahi
Kahe Point (Electric Beach)
Power Plant
Paradise Cove Lu'au
JW Marriott Ihilani Resort & Spa at Ko Olina
Lagoon #1 (Kohola)
Lagoon #2 (Honu)
Lagoon #3 (Nai'a)
Lagoon #4 (Ulua)
Ali'inui Dr
Ko Olina
Ko Olina Golf Course
93
Ko Olina Marina
Barbers Point Harbor

— Highways
— Minor Roads

Map continued on page 100

Farrington Hwy
H-1
93
Unnamed Beach
Kaiholo
Malakole Rd
Exit #1
Kalaeloa Blvd
Hawaiian Waters Adventure Park
Olai
Germaine's Lu'au

0   1 MILE

© 2005 Wizard Publications, Inc.

'EWA

'Ewa is the area below H-1 on your way out to Wai'anae. This is where the county wants to direct future growth. It's hot, dry and not particularly pretty, so there's really not much for the visitor out here other than **Hawai'i's Plantation Village** and **Hawaiian Waters Adventure Park**. See ATTRACTIONS on pages 115 and 111 for more on these.

Two miles offshore of 'Ewa Beach is a giant open ocean fish farm. A company called Cates International has anchored several 80-foot cages 40 feet below the surface to raise moi (a tasty fish found at some island restaurants often served whole). Currents sweep through the cages, which are said to attract sharks and other predators.

KALAELOA/BARBERS POINT

The Navy purchased the land at Barbers Point a century ago for their aircraft. Not planes, however. It was for *blimps*. (Yes, the Navy was a major blimp operator.) When the Navy got out of the blimp business in the 1930s, they converted it to an airfield. At the end of the 20th century, the Navy handed the land to the state of Hawai'i, which now controls it. The area is very industrial, though there are a few decent beaches. See BEACHES for more.

WAI'ANAE

Wai'anae is the name of a town, but it's also the name generally used to describe the coastline leading all the way to Ka'ena Point. Wai'anae is one of the poorer sections of the island, and it has a reputation of being a rough place. In the '70s that was certainly true. A number of violent crimes against visitors created an image among island residents that persists to this day. *Don't go to*

Wai'anae, they say. *You'll get beaten up.* Well frankly, that's ridiculous, and those who espouse that attitude need to come out here more often. Because it's so dry, Wai'anae has some of the nicest water on the island, and you shouldn't let its outdated reputation dissuade you from partaking of its delights. Even the police confirm that today, violent crimes against visitors are extremely rare here. It's mainly petty theft, which can happen anywhere on the island. That means some dirtbag breaking into your car to steal your camera while you're at the beach. When we're out in Wai'anae, we simply don't leave anything valuable in the car. (Frankly, we do that everywhere we go.) There's always a chance someone will break in anyway, but it has never happened to us anywhere in Hawai'i. (And we've left our car in a *lot* of places.) As for safety, common sense needs to be applied, no matter where you are. If you're at a beach park after dark and the parking lot is filled with young toughs drinking copious amounts of beer, you don't need us to tell you that now is not the right time to go over and show them your fancy Rolex watch. The biggest problem we've found with Wai'anae isn't the people, it's the bad restaurants. There are a few places to

An Oversight Leads to a Spared Gas Station— and Victory in WWII

Say what you want about the Japanese attack on Pearl Harbor, militarily the plan was brilliantly conceived and executed. The level of surprise was only matched by the level of destruction, and Japanese losses were minimal. Although our aircraft carriers weren't there (by chance, not design), the Japanese nonetheless achieved their goals and didn't make any mistakes…except for one—a mistake so giant, so glaring and so important that it possibly ended up costing Japan the war.

When the Japanese warplanes were swarming around during the attack, their pilots were so single-mindedly focused on destroying ships and planes, that they totally ignored row after row of conspicuous white fuel tanks above the ground. In them was the fuel that powered all of America's Pacific Fleet. If a single bomb had been dropped on just one of the tanks, it could have set them all ablaze. It would have taken a year to replace that fuel. A year that our aircraft carriers would have sat idled without any gas. A year when the Japanese navy would have had free reign. A year that could have changed the outcome of WWII.

Having dodged that potentially fatal bullet, the Navy accelerated a plan that was already in the works—building giant gas tanks underground beneath Red Hill to hold the quarter billion gallons of fuel that was needed to power the Navy's Pacific Fleet. (Large naval ships can only travel a few feet per gallon.) To this day if you're near the H-3 and Hwy 78 freeway intersection and look mauka (toward the mountain), you'll see Red Hill, the Pacific Fleet's gas station and the Navy's response to the biggest blunder of the Pacific war.

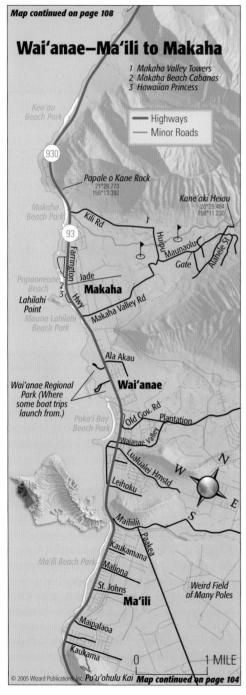

Wai'anae—Ma'ili to Makaha

1 Makaha Valley Towers
2 Makaha Beach Cabanas
3 Hawaiian Princess

— Highways
— Minor Roads

Map continued on page 108

Kea'au
Beach Park

930

Papale o Kane Rock
21°28.773
158°13.392

Kane'aki Heiau
20°29.484
158°11.230

Makaha
Beach Park

93

Kili Rd

Huipu

Maunaolu

Gate

Atanele St

Farrington

Jade

Makaha

Papaoneone
Beach

Lahilahi
Point

Mauna Lahilahi
Beach Park

Makaha Valley Rd

Hwy

Ala Akau

Wai'anae Regional
Park (Where
some boat trips
launch from.)

Wai'anae

Poka'i Bay
Beach Park

Old Gov. Rd

Plantation

Waianae Valley

Lualualei Hmstd

Leihoku

Mailiili

Paakea

Kaukamana

Ma'ili Beach Park

Maliona

St. Johns

Ma'ili

Weird Field
of Many Poles

Maipalaoa

Kaukama

0   1 MILE

Pu'u'ohulu Kai
Map continued on page 104

---

eat, but many people may stick with fast food out here. And like all beaches on the island, avoid them on weekends when they're crowded with locals.

Before the towns start rolling by, the resort area of **Ko Olina** is the main resort out here. Their four man-made lagoons offer super-protected swimming and some surprisingly good snorkeling.

As you pass by the power plant, keep an eye out for **dolphins** here. You may get lucky. We've seen them more often here than just about any other place on the island.

The first town is **Nanakuli**. One explanation of how Nanakuli got it s name is out of local embarrassment. In ancient times this was a dry, inhospitable place to grow food. Residents had little spare water or food. When travelers walked by, it was customary to give them nourishment. Residents here hid from approaching travelers, fearing shame if they had to refuse to be hospitable. When they couldn't avoid passing travelers, residents pretended to be deaf so they'd be able to feign a lack of understanding. When puzzled travelers moved on, they'd comment on the strange village full of nothing but deaf people who just stared at them. Nana-kuli means to *look deaf.*

Next, the town of **Wai'anae** is where some boat tours leave from. The waters off the Wai'anae Coast can be particularly blue due to a lack of runoff and the steepness of the underwater terrain.

MAKAHA

Makaha is the last town along here. In talking about this part of the island and its rough reputation, you should realize that this is not a recent development. Even in ancient times Makaha—which means "savage" or "fierce"—was a place travel-

Tucked away in a quiet part of Makaha Valley, Kane'ahi Heiau is a nicely restored Hawaiian Temple.

ers feared. A notorious band of robbers and cutthroats lived up in the valley and ambushed groups passing by. These robbers were skillful at a type of fighting called lua (bone-breaking). They plucked all the hairs from their bodies and smeared themselves with oil so they'd be hard to grab in a fight. At the north end of Makaha Valley on the *mauka* (mountain) side of the road across the street from Makaha Shores Apartments, you'll see a tall, upright rock. The top of that very rock, called *Papale o Kane*, was where the gang's lookout waited. When an approaching group was within striking range, the lookout would yell *low tide,* which signaled that the group was beatable. If he yelled *high tide,* it meant the group was too big or too well-armed to take advantage of, so the robbers would let them pass.

Hawaiians of old created temples, called heiaus, to worship their gods. Up in Makaha Valley is a somewhat mysterious heiau called **Kane'ahi**. This was built as an agricultural heiau—where growers prayed for good conditions—but for some reason it was eventually converted to a heiau to the war god, Ku—where chiefs prayed for victory over their enemies. It's been nicely restored, and you can visit it Tue.–Sun. 10 a.m. to 2 p.m., unless it rains (which doesn't happen often in Makaha). Take a right on Makaha Valley Road, it'll turn onto Huipu Road. Then left on Maunaolu Road. You'll have to sign a waiver at the gate, show license and proof of insurance. After leaving the heiau on Alahale Street, if you were to accidentally turn left instead of right onto Maunaolu, the road goes a little higher and exposes pretty views of Makaha Valley from behind.

A REAL GEM

The least known resorts *on the entire island* are in Makaha. **Makaha Beach Cabanas** and **Hawaiian Princess** both

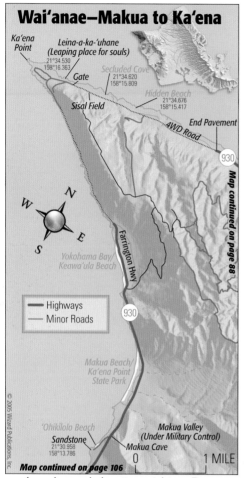

Wai'anae—Makua to Ka'ena

Ka'ena Point

Leina-a-ka-'uhane
(Leaping place for souls)
21°34.530
158°16.363

Gate

Secluded Cove
21°34.620
158°15.809

Sisal Field

Hidden Beach
21°34.676
158°15.417

4WD Road

End Pavement

930

Map continued on page 88

Yokohama Bay/
Keawa'ula Beach

Farrington Hwy

— Highways
— Minor Roads

930

Makua Beach/
Ka'ena Point
State Park

'Ohikilolo Beach

Sandstone
21°30.958
158°13.786

Makua Valley
(Under Military Control)

Makua Cave

0   1 MILE

© 2005 Wizard Publications, Inc.

Map continued on page 106

state government, the highway keeps going around Ka'ena Point and on to Dillingham Airfield on the North Shore. The only thing missing from the government's version...is 5½ miles of connecting road they haven't gotten around to building yet.)

A REAL GEM

Drive these last miles slowly and soak in the views. You'll be amazed at how little use beaches like Makua Beach and Yokohama Bay get during the week.

Makua Cave is an old sea cave gouged out by the ocean during a time when the world was warmer and the oceans higher. Now high and dry, it's on the mauka side of Hwy 93 just past the 17 mile marker. Legend says that a shape-shifting shark god lives in the area and visits the cave via an underground tunnel to the ocean. If you're looking for a secluded beach or a short hike to a tortured sandstone bench, see 'Ohiki-lolo Beach on page 128 or the hike on page 186.

Once at Yokohama Bay, the road ends. The western tip of the island at Ka'ena Point is almost 2½ miles away. You can hike it, see ACTIVITIES on page 187.

have heavenly locations right on Papaoneone Beach, one of the lesser known beaches, and they're very reasonably priced for what you get. If you're not interested in staying in Waikiki, these resorts have an incredible beachfront setting. See WHERE TO STAY on page 294 for more.

THE END OF THE ROAD

The best part of Wai'anae is the last 5 miles, before Farrington Highway seemingly ends at Yokohama Bay. (We say *seemingly* because, according to the

WAI'ANAE & CENTRAL O'AHU BEST BETS

Best Place to Impersonate a Rat in a Maze—Dole Plantation

Best View of a Lake You Didn't Know was There—Jimmy's Lakeside Café

Best Beach—Makua Beach

Best Garden to Avoid—Wahiawa Garden

Best Hawaiian Relic—Kane'ahi Heiau

Best Forgotten Resort—Hawaiian Princess

Woe to any enemy that ever saw the business end of these USS Missouri guns, which could hurl a 2,700 pound projectile 23 miles.

You gotta drive there or take a bus there, and it's the only reason you're in that area. This is what the ATTRACTIONS chapter is all about. We don't have an ATTRACTIONS chapter in our neighbor island books because, frankly, we didn't need one before. But O'ahu has tons of attractions that you'll drive to. This chapter excludes lu'aus (covered at the end of DINING), but includes Polynesian Cultural Center, Hawaiian Waters Adventure Park, Bishop Museum, Iolani Palace and more.

POLYNESIAN CULTURAL CENTER
293–3333

It's as far from Waikiki as you can get—both literally and figuratively. Be-

cause the Polynesian Cultural Center (PCC) is *so* popular, a lot of preconceived misconceptions exist. This is not a Hawaiian Disneyland with rides and dolphins leaping out of the water. This is a laid-back collection of recreations from various island villages from around Polynesia. They don't pretend to be completely authentic. Power outlets and plywood, electric lights and cell phones are ever-present. What they've attempted to do is to create a non-frantic environment where you can wander around at your leisure and see various styles of huts, lots of dancing demonstrations, education of all-things Polynesian, spear throwing and more. Coconuts, drums and palm fronds along with a meandering cement-lined

The Polynesian Cultural Center has shows and demonstrations throughout the day.

lagoon create an island atmosphere that's certainly closer to reality than anything you'll find in Waikiki.

The Mormon Church created and runs this place in association with Brigham Young Hawai'i University. Basically, your entrance fees help subsidize students from all around the Pacific. In exchange, those students **A REAL GEM** work here at PCC, so it's likely you'll come in contact with many young people from the very countries that are represented in the faux villages. Hearing them sing in their various languages is a real treat.

Start by taking a canoe trip to the other side of PCC and walk your way back, stopping along the way whenever something strikes your fancy. You may find yourself playing drums in Tonga or getting a fake tattoo in the Marquesas Islands. Wear a wide-brimmed hat since even on windy days there are areas where the winds are blocked, and it can get hot.

The PCC also has a lu'au (which we found to be the best on the island) and an excellent evening show called Horizons. (See LU'AUS on page 258 for more.)

The PCC is worth the time if you have any interest at all in learning about the Polynesian way of life. And although it's very popular with visitors, they've managed to keep a good and friendly attitude. It doesn't feel like a mob scene, and the staff is top-notch. You can tell they feel honored to be working here, showing you their way of life. We thought it was a class act, through and through. There are many, many shops inside. Our only dig is that there are probably a few *too* many opportunities for you to buy your picture taken at various times during your stay.

Price is pretty steep at $64, but that includes buffet dinner at one of their restaurants and unguided entrance to everything, including the on-site IMAX theater and the evening show. It's an extra $14 for bus transportation to and from Waikiki (which is a 60–90 minute drive away). It's $109 or $175 for guided tours and the lu'au is included. On Hwy 83 in La'ie on the windward side of the island. They open at noon, but demonstrations are more numerous after 1:30 p.m. There's too much to see in one day, but if you're so inclined, you can come back free within three days. Closed Sundays.

HAWAIIAN WATERS ADVENTURE PARK 674–9283

Waterslides and other ways to get wet. This place is usually packed on weekends but often uncrowded (unless there's a group function going on) Monday–Thursday. It's not exactly massive, but it's an easy place to spend half a day or more sliding into various pools and getting hammered in the wave pool or simply floating along in the current-driven whirlpool. Although conceived for families with kids, adults who still have that child-like spark will have fun here, too. It's $34 to get in, which includes most of the attractions. Kids 3–11 are $23. (Tots are free.) They have lockers to keep your junk, and a few things, such as bungee-bouncing and rock climbing, cost extra. Remember to keep your legs crossed when you come down the Cliffhanger (we won't go into detail as to

why), and if you have big shoulders, it might rake your back (you have to experience it to understand it).

WAIKIKI AQUARIUM 923–9741

You can walk to this from most Waikiki hotels. This is a tiny aquarium in Kapiolani Park on Kalakaua Ave. Entrance is a cheap $7. (13–17 year-olds pay $3.50, 12 and under are free.) But if you're expecting the same kind of *ooh-ah* value you'd get at a bigger aquarium, you're likely to be disappointed. An hour or so is probably about enough to see this place.

We don't mean to be disrespectful, but just about any aquarium built on the mainland in the past 20 years outshines the Waikiki Aquarium. There are no giant tanks with scuba divers feeding the fish. Just a series of smaller tanks with colorful fish and coral (from around the Pacific—not just Hawai'i) and a spartan seal enclosure with one very bored monk seal. Kids will probably find it interesting here, but others may not, especially if you've seen nicer aquariums elsewhere. At press time they were planning a large aquarium in western O'ahu at Ko Olina. We doubt that Waikiki Aquarium will survive its emergence. In fairness, the $7 entrance fee certainly doesn't imply opulence.

HONOLULU ZOO 971–7171

We don't mean to sound negative after giving the nearby Waikiki Aquarium a lukewarm review, but the Waikiki Zoo is merely so-so. It's 42 acres of cages, but there are problems. For one, the mesh they use on some of the cages makes it difficult to see the exhibits. Too much metal, too little openings. Also, the zoo doesn't exactly seem scrupulously well-cared for. The bird exhibit is good, but again it's kind of hard to see when sunny. The hippo exhibit is a hit, however. Bottom line—adults without kids won't find it compelling. With kids? Hey, it's a place with animals; they'll be entertained for a bit. Avoid at mid-day due to heat. Entrance is on Kapahulu Ave. Cost is $6, kids 6–12 is $1. Open 9 a.m to 4:30 p.m.

'IOLANI PALACE & HISTORIC BUILDINGS

The United States has been a republic since we broke from England, so we don't really have any examples of royal palaces—except for 'Iolani. These islands were a kingdom until 1893, and in 1882 Hawai'i's last king, David Kalakaua (who was actually elected by the Legislature), ordered **A REAL GEM** this palace to be built to show all the world that Hawai'i had a royalty just as grand as any other. There are many historic buildings downtown, but this is the finest of them all.

'Iolani (522–0832) is as much a testament to the desire to restore as it is to the king who built it. It was only used as a royal palace for 11 years. For the next 75 years a series of governments used it as government building and frankly let it deteriorate to the point that some wanted to bulldoze the building in the late '60s. Most of its artifacts were auctioned off over the years. Once the bureaucrats got their own building next door in 1969, local volunteers worked for years to retrieve many of the artifacts and restore the palace to the glorious condition you see today. The beautiful woodwork, the grandness of design and the great info conveyed along the way make it a worthwhile diversion.

'Iolani is open Tuesday–Saturday 8:30 a.m to 3:30 p.m. Reserve in advance since only 20 people are allowed per guided tour, which is $20 per person. (Self-guided tours are free, but you're not allowed to see the good stuff that way.) The quality of your tour depends on the quality of the docent guide, which varies, but the ones we've seen were incredibly enthusiastic and—although it's a cliché—really made the building come alive. Park in the metered lot on the grounds and stuff at least two hours worth of quarters into the meter. At King and Richards. Take Ala Wai Boulevard right on Kalakaua to the end, left on Beretania, left on Richards, left on King and left into the parking lot.

After 'Iolani Palace, if you have some extra quarters for the meter, you can leave your car and check out some of the other historic buildings, though they aren't as compelling as the palace. See map on page 50.

Kawaiaha'o Church at King and Punchbowl was completed in 1842 and is made from 1,000 pound chunks of coral chiseled from reefs 10–20 feet deep. It is still used as a place of worship. On the grounds is the tomb containing the remains of a lessor known king from the 1800s, Lunalilo, who wanted to be buried next to his people rather than in the royal mausoleum.

The **Hawai'i State Art Museum** (586–0900) is on Richards at Hotel Street. It has art from Hawai'i artists, as well as other from around the world. Entrance is free. If you're an art buff, it's worth your time. Others may not be so impressed.

At Beretania and Richards Street is **Washington Place**. This is where the governor used to live and they still use it for political functions. It's not open to

Using Howitzers, soldiers fire off a twenty-one gun salute during a ceremony at Punchbowl.

the public and you *ain't* on the invitation list, so move along.

At Punchbowl and King Street you'll find **Mission Houses** (531–0481), some of the earliest living quarters that the missionaries built upon their arrival in 1820. The 1-hour tours are a bit pricey at $10. Think of is as more of a lesson on early missionary life and their effort to create a written Hawaiian language. The whole experience is educational, if a bit dry.

PUNCHBOWL CEMETERY 532–3720

National Memorial Cemetery of the Pacific at Punchbowl is an incredibly moving place. In ancient times Hawaiians buried their royalty here and also used it as a place of human sacrifice. The Hawaiian name for this crater is Pu'u-o-waina—hill of human sacrifices.

It's eerily fitting that since 1949 it's been used as a cemetery for those in the military who sacrificed their lives in the Pacific.

Driving into the crater is an experience that is guaranteed to put a lump in your throat. At the far end is a giant statue of Columbia holding a laurel branch. Between you and her are the graves of over 44,000 men and women. No large tombstones or even crosses here—just simple slabs marking the final resting places. Drive up to the statue and look at the walls. In addition to these graves, you'll find over 28,000 names carved into the walls. During the wars of the mid-20th century, young men died in such vast numbers and so rapidly that there wasn't always time to keep track of them. These 28,778 names are of those "whose earthly resting place is known only to God." Under the sculpture of Columbia is a quote from Abraham Lincoln when he wrote to the mother of five sons lost in the Civil War: "The solemn pride that must be yours to have laid so costly a sacrifice on the alter of freedom."

There are some interesting displays of the various battles that claimed these lives. Look at them from the left side to the right. The cemetery is open from 8

Bustling Chinatown is the place to be if you want to pick up fresh fruit—or simply haggle for fun.

a.m. to 6:30 p.m. Entrance is free.

The simplest way to get there from Waikiki is to take Ala Wai Boulevard, right on Kalakaua, left onto Beretania, right onto Queen Emma. It'll pass under H-1 and become Lusitana. Look for San Antonio angling back on your right. Take it, then go left on Puowaina, and it'll eventually fork into the cemetery. There should be signs pointing the way, but they can get faded.

HAWAI'I MARITIME CENTER
536–6373

This rather well-stocked museum to all things nautical in Hawai'i is part of the Bishop Museum. Parked here you'll also

find a four-masted sailing ship called the *Falls of Clyde*, built in 1878. Overall, this is one of those attractions that *sounds* better than it *is*. We *like* this kind of thing, and yet we found this particular experience rather dull and kept hoping that the narrative tape that guides you through the exhibits would hurry up. If you're a hard-core nautical fan, you'll probably like it, but others might want to pass. It's $7.50 for the entrance fee. Near the Aloha Tower at Ala Moana Boulevard and Bishop Street.

If you're in the area, there's a nice view of Honolulu Harbor from the 10th story top of nearby **Aloha Tower**.

CHINATOWN

If you're expecting a made-for-tourist Chinatown, you ain't gonna get it. This is the real deal. Having worked in China for a few years, going to the markets here was like going back to the Orient. Stroll the aisles of the markets, and you come across raw chicken feet, tank after tank of various live fish, whole pig heads, more fruits and vegetables than you even knew existed, Asian orange soda (which is amazingly ubiquitous in China), salted duck eggs and more—all with the sound of Cantonese in the background and the ever-present haggling: *How much? Figh dallah!*

That guy you just bumped into might have been the star chef at the fancy restaurant you ate at last night. Chinatown is where many of them get their fresh seafood and veggies. This is also where much of the Kahuku Shrimp from the north shore ends up—still live and wiggling in the early morning.

More than China is represented here, and you'll see stores that sell Vietnamese food next to their jewelry selections. Don't just hit the stores on the street.

The real fun is in the Kekaulike Market (between King and Hotel on Kekaulike St) and Maunakea Market.

If you get hungry (and you will), stroll over to **Legend Seafood** (see review under Dining) at River and Beretania for the best dim sum on O'ahu. Or try the Asian food court at the Maunakea Market. Lots of Filipino fast food along with some Thai, Vietnamese, Korean and Japanese. It's cheap and there's lots of variety. Locals love Tô-Châu Vietnamese Restaurant at River and Hotel Street.

You'll want to arrive in Chinatown by 10 a.m., before it gets too hot and when the merchants are still hungry. Park at the garage on Maunakea between King and Hotel Street if you can.

HAWAI'I'S PLANTATION VILLAGE
677-0110

We've lived in Hawai'i for a number of years now, but we got more of a feel for the essence of plantation life during this 1½-hour tour than in all the time we've lived here.

In the 1990s the county took this parkland and attempted to re-create what a typical sugar plantation camp was like, and they did a pretty good job. In real life each plantation camp represented a single ethnic group. Here what they've done is create regions of camps representing Chinese, Portuguese, Puerto Rican, Japanese, Filipino, Okinawan and Korean camps. To us, what's special are the guides. You'll spend 60–90 minutes with old-timers who lived this life here. Don't hesitate to engage your guide because that's what makes the experience so cool—at least for us it was. It's $10. The last tour starts at 3 p.m. Located at the west end of Pearl Harbor. Take H-1 to exit 7, left on Paiwa toward the ocean, right on Waipahu. Look for it eventually on your left.

BISHOP MUSEUM 847-3511

This is Hawai'i's most comprehensive museum. Established by the husband of Bernice Pauahi Bishop, the last descendant of King Kamehameha the Great, much of Hawai'i's culture and heritage is stored here. Priceless items such as the royal feathered cape worn by Kamehameha himself along with more common items like lava poi pounders sit side by side. Other examples include the feathered war god Kuka'ilimoku, combs made from coconut leaflet ribs, a grass hut, royal jewelry, kapa cloths, miniature representations of heiaus (temples), leiomanu (shark's tooth-studded wooden weapons that were kept hidden and then used to disembowel unsuspecting enemies), a 55-foot sperm whale skeleton, scrimshaw, and a conch shell that's over 600 years old and wonderfully worn down from all the generations of Hawaiians who rubbed it while blowing through it like a bugle.

The museum also has exhibits from other parts of Polynesia, exhibits from cultures that immigrated to the islands, a hall of natural history, temporary exhibits, hula demonstrations and an awesome Kahili room that is especially regal—don't miss that one.

Parts of the museum seem to be in need of a maintenance boost, and you might not find may people around the exhibits to answer questions, but anyone with an interest in history or the Hawaiian culture will want to devote at least a couple of hours to this museum. $10 per person, kids 4–12 and seniors are $7. In Honolulu at 1525 Bernice Ave. From Waikiki get on H-1 West, take exit 20B, go right on Houghtailing, immediate left on Bernice Street.

BISHOP MUSEUM–HILTON HAWAIIAN VILLAGE 947-2458

This is only a fraction of the size of the real Bishop Museum downtown but this one has a good perspective of Waikiki and how it was developed. The second room is more interesting than the first. Stop to watch the footage shot in 1906 showing that in some ways people are the same throughout time—splashing each other, goofing around and generally frolicking at the beach. But also note how they dressed when walking along the beach, covered from head to toe in suits and dresses. $7 per person. Entrance is at the Hilton Hawaiian Village off Kalia Road. Open 9 a.m. to noon.

SEA LIFE PARK 259-7933

This is O'ahu's version of Sea World, though it's *far* smaller than most mainland aquarium parks. And that's probably the thing you'll notice most. Even the tanks that the dolphins live in seem small. Though it costs $26 to get in ($13 for kids 4–12), you can see this whole park in a couple of hours. Things included with admission include a so-so dolphin show, a pretty good sea lion show and several feedings. (Though you pay extra if you want to be the one feeding them.) You'll notice *many* opportunities here to spend

The dolphin show at Sea Life Park is their most popular attraction.

more, some of them worthwhile. For instance, you can pay an extra $60 to walk around in their giant glass-walled aquarium wearing a diver's helmet with air hose. It's kind of cool to take a picture with the included underwater camera of your dry companion outside the glass. (Granted $60 is *a lot* for this, but it's a pretty unusual experience.) You can snorkel with sting rays for $14 or participate in their dolphin program for $55 or $110. (Though we recommend Dolphin Quest's program more—see page 219.) When you go to their activity booth to sign up for these things, it seems like they're usually pushing "specials" to make it cheaper.

Sea Life Park isn't usually too crowded and seems to be a hit with kids. More than half of their customers are Japanese tour groups, and some of the narrations are in Japanese first. You can drop a lot of money fast here, but it's not a bad attraction.

Near the easternmost tip of the island on Hwy 72 near Waimanalo. Open 9:30 a.m. to 5 p.m.

MILITARY HISTORY
USS Arizona Memorial,
USS Missouri Battleship &
USS Bowfin Submarine

There are three historic Navy vessels all next to each other. And, frankly, all three are worth your time. The sunken USS Arizona is the most somber of the three, the USS Missouri the most impres-

NOT TO BE MISSED!

sive in its scale, and the Bowfin the most interesting to observe how life in a submerged vessel must have been like.

Directions to all three are the same: From Waikiki, get on H-1 West. Take exit #15A *(not 15B)*, which says ARIZONA MEM./STADIUM and stay on Kamehameha Hwy (99) West, past Radford, past Arizona/Halawa Road, then left on Arizona Memorial Place/Kalaloa. (If you get to the stadium, you went too far.) You'll see signs. (See map on page 101.)

If you're coming from the *other* way, it's more complicated. Driving east on H-1 take exit #15, then the Nimitz East part of the exit (which will *feel* wrong). After an overpass, use Valkenburgh to

For only $8 you'll get to see the USS Bowfin submarine the way her crew saw her—without the two-year stint.

make a U-turn, going back on 99 West (toward the stadium) past Radford, past Arizona/Halawa Road, then left on Arizona Memorial Place/Kalaloa.

Parking can be difficult at peak times. If you don't see a spot, keep driving and there's often an opening or two in a parking lot on your right next to a pool before the overpass.

Because of security (this is an active Navy base), you can't bring anything into these attractions other than a normal-sized camera—no purses, backpacks, camera bags, etc. They'll charge to store your stuff, so don't bring it along.

The **USS Arizona Memorial** is the single most popular visitor attraction on Oʻahu. When the Japanese attacked Pearl Harbor in 1941, 21 vessels were damaged or sunk. But it was the USS Arizona sinking that caused the most

deaths—1,177 young, promising lives were cut short when an armor-piercing bomb dropped from a kamikaze plane drilled through her top deck and ignited the battleship's own ordinance. The vessel sank in 9 minutes, and only 337 were able to escape. In all, over 2,400 people were killed during the sneak attack here, a figure that would stand as an unwelcome record for six decades and seemed like the kind of event that could only happen in the distant past, until today's generation experienced their own sneak attack. And like September 11th, America rode a roller coaster of emotion after Pearl Harbor— from shock to anger to resolve. For Pearl Harbor it took an empire's entire military might—a whole fleet of ships and subs, including six aircraft carriers, 353 planes and thousands of soldiers. September 11th required four planes and 19 men with boxcutters. But whatever the source, it awakened a nation that had previously felt safe and isolated from the harshness of the world.

Visiting the memorial is one of those must-dos on O'ahu, and for good reason. Since there are so few WWII vets left, it makes WWII real for the rest of us. *We* know how WWII ended because we've lived our lives *after* the attack. But those men still entombed under your feet at the memorial only knew the shock and awe of how they died. And it's not until you're standing on the memorial, perched over the sunken ship that the echo of their lives can be heard. And when you see the massive marble wall with their names engraved, only then does the beginning of WWII turn from an event that happened as part of our history to an assault that stole the lives of people like you and me and galvanized a nation.

The memorial visit includes an excellent 23-minute film, a short boat ride and time at the memorial. It'll take 75 minutes *plus* whatever time you wait. And that wait could be anywhere from 1–3 hours, sometimes more. You can't get your free ticket in advance (and the Arizona museum and bookstore aren't enough to keep you occupied for *that* long), but you can grab your tickets and leave for awhile. See one of the other attractions mentioned below or go have lunch. To minimize your wait, either get there first thing in the morning (7:15–8:00 a.m.) or around 1–2 p.m. If it's Wed., Sat. or Sun. and you're facing a wait, there's a swap meet at the nearby Aloha Stadium until 3 p.m. (or earlier).

The **USS Missouri Battleship** (877–644–4896) is a short distance away from the sunken Arizona. When the Navy was looking for the final resting place for this proud warship, the symbolism of this location wasn't lost on them: placing the floating ship that ended WWII next to the sunken ship where the war began. Because it was on the Missouri's deck that the Japanese signed the surrender agreement, bringing the bloody fighting in the Pacific to a close.

The "Mighty Mo" was launched in 1944, near the end of the war. It was the last battleship ever built, and after only 11 years in service was considered obsolete and mothballed in 1955. It seems hard to imagine how a state-of-the-art battleship—the toughest and most visually menacing ship ever built with guns that could fire a 2,700 pound projectile *23 miles*—could be considered obsolete. In essence it comes down to this: It's more effective to *drop* things on the enemy than to *throw* things at 'em. Once ship-based aircraft had matured, aircraft carriers were far more efficient at projecting power than the greatest battleship could ever be. Even though the ship was brought back to service in the mid-'80s for a short time and armed with Tomahawk missiles, the usefulness of battleships had long since passed, even for a giant that's 887 feet long and weighs over *100 million* pounds.

It costs $16 to self-tour, $7 for kids 4–12. Or you can take guided tours, which are much more interesting. They have several. We liked the $49 Explorer's Tour (90 minutes) since it went into the firing rooms, engine room and other nuts and bolts areas that self-tours can't visit. Ironically, at least half the ship is off limits, even to guided trips. The reason? It's dirty. And although conditions were good enough for sailors who were there on the ship's final tour, it's not clean enough for the EPA to sign off.

However you tour it, it's a real treat to peer into this symbol of America's might during the mid-20th century. The sheer scale of this vessel can only be appreciated in person. It's amazing to stand on its giant teak deck, under the massive guns capable of such destruction, and try to imagine the dread that must have been felt by any enemy that watched this warship coming at them in anger.

The almost forgotten attraction here is the **USS Bowfin** (836–0317). Launched in 1942 (and nicknamed the Pearl Harbor Avenger), this submarine sank 44 enemy ships and now is available for self-guided tours for $8 ($3 for kids 4–12). The latest you can start the tour is 4:30, and it'll take about 30 minutes. They'll give you a narrative tape recorded by the ship's last WWII captain. And it's great to walk through this sub and see the instruments and see how the sailors lived and fought. From the turrets to the torpedoes to the toilets—you'll see it all. When you're done, the nearby **Submarine Museum** (423–1341) is *excellent—* much better than the Arizona's museum. Kids under 4 are not allowed on the sub or the museum.

GARDEN TOURS

There are several gardens on the island and they are by no means equal. The best are the **Waimea Valley Audubon Center** and **Foster Botanical Garden**.

Longtime visitors will be puzzled to see **Waimea Valley Audubon Center** (638–9199) listed under gardens. It used to be called **Waimea Falls Adventure Park** and was where people came to see cliff-diving shows, ride ATVs, horses, trams and kayaks. After a messy dispute, the city condemned it and in 2003 gave control to the Audubon Society, which did away with all of the adventure stuff and converted it to a simple botanical garden with a waterfall you can swim to when it's flowing.

Although much of the infrastructure here shows obvious neglect, the giant garden itself (1,875 acres) is still beautiful, and the setting on the Waimea River is tranquil. Take the opportunities to veer from the main road and walk along the river. (If you don't bring mosquito repellent down near the river trail, you'll donate more blood than you ever knew you had.) Most people make a beeline to the falls ¾ mile away (and slightly uphill) and take their time coming back. There are changing rooms at the falls if you brought your suit. The 40-foot high falls dries up at times, especially in the summer. $8 to get in, $5 for kids 4–12. It's $2 to park. At the mouth of Waimea Bay north of Hale'iwa on Hwy 83. You'll probably spend about 1½ hours here.

Foster Botanical Garden (522–7060) is small—only 13½ acres. But it's pretty, has some of the largest trees we've seen in Hawai'i—one with a diameter of 10 feet—and their hybrid orchid collection is particularly nice. It's $5 to get in, $1 for kids 6–12. At 50 N. Vineyard Blvd. From Waikiki, take Kalakaua out, left on Kapiolani, right on Ward, left on Beretania, right on Nuuanu, left on Vineyard.

Nearby is the almost useless **Liliuokalani Garden** (522–7060). It's a pathetic excuse for a garden, and normally we'd steer you away from it. But it has one thing going for it—a small waterfall. (Of the four major Hawaiian islands, O'ahu is the poorest when it comes to accessible waterfalls, so beggars can't be choosy.) From Foster, make a U-turn on Vineyard, left on Nuuanu, left on School,

right on Waikahalulu and park at the end of the street. Visit the falls and then leave—there ain't much else here for you. Admission is free, as it should be.

You next best bet is the **Ho'omaluhia Park Botanical Garden** (233–7323) in Kane'ohe on Hwy 83 just north of its intersection with H-3 is Luluku Road. This 400-acre garden (built by the U.S. Army Corps of Engineers as a flood protection tool to protect Kane'ohe) backs up against the Ko'olau Mountains, which are simply gorgeous in the morning light. It's run by the county, and admission is free. You don't need to do a lot of walking here since you can drive to the many parking lots, each of which

The Waimea Valley Audubon Center, once a well-known adventure park, is now the island's prettiest botanical garden.

is meant for areas featuring plants from different parts of the world. Even if garden's aren't your thing, it might be worth a quick drive along the main road to get a vantage point of the mountains that is hard to achieve otherwise, and the health of the plants in this area is impressive. Pets aren't allowed, but they stress that you're "allowed to bring your own horse." We mention this on the off chance you brought one along with you on the plane.

The last two gardens, operated by the county, are must-misses. In central O'ahu is the **Wahiawa Botanical Garden** (522–7060). It's a 27-acre site that's hillier than the other gardens. The plant variety is nice, but overall, it's disappointing to anyone looking for a garden experience. That's because what this *really* is, is an arboretum experiment that the county inherited in the 1950s and they seem to put very little effort into maintaining it—especially the lower level. Not worth the drive, but if you do, see map on page 96.

And lastly (in every way) is **Koko Crater Botanical Garden** (522–7060). Government literature stresses their "long-term plans of continuing to grow plants." In the short term it's 60 acres of unremarkable, unmarked plants in the hot, dry, dusty Koko Crater. It's free (and worth every penny). See map on page 63.

DORIS DUKE'S SHANGRI LA
(866) 385–3849

It's the 1930s, and one of the richest women in the world, the sole heir to a tobacco empire, buys a scrumptious oceanside piece of property at Black Point. She has an obsession with Islamic art and architecture. This is a time be-

fore oil becomes synonymous with the Middle East. A time when someone, with enough money, could travel to Iran, Iraq and neighboring countries and buy what is now priceless art and architectural pieces for a relative pittance. And that's what Doris Duke did. Today, her 5-acre palace is what results when you mix 150 workmen, 50 years of effort, limitless money and a reverence for antiquities.

A REAL GEM

Three times a day two groups of 12 people are guided through Doris's estate for $25, and it's nearly always sold out a week or more in advance. You'll meet at the Honolulu Academy of Arts at the corner of Beretania and Ward Avenue and be driven to the estate. It'll take 2½ hours (1½ hours at the house). There's no a/c in the house, so try to get an early tour.

We didn't expect to be so impressed. Though touted as Islamic, there are plenty of non-Islamic pieces, some as old as 1,000 years. And we're not talking about paintings on the walls, but rather a sensory overload of Middle Eastern history that is simply astounding. Forget what's happening in the world right now. These pieces predate the tensions that define our relationship with that part of the world today. The tour ends in the Turkish Room—an overwhelming experience for the eyes that'll make your heart beat faster.

Where you board the van at the **Honolulu Academy of Arts** (532–8701), you'll find Doris's jewelry collection, including some amazing pieces. At the art academy you'll also find a healthy mix of interesting 2,000-year-old artifacts and self-indulgent abstract junk that only an artist's mother can love.

Ask any local on O'ahu where Kawela Bay is and they'll probably say Kaua'i.

The biggest surprise about O'ahu is how many beautiful beaches there are and how often they're utterly uncrowded. Residents and visitors alike tend to congregate at the same popular beaches, leaving beautiful stretches of sand lightly touched. So we gave ourselves the difficult and thankless job of visiting every sand beach on the island to swim, snorkel and frolic. (See, and you thought all we did was *frivolous* stuff.)

No matter what kind of beach experience you're looking for, O'ahu has something for everyone. In trying to pick a beach, you should consider the island's geography. The **windward** side has some of the most underutilized and lovely beaches on the island, but it didn't get the name *windward* for nothing. If the trade winds are smoking along at 15–30 MPH, these beaches tend to be windy. But if it's a 10–20 MPH day, the cool breezes might be just right.

Wai'anae has lots of beaches that are protected from the wind thanks to the mountain behind them, and the waters tend to be clean and clear. But some of their beaches, especially near the Wai'anae towns, might be more crowded. Keep driving past the towns toward Ka'ena Point for the best Wai'anae beaches.

North Shore beaches can be a wonderful playground in the summer with calm waters and beautiful vistas along with breezes that tend to be slightly *offshore* until you get to Hale'iwa, keeping nearshore waters smooth. But winter can bring monstrous waves that would rip you to pieces if you got careless.

And finally the leeward side with Waikiki, Ala Moana and Hanauma Bay tends to have calmer and safer water than the rest of the island, but you sure ain't gonna have 'em to yourself.

BEACH SAFETY

The biggest danger you will face at the beach is the surf. Though it is calmer on the leeward side of the island (where Waikiki is), that's a relative term. Most mainlanders are unprepared for the strength of Hawai'i's surf. We're out in the middle of the biggest ocean in the world, and the surf has lots of room to build up. We have our calm days when the

So much reef, so little time.

water is like glass. We often have days when the surf is moderate, calling for respect and diligence on the part of the swimmer. And we have the high surf days, perfect for sitting on the beach with a picnic or a mai-tai, watching the experienced and the audacious tempt the ocean's patience. Don't make the mistake of underestimating the ocean's power here. Hawai'i is the undisputed drowning capital of the United States, and we don't want you to join the statistics.

Other hazards include rip currents, which can form, cease and form again with no warning. Large "rogue waves" can come ashore with no warning. These usually occur when two or more waves fuse at sea, becoming a larger wave. Even calm seas are no guarantee of safety. Many people have been

caught unaware by large waves during ostensibly "calm seas." We swam and snorkeled most of the beaches described in this book on at least two occasions (usually more than two). But beaches change. The underwater topography changes throughout the year. Storms can take a very safe beach and rearrange the sand, turning it into a dangerous beach. Just because we describe a beach as being in a certain condition does not mean it will be in that same condition when *you* visit it.

Consequently, you should take the beach descriptions as a snapshot in calm times. If seas aren't calm, you probably shouldn't go in the water. If you observe a rip current, you probably shouldn't go in the water. If you aren't a comfortable swimmer, you should probably never go in the water, except at those beaches that have lifeguards. There is no way we can tell you that a certain beach will be swimmable on a certain day, and we claim no such prescience. There is no substitution for your own observations and judgment.

A few standard safety tips: Never turn your back on the ocean. Never swim alone. Never swim in the mouth of a river. Never swim in murky water. Never swim when the seas are not calm. Don't walk too close to the shorebreak; a large wave can come and knock you over and pull you in. Observe ocean conditions carefully. Don't let small children play in the water unsupervised. Fins give you far more power and speed and are a good safety device in addition to being more fun. If you're comfortable in a mask and snorkel, they provide considerable peace of mind, as well as opening up the underwater world. Lastly, don't let Hawai'i's idyllic environment cloud your judgment. Recognize the ocean for

what it is—a powerful force that needs to be respected.

If you're going to spend any time at the shoreline or beach, **reef shoes** are the best investment you'll ever make. These water-friendly wonders accompany us whenever we go to any beach. You can get them at lots of places, including the ubiquitous ABC stores. Even on sandy beaches, rocks or sea life seem magnetically attracted to the bottom of feet. With reef shoes, you can frolic without the worry. (Though don't expect them to protect you from everything.)

The ocean here rarely smells fishy since the difference between high and low tide is so small. (In other words, it doesn't strand large amounts of smelly sea plants at low tide like other locations.)

Theft can be a problem when visiting beaches. Visitors like to lock their cars at all beaches, but piles of glass on the ground usually dissuade island residents from doing that at secluded beaches. We usually remove anything we can't bear to have stolen and leave the car with the windows rolled up but unlocked. That way, we're less likely to get our windows broken by a curious thief. Regardless, don't leave anything of value in your car. (Well...maybe the seats can stay.) While in the water, we use a waterproof fanny pack (available at many outdoor stores) for our wallet, checkbook and keys, and leave everything else on the beach. Sometimes we only bring car keys and tie them to bathing suit drawstrings. (Though you can't do that with electronic keys.) We don't take a camera to the beach unless we are willing to stay there on the sand and baby-sit it. This way, when we swim, snorkel or just walk, we don't have to constantly watch our things.

Consider buying one of those disposable underwater cameras. Even if you don't go in the water, they will withstand the elements. Their quality is better than most people think. You can find disposable film cameras, as well as disposable digital cameras.

Use sunblock early and often. Don't pay any attention to the claims from sunblock makers that their product is waterproof, rubproof, sandblast proof, powerwash proof, etc. Reapply it every couple of hours and after you get out of the ocean. The ocean water will hide sunburn symptoms until after you're toast. Then you can look forward to agony for the rest of your trip. (And yes, you *can* get burned while in the water.) Gel-based sunblocks work best in the water. Lotions work best on land.

People tend to get fatigued while walking in sand. The trick to making it easier is to walk with a very gentle, relaxed stride while lightly striking the sand almost flat-footed.

Always remember that in Hawai'i, all beaches are public beaches. This means that you can park yourself on any stretch of sand you like. The trick, sometimes, can be access. You might have to cross private land to get to a public beach. We've pointed out a legal way to every beach on the island, and some of the maps have access routes in yellow to show you the way.

In general, surf is higher and stronger during the winter, calmer in the summer, but there are exceptions during all seasons. When we mention that a beach has facilities, it usually includes restrooms, showers, picnic tables and drinking water.

You might want to pick up a cheapo beach chair at ABC store and donate it to your hotel when you leave the island.

Lastly, remember that just because *you* may be on vacation doesn't mean that residents are. Monday through Thursday is best the best time to go to the beach. Locals *love* their beaches, and show their affections every weekend.

Beach conditions around the island are almost entirely determined by what what direction they face, and the dividing lines around O'ahu are rather dramatic. From Makapu'u in the east to Kahuku in the north, you'll often find moderate, onshore winds and somewhat choppy seas year-round—being the *least* windy in the winter months—and waves sizes are rarely monstrous but often respectable. From Kahuku in the north to Ka'ena Point in the west, giant surf in the winter and calm seas in the summer are often combined with light winds at the shore or winds coming from right to left, with windier conditions just offshore. (But onshore winds increase if the trade winds become more northerly.) From Ka'ena Point in the west to Barber's Point in the south, much of the winds are blocked by the mountains, and the surf tends to be big when there's a westerly swell, usually in the winter. The south-facing shoreline, including Waikiki and Hanauma Bay, tends to get small to flat surf in the winter and somewhat larger surf in the summer, but rarely gets the towering waves that the North Shore is famous for.

But remember, these are generalities. We've seen huge surf from the north in June, and we've seen the North Shore flat in February. Nothing can substitute your own eyes and judgment. Ultimately, that's what'll keep you out of trouble.

We're going to start our beach descriptions from the westernmost tip of the island at Ka'ena Point on the left side of the main map and work our way around the island counter-clockwise.

WAI'ANAE BEACHES

❖ Yokohama Bay/Keawa'ula Beach

This is are far as you can drive in Wai'anae, and it's a worthy destination. This long, glorious beach is lightly used during the week because locals will usually congregate at beaches closer to the Wai'anae towns and be-

A REAL GEM

cause visitors are usually told to avoid the Wai'anae Coast. (Which we consider bad advice. See explanation on page 104.) The result is a heavenly stretch of sand with impossibly blue water, drop-dead gorgeous views and no weekday crowds. The offshore waters are clean and clear, and the beach is usually protected from strong winds by the mountain ridge behind you.

The beach tends to be wider in the summer and narrower in the winter, which can sometimes expose more sandstone beachrock, but this is always a sandy beach, never stripped bare by big surf. Large waves can, however, create strong currents, so avoid the water when the ocean's angry. There's no shade, but there are full park facilities, such as restrooms and showers.

Yokohama is really a nickname that has stuck to the point that few islanders even recognize its real name, Keawa'ula Beach. Early Japanese immigrants used to come here in large numbers to fish, and other immigrant groups began referring to the area as Yokohama Bay.

If you're in the mood for a hike, check out the Ka'ena Point hike on page 187.

❖ Makua Beach/Ka'ena Point State Park

One of our favorite beaches on the island, and during the week it's *never*

You can't drive any farther along the Wai'anae coast than Yokohama Bay. Then again, would you want to?

crowded. Here's the story. The U.S. military trains in the valley *behind* the beach, though they rarely visit the beach itself. Because of this, and the fact that it's several miles from the nearest town, locals rarely come here in numbers. And even fewer visitors come here. The south end has a super-convenient access via a dirt road ½ mile past Makua Cave (but before the tall observation tower on the mauka side of the road). This dirt road isn't easily noticeable, so most people drive right past it. Whether the ocean's calm or pounding, this beach stands apart as one of the most achingly beautiful on the island with clear blue waters, and it never fails to astonish us how lightly it's used during the week. Moderate to high surf

A REAL GEM

can create currents and surge, so be cautious. Access to the northern end of the beach is from the pullout right next to the sand. No facilities but there's some shade.

Makua is the second to last beach on Hwy 930 in Wai'anae several miles past the town of Makaha.

By the way, many residents refer to this beach as "pray for sex" beach in reference to the still-visible 1960s graffiti written onto a rock at the south end of the beach.

❖ 'Ohiki-Iolo Beach

Huh...where? Few locals and even fewer visitors have ever heard of this beach. It's a few miles from the end of the road in Wai'anae. Just before Makua Cave, a fence on the ocean side of the road causes most people to think the shoreline isn't accessible here. But many years ago the county set the shoreline aside as a beach park; they just never

'Ohiki-Iolo Beach is probably the least known beach in all of Wai'anae.

A beachgoer battles the mid-week crowd at Makaha Beach Park.

marked it or mentioned it. So although the land mauka of the beach is private, *the beach itself* is all yours. The lovely and secluded pocket of sand is mostly protected by a sandstone bench and is often deserted during the week. At high tide a large pool forms where fish and crab make a living.

There are plenty of turtles in the nearshore waters, but access to the open water is awkward and should only be attempted when the ocean's completely calm. Just past this beach is a peninsula composed of an intricate sandstone lattice. See HIKING on page 186 for more on that.

Access is via a 10-minute walk from your car. Park across from Makua Cave after the 17 mile marker on Hwy 93 in Wai'anae. Take the trail at the left end of the lot down to the shoreline, then walk left along the shore. Don't leave anything valuable in your car here.

By the way, 'Ohiki-lolo is Hawaiian for either *prying out your brains* or *crazy sand crab*. (It's commonly translated both ways.) Don't know why, but

either way someone was having a pretty bad hair day when they named it.

❖ Kea'au Beach Park

Most of this beach park has a sandstone ledge or a sandstone bench lining the sand beach, creating difficult swimming. The park is mainly used by campers (camping is allowed with a free county permit) and surfers who ride a very nice break on the southern (left) end. Determined SCUBA divers can straggle over the sandstone bench when the ocean's dead calm. Otherwise, the park doesn't offer much. It's after the town of Makaha and the large hill that approaches the shoreline.

❖ Makaha Beach Park

A nice, wide beach that is rarely too crowded during the week. Summer is the best time to visit because the wide sand is usually complemented by gentle water. Sometimes small surf can make for some nice, long boogie board

A REAL GEM

You'd think with all those houses around that Papaoneone Beach would be crowded—yet it never is during the week.

rides. If the surf's up, however, longshore currents converge in the center, then a rip current heads out to sea, so avoid if it's not calm. In the winter large waves create dangerous conditions, but that's also when you'll see some of the prettiest waves on this part of the coast. Local expert surfers *love* Makaha's winter waves. Full facilities and lifeguard. A good SCUBA site called Makaha Caverns is a few hundred feet offshore, and boat companies often take divers here.

Located across the street from Kili Rd. and Hwy 93 in Makaha. See map on page 106.

❖ Papaoneone Beach

The beaches near the Wai'anae towns tend to be more heavily used, but this one is visited less than most because it's backed by three resort buildings that seem

A REAL GEM

to have the effect of discouraging non-residents (of the apartments) from coming here. We've never seen it crowded during the week. The beach is excellent, and the shorebreak is steeper than most beaches, so decent-sized waves rip up and down the beach, which can be a blast to ride if you're careful. Even bodysurfers will enjoy them if the waves are not too big and powerful. Just beware of undertow here, and don't try riding waves that are too big for you. Winter brings big surf; summer usually has flat waters and excellent snorkeling. Easy access from the pullout across the street from Jade Street in Makaha, or take Moua St. and look for a *less* convenient public access next to 84–879 Moua Street. No facilities and no shade except for the shadow of the apartments in the morning. Nearby locals sometimes call the beach Turtle Beach, not to be confused with a beach of the same name on the North Shore.

❖ Mauna Lahilahi Beach Park

Very pretty with Mauna Lahilahi hill standing guard at one end, picnic tables near the road and easy access. Water entry is awkward and difficult due to a rocky bench, so water activities aren't much to speak of. Park at Hwy 93 near Makaha Valley Road in Makaha.

❖ Poka'i Beach Park

This is one of the safest places to swim on the Wai'anae coast due to a protective breakwater. Even when surf's high elsewhere, Poka'i may be relatively calm. For this reason, it's often packed, even during the week, with parents who bring their keikis to swim. Poka'i is also a popular canoe launching location. Full facilities, some shade and a lifeguard. One note—we've often seen reef sharks cruising inside the breakwater, though these animals, which rarely exceed 6 feet, are generally not considered dangerous to people.

In Wai'anae. Turn toward the ocean where Wai'anae Valley Road meets the highway (93).

❖ Ma'ili Beach Park

This beach is over a mile long with a nearly mile-long grassy lawn lined in parts with palm trees. Camping is permitted. Although the facilities aren't in tip-top shape, this beach is lightly used during the week, and it's a short walk from your car. During the winter some of the sand erodes away, and high surf can bring strong rip currents.

In Ma'ili; can't miss it. See map on page 106.

If you can overcome the ugliness driving in, the unnamed beach at this remote part of Ko Olina Park has a charm all its own.

❖ Ulehawa Beach Park

This one's also over a mile-long beach, but don't let that get you too excited. The beach park where Princess Kahanu Avenue meets the highway is the worst part of the beach. A sandstone bench makes the swimming poor. You're better off to the left (south) where the conditions are sandier, but overall, this isn't a great beach to spend some time. By the way, Ulehawa is Hawaiian for *filthy penis*, and was named in honor of a not-so-loved chief from the area.

❖ Nanakuli Beach

This is a small beach with a very steep shorebreak, which is lots of fun if you want to rake up and down the shoreline feeling the ocean's raw power. It's not so fun if the surf is too strong, or you're skittish about the ocean and don't want to feel the ocean's force unfiltered by more gently sloping shorelines else- where. High surf, especially in the win- ter, creates dangerous conditions. The right (north) end of the park has a lawn, ballfield and playground. At the extreme north end where the cyclone fence forms a 90° angle, you'll find a sand- stone blowhole that snorts, gasps and spouts when the surf's up.

Camping is allowed with free county permit. Located where Nanakuli Ave. meets the highway (93) in Nanakuli.

❖ Electric Beach/Tracks/ Kahe Point

Just before the impossible-to-miss power plant on Hwy 93 before Nanakuli is a tiny pocket of sand called Electric Beach. It's a popular SCUBA diving and snorkeling spot. Good snorkeling when calm, but visibility can be poor. The long beach just past the power plant is know locally as Tracks (after the nearby now- abandoned railroad tracks). The surf is

Who cares if they're manmade? The lagoons of Ko Olina are exceptionally good beaches.

often fairly gentle here, making the swimming good much of the time.

❖ Ko Olina Lagoons

In the 1990s the developers of Ko Olina created four semi-circular lagoons mostly protected from the open ocean. The swimming is excellent and ultra-protected near the beach. Swim from the sandy shoreline to **A REAL GEM** the open end where the snorkeling can be outstanding around the rocks. Watch for currents flushing in and out of the openings. These lagoons are extremely pretty, and sunsets from here are fantastic. At press time there were two resorts at Ko Olina, one at Lagoon #1 and one at #3. Lagoon #4 has the most parking spaces—about 100. That means Lagoon #2 (the Honu Lagoon) is the least crowded most of the time. Lagoons

1, 2 and 3 have only 18 parking spaces (plus 18 at parking lot 1B). Bottom line, whichever lagoon you choose, you should arrive before 10 a.m. or go in the late afternoon if you want to get a parking space. A concrete path connects them.

Take H-1 west until it becomes Hwy 93 (*after* exit #1) and look for an entrance to Ko'olina on the *mauka* side of the road. The roads to the lagoons are labeled.

❖ Unnamed Beach

OK, here's the deal. This beach is in an ugly area (power plant, shipping containers and other industrial doodads nearby). Perhaps because of this, it's unknown to visitors and darned near unknown to locals during the week. (Notice how we always cover ourselves by saying "during the week"—you should assume that *every* beach will be frequented on weekends.)

It doesn't even have a name because it was once part of what is now Ko Olina Beach Park but was cut off from that area when the nearby marina was constructed. Nonetheless, this beach has three things going for it: 1—Access is easy. (You park next to the sand.) 2—It often has unusual-looking waves (thanks to a sandstone bench that the waves smack into and prevailing offshore breezes that push the tops of the waves backward). 3—No crowds. You may have it to yourself. You ain't gonna be snorkeling here, and swimming can be awkward. (Your best entrance is at the harbor side.) But it's a sand beach, and the wave watching can be fun.

There are no facilities out here, and that same offshore breeze tends to be dry and hot. Take H-1 west to exit #1 (Kalaeloa Boulevard) toward the shore.

Right on Malakole Road, left on Kaiholo. Stop when your wheels touch sand.

'EWA & LEEWARD BEACHES

❖ Nimitz Beach

Lining the south end of Kalaeloa Airport, the water's better than 'Ewa Beach
(below), and in winter the seas can get
exceptionally calm, though swimming
can be awkward due to reefs offshore.
There's some shade, and it's not a bad
place to stake your claim and stretch out
on the sand. The beach park itself (where
the facilities are) has beachrock at its
shoreline, but it's sandier at the eastern
end. The best portion of the beach is
near the campsites. Where Coral Sea
Road veers right, there's an unpaved
road on the left. See map on page 100
and take exit 5.

❖ One'ula Beach Park

There's even less reason to come
here than 'Ewa Beach. It's lined with
beachrock that's hard on your feet and
anything else that comes in contact with
it. This is also where the area's...less-
than-savory characters tend to hang out,
from what we've observed.

❖ 'Ewa Beach

This beach doesn't really look very
Hawaiian. If you were transported here,
you might think you ended up in Florida.
With its long, yardstick-straight sand
beach, no shade and a sandy lawn
behind it, the beach is appreciated by
nearby residents but doesn't attract
much attention by visitors spoiled by better offerings elsewhere. The water is
always less-than-clear since so much of it
originates in mucky Pearl Harbor and
gets carried here by currents. And the
surrounding 'Ewa Plain is just what the

name implies—plain and featureless
except for the development. See map
on page 100.

❖ Ke'ehi Beach Park

This park has tennis courts, a giant
lawn and playgrounds and is adjacent to
flat, calm water, though it's less than
sparkly. Near the airport on Lagoon
Drive, turn left onto Aolele.

❖ Sand Island

Sounds like a great place to go to the
beach, but it's actually an industrial area
(where much of our imported cargo
comes in). The bottom half of the island
is ringed with a beach park. The water's
not the clearest, but it's mostly dead
calm. The west end is actually kind of
pretty, and from here you can take a jet
ski tour. The southern portion that faces
the open ocean has a nice sand beach
and large lawn area, but it's backed by
cranes and shipping derricks.

❖ Kaka'ako Beach Park

This park makes a rotten first
impression when you're driving up past
an industrial area and a fleet of garbage
trucks. But the park itself is actually a
nice place to sit at the shoreline and
watch the sunset, because if there's any
surf, it comes crashing into the lava
rock wall. Watching it can be surprisingly relaxing. It'll be almost all locals—
this place is unknown to most visitors.
Just west of Waikiki, take Ala Moana
Boulevard to Ward to Ahui toward the
ocean.

❖ Ala Moana Beach Park

These beaches are the main nearby
alternatives to Waikiki beachgoing. If
Waikiki feels a little small to you, Ala
Moana is an ultra wide beach with end-

Ala Moana (in the distance) and Magic Island are within walking distance to Waikiki and have ultra-protected waters most of the time.

less sand and shallow, very protected water plus a lifeguard. The southeast end can be like a bathtub. Just be aware of where the sea-floor drops off to deeper water.

A REAL GEM

Behind Ala Moana is a gigantic lawn where locals bring their volleyballs, Frisbees, croquet and just about every other plaything you can imagine. The only shade on the beach is from the moving shadows of palm tree crowns. While visitors gravitate toward Waikiki, Honolulu residents tend to be the most frequent users of Ala Moana, and on weekends and holidays they pack the place.

Because it's so calm most of the time, it's popular with timid swimmers and families with kids. Of course, if the sound of screaming kids is what you're trying to get *away* from, you might want to go elsewhere.

❖ Magic Island

This is that peninsula on the Diamond Head side of Ala Moana. It was created in 1964 and was slated to be a resort, but the developers ran into money problems, and it was eventually turned into parkland. Even fairly large waves are usually diffused here and at Ala Moana, creating another bathtub backed by sand, lawn, palm trees, the city skyline and finally the Ko'olau mountains. This is classic Honolulu. The only areas you want to stay away from are the breaks in the wall that allow ocean water in. Water shoes are a good idea here as the bottom is not entirely sand-lined. No snorkeling—just swimming. From the south end you can watch the small boats coming into Ala Wai Harbor.

Overall, we prefer Ala Moana over Magic Island due to its better water quality and sandier sea bottom.

❖ Waikiki

Since this is the heart of where most people stay, we've put the description in the WAIKIKI AND HONOLULU SIGHTS chapter. The beach areas from Kahanamoku to Sans Souci are covered there.

A REAL GEM

❖ Kaluahole/Makalei Beach

Not too many people staying in Waikiki come to this small pocket beach because it's a ¼ mile walk from the nearest parking at Kapiolani Park. It's used mostly by residents whose houses line the shoreline. If you're up for a walk (or you have someone to drop you off), the swimming is good, and you're likely to be the only non-resident there. See map on page 62.

❖ Diamond Head Beach Park & Kuilei Cliffs Beach Park

These two parks are at the shoreline of Diamond Head. There are only intermittent pockets of sand, and the surf is usually ridable here. Longshore currents heading toward Waikiki often form, meaning surfers might not be able to effortlessly bob in place. Swimming and snorkeling isn't very good. Consider these pretty to look at but not overly user-friendly for most water activities.

❖ Ka'alawai Beach

One of the least appreciated beaches near Waikiki. The section of sand closest to Black Point (the far, eastern end) has excellent swimming that's fairly protect-

If you're looking for a quieter beach experience than Waikiki, Ka'alawai Beach is a short drive away, and the pace is waaaay calmer.

Though this part of Wai'alae Beach is right next to the Kahala Mandarin resort, it never seems crowded or frantic.

ed most of the time, and there are good snorkeling opportunities. The beach access is not well-known, so it stays off the radar screen of most visitors. You get there either by walking along the shoreline from the easternmost Kuilei Cliffs Beach Park lookout, or take Kahala to Papu Circle to Kulamanu. No facilities. Some shade is available only in the summer due to the shifting sun. See map on page 62.

A REAL GEM

❖ Kahala Beach

Kahala is where the rich and not-so-famous live on O'ahu. Huge oceanfront mansions line parts of the shoreline here. Kahala Beach is the intermittent sandy strip on the far side of Diamond Head, from Black Point to Wai'alae Beach. You access it by driving from Waikiki until Kalakaua Avenue turns into Diamond Head Road then Kahala Avenue. Continue and park

A REAL GEM

near the intersection of Kahala and Elepaio Street where the curb isn't painted red and take the first beach access you see.

The snorkeling here is different than places like Hanauma Bay. Forget big fish eyeballing you. Most of them have been taken by local fishermen. What's good about the snorkeling here is the small, intricate marine life making a living over this flat, shallow reef. Most of the time you're swimming in only a couple feet of water, gliding just over the reef. Once away from the shore (and nearer the outer reef edge) the observant and patient snorkeler will notice tiny shrimp passing by, small blennies sticking their heads out of holes and a host of other small 1–2 inch fish going about their business. You'll want to wear a T-shirt to protect you from times the water gets too shallow. Some cheap gloves wouldn't hurt either. The general flow of water is over the reef (it will resist your advances the closer you get to the edge), along the shore and out the channel at Hunakai Street. (So avoid the channel.) The closer to the reef edge, the more fish. (They're almost completely absent at the shoreline.) If the fish seem unusually skittish, remember: They've watched their bigger siblings get nabbed by critters that look *just like you*.

Near Black Point there's a small sand pocket where the point starts. As you approach it, you'll see lots of distortive perturbations in the water and notice rapid temperature changes. There are basal springs of brackish and fresh water percolating from the ground here. Fresh and saltwater don't like mixing, so you can literally see them rubbing against each other, and the lighter (and colder) freshwater tends to stay on top. Quickly push your flat hand through it, and you'll see the kind of roiling turbulence you normally make as you pass though the water, but is usually invisible to you. Dig a hole in the sand just above the surf line and notice how it fills with water. The sand is saturated from the spring, and your feet sink faster in the sand here. If you've taken the beach access we suggested, you can swim to this pocket, then out toward the reef edge, let the current take you along toward (but stop before!) the channel, then take another beach access from the beach to Kahala Avenue and walk back to your car.

Experienced body surfers only need apply at Sandy Beach. All others will be pounded into oblivion by the shorebreak.

❖ Wai'alae Beach Park

Calm, protected waters most of the time make it a very good swimming beach, but snorkelers need not apply since the water isn't very clear. The best part of the beach is a few minutes walk to the left, near the Kahala Mandarin Hotel and its tiny offshore island. It's very pretty, and though that area is a resort beach, it's got a much more relaxed atmosphere than most resort beaches and they have beach toys for rent. (It's not a bad place for a windsurfing lesson when the winds are right.)

At the beach park itself, over the bridge to the right the sandy shoreline is lightly used except by the beachhouse owners. (Remember, *you* own the beach, not the nearby homeowners.) Ironically, the worst part of the beach is the narrow sandy stretch fronting the park itself due to stream runoff and the crumbling remains of an old sidewalk that occasionally poke through the sand. On Kahala Avenue near Kealaolu Avenue. Full facilities.

❖ Wailupe Beach Park

Very easy access off Hwy 72 near Aina Haina, but the uninviting water makes it a must-miss.

❖ Kawaiku'i Beach Park

A good place to launch a kayak if you just want to paddle the super-calm, protected water from here to Koko Head. The water quality for swimming is poor thanks to runoff from Hawai'i Kai. But it's pretty with lots of shade trees, picnic tables and facilities. At Hwy 72 and Puuikena Drive.

❖ Maunalua Bay Beach Park

At Hwy 72 and Keahole in Hawai'i Kai, this is a popular boat launching

place, and you can launch a kayak from here. Otherwise, there's not much for you.

A REAL GEM

❖ Hanauma Bay

The snorkeling mecca of the island. We've described it in detail on page 63.

❖ Halona Cove

This is an idyllic Hawaiian sandy cove. So idyllic, in fact, that in 1953 they

A REAL GEM

filmed a now-famous roll-in-the-sand-while-kissing scene for the movie *From Here to Eternity*. When calm, the cove makes for

great swimming. If there's a little surf, it provides good body surfing. And when the surf is stronger, it becomes a washing machine that will clean your clothes by banging them into the side rocks—with you in them.

You park at the Halona Blowhole Lookout 1⁴⁄₁₀ miles past (east of) the entrance to Hanauma Bay on Hwy 72. Walk down the short, natural boulder stair-step path near the road. If you want to make a more dramatic entrance, the back of the bay has a tunnel to it. It starts from the mauka side of the road and passes under the highway. (You'd have to cross the highway and draw an imaginary line from the cove to the mountain). The first part of the tunnel is pretty low, but you'll emerge rather theatrically into the cove.

❖ Sandy Beach

Pretty obvious name, huh? Like identifying a "wooden tree." For years locals called it the "sand beach near the blowhole," and it was eventually shortened to

Sandy Beach. Some call it Sandys. Anyway, this beach is ultra-popular with locals for its bodysurfing. Note that we said *locals*. That's because the sandy shoreline is steep and the waves have a wickedly powerful shorebreak. Anyone who isn't very experienced is likely to (and often does) get pile-driven into the sand, resulting in some terrible neck injuries. Unless you know what you're doing, consider bodysurfing elsewhere. We often use the giant lawn next to the beach to launch our ultralight, and too many times we've seen ambulances here carting away injured bodysurfing visitors.

The park has full facilities and that same lawn is popular with kite fliers, hang gliders (for landing—they *launch* off the cliff above Kaupo Beach Park) and other lawn sports. On Hwy 72 just before the road reaches its easternmost point. By the way, it's not uncommon to be asked by hang gliding beggars to drive them up the mountain and drive their cars back to Sandys.

WINDWARD BEACHES

❖ Makapu'u Beach Park

This is the first beach on the windward side after you've rounded Makapu'u Head, and the boogie boarding and bodysurfing can be excellent here. Conditions are similar to those at Sandy Beach—fantastic, but only for the experienced or the lucky, unless the ocean's pretty calm. During high surf the waves can wash up the entire beach. At times like that the raging surf scratches and claws at the cliffs to the right, producing quite a sight. Even during smaller seas the waves will feel pretty powerful for their size due to the shape of the nearshore seabed, making it fun to get

tossed around as long as you're aware of the ocean's potential to rough you up.

There's a great lookout above the beach, as well as a convenient access at the bottom of the hill across from Sea Life Park. The offshore islands of Manana (AKA Rabbit Island) and Kaohi-ka-ipu add to the scenery. Full facilities.

❖ Kaupo Beach Park

After Sea Life Park, across from the Oceanic Institute (they farm shrimp), is a beach access and a small lawn which is used as a hang glider landing spot (hence the windsock). This is mainly a surfing beach since the shoreline is pretty rocky, but there's a nice tide-pool here. To the left of the nearby pier is where some introductory SCUBA dives take place, but frankly the water conditions there are pretty poor, and you'd be wise to do your SCUBA diving somewhere else.

❖ Kaiona Beach Park

You probably won't see this name, but you will see a sign saying, WAIMANO CANOE CLUB. And indeed this is a good place to launch a canoe or kayak. A long reef offshore protects you from most of the ocean's force. Snorkeling can be good at times, but water visibility might be poor. Consider snorkeling about 700 feet off a house with a light green tile roof (which is far to the right of the park entrance) for fairly good fish life and reef structure. If you ever saw the TV show *Magnum PI,* walk along the beach to the right and you'll see a house with a tennis court. That's the smaller-than-you-expected Robin Masters estate. (Of course, if you never saw the show, you couldn't care less.) Showers and restrooms available. Packed with local campers on weekends. If you drive past the park, a much less used

A future developer gets his first lesson on how close to build to the shoreline.

part of the beach is easily accessible from the road just before it peels away from the shoreline. Just pull over and grab a spot. Gobs of nice sand, if not the clearest water.

❖ Waimanalo Beach Park

A long, very pretty strip of sand with very good swimming much of the time. The ocean's usually clearer than Kaiona, though snorkeling is still pretty poor. There are picnic tables, facilities and some ironwood trees for shade. Weekends are particularly crowded, but on weekdays it's lightly used. Car break-ins can be a problem here, so don't leave anything valuable in your car.

The nearby baseball field attracts lots of BBQers on weekends. Camping is allowed with free county permit. Easy to find on Hwy 72.

❖ Waimanalo Bay Recreation Area

The beach has a pretty thick pad of sand which drops to depth fairly quickly, making it fun to splash around in the water if you respect the fact that the waves will have a bit more force. Currents can form parallel to the shoreline (called longshore currents), but they're usually easy to get out of by swimming perpendicular to them back to shore. Full facilities. Very nice beach for a long walk. Heavily used on weekends. Located halfway between Kailua and Makapu'u (the easternmost point) off Hwy 72. Camping is allowed with free county permit.

❖ Bellows Beach

This is an unusual beach because it's only open to the public from noon Fridays to midnight Sunday. (It's a county park that fronts a closed military base.) As

Kailua Beach goes on and on and on...

a result of the weeklong pent-up demand, weekend use tends to be unusually high.

The waters offer pretty good swimming most of the time (though not good snorkeling), and the forest of ironwood trees behind the beach gives it an undeveloped feel.

The beach has one historical high point. The first Japanese prisoner was taken here during WWII when a mini-submarine washed up on the reef and the officer straggled ashore. Camping is allowed on weekends with free county permit. Look for the entrance off Hwy 72 in Waimanalo town. There will be a military guard.

❖ Lanikai Beach

Lanikai has that dreamy, tropical look that postcards and paintings are made of. Beautiful sand, stunning blue water and two idyllic offshore islands combine to create the quintessential island atmosphere. Lanikai's no secret, and one thing that you need to know is that many of the descriptions you read about this beach are outdated. The last decade hasn't been kind to Lanikai. More than half of the beach that lives in the memory of residents—and those who have created the paintings—is gone. It's ironic. House lots on the beach might sell for $5 million and up. These wealthy landowners built seawalls to protect their precious investments. According to many observers, seawalls cause the very kind of beach erosion that people try to prevent. The result? What was once a beach well over a mile long is now less than half a mile long. Much of the generous sand

A REAL GEM

that once defined Lanikai has now shifted over to Kailua Beach, whose residents, no doubt, thank the Lanikai community for inadvertently donating their sand.

But even smaller, Lanikai is still a feast for the eyes. And the snorkeling along the stretch of water between Mokumanu Drive and Haokea Drive can be great, featuring a healthy community of coral and fish—mostly small fish, but lots of 'em. The only thing that keeps this area from being world class snorkeling is a general cloudiness in the water. That shouldn't dissuade you; just don't expect it to be as crystal clear below the surface as it *appears* from above the surface.

By the way, the offshore islets are called Moku-lua, and the name applies to both. This is fitting since Moku-lua means *two islands*.

There are beach accesses all along Lanikai. If you have a kayak to launch, go to the far end at Lanipo Drive. If you're looking for a larger patch of sand go to Kuailima Drive. There's usually enough parking along Mokulua Road and on the side streets. No facilities and no shade. In Kailua, take the Pali Highway until it becomes Kailua Road then see map on page 70 to see which feeder street to take to Lanikai Beach.

❖ Kailua Beach

This lovely 2½ miles of delicious sandy beach fits nearly everyone's profile of a beautiful, tropical paradise. This is one of the best beaches on the island to simply stroll along as the waves splash your legs. Four different offshore islands beckon the adventurous. And Kailua rarely gets the monstrous 30-foot surf that pounds the North Shore.

A REAL GEM

The swimming, boogie boarding and bodysurfing at Kailua are good when conditions cooperate—which is most of the time. Snorkeling isn't worth your time, thanks to the runoff from Enchanted Lake and the Kawainui Canal.

The kayaking here is particularly good, and you can rent kayaks right at Kailua Beach Park. See KAYAKING on page 193 for more.

This beach is your best opportunity to spot the elusive **mole crab**. These quarter-sized buggers live under the sand beneath the surf line and can only be pinpointed by subtle clusters of V-shaped water wakes as waves recede from their barely-exposed eye-stalks. (They're different than the ghost crabs that live in holes above the surf line.) On those occasions that Portuguese man-o-wars drift in, mole crabs will snag a passing tentacle and pull it under the sand, munching away on it like spaghetti. Speaking of man-o-wars, they are unfortunately more common here, especially during summer months (April–October) than at most other beaches, one of the few dings to this otherwise great beach.

You can either park at Kailua Beach Park at Kalaheo and Kailua Road, or at Kalama Beach Park (less used) at Kalaheo and Kapaa, which gets you closer to the center of the beach. There are also several rights-of-way along Kalaheo (shown on map), but parking might be a problem with them.

As an aside, during WWII the island's police chief, for some reason, set a rule that "prostitutes can only swim at Kailua Beach." He also banned them "from all golf courses."

❖ Kualoa Beach Park

A truly kickin' windward beach park. Straddling the point at the north end of

Kaneʻohe Bay, the park features endless lawn, plenty of facilities, camping, shade, picnic tables and an uninterrupted sandy strip of shoreline with usually calm waters, a gorgeous mountain backdrop and a tempting and utterly

A REAL GEM

picturesque island. Chinamanʻs Hat Island is 614 yards offshore. About the only thing this park *doesnʻt* have is crystal clear waters. The ocean gets some runoff from nearby streams, so the water tends to be a bit cloudy. But the shoreline is usually so protected that swimming can be great here—just not the snorkeling.

If you walk along the beach to the right, the sand keeps going, leading to land fronted by Kualoa Ranch. Although they sell that as their "private beach" calling it a "secret island" that theyʻll take you to for $30, you can have it for free just by strolling onto it from Kualoa Beach. Remember, all beaches are *public*. Kualoa Ranch only owns the land *behind* the beach. (But donʻt tell that to any of the beachgoers that Kualoa charged to take them there—itʻll just antagonize ʻem.) Camping is allowed with free county permit.

❖ Kualoa Sugar Mill Beach/ Kanenelu Beach/Kalauʻoʻio Beach

As soon as you leave the entrance to Kualoa Park heading north, the road starts hugging the shoreline and sandy beaches present themselves. Although theyʻre tantalizing (heck, we even used a photo of one to start the NORTH SHORE SIGHTS chapter), they arenʻt the best beaches youʻll find—theyʻre just the *first* beaches lining the highway. Swimming is not bad but can be better elsewhere. Access is easy and totally obvious—just pull over when you want and dig in.

These beaches tend to be fairly narrow.

❖ Kaʻaʻawa Beach Park

The sand is wider here than the beaches to the south and the swimmingʻs pretty good. Visibility is better too, but often not good enough to encourage snorkeling. In Kaʻaʻawa. (We just love saying that word.) Access? Right next to the road.

❖ Swanzy Beach Park

There are good park facilities, and camping is allowed on weekends with free county permit. And although the waters are fairly protected and reefy, the fish count is pretty poor (probably overfished by local spearfishermen) and thereʻs little sand here. A dozen miles north of Kaneʻohe on Hwy 83 in Kaʻaʻawa.

❖ Makaua Beach

This beach is the easy-to-access strip of sand just before the Crouching Lion between Kaʻaʻawa and Kahana on your way to the north shore from Kaneʻohe. One of those beaches along the windward coast where you can just stop your car and hop right in, but it doesnʻt offer much other than an easy presence in sand. The nearshore waters are rocky and pretty shallow.

❖ Kahana Beach Park

Kahana is a pretty arc of sand fronting Kahana Valley. The water is

never pristine due to runoff from the Kahana Stream, but if you donʻt care about snorkeling, itʻs a nice place. There are trees for shade and

A REAL GEM

picnic tables, and thereʻs rarely more than a handful of people during the

Kahana Beach doesn't have the clearest water on the island thanks to the nearby river, but if you're looking for delicious scenery or good kayaking, you've found your destination for the day.

week. And if you want to kayak, the river feeding the bay makes for a very enjoyable kayak trip. See KAYAKING on page 194. Can't miss it in south Kahana 15 miles north of Kane'ohe on Hwy 83.

❖ Punalu'u Beach Park

Here's the perfect beach for the lazy beachgoer. You drive up and...well, that's it. The beach liter- ally touches the road. No muss, no fuss. And what a beauty it is. Long, inviting stretch of sand, lots of shade, full facilities, partial protection from an off- shore reef and surprisingly few visitors during the week. In the winter the beach

A REAL GEM

narrows during periods of high surf, but overall, this is an underappreciated windward beach. The snorkeling isn't world class, but the swimming much of the time is over a sandy bottom. Just stay away from the channel to the left (north) where currents can form. In Punalu'u on Hwy 83, can't miss it.

❖ Makao Beach

Another one of those ridiculously easy beaches to access. The road's right next to the sand beach. Just find a place to pull over. The sand is narrow and almost disappears at high tide. The water is very protected by an offshore reef. Only at the extreme north end does current start to form as the water exits through the channel. Snorkeling can be good, though wintertime brings cloudy water and overall, the area seems to have been overfished by locals. On Hwy 83 just south of Ha'aula.

❖ Hau'ula Beach Park

The good news is that access is easy and convenient, and the park has full facilities. Camping is allowed with free county permit. The bad news is that the water tends to be cloudy and it's over-fished. Overall, not a must-see beach. On Hwy 83 in Hau'ula.

❖ Kokololio Beach Park

There are a few beach estates just north of the park. In case you're wondering what kind of people can afford an estate on a lovely beach like this, here's one example: The estate just south of

Instructions for Punalu'u Beach: Drive up, open door, fall out onto the sand...repeat if necessary.

the stream near Pali Kilo I'a is owned by our local electric company and used as a perk for its executives. (Apparently, we lowly rate-payers aren't invited.) Anyway, the beach is very pretty and there are full facilities. There's a small area with good snorkeling some of the time for adventurous snorkelers. If you follow the large wall that bisects the park to where it *would have* touched the water, and enter slightly to the right and paddle out a short way, longshore currents will carry you to the left along a short reefy wall that sometimes has an impressive amount of fish. It's like being on a conveyer belt. Then in a hundred feet or so swim perpendicular to the current (toward the shore) and walk back to where you started. (This is typical current—we imagine that stronger currents could prove problematic if the surf's raging.) Sometimes, inexplicably, we've seen the fish almost completely absent. Other times they're everywhere. The far

Pounders Beach when it's not too pounding.

north end has a protected area sometimes called Bathtub Beach. (Not to be confused with the Bathtub Beach below.)

Camping is allowed with free county permit.

❖ La'ie Beach Park/Pounders

In La'ie, 1 mile past (north of) Ha'ula Kai Shopping Center is an unmarked park called La'ie Beach Park. (It's also known locally as Pounders.) This is an attractive beach with a sandstone cliff defining the right

A REAL GEM

(south) end. It's the waves at that end that inspired the name *Pounders*. When the surf's decent, the pounding waves can make for some good bodysurfing.

But if you're not careful, they can also pound the living daylights out of you. Better and safer swimming is at the north end near the old pier pilings.

If you walk to the left along the beach for a few minutes, past the old pier pilings and around the corner, a wonderful treat awaits. Except during high tide and high surf, a wonderfully protected set of ponds creates bathtub-smooth water; hence it's nickname—**Bathtub Beach**. (Separate from the other Bathtub Beach at Kokololio Beach.) This is a fantastic place to splash about in the ocean while still feeling protected. (Of course, you're still in the ocean, so anything can happen, and high surf means that all bets are off and you might not even be able to reach it by walking along the shoreline.)

❖ Laniloa Beach

In Laʻie town there's an easy-to-miss public access 2/10 mile past the Laʻie Inn (toward Kahuku). We usually park on the other side of the street. The 60-second path takes you to a lovely ribbon of sand that overlooks impressive Laʻie Point. Though the waters have a mostly reefy bottom, the swimming is usually safe due to a protective reef. There is a sandy patch in the water to the left of the shoreline access point. That, along with its mostly forgotten status, makes this a great beach to spend an afternoon. A few trees provide shade.

❖ Hukilau Beach/Laʻie Beach

If you go to a luʻau or listen to anyone play Hawaiian music for very long, you'll hear it. *Oh, we're going / to a hukilau /*

It's not hard to see why this hidden stretch of shoreline, which you can't see from the road or from nearby Laʻie Beach Park, is affectionately called Bathtub Beach.

a huki huki huki huki hukilau… This refers to the age-old practice of circling

A REAL GEM

a portion of the ocean in with a net, driving the fish in, and then a group of people hauls the fish-laden net out. That's what used to happen at this beach, and it was quite a sight to see—until the taxman heard about it. See page 81 for more.

Anyway, Hukilau Beach is yet another beautiful windward beach with fantastic views of Goat Island to the left, Pulemoku Rock directly offshore, and Laʻie Point on the right. There's not much shade here. The right side of the beach is partially protected by reef and is often safe to swim. That end also has its own beach access at the end of Halelaa Street, but the NO PARKING sign usually convinces people to park at Hukilau Park. If you feel like walking, you could stroll 2/3 mile along the beach to the point nearest Goat Island, then wade to

What makes the beach on Goat Island so special? 'Cause ya gotta earn it, brah...

its offshore beach. Or park closer—see Malaekahana Beach. Most of the beach users here are students from nearby Brigham Young University. Showers available. Closed Sundays.

❖ Goat Island/Moku'auia Island

This island is 720 feet off Malaekahana Beach. It has two beaches of its own, and the one to the left is fantastic. It's a classic, curving sandy beach with awesome swimming most of the time, thanks to the protection offered from the two points and an offshore reef. And since you need to swim to it (really wade to it up to your chest unless the ocean's raging—you'll need reef shoes since the bottom's

A REAL GEM

uneven and sharp), it's never crowded. What a *great* getaway. See directions to Malaekahana Beach below. Sometimes, especially in winter, waves can wrap around Goat Island and slap each other right where you'll be wading. You may get bumped around a bit if that's happening. Huge surf means you don't go.

In the mid-1800s, this small island was the home of a Hawaiian lawyer who kept two mistresses here. When the King of Hawai'i learned of this, he ordered him arrested. You know what they say...never mess with a lawyer, even if you're a king. The attorney did some research and found out that his offshore island wasn't recorded on any of the king's maps. So he declared that it wasn't part of Hawai'i and that he was now king of his own island. (Even in the 1800s, lawyers will be lawyers.) The ploy worked, and the Hawaiian king left him alone.

❖ Malaekahana Beach

One of the less appreciated beach parks near the northern tip of the island. The beach is a mile long and has pretty good swimming if you wear reef shoes (since the nearshore waters are rocky). Near the northern (left) end there are several beach cabins. You can actually rent these—see CAMPING on page 162. Malaekahana seems to be one of those beaches that stays unknown to most visitors, so odds are you'll be sharing it with mostly residents. Offshore is Goat Island (see above) with its exclusive beach that you need to wade to.

Between the towns of La'ie and Kahuku on Hwy 83. There are two entrances. The first (southern) one is closest to Goat Island and has more facilities. The second one leads to the cabins.

❖ Kahuku Golf Course Beach

Think of it as a rose with thorns; look but don't touch. More specifically, don't swim. That's because there's a pretty impressive rip current that's usually present here. But the good news is the beach is often empty and exhibits a certain wildness to it. Sand and sandstone beachrock are the ingredients topped off by everpresent wind. You can walk along the shoreline for miles here—so much so that we've detailed it as a hike on page 185 since access to it is a bit awkward. At the northern tip of the island.

❖ Kuilima Cove

The snorkeling off the middle/right behind the semi-protective reef can be exceptional, even Hanauma Bay-like in terms of fish count, although this bay is much smaller and not as protected and so the snorkeling isn't as reliable. Stay away from the channel at the right end where the reef ends, and avoid the left side where the bay empties into the open ocean.

A REAL GEM

Visibility won't be stellar—it's often somewhat cloudy. But the fish life can be extraordinary at times.

To get here, drive past the northern tip of the island and Kahuku, and turn into the impossible-to-miss Turtle Bay Resort. The cove is to the right of the hotel. See map on page 82.

❖ Turtle Bay

Past the Turtle Bay Resort, the western part is lightly used and beautiful. There's even an island to wade to when it's super-calm (which sometimes happens during summer months). The snorkeling around that island can be good, but currents can be a problem here, so be cautious. Much of the beach is fronted by beachrock, so swimming is often awkward. Winter waves make swimming impossible.

The name Turtle Bay comes from years ago when green sea turtles used to lay eggs on the beach. They don't do that anymore, and the bay is not necessarily more turtle-infested than any other beach. (Just so you don't get your hopes up.) Don't confuse Turtle Bay with Turtle Beach, described on page 156.

❖ Kawela Bay

There aren't many places like this on O'ahu: a beach so little known that it's essentially a secret. If you don't live nearby, you probably don't know about this one. We first saw this beach from the air in an ultralight and wished there was a way to get to it other than a 30-minute walk from the Turtle Bay Resort. One end of the beach has a few houses on it, but it's a gated community—can't go there. From Hwy 83 it's not visible; there's only jungle and an unattributed No Trespassing sign.

A REAL GEM

After digging a bit, we found that the sign is on land the county actually designates as a park (though they don't own it). Further digging showed the access parcel is owned by Turtle Bay Resort. When we confronted security personnel at the resort itself, they eventually admitted that "It was OK to walk the trail" to the beach. So it's apparently OK to disregard the unattributed No Trespassing sign and walk for only 3 minutes to a lovely and heretofore difficult-to-reach beach which rarely, especially during the week, has more than a handful of people on it. The trailhead is 1 mile past (toward Hale'iwa) the prominent Turtle Bay Resort entrance near the northern tip of the island. See map on page 82. (Another trailhead is farther down at a small bridge.) Walk through the fence, past the sign, and when you get to some *incredible* banyan trees, go straight to the beach and head right along the sand.

The middle/right portion has the best swimming with its sandy patches. (Bring polarized sunglasses to see though the surface better.) The left (west) end, where the houses are, has some weak basal springs that gurgle out of the sand above the ocean line. But it's the far *right* end that you want. It has your best snorkeling, though overall, the bay isn't a great snorkeling spot due to some sediment that

A Kuilima Cove sunrise from the Turtle Bay Resort. Not a bad way to start the day.

comes out of the river. That side also has calm, lapping waves, abundant shade and striking beauty, along with a serenity that you'll remember for years. In the winter, big rains often cloud up the water for days at a time, but it never keeps this beach from being lovely.

❖ Waiale'e Beach Park

Unmarked at press time, this pretty little park has a small island 153 feet offshore. (Standing at the point, you'd *swear* it was closer.) When it's calm (and *only* when it's calm), the snorkeling to the right of the island can be exceptional. Lots of big and small fish and even occasional barracuda and octopus swim around this tiny area. If it's flat calm, consider swimming around the back side of Kukaimanini Island, which is intricate and lattice-like and very different-looking than the front of the island. See if you can find the basal spring barely percolating from the beach sand area closest to the island. Located on

Hwy 83 almost 2 miles southwest (toward Hale'iwa) of the entrance to Turtle Bay Resort (but northeast of Sunset Beach).

NORTH SHORE BEACHES

These beaches are quintessential dual-personality beaches. During the winter (October–April) they can produce staggering waves that keep all but expert surfers out of the water—classic *look but don't touch* beaches. During the rest of the year, seas are *usually* small to calm.

❖ Sunset Beach Support Park

During summer months (May–September or October) this is an exquisitely beau-

A REAL GEM

tiful beach that is irresistibly inviting. You won't find a better-looking beach to frolic on than Sunset on a calm day. Though mostly sand-bottomed, there are some reef areas near the lifeguard station and on the

The endless sands of Sunset Beach Park are like a dreamy stroll down tropical lane.

right (north) side that can offer downright kickin' snorkeling, very clear water and lots of fish. Otherwise, just wade in the crystalline water till you're waterlogged. The sand drops quickly, so you can be in chest-high water only a few feet from shore. Check with the lifeguard for conditions. Restrooms across the street, as well as showers (which are unusually cold—we wonder if the pipes are ensconced in a chilly basal spring).

This steepness, along with fairly coarse sand, creates good conditions for Monastery Tag (named after a beach in California where we accidentally invented one day after a SCUBA dive). Now bear with me, it'll sound a bit strange, but we've shown this to others and they *love* it. The three ingredients you need are unchecked waves, a steep beach and a padded (sandy) bottom. Basically you lie in the water at the surf's edge and zip up and down the beach up to 30 feet each way on a thin cushion of water, digging feet and hands into the sand to control your ascent and descent. Like a low-to-the-ground sports car, the sensation of speed is greater. Here, you're only inches above the sand, and the trick is to go as far up the shore as possible without getting stranded. To people on the beach it looks like you're mindlessly scraping along the sand, but actually you're unscathed as you orient the shape of your body for maximum efficiency. A mask and snorkel make it much easier. As with all *worthwhile* and important endeavors, it takes years of practice and dedication. On your back, front, head first, feet first, it's important to master them all. You really feel the power of the ocean this way. Obviously you can't do this when the ocean's flat, and you'd be crazy to do it when the ocean's raging. Only during those in-between times.

❖ 'Ehukai Beach Park

Few locals refer to this beach by this name, but that's what's on the sign out front. During summer months the ocean transports mountains of sand here, making the beach wide and thick with good swimming.

But it's the winter when this spot occupies its special place in the world of surfing. Because 'Ehukai is the home of the most famous surf site in all Hawai'i—the **Banzai Pipeline**. Classic tube-shaped waves roll ashore from the surf break to the left of the beach park, and experienced surfers and boogie boarders ride them with undisguised glee. If you're looking for a great surfing photo and the area is getting a west/northwest swell, Pipeline is the place to be. Just sit on the beach and watch *da buggas shred 'em*.

Between Sunset Beach Park and Waimea Bay on Hwy 83. (See map on page 82.)

❖ Pupukea Beach Park

This park is divided into two main areas: Sharks Cove and Three Tables.

❖ Sharks Cove

First of all, it's ain't overly sharky. It was so named by divers years ago because it sounded more exciting than "the area to the right of the tidepool at Pupukea." This tiny cove offers fantastic snorkeling and SCUBA

A REAL GEM

much of the time during the summer (May–September) months. Yeah, it's popular and sometimes crowded with people. But it's also crowded with fish since this area is a preserve. You may find gobs of fish and the occasional turtle, hard-to-find octopus and even bait balls at times. Entry can be awkward over the slippery rocks.

During calm days (usually from May to October) Sharks Cove can offer insanely good snorkeling opportunities.

Most people enter from the left side, so if you want some wiggle room, consider entering from the right side of the cove. Snorkelers should stay inside the cove.

SCUBA divers will love the shallow but interesting diving inside the cove. It's very relaxing since you don't need to kick far too see good stuff. Just slowly meander around the clear water, looking under rock shelves. Good for underwater photos. The more adventurous will wander out the cove, staying to the right where walls, small caves and chasms await. Even inside the cove, experienced divers will enjoy the relief of big ol' boulders, overhangs and sandy patches. And since it's so shallow (under 30 feet), even heavy breathers will have staying power. Consider getting 63s instead of 80s to make it easier. One caveat: The cove is not at all tolerant of swells. Even a 2-foot swell, if aimed straight into the cove, can stir up the shallow water and make conditions annoyingly cloudy and surgy.

During high tide the tide-pool to the left gets deep enough to become a giant swimming pool when seas are calm. Visitors mistakenly think *this* is where they're supposed to snorkel. Granted, it looks interesting from the shore. But there are relatively few fish in there. Stick with the cove unless you hate the thought of venturing into deeper water. Big surf makes this tide-pool area dangerous and, of course, ruins the cove itself for swimming.

The rock defining the left side of the cove is often used as a place to jump into the water. Remember to look before you leap.

Across from an old gas station next to Puula Road. Snorkel gear can be rented across the street near the Foodland.

❖ Three Tables

Good snorkeling when calm around the little table islands (there are more than three at low tide). It can be a little surgy, and you'll want to avoid this place when the surf's up. SCUBA intros take place here. It's shallow (35 feet max) but has interesting underwater terrain with lots of over-hangs, crevices and boulders off to the left,

A REAL GEM

though divers are still better off over at Sharks Cove. Overall, a nice sandy beach with no facilities or lifeguard. Unmarked, it's where tiny Kapuhi Street meets Kamehameha Hwy (83) just north of Waimea Bay.

❖ Waimea Bay Beach Park

Say the words "Waimea Bay" to any surfer and their eyes will light up. This is the most famous *big wave* surf site in the world. In the win-ter, waves 20–40 feet high are not uncommon.

A REAL GEM

Visitors and locals alike delight in coming here during these waves, lining the shore-line and road, and watching the best surfers in the world take their chances slid-ing down these four-story walls of water. A collapsing wave can snap boards, snap people, or hold 'em underwater for min-utes at a time. If you're on O'ahu in the winter and the surf is giant, *this* is where you want to go. (Other surf sites close out with big surf—see box on page 208.) Needless to say, you don't want to get anywhere near the water during big winter surf. You'll die…period…no kidding.

What a shock to come here in the summer and find placid, lake-like water. The area around the southern end (left side) of the bay offers utterly magnificent snorkeling when calm. The entire area leading to the off-shore islets is studded with fish, interesting terrain and turtles. In fact, turtles are plentiful from here all

This lovely part of Pupukea Beach Park, called Three Tables, is named after the offshore reefs.

Waimea Bay in the summer when the swimming is peaceful.

the way to Turtle Beach, but the water gets cloudy after you leave the bay—from Uppers to Chun's Reef—due to intruding basal springs. Stay in Waimea Bay and around the islands for the best snorkeling during calm seas.

The giant rock near the left end of the beach is a popular cliff-diving spot. People often climb up from the shore-facing side and leap off the back/right end. It's a pretty far drop, and you're on your own in evaluating it. Jumpers have to walk past the NO JUMPING sign to get to the top.

Waimea Bay Beach Park has full facilities and a lifeguard. It's 5 miles north of Hale'iwa or 36 miles from Kane'ohe on Hwy 83.

❖ Chun's Reef

Most drive right by this park without noticing it. This is a decent place for beginner surfers when surf is light, because the ideally shaped reef creates waves in nearly any size swell. Or park there and walk to the right along the sand to rarely visited **Kawailoa Beach**, AKA **Leftovers**. Although there are houses on it, you'll almost never see many visitors here. Chun's Reef Park is near the 61-500 address across from Ashley Road between Waimea Beach Park and Hale'iwa.

❖ Turtle Beach/Laniakea Beach

This beach is famous. Not among people, but apparently in the turtle community. Because the

A REAL GEM

buggers sometimes congregate here in impressive numbers and seem so tolerant of people that we've seen swimmers get bored and swim away, only to have the turtle swim after them. This is the only place we've ever seen in Hawai'i where the turtles do this. (We suspect that some nearby resident might be feeding them to get this result.) Naturally, the turtles aren't *always* here (turtles *hate* to get into a predictable rut) but they're here *most* of the time. And when they are, it's great. Water visibility here is often poor. On Hwy 83 between Waimea Bay and Hale'iwa, south of 61-500 address and at the south (toward Hale'iwa) end of a loop road called Pohaku Loa Way.

Although the beach keeps going south, the swimming is not very good due to currents and the beachrock that lines much of the nearshore waters. Go for the turtles, not for the swimming.

By the way, Turtle Beach is a modern name. It sure beats the ancient Hawaiian name for this beach, which was Kukae'ohiki meaning *excrement of the sand crabs*. (Just doesn't have the same ring to it, does it?)

❖ Hale'iwa Beach Park

Nice big lawn and usually a calm, protected shoreline, but the proximity to the river and harbor creates less-than-pristine water. It's popular with the local community. On Kamehameha Highway (83) in the heart of Hale'iwa.

❖ Mokule'ia Beach Park/ Kealia Beach

Across from Dillingham Airfield near the northwestern tip of the island, this is a great place for kite surfing (or watching it). Near-constant winds and a sandy shore-

Waimea Bay in the winter, when the swimming is a tad more challenging.

line create excellent conditions. Mokuleʻia stretches for miles in both directions.

Just past (west of) the beach park you'll find a series of usually deserted beaches. Even when other North Shore beaches are packed, you may be shocked to find these beaches completely empty. Sure, it tends to be windy here, and the swimming is dicey in the winter due to longshore currents, perhaps a bit better in calmer seas. But if the idea of an empty sandy beach is appealing, you have a good shot here, and access is a snap. These are Oʻahu's forgotten beaches, and it's ironic since you can drive right up to them. Some of the stretches have sandy nearshore waters; others have waters lined with sandstone beachrock. Biggest downside

here is that litter from local weekend use seems to occur more often than at most beaches.

Camping is allowed with free county permit.

❖ **Hidden Beach**

How fitting that we end the BEACHES chapter with this beach. Few people on the island even know about it. It's past the end of the pavement on Farrington Highway (930) on the North Shore, about 1¼ miles into the dirt 4WD road, 15 telephone poles past the metal gate you went around and across from pole #196. You might even have this small, sandy cove to yourself. Snorkeling is possible when the ocean's not too pounding. Otherwise, just enjoy the remoteness, our reason for giving it a GEM.

A REAL GEM

Although locals drive their 4WDs to it on weekends and afternoons, Hidden Beach is often deserted during weekday mornings.

In a sudden burst of clarity, the boogie boarder realized that the guy at the rental counter was only kidding when he suggested Bonzai Pipeline would be the perfect place to ride his first wave.

If you want more from your Hawaiian vacation than a suntan, O'ahu offers a multitude of activities that will keep you happy and busy. Among the more popular activities are glider rides, ocean tours, golfing, hiking, SCUBA diving and kayaking.

We've listed the activities here in alphabetical order. Beware of false claims on brochures. We've seen many fake scenes in brochure racks. Computers have allowed photo manipulation to create realities that don't exist (which, by the way, we don't do).

Activities can be booked directly with the companies themselves. Ask them if they have any coupons floating around in the free publications, or if there is a discount for booking direct. You can also book through **activity brokers** and **booths**, which are numerous and usually have signs such as FREE MAPS or ISLAND INFORMATION. Allow me to translate: The word FREE usually means I WANT TO SELL YOU SOMETHING.

What we're about to tell you has gotten our other books pulled from some shops and badmouthed in some circles, but the truth's the truth. The objective at activity booths, as is the case with many concierges, is to sell you activities for a commission. *Occasionally,* you can get better deals through activity booths or your concierge, but not often, because 25–35 percent of what you're paying is their commission (which they call a "deposit") for making the phone call. That's why calling direct can sometimes save money. Companies are so happy they don't have to give away ¼ to ⅓ of their fee to activity booths, they'll sometimes give you a discount.

Many of the activity booths strewn about the island are actually forums for selling timeshares. We are not taking a shot at timeshares. It's just that you need to know the real purpose of some of these booths. They can be very aggressive. (To use a wilderness analogy— they are the hunters; you are the hunted. Don't let them see the fear in your eyes.)

Selling activities is a *big* business on O'ahu, and it's important to know *why* they're pitching a certain company. If an activity booth or desk steers you to XYZ snorkel cruise and assures you that it's the best, that's fine, but consider the source. That's usually the company that the booth gets the *biggest commission* from. We check up on these booths frequently. Some are reputable and honest, and some are outrageous liars. Few activity sellers have ever done any of the activities unless they got it *free* and the company *knew* who they were. On the other hand, we *pay* for everything we do and review activities *anonymously*. We have no stake in *any* company we recommend, and we receive *no* commission. We just want to steer you in the best direction we can. If you know who you want to go with (because you read our reviews and decided for yourself), call them direct first.

A WARNING: Many of the companies listed have a 24-hour cancellation policy. Even if the weather causes you (not them) to cancel the morning of your activity, *you will be charged.* Some credit card companies will back you in a dispute if the 24-hour policy is posted,

some won't. Fair? Maybe not. But that's the way it is.

Consider booking by e-mail before you come. Good companies can fill up in advance, and the Web can pave the way for your activities. Our site at **www.wizardpub.com** has links to *every* company listed here that has a site, even the ones we recommend *against*.

If you've read many travel books, you're familiar with the grumpy and pretentious travel writer. The kind who's impressed by very little because he's so much more advanced than peons like you and me. Well, we pride ourselves in not being like that. We're all here to have fun! But having written our neighbor island books *before* O'ahu Revealed, we've noticed that, relative to the outer islands, there's a complacency that permeates many of the Waikiki activity providers. A constant influx of potential customers has bred a less-than-hungry attitude. That doesn't mean you won't get good service, it's just that you might need to look harder for it.

These are those four-wheeled things that look like Tonka Toys on steroids with knobby tires. They're pretty fun to ride, though at press time there was only one company giving tours on these.

Kualoa Ranch (237–7321) on the windward side north of Kane'ohe has rides on their ranch. Though the ranch is pretty, they use relatively small 400 cc bikes and take up to 16 riders per group, keeping them in single file. It's $47 for a one hour tour, $87 for 2 hours.

BOAT TOURS
See OCEAN TOURS on page 195.

Catching a wave isn't the biggest challenge. The hardest part is holding onto the board and your pants at the same time.

Boogie Boarding

Boogie boarding (riders are derisively referred to as *spongers* by surfers) is where you ride a wave on what is essentially a sawed-off surfboard. It can be a real blast. You need short, stubby fins to catch bigger waves (which break in deeper water), but you can snare small waves by simply standing in shallow water and lurching forward as the wave is breaking. If you've never done it before, stay away from big waves; they can drill you. Smooth-bottom boards work best. If you're not going to boogie board with boogie fins (which some consider difficult to learn), then you should boogie board with reef shoes or some other kind of water footwear. It allows you to scramble around in the water without fear of tearing up your feet on a rock or urchin. Shirts or rashguards are very important, especially for men. (Women

already have this problem covered.) Sand and the board itself can rub you so raw your *da kines* will glow in the dark.

Boards can be rented just about anywhere for $7–$15 per day. See the BEACHES section for descriptions of specific beaches. Popular boogie boarding spots for visitors include the **Kapahulu Groin** in Waikiki and **Ala Moana Beach Park**. Those with experience should check out **Makapu'u Beach** and sometimes **Sandy Beach**. Many of the **Wai'anae** beaches offer great boogie boarding when the ocean's cooperating. **Kailua Beach Park** on the windward side is good and they rent boards there from **Hawaiian Watersports** (255–4352) and **Kailua Sailboard and Kayaks** (262–2555).

CAMPING

The ultimate in low-price lodging is offered by Mother Nature herself. O'ahu is a great place to camp with 16 different areas—four state camping areas

Maleakahana State Rec.
Kokololio Beach Park
Hau'ula Beach Park
Ahupua'a O Kahana State Park
Swanzy Beach Park *(weekends only)*
Kualoa Park
Kaiaka Bay Beach Park
Mokule'ia Beach Park
Kea'au Beach Park
Keaiwa Heiau State Rec.
Lualualei Beach Park *(summers only)*
Bellows Field Beach Park *(weekends only)*
Nanakuli Beach Park
Waimanalo Bay Beach Park
Waimanalo Beach Park
Sand Island State Rec.

and twelve county campsites. See map above.

County sites require a *free* county permit. You have to show up *in person* to the **Division of Parks and Recreation, Permit Section**, 650 South King Street, Honolulu (523-4525) or a satellite city hall, such as the one in Ala Moana Shopping Center (973-2600).

For state sites the rules are more complicated and the system more rigid. (We fell asleep halfway through the process description.) Call **Division of State Parks** (587-0300) at least 30 days in advance for details or use the link from our Web site. It's $5 per night per family.

At all campsites you can only camp Friday through Tuesday (unless otherwise noted on map).

The cheapest place to buy your camping gear and supplies is the **Sam's/Wal-Mart Superblock** just outside of Waikiki on Keeaumoku and Makaloa.

One of the more interesting camping opportunities is the **cabins at Malaekahana** near the northern tip of the island in La'ie. These were private beach cabins until the state made this area into a park. While they're certainly *not* upscale, they're next to (and in some cases right on) the beach at

Malaekahana Beach. The concessionaire is called **Friends of Malaekahana** (293-1736). These are highly sought after, so call as far in advance as possible. Rates range from $60-$80 per night (more for big groups), depending on the cabin. Cabins 6/7 and 4 have the best beach locations.

Deep sea fishing is synonymous with Hawai'i. Reeling in a massive marlin, tuna or tough-fighting ono is a dream for many fishermen. When there's a strike, the adrenaline level of everyone on board shoots through the roof. Most talked about are the marlin (very hard fighters known for multiple runs). These goliaths can tip the scales at over 1,000 pounds. Also in abundance are ono, also called wahoo (one of the fastest fish in the ocean and indescribably delicious), mahimahi (vigorous fighters—excellent on light tackle), ahi (tasty yellowfin tuna) and billfish.

Most boats troll nonstop since the lure darting out of the water simulates a panicky bait fish—the favored meal for large game fish. On some boats, each person is assigned a certain reel. Experienced anglers usually vie for the corner poles with the assumption that strikes coming from the sides are more likely to hit corners first.

You should know in advance that in Hawaiʻi, the fish belongs to the boat. What happens to the fish is entirely up to the captain, and he usually keeps it. You could catch a 1,000-pound marlin and be told that you can't have as much as a steak from it. If this bothers you, you're out of luck. If the ono or other small fish are striking a lot and there is a glut of them, you might be allowed to keep it—or half of it. You *may* be able to make arrangements in advance to the contrary.

Most charters leave Kewalo Basin near Waikiki with some departing from Waiʻanae and Haleʻiwa on the North Shore in the summer. Most have 4-, 6- and 8-hour charters. Mornings offer best conditions. Prices are $80–$120 per person for a 4-hour shared charter. You can do a private 6-hour charter for $350–$600. 8-hour private charters go for $600–$900 or more for the big boats. Usually, the bigger the boat, the higher the price since most are licensed to take only 6 passengers. Individual boat rates can change often depending on the season, fishing conditions and whims of the owners. Consequently, we'll forgo listing individual boat rates since this information is so perishable and instead list a few companies that we recommend. Call them directly to get current rates. If you have 4 or more people, make it private so you can exercise more control.

If you're easy-queasy, take an anti-seasickness medication. There are people who never get sick regardless of conditions, and those who turn green just

watching *A Perfect Storm* on DVD. Nothing can ruin an ocean outing quicker than being hunched over the stern feeding the fish. Scopolamine patches prescribed by doctors can have side effects including (occasionally) blurred vision that can last a week. Dramamine II or Bonine taken the night before and the morning of a trip also seems to work well for many, though some drowsiness may occur. Ginger is a mild preventative. Try powdered ginger, ginger pills or even *real* ginger ale—can't hurt, right?

Tipping: 10–15% split between the captain and deck hand is customary if you are pleased with their performance. If the captain is a jerk and the deck hand throws up on you, you're not obligated to give ʻem diddly.

Because boat slips are so hard to get near Waikiki (Kewalo Basin), companies share boats or swap customers constantly and shared charters are sometimes hard to arrange. (They like you to charter the whole boat.) These guys do take shared charters: **Maggie Joe's** (591–8888) has 3 nice boats. **Monkey Biz** (591–2520) has 2 nice 38' Bertrams. Both charge $150 per person for a full day, as does **Kuu Huapala** (596–0918) and **Magic Sportfishing** (596–2998).

Sashimi Fishing (955–3474) has several boats at Kewalo Basin. They do some exclusive charters and some shared. One boat is a powerful 43' Scarab, and they do shark hunts at night.

Companies that only do exclusive charters at Kewalo Basin (you'll need to rent the whole boat) are **Pacific Blue** (396–4401) and **Wild Bunch** (596–4709).

Out of Ko Olina on the west side, **Deep Blue** (368–3765) has a 44' Phoenix. Half-day charters are $500 for up to 5 people.

In Wai'anae, there's **Boom Boom** (306–4162) and their small (28') cabin cruiser. Shared full day is $125.

In Hale'iwa call **Chupu Charters** (637–3474) with a 42' Uniflite. $135 per person for full-day shared charters.

GLIDERS

Gliders, sailplanes, skysurfing—whatever you call it, these engine-less aircraft offer a fun way to see the western tip of the island. You get towed up by airplane, then during typical trade winds, ridge lift from the nearby mountains provide the buoyancy necessary to keep you aloft. Most people assume that glider rides are nearly silent. Sorry to burst your bubble, but most of these are 30-year-old gliders, and the wind noise can be loud enough that it might be hard to

Soaring in a glider is fun, but not as quiet as most people think.

hear some of the things your pilot is saying to you. (Newer quiet 3-passenger gliders are obscenely expensive and companies are hesitant to invest in them.) One thing we strongly suggest is that you spend the extra $5–$10 to sit in front. From there they'll let you take control if you want. (Don't worry, the pilot can control it from the back seat, as well.) Another consideration is size. Although these are 3-person craft, the back bench is crowded with two people unless you're *real* small. If there are two of you, consider tacking on another $5 and taking separate rides.

Two companies are out at Dillingham Airfield on the North Shore. **Mr. Bill's** (677–3404) and **Soar Hawaii** (637–3147) provide similar rides for $40–$60, plus the extras listed above, and you're in the air for about 20 minutes. (If these prices seem especially fluid, it's because both companies *seem* to charge different prices depending on how they feel. Frankly, we're not sure *what* you'll pay.) They want you there super early

(assuming you'll be late). Ask them what time you'll *actually be flying*. It's not an aerobatic ride (that's extra, too), but it's lots of fun and it's gentle. Generally, the earlier in the day you go, the smoother the air.

GOLFING

With its balmy trade winds, sunny skies and rich soil, O'ahu is an absolutely ideal place to build a golf course. And we're not the only ones who think so. More than *three dozen* courses carpet this tropical island. No matter what kind of golfing animal you are, O'ahu surely has a course that'll fulfill your dreams.

The one area where O'ahu courses come up short relative to their neighbor island brethren is with oceanside courses. There are only four: one's a military course, one's a private club, the third—Turtle Bay—inexplicably lets a thick grove of trees block your view most of the time. Only at a crusty 9-hole municipal course—Kahuku—does the promise of playing near the ocean come true. But don't fret. With *so* many courses on such a beautiful island, golfing on O'ahu will keep you smiling.

It's impossible to review all the courses—hey, we've only got so much space here. So below are some of the more notable courses.

Luana Hills (262–2139)

In a state filled with pretty golf courses, this one stands apart as one of the loveliest. Simply put, it's achingly beautiful. Set in the center of Maunawili Valley

behind Olomana Peak near Kailua, the back nine in particular are draped in such a verdant setting, that its nickname of Jurassic Park seems totally appropriate. Even the golf paths are so mouth-wateringly lush, you'd expect dinosaurs to come strolling by.

But this is also a hard course. Make that humiliatingly hard. There isn't a flat piece of ground on any of the narrow fairways. It's the perfect course to accidentally lose your scorecard on the first hole so you can enjoy the course for the purity of the play and the serenity of the scenery. Then you can exercise selective memory to convince yourself that you did well. The only evidence to the contrary will a much lighter supply of balls at the end. (Bring *plenty*.)

One downside is that it does rain more here than on leeward courses, though not as much as other course-keepers might lead you to believe. Having lived in Kailua, we can tell you that its reputation among leeward residents as being too rainy is way overstated.

Bring your laser-guided ball for number 3. It requires the precision of a smart bomb to drive it onto the isolated green. Eleven is their signature hole—a drive across water onto an island green fronted by fountains. They close it several days a week since the island green gets unusually soft. If you drive up to sneak a peek during its closure, smack a ball onto the green if you want. They don't mind. It's so striking that they often use it for weddings. (You'll be penalized a stroke if you hit the bride.)

Number 13 is a cruel joke. Try to launch it into the gully, then drop on the other side and take your punishment like a grown-up.

You'll put a lot of miles on your cart at this flawlessly maintained course, and you'll love every minute of it. The course is relatively short but calls for extreme accuracy. The front nine are the most open and forgiving. It's the back nine where egos are smashed and memories are made. Rates are $109, including cart.

Turtle Bay (293–8574)

Way out near the northernmost tip of O'ahu off Hwy 83, two resort courses provide an amazingly uncrowded golf experience. During the week, tee times before noon often result in a nearly private golf game. There's often no one behind or in front of you. (Weekends are busy and afternoons, especially Fridays, also bring locals who cut work early.) The **Palmer Course** (also called The Links at Kuilima—it was designed by Arnold Palmer) is the better of the two. It's well-marked, pretty wide open and not a wickedly challenging links-style course. Check out the giant ficus trees before the 9th green. This is not an overly sandy course, but at 17 it's as if they needed to use up their supply. It's bunker city.

The other course, called the **Fazio Course** (designed by George Fazio), gets less respect—and seeming less maintenance. Play this one only after you've played Palmer. It's extremely open and pretty easy on the ego. At 6 and 7 you *finally* get to see the ocean. In fact, both courses suffer the same shortcoming. With so much splendid oceanfront real estate to work with, they made surprisingly little use of it. Throughout the bulk of your play, you're totally detached from, and unaware of, the glorious Pacific Ocean so near and yet so far.

Turtle Bay ain't cheap, but it's a real treat to play courses of this caliber and maybe feel like you've rented the fairways for yourself. It won't happen every

weekday, but it's more the norm than the exception.

Palmer is $160 for off-property players, $125 for Turtle Bay guests. Fazio is $155 and $110. This includes cart (walking is allowed).

Pali Golf Course (266–7612)

A municipal course that often has fairly mangy fairways but nice views. Lots of uneven lies here and it's not real sandy, but it's a fun course, nonetheless. Par threes tend to have pretty big dips before the green. Hole 9 is one of the most beautiful municipal holes you'll ever see—right toward a pali pinnacle with H-3 terraced on the slopes. $42. No driving range. Off Hwy 83 near Hwy 61 in Kailua. See map on page 68.

Pearl Country Club (487–3802)

Some courses excel at views; this course excels at staying in tip-top shape. Conditions are fantastic. (The fact that your cart has to stay on the path—not even a 90° rule here—helps keep the fairways in awesome condition.) The course is owned by the Honda family—as in Honda automobiles—and they obviously spend a great deal on maintenance. It's been here since 1967, so the trees are mature. Rolling hills and a surprisingly varied layout keep it interesting. Hole 4 is a tough par 4—uphill and into the wind for 411 yards. Swing for your life here. And at #5, don't aim for the fairway—aim for those coconut trees to the left to cut your distance.

Although you won't get those classic Hawai'i views, this is the course to play if you want to get pampered by the groundskeepers. Most of your fellow golfers will be residents since this course isn't on most visitors' radars. Fees are $90–$100; it's $40–$50 for kama'ainas.

Carts included and mandatory. Near Aiea. From H-1 going west, take exit 13A, stay left onto Hwy 99. Then turn right onto Kaonohi; you'll see their driveway. See map on page 101.

Kahuku Municipal Course (293–5842)

Bad news and good news at this municipal course. The nine fairways are more like one big stressed-out lawn with some greens and a smattering of sand traps. The grass is only as green as the last rain (no sprinkler system). Now the good news: It's *right on the ocean,* and the views of the water are relaxing. Plus it's dirt cheap. $10 per 9 holes. No power carts—push carts only; club rentals available (don't expect Pings). It's virtually never crowded during the week. If you can get over the skanky greens that only a groundskeeper's mother could love, it's a cheap way to walk and whack at an oceanside course. In Kahuku on Hwy 83 *waaaay* up at the northern tip of the island. See map on page 81. Theft can be a problem here, so don't leave anything valuable in your car.

Coral Creek (441–4653)

An awesome O'ahu course nestled between housing tracks. Some of the roughs are stiff enough to snap your club, but the fairways are pretty wide open and well cared-for, and greens tend to be fast and not too flat.

O'ahu may have fewer oceanfront courses than the neighbor islands, but the beauty of the tropics is never far away.

You'll start at either the front or back nine. Don't get greedy on hole 3; lay up or curse yourself afterward when you dump into that gully on the right or roll into an easy-to-miss hole.

At signature hole 10, a 3-par over water with a manmade waterfall behind the green makes for a pretty scene. As with most of the harder holes, it faces into the trade winds, so you'll want to account for that in your club selection.

Fees are $125 ($75 after noon); kama'aina is $47–$58. Carts are included. Walking is allowed "but not recommended."

Take H-1 West past the airport, exit 5A to Kunia Road, which becomes Fort Weaver Road, then right on Geiger Road and look for course on your left. See map on page 100.

Ko Olina (676-5300)

Waterfalls and black swans are the hallmarks of this beautiful course (though their symbol is a ladybug). The course is relatively forgiving, so it's not too hard on your ego, and it's extremely well-maintained. Nice touches abound like the GPS in the cart, which also allows you to order lunch so it's waiting for you after the 9th and 18th hole. (Way cool.)

They have a particularly nice variety of rental clubs, which are pricey, but several manufacturers are represented and you get a choice of steel or graphite.

At hole 12 you'll drive your cart behind a waterfall. (Hold your club out, and you can actually rinse it off.) It's a 3 par overlooking a pond with three waterfalls—very beautiful. At 18 there's a lake—lay up before it, then shoot to the back of the green; otherwise, you'll be putting uphill.

In all, this is an easy course to recommend. Fees are $150. Carts are included

and mandatory. Kama'ainas pay $70. Marriott guests pay $125. Take H-1 west past the airport. When it becomes Hwy 93, take Alinui Drive into Ko Olina.

Royal Kunia (688-9222)

If the hallmark of Ko Olina is swans and waterfalls, this course can be described as the land of sweeping vistas and limitless bunkers. The developer must have owned an atoll somewhere in the South Pacific because he used enough sand to create his own island. We're talking 101 bunkers. And that's just the bunkers *above* the ground. This area used to be controlled by the military, and beneath your feet are numerous old naval *ammo* bunkers.

Opened in April 2003, the course might seem more mature. That's because it was built almost 10 years earlier, but they weren't allowed to open because they didn't pay a county demand of $25 million in the form of an "impact fee." (When the developer went bankrupt and then their *lender* went bankrupt, the county *graciously* shaved $10 million off their shakedown demand.) So ironically, for a decade the only people who could play this course were the very politicians who wouldn't let them open.

Overall, it's an awesome course with some glaring shortcomings. Let's get the downside out of the way. The clubhouse is very unimpressive. (But at least their rental clubs are nice.) And the driving range is far enough away that you can't walk to it. But they won't let you take a cart. So they'll drive you to the range, but there's no way to tell them when you want to come back. You'll have to wait until they bring someone else. And oddly, you buy your tokens back at the clubhouse, so if you hit all your balls, you'll either putt or sit and twiddle your thumbs until they return.

Once on the course, the views are particularly expansive. Don't be fooled by your eyes at hole 16. Sure, you can see the green. But you can't see a water hazard on the right side. Don't slice or you'll either get wet, or you'll be playing at the beach bunker next to it.

At the 18th, your long journey to the flag leads to a green backed by a waterfall pretty enough to stop and picnic at. What a way to end the game.

Fees are $125–$135; kama'ainas pay $50–$55. Carts are included and mandatory.

Take H-1 east past the airport, exit 5B to go right onto Kunia Road then right on Anonui. The course is on the right. See map on page 100.

Ala Wai Municipal Course
(733–7387)

We mention this 18-hole course because it's right across the Ala Wai Canal from Waikiki, and as a result it's the busiest course in the state, *by far*. They get an average of 500 players *a day*. It's also one of the least impressive courses. It's like one big lawn with its wide fairways, flat ground and lack of personality. Unless you're set on playing as close to Waikiki as possible, consider playing elsewhere. Rates are $42; carts are $16 extra.

First, I need to get something out of the way. Flying a powered hang glider (known as a trike) is different than any other type of aircraft. When I was grow-

Rock your world by flying along the coast in a powered hang glider.

ing up, I used to have a recurring dream that I could flap my arms and fly like a bird. My father flew little Cessnas, which, though fun, felt more to me like a car in the air than flying like a bird. I had forgotten my flying dreams until I reviewed a company on Kaua'i that gave lessons in this odd little craft. As soon as my instructor and I took off, I realized that a person *really could* fly like a bird. *This* was what the flying bug felt like! I was so smitten with the craft that I eventually hired the instructor on Kaua'i to teach me, and now I fly trikes myself. So although I have no personal interest in any company teaching trikes in Hawai'i, my perspective isn't as remote as it is for most activities. After all, it's not possible to anonymously review some companies, like Paradise Air, because I know the pilots. (We're all members of the small ultralight community.)

With that explanation, powered hang gliding is an activity I recommend. Don't confuse this with hang gliding. This craft has an engine, it's bigger and more stable, and some even have a powered parachute attached to the craft...just in case (a safety feature they're just beginning to install on traditional airplanes). Trikes take off and land on regular runways, and the ease and grace of the craft is glorious. (Rent the movie *Fly Away Home* if you want to see what they're like.) It's as close to flying like a bird as any form of flight I know. Trikes are what I have come to love so much and, in my opinion, are the safest form of ultralight flight available. (I'm not a daredevil and wouldn't fly them myself if I felt unsafe in them, though any time you're in the air you're potentially at risk, even on the airlines.) I grin like a fool every time I fly and have never reviewed an activity that generates more enthusiastic responses from other participants. It seems that whenever I see people coming off a trike, its passengers are frothing at the mouth with excitement, proclaiming that it's the best thing they've ever done on vacation. (Unless they're on their honeymoon, of course; then it's the *second* best thing.)

There are a couple of local companies. **Paradise Air** (497–6033) is out of Dillingham Airfield on the North Shore. The pilots, Denise and Tom Sanders, are professional sky divers who have recently opened up this trike ultralight business. From what we've observed, they're methodical in their approach to giving lessons in their high-end aircraft and maximize your time in the air. They charge $115 per half-hour, $190 per hour. They have a camera mounted to the wing (still or video) to get shots of you that no one back home will believe.

Another company is **Birds Eye View** (381–4296). They use a trike on water floats and operate out of Kane'ohe Bay. Though the air tends to be a bit smoother in Kane'ohe Bay, you only get about 30 minutes in the air for your $175, and their trike isn't as comfortable or as high-end, though the water floats do add a coolness factor to the flight. We've also had problems at times getting calls returned.

We've been unabashedly enthusiastic in our recommendation of helicopter tours of Kaua'i and the Big Island and lukewarm about them on Maui. Consider us lukewarm about these tours on

If you opt for a helicopter flight, get one that showcases more than just Waikiki. The Koʻolau Mountain range is the star of any aerial tour.

Oʻahu, as well. Compared to the other Hawaiian islands, Oʻahu helicopter tours are a bit less compelling. Kauaʻi, the Big Island and even Maui all have more nooks and crannies to explore than Oʻahu due to the physical structure of the mountain ranges here. Although the Koʻolaus are beautifully sculpted and corrugated, they don't lend themselves to aerial exploration as well—they just don't *feel* as mysterious from the air—at least the way companies do tours here. They're incredibly beautiful, but a drive along H-3 from Kailua to Honolulu can give you a view that rivals some of what you'll get from a helicopter. For the money, it's hard to recommend a helicopter flight on Oʻahu.

That said, if you want one anyway, the company we prefer is **Paradise Helicopter** (293–2570). They use 4-seater Hughes 500s and leave from the Turtle Bay Resort on the North Shore. They're *totally* flexible and will pretty much fly where the passengers want. Call in advance since they need 4 people to book the 60-minute flight (which is $185). Unlike others, they'll visit the Waiʻanae Coast. You can also charter it for $725 an hour, which can be split four ways.

Other companies, which leave from Honolulu Airport, are **Heli USA** (866 936–1234), **Makani Kai** (834–5813) and **Hawaiian Odyssey** (833–4354), which use 6-passenger A-Stars for their

60-minute tours for around $180, plus some shorter flights. We don't recommend their longer flights because of their route, which avoids the Wai'anae Coast. (They tell us they *can't* tour the Wai'anae Coast because it's restricted military space. We'll spare you the details, but that's not an accurate statement; it's more of a business choice.)

AIRPLANE TOURS

If helicopters aren't your thing, a surprisingly good air tour is **Island Seaplane** (836–6273). They have two float planes—a Cessna 206 and a DeHavilland Beaver. Although some of the facts are a bit shaky, the pilot does a pretty good job on the narration. They try to fly their route so that both sides get good views, but overall, the left side is the best due to the counter-clockwise direction of

the tour. They have a 30-minute flight for $99 and a pretty good 60-minute flight for $169. (We just wish they'd do Wai'anae, too since central O'ahu is uninteresting.) Co-pilot seat available upon request. Earlier flights are usually smoother. Most of the time the pilot stays at about 1,500 feet.

The larger Beaver is the better plane for the tour due to its better visibility and bulbous windows. They use the Cessna when they have 4 passengers; the Beaver holds 6. They'll try to work you into the Beaver with others if you request it. They were contemplating selling the company at press time, so things may change.

You can also take an open cockpit flight in a **Stearman Biplane** (637–4461) at Dillingham Airport on the North Shore. One passenger per flight. Frankly, the tours are handled pretty con-

Hiking some of O'ahu's less trampled trails, like the Maunawili Trail, can reward you with tropical visions that will stay with you for a lifetime.

From the top of Diamond Head, Waikiki and Honolulu take on a whole new perspective.

servatively—not much wildness, just a straightforward 40-minute tour for $195. (Short flights available.) If you want them to do any aerobatics during the flight, you have to cough up (if you'll pardon the expression) an additional $50.

Because O'ahu has such a large and active population, hikers will find the island *filled* with good hiking trails. This presented a problem for us. Which ones do we include? What we ended up doing was including a few of the more popular trails (Diamond Head and Manoa Falls are examples) along with some lightly used trails, some of them never seen in any book. If you're an ultra-serious hiker who wants more options than our hiking section allows, there are a number of hiking books for O'ahu. Probably the best one is the *Hikers Guide to O'ahu*.

HIKING NEAR HONOLULU

Diamond Head

Many vacation destinations have that *one* thing that you're supposed to do. In New York, you're supposed to visit the Statue of Liberty. In San Francisco, you're supposed to see the Golden Gate Bridge. And in Honolulu, you're supposed to climb to the top of that ultra-prominent circular landmark that dominates Waikiki, Diamond Head. You're *supposed* to do this because from up top, the view is *da kine, brah!*

Though you'll read that Diamond Head Crater was created 300,000 years ago, that's no longer accepted as correct. The truth is, we don't know how old da bugga is. Scientists debate whether the last eruption on O'ahu took place 400,000 years ago...or 5,000 years ago, as some of the radicals suggest. Most think it's been about 100,000 years, but that's a stab in the dark.

There are two great reasons to do this hike early—avoiding heat and assuring yourself a parking space. It's $5 per car. If the parking lot's full, they'll allow five cars at a whack to circle like vultures looking for a space. Otherwise, you'll have to park outside at Kapiolani Community College and walk an additional 1¼ uninteresting miles up the road.

The buildings inside the crater—shaped like a fluted bowl—belong to the FAA and until 2001 housed their air traffic controllers for Honolulu Center. (Doesn't it seem odd that the government agency in charge of the sky would choose to put its main office in a hole?)

On the trail you'll gain 560 feet over 1 mile (according to the GPS), and it'll take most people about 1½ hours. That's 30 to 40 minutes to go up, 20 minutes at the top, then the return. On this trail we've seen everyone from Ironman triathletes to people literally using walkers (though they didn't exactly hike it at the same speed). The trail has sections of unevenness, so wear shoes instead of flip-flops. Short marching steps work best along the constant incline. Near the end, it's the 99 steps plus a spiral staircase followed by more steps, then a low duck that tuckers most people out. (Ignore advice to bring a flashlight—the interior portions are now lighted.)

Once at the 761-foot summit it's all worth it. What a grand view. Waikiki is such a beautiful place from up here. From Barbers Point almost 20 miles to the west to Koko Crater 9 miles behind you, it's easy to see why the military bought this landmark in 1904—it's the perfect place to watch over all of leeward O'ahu. Look down on the ocean side, and you'll probably see lots of hats piled up below the lookout. We see somebody lose one almost every time we come up here, so hang onto yours.

It's crowded at the top—this wasn't designed to accommodate 1,500 hikers per day; it was designed for a few eagle-eyed lookouts.

To get here, take Kalakaua down to Monsarrat and head up that street for over a mile to the entrance on the right. (Monsarrat changes to Diamond Head Road.)

Top of the World Hiking

The Ko'olau Range is the long mountain that stretches 36 miles, effectively defining the windward side. (See fold-out back map to orient you.) From its meandering summit you'll find some of the best views on the island. Look one way, and most of the windward side stretches before you. Turn around, and the leeward side from Honolulu to Makapu'u Point is all yours.

The leeward side of this range gently slopes toward the sea, so that's where all the trails to the summit are. (The windward side of the ridge is cliffy.) Erosion has created a repeating pattern of ridges and valleys. What does this mean for the hiker lusting after the views up there? It

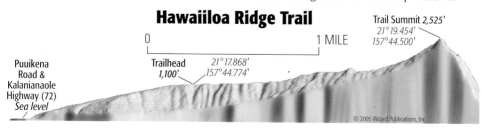

Hawaiiloa Ridge Trail

0   1 MILE

Trail Summit 2,525'
21°19.454'
157°44.500'

Puuikena
Road &
Kalanianaole
Highway (72)
Sea level

Trailhead
1,100'
21°17.868'
157°44.774'

© 2005 Wizard Publications, Inc.

The Hawaiiloa Trail (lower right side) ends at a view overlooking the windward side that is as sweeping as any place you'll find on the island.

means you'll be walking up one of the many ridges until you get to the summit.

Weather is the big question mark. More specifically, cloud cover, which would turn your grand, expansive view at the summit into a white out. Mornings are usually your best chance of cloud-free conditions, but sometimes it's only in the afternoon. Bottom line, you need to look to the summit before you go and, if it's clear, cross your fingers and hope that it'll stay that way.

Knowing that you don't have the time or desire to hike all the trails to the summit, we've spent considerable effort viewing the windward side from *all* the summit trails. In our opinion, **Hawaiiloa Trail** offers the best views. That's because it's far enough north to get the wicked views of the windward side, without being so far north that your sweep-

ing vistas begin to get clipped by a peak called Konahuanui. Hawaiiloa Trail is also favored because the trailhead starts at the 1,100 foot level, so your car will be able to pay part of the elevation bill. The unfavorable part of this trail is the steep ending, which can be tricky, especially for those afraid of heights.

Hawaiiloa Ridge Trail

You'll climb a total of 2,000 feet over 5 miles (round trip), and your reward is one of the grandest views on the island overlooking both the windward and leeward side.

Drive about 7 miles east of Waikiki, after H-1 becomes Kalanianaole Highway (72). Several miles before you get to Hawai'i Kai, you'll see Puuikena Drive on your left. (But you'll have to turn right and do a U-turn since there's no left lane onto Puuikena Drive.) Going into this affluent gated community (you'll have to sign a waiver), you'll drive 1¾ miles up the steep road to the top. Smile as you press hard on the gas pedal, because every foot of elevation gained by your straining car is one less foot your legs will have to climb.

At the lightly used trailhead go right, onward and upward. It'll be quickly apparent from looking at the trail that the most aggressive elevation gains will occur during the later portion.

Winds can be strong and gusty at times here, probably coming from your right on the way up. If this is the case, you'll want to leave your big, floppy hat in the car, lest it become a sail that'll drag you off the ridge.

Almost ½ mile into the trail, there's a spot where the valley to your left is exposed and, if it's nice and windy, the treetops below you form ocean-like waves which are quite mesmerizing to watch. The windier and gustier, the better.

Although the trail does undulate up and down at times (adding to the overall elevation tally that your legs will have to pay), it doesn't undulate as much as some of the other ridge hikes.

Before the steep part, you're treated to a very pretty field of ferns, 'ohi'a and ti plants. You never knew there were so many shades of green along here, and photo ops abound. Some of the ferns might scratch a bit at your legs and conspire to untie your shoes.

Once at the steep part, some people turn around and head back, which is a shame. Sure, this is the hard part. And even before the steep part, there are some short steep stretches that might make life interesting if it's raining. As a precaution we always bring rope on hikes, and on these stretches we've wrapped it around trees to help us go down some short, slippery areas, though it's not a necessity. The steep area has steps built into the mountain at many of the steepest parts. Use your best judgment, but we're hoping that you make it to the top. Of course, if the summit's socked in with clouds and it doesn't look like that will change, no sense proceeding any farther. That's one reason why we like to start this hike early, to maximize our chances of getting to the top before late morning or afternoon clouds form.

Halfway into the steep part, turn around. Lo and behold, tall buildings from Honolulu will begin rising above the ridges.

Once at the top (if nature is cooperating), you can see from Chinaman's Hat Island to your left, all along the coast to Rabbit Island. Turn around, and you see Honolulu and Diamond Head to Koko Crater. If it's cloudy, consider waiting—it can change fast up here. Clouds rip in and out of the ridge area, giving you a very graphic feel of the wind speed.

The Ko'olau Ridge Trail continues both ways along the ridge, but it's a *very* advanced trail. Only use it on calm, sunny days, only if you're feeling lucky and only after you've verified that your life insurance is up to date and includes your humble authors as beneficiaries. (We'll do good things with the money, we promise!)

You're at 2,500 feet. Although you started at 1,100, the undulations will cumulatively add about another 600 feet or so of climbing. Going back provides wonderful distant leeward views.

Manoa Falls Trail

Though this is generally considered the second most popular hike on the island (after Diamond Head), we haven't seen nearly as many people on it as its reputation suggests. It's popular for good reason. The surrounding forest is staggeringly beautiful, it's only a mile (each way), it's such a gentle slope that nearly anyone can do it, and it rewards you with a very pretty 160-foot high waterfall.

Right from the get-go, it's obvious that this is an impossibly lush area. Giant trees with luxuriant clinging vines, elephant-eared ape plants and every shade of green you could want along with a soundtrack of tropical birds create an Eden-like atmosphere. The stream is always nearby, and the verdant growth is ever present. Once at the falls, there's a bench to sit at and listen to the hissing water. All in all, a very rewarding hike for relatively little effort.

It's only a mile walk to Manoa Falls. Long enough to dissuade casual visitors, but close enough for almost any hiker to visit.

To get there, either take McCully out of Waikiki, past H-1 and onto Metcalf then right on University Avenue, or if you're on H1 take the University Avenue exit (#24B) and head mauka (toward the mountains). University will become O'ahu Avenue. Then take the right fork onto Manoa Road and drive to the end, past the pay parking lot (for now), and keep going till the blacktop ends and the trail begins. If there's parking available, grab it. If not, drop off your passengers and head back to the pay parking ($5 at press time). Car break-ins are a problem here, so don't leave anything valuable in them. Bring mosquito repellent, and expect some muddiness if it's been raining lately. (Which it probably has—that's why it's so lush here.)

Kapena Falls

This is the hike with the most bang for your hiking buck. Only a 5–10 minute walk leads to a waterfall that is often deserted during the week—a rare thing on O'ahu. Kapena Falls is a 15 or 20-foot high waterfall that plunges into a broad pool, and it's a pretty sight. Two things you need to remember: Don't drink the water (see BASICS on page 31

for an explanation), and bring mosquito repellent, or you'll lose enough blood to make an elephant dizzy.

There are two ways to get to this waterfall, and they'll put you on opposite sides of the stream. See map on page 50. You'll want to get on Hwy 61 (Pali Highway) heading north. Only about 1 mile from H-1 you'll pass a scenic overlook on your left, but you can't get to it. Keep going and take the Wyllie exit, then turn left on Nuuanu Avenue. Drive down into the Nuuanu Cemetery. Go to the end of the road at the bottom, and a trail leads through the brush for about 5 minutes to the falls. The signs are inconsistent as to whether this is allowed. (The first one says don't go, then the one on the trail says hike at your own risk.)

The better view of the falls is from the other side of the stream. If you don't want to walk through the cemetery, use

In the movie Rundown, *they tossed a* JEEP *off Kapena Falls.*

it to turn around on Nuuanu Avenue. Head back toward Wyllie, get back on Hwy 61 this time going south (back toward Honolulu), and look for a SCENIC OVERLOOK 500 FEET sign. That's where the trail goes into the jungle, but you'll have to park at the scenic overlook (which actually overlooks nothing even remotely scenic) and walk along the side of the highway. (Don't get whacked!) Take the trail inland, and take the right fork at the top of the ridge. The falls are down below you.

By the way, the falls and stream are on state conservation land, and you aren't forbidden from visiting it.

If you saw the movie *Rundown*, this is where the JEEP came hurtling down into the water. They used an empty JEEP shell (no engine or transmission) and hurled it off a ramp. The highway bridge behind the falls was magically removed by special effects.

Pali Trail

Who'd have thought an abandoned highway filled with the traffic noise of its newer replacement road below could make such a pleasant hike? From the Pali lookout, the old Pali Road snakes its way to the right. It meanders downhill 600 feet over a span of 1⅓ miles and, in the process, shows you a side of Kane'ohe and especially Kailua you won't see from the lookout.

About ½ mile into it is an intermittent stream flowing under the old bridge that you're walking on. Look straight down from the curved bridge, and you may see a waterfall beneath you *if* Mother Nature is cooperating. Note how plants such as banyan trees are reclaiming the old roadbed and guard-rails.

About ⁸⁄₁₀ mile into the hike you've lost 450 feet of elevation. You'll come to

a section of old road that seems to have sheared away from the mountain in a dramatic way. You can get past this, but from here this becomes a real trail. You'll have to get to the right side of a protective cyclone fence and walk along the mauka side.

Soon the forest has completely paved over the old road, and it'll veer inland. The traditional shades of every green adorn the scenery. If you haven't gotten used to the traffic noise below you, it may seem a bit more annoying here because, after all, this is a forest and the noise seems out of place. A sometimes-babbling brook will soon alleviate some of the noise.

When you come to an intersection, to the right is the Maunawili Hike described on page 182. To the left is a short trail to a highway turnout where the lazy (and well-funded) hiker could have left a second rental car. And behind you is where the rest of us poor slobs will have to walk to regain that 600 feet you just lost.

To get here, take Kalakaua Avenue west out of Waikiki. Left onto Beretania, right onto Bishop/Pali Highway. Take Pali (61) toward Kailua and look for the Pali Lookout sign toward the top. See maps on pages 50 and 68.

EAST O'AHU

Makapu'u Walk to The Dragon's Nostrils

There's an old abandoned road that heads to the top of Makapu'u Head, the easternmost point of the island. During its 1¼ mile distance (each way) it gains 520 feet at a reasonably constant pace. This is a very popular hike with locals and visitors alike due to the sweeping views from up top. What's less known is what lies at the foot of Makapu'u Head.

The Dragon's Nostrils aren't as reliable as the Halona Blowhole, but when they're going off they're far more interesting. Here a visitor from Kaua'i gets exposed to the dragon's fury.

It gets hot by late morning here, so start this hike early. We like to walk up for the sunrise with flashlights, though it might be hard to motivate yourself to get up *that* early. Take McCully out of Waikiki, then right on Kapiolani and up to H-1 east. Drive till you're past the 9 mile marker on Hwy 72, east of Waikiki. Park on the side of the road where a turnout and gate mark the trailhead. You're allowed to go past the gate on foot. The abandoned road ascends the back side of the hill first, then slithers around to the windward side halfway up. Stop at an information plaque about whales and look for the buggers below if it's whale season (December–April). Remember that plaque on your way down.

Once at the top, a lookout presents an unexpectedly dreamy view of Manana (AKA Rabbit Island) and Kaohi-ka-ipu islands and Waimanalo beyond. *Wow!*

The vista is fantastic. All around you are reminders of the military significance of this hill during WWII. Old bunkers and gun emplacements are all over this mountain. Wild cactus dot the mountain top. The Makapu'u Lighthouse is below you on a bluff, but it's off limits.

Now here's the surprise. On your way back down, before you get to that whale plaque we talked about, keep an eye out below you. There's a lava bench that's only partially visible in spots. Do you see any mist? How about water shooting into the air? Maybe, maybe not. The hill blocks most of the view of it. But from the whale plaque, a faint trail works its way down the mountain to the lava bench below. And there you will find, *some* of the time (though not *all* of the time), a cluster of blowholes.

We've seen lots of blowholes in the islands. But this stands out as the most numerous in one spot, and they successfully convey a feeling of barely contained violence. It's as if there is a giant, furious beast pounding at his confines to get out. Sit a while and you'll realize that there may be as many as seven blow-holes down here on a good day. Some go off only occasionally. The snorting twin nostrils sound frightening and dangerous, and you can feel the ocean several feet below the lava shelf you're standing on, pounding away at the lava. This great beast will escape someday, you can feel the inevitability in the air. Take your time here, but never take your eye off the violent ocean. Unlike many blowholes around Hawai'i, the opening is probably too small for someone to fall into. One of the twin nostrils separates the spray on the way out, creating three eruptions.

There's a good chance that the ocean may be too calm for the blowholes to work. Probably 60% of the time they're *not* going off. East swells and long period swells work best, but it'll be hard for you to know if that's what's hitting the island. Low tide seems to *diminish* the blowholes, but that's when the waves may smash against the shoreline the most dramatically, creating explosions of water shooting well over 100 feet into the air when the surf is really high. What we're saying is you won't really know what to expect until you start going down the trail. If the ocean's calm, there *is* a nice consolation prize. Some deep tide-pools make wonderful bathing. But only use the tide-pools if the ocean's calm. Pounding seas would make them hazardous.

The trail can be a little slippery going down and faint going back up—try to keep a mental note of it. Also, don't tempt fate by getting too chummy with the ocean down here. Keep your distance unless you're *sure* you're in a safe place. Bring water for that climb back up to the 400-foot level.

A pack-laden hiker marvels at the fluted walls of Maunawili Valley.

Maunawili Trail

There's a bowl-shaped valley called Maunawili tucked into the Ko'olau Mountain range that's mauka (toward the mountains) of Kailua town. The northeastern tip of this valley is defined by Olomana peak. The northwestern tip is what the Pali Highway punches through. In between is a wonderland containing one of O'ahu's finest hikes.

Now there are several ways to skin this cat. The best way, *by far*, is as a shuttle hike—starting from the west and ending in the east. Now, we realize that renting a separate cheap-o car for the day and leaving it at the other end is a burden that many won't bear. Fair enough. We'll describe it from one end to the other and, if you only use one car, you can hike it one way until you're half-way to satisfied, then turn around and go back. But consider

springing for the extra car; this one's worth it.

You may read elsewhere that this hike only climbs a few hundred feet. Don't you believe it. That false notion is obtained by casually looking at topographic maps, noting that the trail starts at 600 feet, tops out at 1,000 or so (it's actually 1,120), never deviates from the contour lines *too much*, and guessing. Sounds good. But when we used a GPS with a built-in altimeter to keep track of all the "little hills and dales," we got very different results. You may only climb a hundred or so feet with each wiggle on a map—which barely shows up on a topo. But do that 25 times or so, and together those little climbs add up to 2,460 feet of climbing over 9½ miles. And that's *without* the side trip to the falls. It's not until the second half of the trail that those climbs start to get tiring.

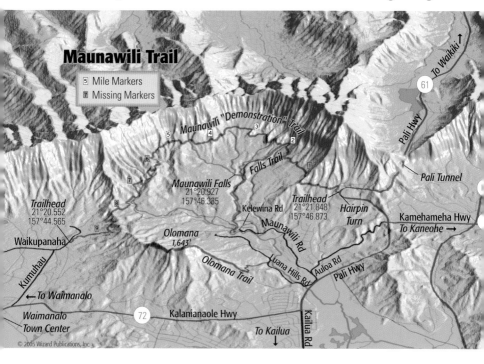

Maunawili Trail

- 5 Mile Markers
- 7 Missing Markers

Maunawili "Demonstration" Trail

Falls Trail

Maunawili Falls
21°20.927
157°46.385

Trailhead
21°20.552
157°44.565

Trailhead
21°21.848
157°46.873

Kelewina Rd

Hairpin Turn

Olomana
1,643'

Olomana Trail

Luana Hills Rd

Auloa Rd

Maunawili Rd

Pali Hwy

Pali Hwy

Pali Tunnel

To Waikiki

61

Kamehameha Hwy
To Kaneohe →

Waikupanaha

Kumuhau

← To Waimanalo

Waimanalo
Town Center

72

Kalanianaole Hwy

To Kailua
↓

Kailua Rd

© 2005 Wizard Publications, Inc.

Read these two paragraphs slowly—there's a lot of meat in them. Start at the long, hairpin turn pullout on the Kailua side of the Pali Tunnel. From H-1 near Waikiki, you'll go 7 miles up the Pali Hwy, though the second tunnel and pull over at the marked lookout after the runaway truck ramp. The trailhead starts here toward the right of the turnout.

If you're leaving a car at the other end, take Kalanianaole Highway (72) to Waimanalo. Go mauka (toward the mountain) at Kumuhau Street, right when it ends at Waikupanaha, then go ¼ mile until you see a turnout on the right side at the trailhead. Driving back with your *other* car to that hairpin turn from here, you'll get back on the Pali Highway going mauka, drive past the hairpin (which you can't turn into from that side) through the tunnels, eventually turn right at the exit for the wayside park, back up the mountain, around through the wayside, back onto the highway going toward Kailua, and back through the tunnels again to the hairpin turn. (Phew!)

After a couple minutes on the trail you'll continue straight at the intersection of the Pali Trail. As you start to leave the traffic noise behind, the trail starts to wind though lush forest, and the views can change rapidly. In one moment you're overlooking Kailua and the coast, then turn a corner and you're looking at a wild and lush valley. Around another corner is a mountain carpeted with lush ferns, another and you're overlooking a pretty banana farm. Many hikes on O'ahu require a long climb, culminating in a grand view at the top. This hike rewards you incrementally along the way. You never have to go too long without a treat.

Shortly after the 2 mile marker (these markers aren't all present—we labeled the ones we've seen), you'll come to an intersection...and a decision. Up until now you've had it fairly easy in the elevation department—somewhat gradual climbs. About 8/10 mile down that optional ridge is **Maunawili Falls** (see page 184 for more), a small but pleasant falls to spend some time. But it means giving up (and then reclaiming) 500 feet of elevation quickly. If you're doing an out and back hike, it's worth a stop. If you're going all the way to Waimanalo, you may not have the time or juice to go to the falls. Either way, at least go down the trail about 5 minutes, then turn around. The perspective of the fluted cliffs of Ko'olau is mind-boggling.

Staying on the Maunawili "Demonstration" Trail (as it's called), the variety of plants is amazing. Ti plants, tree ferns, kukui trees, wild orchids, 'ohi'a trees, koa trees—such a nice mixture in this valley. And the birds are more numerous than at almost any other place on the island. Especially delightful are the shamas, with their beautifully complex song. In places the bird life is intense enough, depending on the time of day, to drown out conversation.

Mile after mile, the views and forest just keep getting better and better. About halfway in, you've now left nearly all traces of civilization behind. The trail zigzags over and over again into Eden-like lushness. You may even come across a small waterfall or two along the way, if it's been raining recently.

After 8 miles or so the visions of beauty might start getting supplanted by visions of cold beer. At least they did with us. You'll arrive at an intersection underneath powerlines. Go to the right here and at the other two intersections ahead and you'll eventually reach your car, and soon those cold beers.

This 9⅓ mile trail is on the side of a mountain much of the time, giving opportunity to take a tumble if you were particularly clumsy. Also, keep track of the time it's taking. You want to leave early enough to take your time and to ensure you're not on the trail in the dark. Hiking shoes are best as several areas may be muddy, especially the second half. But overall, this is a well-cared for and easy-to-follow trail.

Kaiwa Ridge Hike

It's short—only about ⁴⁄₁₀ mile each way. And over that distance you'll gain almost 500 feet, so expect to puff and pant and wheeze and whine. But the views of the Moku-lua Islands 1¼ miles away and dreamy Lanikai Beach make it worth the sweat. Best times are either sunrise (if you're so motivated) or late afternoon. Don't hike it in the midday heat—there's not enough air in all Kailua to fill your lungs.

In Kailua—see directions to Lanikai Beach Park under BEACHES and the map on page 70. Then take a right on Kaelepulu Drive. Just before it ends at a private gate, look to the left for a cyclone fence. The trail is at the top of that unnamed road along the fence.

Kawainui Marsh Path

This is a 1⁴⁄₁₀ mile (each way) dead flat cemented path through the Kawainui Marsh—sort of Hawai'i's version of the Everglades on a tinier scale. It's not much of an exaggeration to say that once you've seen the first 60 seconds or so, you've seen it all. Swamps are not exactly a hotbed of variety when it comes to scenery. Nonetheless, it's popular with walkers and joggers, and the views of the distant mountains are pleasing in the morning or afternoon. There

are two places to park. The north end is the better of the two. In Kailua, take Oneawa to Kaha. See map on page 70. The path hooks from the right side.

Maunawili Falls Hike

This is a small but pretty and user-friendly waterfall on the windward side, and the hiking is straightforward. It's 1³⁄₁₀ miles each way and will involve 500 feet of climb round-trip. Most people will take 40–60 minutes each way. You'll have to cross the Maunawili Stream four times, though during normal flow you'll *probably* be able to boulder-hop and keep your feet dry.

See map on page 68. The trailhead starts at the intersection of Maunawili Road and Kelewina Road in Kailua. From the Pali Highway (61) turn onto the *second* Auloa Road (the one that's *not* across from Kamehameha Hwy) and stay on the left fork to veer onto Maunawili Road. Take that to the end to Kelewina Road and park around the corner on Lola Road.

The trail is beautiful, jungly and easy to follow. (Bring bug spray.) It's a fairly constant incline upward for the first mile. Ginger, heleconia and banana are sprinkled along the way. Some of the trees have exotic vines all over them. Note the wild coffee trees after the second stream crossing. They have dark, slightly wrinkled leaves and small white blossoms at times. On the Big Island, where coffee is grown commercially, the blossoms are so numerous when blooming it's sometimes called Kona snow.

Before the third stream crossing you'll see a small concrete channel. This was built long ago to harness spring water from Api Spring, which you'll see coming out of the mountain

After a bench, the trail goes down to

the river 110 feet below. Turn left at the fork, cross and then parallel the stream for a couple of minutes to claim your prize—a waterfall that you can wade under. Since there aren't a huge number of accessible waterfalls on O'ahu, you probably *won't* have it to yourself. We've seen it empty for 20 minutes at a stretch *at most*, and we've seen it packed with locals on weekends. There's a trail on the far side of the falls that leads up to a platform that locals jump off, but it's steep and treacherous and we don't recommend it. If you do it anyway, check where you'll be jumping *before* you jump.

NORTH SHORE

Northern Tip Empty Beach Walk

Although the beaches on O'ahu are rarely deserted, here's an exception. The northern tip from the Kahuku Golf Course almost to the Turtle Bay Resort (about 5 miles) is beach and beachrock (sandstone). And since there's no convenient access (except for a club that has the keys to the James Campbell Estate locks), it's nearly always deserted during the week. Though not technically a public access, for years locals (mainly surfers) have been parking at the public golf course at the end of Puuluana Road (see map on page 81) and discretely walking across the golf course, careful not to interrupt any of the golfers' play. And although the county has their typical NO TRESPASSING signs at the golf course, the wink and nod system seems to be in effect, from what we've observed. We've even seen surfers carrying their surfboards across the fairways to the beach. At any rate, perhaps you can get around this limitation by simply buying a round of

O'ahu has fewer waterfalls than Kaua'i and Maui, and it's a treat to find one with no visitors. Maunawili Falls is occasionally deserted for short stretches.

The wild, windy beach near the northern tip of the island makes an ideal secluded beach walk.

golf at the course (it's $10) and walking to the beach. (Theft can be a problem here, so don't leave anything valuable in your car.) From there, head left along the shoreline. Although the land *behind* the beach is private, all beaches are public in Hawai'i, so stay at the shoreline to stay in a public area.

Winds are virtually always blowing along here, and the frothing whitecaps, smell of the sea spray and the empty shoreline all combine to make a memorable walk. Remember the trick to walk-ing in sand—gentle, relaxed strides while lightly striking the sand almost flat-foot-ed. You probably won't want to swim here since rip currents are common.

WAI'ANAE COAST

'Ohiki-lolo Point

This is a short hike—only 10–15 min-utes out to it. But it leads to one of the most interesting lattice-like sandstone benches we've seen in Hawai'i. Once you get to the stony peninsula, walk out as far as the ocean safely allows toward the water. This is all lithified sand, and the ocean is dissolving this former sand dune, creating sharp, awkward footing. Think of it as a large rocky bench that's been bathed in acid. Many of the places at the outer edge have holes and tiny arches eaten into the sandstone.

Farther back you'll see lots of salt in the depressions. During the winter giant surf sometimes washes over the entire bench. If that's the case when you're visiting, there won't be much to see here (other than your own demise if you were foolish enough to walk out onto the bench when it's being pounded). Those large boulders that lined the trail on your way out were tossed there during such periods, which gives you an idea how strong the surf can be at times.

To get here, drive to Wai'anae to near the end of the road. After the 17 mile marker is Makua Cave on the right. Park across the street from the cave and take the trail on the left toward the shoreline, then walk left along the shore. The point is just after 'Ohiki-lolo Beach. Don't leave anything valuable in your car here.

Ka'ena Point

There are two ways to hike out to westernmost tip of the island at Ka'ena Point, the long way and the short way (if you have a 4WD). We prefer this long way, which is from the Wai'anae Side. Drive along Hwy 93/930 until it ends at Yokohama Bay (see map on page 108). Nearly every map out there shows a 4WD road wrapping around Ka'ena Point. And nearly every map is wrong. The "road" soon becomes a trail, and it's not possible—nor would it be legal—to drive a car all the way.

Almost immediately into the hike there are opportunities via short paths to amble over to the shoreline, which is dominated by sandstone lovingly sculpted by nature into a series of chasms, arches and holes. It's fun to look down

The beauty of destruction as the ocean dissolves the sandstone bench near 'Ohiki-lolo Beach.

into them as the ocean snakes its way through the maze.

Beware that although the wind may be calm here, you're in what pilots call a rotor from the mountain behind you, and wind gusts can strike from any direction at any time. (That's why pilots *hate* rotors.) Look up and you'll probably see clouds racing by in the *opposite* direction that the wind is blowing on you.

In several areas the road exposes itself for what it really is—a former railroad track, and some of the trestles are still visible. In the old days this was how sugar cane was transported from Hale'iwa to Honolulu.

Yeah, this is our kind of riding!

At $7/10$ mile from your car, near a painted rock, you can angle down to the shoreline. (Vague directions, we know, but there's little to reference along here.) Below are a series of interconnected tide-pools, one suitable for swimming if the ocean isn't raging. It's an interesting place to watch the way the ocean exchanges water into various pools.

Be alert to opportunities to walk along the shoreline or along one of the many trail segments that are on the berm next to the road. It'll take longer, but it's more interesting, and you can always take the faster dirt road on the way back.

At $1^{2}/10$ miles from your car you may hear a sharp-pitched gasping sound. Throughout Hawai'i, blowholes are relatively common, where the ocean undercuts the lava bench, shooting water and sometimes loud air though a hole. Though this one is manmade (probably drilled by the railroad), it produces the loudest horn we've ever heard when the ocean's cooperating.

Up to this point hard-core 4WDers could have made it, but from here on a couple of narrow stretches convert the road to a trail. (Daring local teenagers occasionally try to drive it and often end up rolling their cherished trucks into the ocean.)

As you approach the point, things start to change. During normal trade wind weather you and the nearby ocean have been protected from the wind by the mountain next to you. Near Ka'ena Point a line of demarcation in the form of a distinct wind line abruptly transports you from a protected world to a windy one. The ocean is often a white-capped frothy mess, and you'll feel instantly cool.

Ka'ena Point Natural Area Reserve is where many of the island's albatross birds live. They burrow holes in the sand here. Stay on the trails so you don't disturb them if it's nesting season. At Ka'ena Point itself there's a rock offshore which marks the western-most point on O'ahu. This is called *Pohaku o Kaua'i*. According to legend, a demigod named Maui tried to bring together O'ahu and Kaua'i. Casting his magical hook across the channel, he snagged Kaua'i and gave a huge tug. Unfortunately, the hook came loose, and only a huge boulder from Kaua'i was pulled ashore here—the rock that you see in front of you. Hawaiians so believed in their legends that the channel to this day is called the Ka'ie'ie Waho Channel, named after the towline made from the 'ie'ie root that Maui used in his attempt.

This is a great place to be if the island is getting big surf from both the north and the south. The rocks at this point are getting slammed from north swells that may have originated in Alaska. The south side of the rocks may be assaulted by New Zealand-born swells.

You're $2^{4}/10$ miles from your car back at Yokohama Bay. If you really want to make it to Ka'ena Point but don't want to walk as far, JEEP drivers can come from the *North Shore* end. The 4WD road past Dillingham Airfield gets to within $1\frac{1}{4}$ miles of the point. You'll have to hoof it from there, and it'll be windier. See page 92 for more.

HORSEBACK RIDING

When people envision riding a horse in Hawai'i, they often picture themselves riding along a beach. **Turtle Bay** (293–8811, ext. 36) comes closest to that image. Sure, it's a nose-to-tail experience. You won't be galloping along with sand and salt flying everywhere. But *some* portions are along the fabulous North Shore at Turtle Bay, and there's something inextricably charming about that scene. It's $45 for a 45-minute ride, $65 for a 90-minute version in the late afternoon. Near the northern tip of the island at Turtle Bay Resort on Hwy 83.

A better product is **Kahuku Kai** (293–8081). They have a very relaxed and laid-back attitude (unless you're late). They'll run the horses if you like, and it's along the shoreline. Kids are fine with them; their restrictions seem non-existent. But Kahuku Kai's future here was uncertain at press time. Call in advance to be sure. Near the northern tip of the island in Kahuku behind the golf course. $45 for around an hour.

Kualoa Ranch (237–8515) has 1-hour rides for $45; 2 hours for $79. It's totally nose-to-tail walking, but the mountain scenery is pretty. On the windward side 10 miles north of Kane'ohe on Hwy 83. Not bad; not great.

Happy Trails (638–7433) has hour-long rides in the hills above Pupukea on the North Shore for $50 for 90 minutes.

If you've never (or rarely) ridden horses, remember that horses respect strength. They can smell fear a mile away. Be confident. And if you're not confident...fake it. Don't ever let them feel that they're in charge.

Call them Jet Skis or Wave Runners (which are brand names), these motorcycles of the sea can be rented at several locations around the island. Sometimes you'll be restricted to a small area usually set off by buoys.

Early morning is usually the most smooth. Later afternoons can be choppy from the wind. Late morning seems a good balance of smooth water seasoned by a little texture. Most people get tuckered out after 30-45 minutes, especially if you're like me and you drive it like it's stolen.

Companies like to encourage riders to double up, claiming it's "more fun." Hardly. Of course, having two people on one jet ski brings more revenue to the

company while only using one machine. (Hmm, pretty cynical, aren't we?) Regardless, doubling up increases the chance of someone falling off, from what we've observed.

One thing you might want to consider is wearing goggles. Frankly, riding jet skis without them can be annoying if there's any wind. Companies that won't provide goggles should be avoided.

The best one is **Watercraft Connection** (637–8006) in Hale'iwa on the North Shore. They rent them for $35 per 30 minutes, and you can ride them in the open ocean, not on a circular track like the other two. Goggles provided.

Aloha Jet Skis (521–2446) operates out of Ke'ehi Lagoon, a very sheltered body of water near the airport. No goggles provided; crummy attitude. $35 (cash only) for 45 minutes on a circular track.

Sea Breeze (396–0100) is at Maunalua Bay near Hawai'i Kai, 20 minutes east of Waikiki. They charge $49 for 30 minutes on a circular track.

One of our favorite kayak destinations is the 1,000-acre sunken island in Kane'ohe Bay, lightly used during the week but enjoyed by locals on weekends, like the day this photo was shot.

Some of the reefs of Kane'ohe Bay are so colorful and so close to the surface, you can simply look down and see the fish.

KAYAKING

Ocean kayaking O'ahu's nearshore waters can be heavenly. There's something unmistakingly exotic about watching your kayak shadow slide over coral reef systems on your way to an offshore island.

The two best places to kayak are **Kane'ohe Bay** and **Kailua Bay**. Although many of the resorts rent kayaks for use off Waikiki, this is a relatively dull paddle. Do it for the novelty of kayaking, but not for the sights.

Kane'ohe Bay

One of the most dramatic kayak trips you can take—and the one with the smoothest waters—is one that almost no one does for a simple reason—it's to a sunken island of over 1,000 acres that you can't see from shore. It's Hawai'i's version of Atlantis.

The central part of Kane'ohe Bay has a *huge* barrier-type reef. (Technically it's not a true barrier reef, but has the same effect.) Unlike most reefs around Hawai'i, however, this one is nearly as broad as it is wide and is covered in most areas by sand. During the ice age 12,000 years ago this area was part of O'ahu, 180 feet above sea level. When the earth warmed and the seas rose, it became separated from O'ahu as an island, then vanished, transforming itself into the fringing reef we know today. At low tide part of it is still exposed as a football field-sized beach rising from the sea. At the farthest edge, a stranded sandstone island, the "summit" of this Atlantis, forms the only visible remnant, towering a mere 14 feet above sea level.

You effortlessly put your kayak in at the pier just north of He'eia State Park (see map on page 68). Look behind you at the mountain peak with a powerline pole on it—that's what you'll be paddling toward when you return. The edge of the reef is just over a mile to the north. Look for Kapapa Island—the only part of this Atlantis you can see—and paddle toward it. The waters are almost always smooth here. You may have a headwind going out—which should increase later and help you coming back. Almost immediately you'll go over shallow coral and fish. It's like snorkeling without the mask. Polarized sunglasses help you see through the glare.

Approaching the sunken island is otherworldly. Suddenly there's a sand beach 2–3 feet beneath your kayak, and you seem magically suspended above it as you glide along. To the left, if the tide is cooperating, a short paddle will bring you to the disappearing beach. On weekends locals bring their boats and their BBQs out and make a day of it. Weekdays you may have it to yourself. Even if the island is submerged, get out and walk along the shallows of this "beach." It's a surreal experience. Then look toward Kapapa Island. If you want to visit, head straight toward it from the south.

As you approach Kapapa, a strange phenomenon occurs. East shore surf, if it's up, is pounding at the outer edge of the shoal but Kapapa Island is protecting you from it, creating a corridor of calmness except for the wrap-around swells that are literally colliding with each other right under your kayak as you get nearer. Stay in the center to stay in the corridor. Once near Kapapa, the colliding wrap-arounds may start to become annoying, and you may want to hop out in the shallow water and walk your kayak ashore. (Water shoes are necessary as the ground is reefy here.)

The sandstone island is a good place to have your lunch under the shade of trees and gaze back at O'ahu and the shoal you just passed over. You're now 2⁴⁄₁₀ miles from where you launched your kayak. Exploring the island reveals lots of sandstone overhangs. Unfortunately, it might also reveal litter left by thoughtless local fishermen who are too lazy to haul out what they hauled in.

Return the way you came.

Kailua Bay

A second ocean kayak trip is inside **Kailua Bay**. You can pick up a kayak at Kailua Beach Park and kayak to **Flat Island** or one of the **Moku-lua Islands** off Lanikai Beach. (Only the left of these twin islands is visitable—the other is a bird sanctuary.) Waters are usually fairly protected (but not nearly as protected as Kane'ohe Bay), and these offshore islands, while popular with other kayakers, still make a great destination. The northern Moku-lua Island has a beach to sprawl onto. And Flat Island has lots of pukas (holes) in the outer edge of the island.

If you don't want to paddle as far to the Moku-luas and are transporting your kayak, start from the far end of Lanikai Beach less than a mile from the islands.

For Kailua paddling, you can rent from companies nearby. **Hawaiian Watersports** (255–4352) will deliver the kayak to the beach, but you can't pay for it there. (Regulations—but they *can* take a credit card number over the phone.) $35 for a single, $45 for a double for a *half* day. **Kailua Sailboard and Kayaks** (262–2555) is slightly more expensive, and you'll have to wheel the kayak to the beach yourself from their shop on Kailua

Road. **Twogood Kayaks** (262–5656) rents and will deliver to Kailua Bay.

Other Kayaking Destinations

The **North Shore** has winds that are usually a kayaker's best friend—along the shore from north to south. If you can handle a shuttle paddle (kayak one way, and one of you takes the bus back to your car), put in at Waimea Bay and take out at Haleʻiwa for a nice wind-at-your-back-most-days, 5-mile tour of some of the island's prettiest beaches. Only paddle here when the ocean is calm, usually during the summer months (May–September).

The waters off **Hawaiʻi Kai** tend to be pretty placid most of the time and so paddling is less challenging, but water quality and views aren't as impressive.

The kayaking along the **Waiʻanae Coast**, especially toward the end of the

If the ocean's not your thing, the Kahana River makes a short but sweet jungle paddle.

highway near Yokohama Bay can be good. You probably won't have the same favorable following winds as the North Shore paddle, but the water tends to be wickedly clear.

Kahana River

This is the only river on the island that's worth kayaking, and it's super-relaxing. (Some would point to Haleʻiwa Stream, as well, but it's not as compelling.) Kahana is a mile each way down a tropical, dripping-with-life river with pretty mountain views in the distance and trees overhanging the banks for shade.

You put in at Kahana Bay Beach Park, which is 15 miles (25 minutes) north of Kaneʻohe on Hwy 83. It's an easy walk from the car to the ocean. Then paddle to the right, and enter the river from the right (east) side of the bay. You'll paddle under the highway bridge (on weekends locals fishing off it might not appreciate your presence—we prefer to do this on week-

days). Since it's only 2 miles round-trip, don't dig in and paddle too furiously—it'll be over too quickly. Instead, paddle and glide and soak in the environment for a relaxing 1½–2 hour cruise. When you get to a large patch of grass, this is a good place to turn around. (You can go a bit farther, but you'd be battling hau bush most of the time.) Make sure you bring lunch and repellent for mosquitoes. (If you forget the latter, then you thoughtfully brought *their* lunch.)

Renting a Kayak

For renting *outside of Waikiki or Kailua Beach*, the biggest (and the most knowledgeable) kayak shop on the island is **Go Bananas** (737–9514) just outside of Waikiki at 799 Kapahulu. They'll strap the kayak(s) to your car, and you're off, and they're cheaper than the Kailua companies. They also have a great selection of waterproof items. $30 per full day for a single, $42 for a double, add $10 for a 24 hour rental.

In Hale'iwa on the North Shore, **Surf & Sea** (637–9887) rents kayaks by the hour. Convenient for the area, but pricier than Go Bananas. At press time they had clear kayaks available—pretty cool.

KITEBOARDING

See Windsurfing on page 211.

What's not to love about spending the day on the water? The ocean off the leeward side of the island (meaning near Waikiki) tends to be fairly calm and somewhat protected. Whether you want to do a snorkel tour, whale watch or a sunset cocktail or dinner cruise, there are lots of boating opportunities off O'ahu.

Ocean tours off Waikiki tend to be on giant boats. (It's simple economics—getting a boat slip in Kewelo Basin is so valuable that anyone with a permit tends to use it for a big boat.) The exception are some of the boats that come right ashore at Waikiki.

From Waikiki Beach

Let's start with the most convenient ocean tours. Some boats slide right onto the beach at Waikiki. The best one we've seen is **Outrigger Catamaran** (922–2210). They have a good 45-foot sailing cat. (Winds permitting, they won't just motorsail. They'll kill the engines and sail in quiet.) The 2½-hour snorkel trips are $37. The sailing and sunset trips are $30 for 90 minutes and include a free open bar. It's a hoot to ride the net (from one of their forward trampolines), though it might get wet. And their snorkel spot is a bit bet better than some of the other outfits that snorkel near here. They can hold up to 49 but usually go with less. They land in front of the Outrigger Reef Hotel

At the other end of the spectrum **Maita'i** (922–5665) will put 47 people on their 44-foot catamaran for $23. (No food, and beverages are extra.) No snorkeling on this 90-minute trip. The sunset trip is $34 and includes beverages. Not pricey but not impressive either. They pull ashore between the Sheraton Waikiki and the Halekulani.

The **Manu Kai** (922–3111, ext. 2341) has 1-hour sails for $15 aboard their catamaran. No reserving for this one—you just show up in front of Dukes (next to Waikiki Beach Center), and if they have room they'll take you. A no-muss, no-fuss way of getting on the water, but it's a no-frills trip. No food, and beverages are extra.

Na Hoku II is a similar walk-up situation on a catamaran. $15 for a one-hour sail with cheap beer and mai tais. The yellow boat is near the Royal Hawaiian Hotel. Nearby is a similar $15 walk-up hour-long trip on the **Kepoikai II**. They'll usually cut the motor and sail awhile offshore. Kids under 12 ride free.

Outrigger Canoe Rides off Waikiki

These are available from **Aloha Beach Services** (922–3111, ext. 2341). It's $10 (you get to ride two waves), or you can charter the whole 8-passenger outrigger canoe (includes paddlers) for $225 per hour.

From Kewalo Basin

From Kewalo Basin, a 10–15 minutes west of Waikiki, **Paradise Cruises** Diamond Head snorkel on the **Starlett** (983–7827) is a terrible snorkel tour. The boat's horribly designed for this. Even with half the 160 capacity, bottlenecks are everywhere. (Like getting in and out of the water, and the undersized grill where it takes *forever* to cook your lunch.) The boat also needs a serious cleaning. Finally, they take you to a laughable snorkel spot off Waikiki's Hilton Hawaiian Village. The free sodas, cash bar and floating trampolines can't make up for their shortcomings. (Kayaks and a windsurfer are tethered by a short rope to the boat, so you'll be tugging on it like a dog on a short leash.) Better to think of this as a ride and a BBQ meal, nothing more, for $50. They leave from Aloha Marketplace.

At the other end of the spectrum is American Dream by **Dream Cruises** (592–5200). This is a much nicer boat and crew. While still big—well over 100 people—the experience is much more pleasant and they seem to be a tighter outfit. Their snorkel spot is farther from the shore than Starlett's and is better (though water is still too deep to get close and personal with the reef below). The stairs out of the water can be awkward when the boat's rocking. They do 3-hour morning snorkel trips in the summer and whale watching trips in the winter for $53; SNUBA available for an extra $50. Both trips include breakfast. Cash bar available. They also have other Waikiki trips and a dolphin watch trip plus BBQ lunch out of Wai'anae for $66. The Wai'anae trip seems to cater mostly to Japanese tour groups.

For Kewalo Basin trips bring quarters for the parking meter—50¢ per hour.

From Honolulu Harbor at Aloha Tower Marketplace

Star of Honolulu (983–7827) has a "cultural cruise" May–December. You ride up and down the leeward coast, make leis, take hula lessons, etc. You won't get in the water (unless you fall overboard), you'll just *see* the water. $28 for the 2½ cruise.

From Wai'anae

If you don't mind driving out to **Ko Olina** (35–45 minutes west of Waikiki *barring traffic*), the waters off the Wai'anae Coast can be delightful during summer months (April–October).

An impressive boat trip is the **Ko Olina Cat** at Hawai'i Nautical (234–7245). They have a nice 53-foot catamaran. (Though it's a sailing cat, they'll mostly motorsail.) Good boat—they feed you well and the crew is good. We weren't impressed with their snorkel spot and were disappointed that they *made* you wear a flotation device, even if you're

It's hard to believe that a boat trip so close to Waikiki can still transport you to another world.

an Olympic swimmer. Three hour morning and afternoon trips are $78 and include two alcoholic beverages. (Not a big hit on the morning trips.)

There's also the less impressive **Ko Olina Ocean Adventures** (396–2068). They have 2-hour trips for $95 in their 40-foot power boat. Light meal included. Not a good a deal. They also have a trip that includes SNUBA for $99.

Farther out in at the Wai'anae Regional Park in Wai'anae, **Wild Side Specialty Tours** (306–7273) has a nice 42-foot sailing catamaran. They take 15 people max, so it's not too crowded on board.

Dolphin Excursions (239–5579) is a 32-foot rigid hull inflatable. 16 people max. No shade. They do two trips per day, and their goal is to locate dolphins, then let you slip into the water with them. They *claim* a 90% success rate on the earliest trip and a 50% on the late morning trip. $95. The only reason to take the later trip is slightly more food.

From Hale'iwa

North Shore Catamaran (638–8279) does summer (meaning June-September) 4-hour snorkel trips for $74 in their 40-foot sailing cat. (Includes lunch.)

In Kane'ohe Bay

All Hawai'i Cruises (942–5077) has a 42-foot catamaran (they mostly motor or motorsail). Four hours and a burger lunch for $69.

Dinner Cruises

Navatek I (973–1311) can be summed up like this—great boat, mediocre food and show. The boat is amazingly smooth using swath technology—where the craft floats on two torpedoes that ride below the surface. The buoyancy of the torpedo is constantly adjusted, resulting in a very cushy ride. The buffet has scant choices. The mashed potatoes had no gravy (we cringed at how many people mistakenly covered their potatoes with tarter sauce). The background music is weird for a tropical cruise—elevator versions of *Strangers in the Night*, etc. But when the live music starts, you may long for the canned music you were listening to. If you wander around the boat, you might discover a deck full of passengers you didn't know about. Most will be Japanese, and your first thought is, "Who *are* these people I never saw board—and why are they eating prime rib and lobster as opposed to my bad chicken and fish?" Well, they paid $99 for their cruise, and it's not worth it.

A boat cruise off Waikiki can feel so relaxing, you'll think somebody has stolen your bones.

(Though their music is less lame than yours, your hula show is slightly better.) In all, Navatek has the potential to be a really great product—if only they'd try harder. $60, only 1 drink included. They leave from Pier 6 near the Aloha Tower Marketplace.

Star of Honolulu (983–7827) is a huge, 232-foot, rock-steady (most of the time) ship with 4 decks that can hold 1,500 passengers. (Don't worry, it won't have that many, and it doesn't feel as crowded as some smaller boats.) The fourth deck is where the fancy French food is served in a formal, air-conditioned atmosphere by fancily dressed waiters. But $200 makes the food hard to swallow.

Decks 2 and 3 have the steak and lobster for $105. No A/C (which is fine once the ship leaves the stuffy harbor).

The bottom deck is steak and crab for $66 in an A/C room.

Overall, they do a good job and the crew is professional. The food's OK—not great, not bad. Some drinks are included, then you're on your own. There's also a quasi-Polynesian show, which is kind of cheesy but fun nonetheless. Our only complaint is that they come in too early and finish the show dockside.

Leaves from Honolulu Harbor next to the Aloha Tower Marketplace. If you park in the lot, *make sure* you buy something at a store there and get validated, or it'll cost you an extra $24.

Hawai'i Sailing Adventures (596–9696) is a nice 80-foot sailboat. Their sunset cruises usually only take 6 people. (If there are two of you and you want to pay for a third person, you can have the boat to yourselves.) It's $119 per person for the 2-hour trip, and that includes an open bar, heavy pupus (appetizers) and

very personalized service. Out of Kewalo Basin. Our biggest concern is they're sometimes lax in returning calls.

Parasailing is where you become a human kite, attached to a parachute and pulled by a boat via a long line. It's an 8-minute ride, though, that includes reeling in and reeling out. It's been our experience that parasailing *looks* more fun and thrilling than it really is and doesn't seem worth the money. Think of it as a $40 amusement ride. (People afraid of heights, however, will no doubt be properly terrified.)

One tip (*especially* for guys): Don't wear any slippery shorts, or you may cinch forward in your harness resulting in...the *longest* 8 minutes of your life.

The companies (except Sea Breeze) operate out of Kewalo Basin a few minutes west of Waikiki.

X-treme Parasail (330–8308) is your best bet. They have 3 trips—$40 for 8 minutes on a 700-foot line, $55 for 11 minutes at 900 feet, or $70 and they'll reel out almost a quarter mile—1,200 feet—for 14 minutes.

Aloha Parasail (521–2446) charges $40 for 8 minutes in the air at 300–600 feet.

Hawaiian Parasail (591–1280) charges $40 for 8 minutes (though they want 2–3 hours of your time from start to finish) at 400 feet.

Sea Breeze (396–0100) is out of Maunalua Bay 20 minutes east of Waikiki. It's $39 for 8 minutes on a relatively short 300-foot line.

You'd think that the most populous island in Hawai'i would have marginal SCUBA diving, but you'd be wrong. The diving here is incredible, and this is the shipwreck capital of Hawai'i.

Where to Dive

Although diving takes place all over the island, there are five main areas that most dive companies use. **Wai'anae** in the west, the wrecks off **Waikiki**, **Hanauma Bay**, near **Hawai'i Kai** and the **North Shore** in the summer.

Overall, **Wai'anae** offers the best dive conditions. It's calm most of the year, and visibility is often 100 feet or more. We don't recommend late afternoon dives there since you'll be fighting traffic the whole way. (Morning trips there go *against* the traffic.) One of the more interesting Wai'anae dives is the **Mahi**. You'll get an idea of what happens to a ship after a quarter century underwater with two hurricanes and an embarrassing incident involving a Navy anchor. The ship's collapsing and you can only *partially* enter it, but it's a fun dive and it's often accompanied by patrols of spotted eagle rays flying in formation.

The wrecks off **Waikiki** are probably our second choice, because divers *love* shipwrecks, even if it's a simple sunken fishing trawler, and the visibility once you're away from the shoreline tends can be 100-foot plus with diverse fish life. Waikiki dives are super convenient since the boats leave from Kewalo Basin a few minutes away on Ala Moana Blvd. Describing the individual Waikiki companies seems pointless since there are only a half dozen or so big boats and about 50 companies that charter space on them. (You probably won't have any say as to which boat you're on.) In general, dive operators off Waikiki are diver processing machines, and we found little difference between them. Get 'em in; get 'em out. You'll probably dive one of the three wrecks offshore for one dive, and a shallow dive the second. The Waikiki shipwrecks are the **Sea Tiger**, **YO-257** and the **San Pedro** right next to it. At these later two wrecks you might see the Atlantis Submarine ambling about. Wave at them—some of their customers are probably wishing they were you.

Hanauma Bay is a shore dive, and though shallow (mostly 35 feet or less). It tends to be protected and calm and, though visibility isn't as good as other parts of the island, the fish life is excellent. Hauling heavy SCUBA gear to the shore (even using the trolley service to the bottom) is a bit daunting, so guided trips are recommended. **Hanauma Bay Dive Tours** (256–8956) does guided shore dives here, both introductory and certified dives. $89 for a 1-tank dive. See page 63 for more on Hanauma Bay.

Although the **Hawai'i Kai** area has some good dives, it comes in fourth for us because the visibility tends to be less and the terrain of most of their sites a bit less interesting. (Though some of the sites are fantastic, we're playing the odds here.)

The **North Shore** has a fairly short window, and we're not impressed with the companies operating there, especially **North Shore Diving Headquarters/Deep Ecology** out of Hale'iwa.

If You've Never Dived Before

Nearly every diver starts their diving life with a supervised intro dive. And, like us, you might be motivated to continue diving and become certified. You'll get instructions on land, then your instructor will take you and a few others down and should stay with you the whole time. Some companies do intro dives off boats, but personally we recommend shore dives for your first time. It'll seem less rushed, and new divers can get intimidated jumping into water over their heads from a boat. Introductory dives cost $75–$110. Some companies, like **Diamond Head Divers** (732–9797), will take you on their two-tank boat dives, and while the certified divers are sucking their first tank, you'll be learning the basics on the boat, then hopping into the water during the second tank. Not a bad plan if you don't mind having your first dive off a boat.

For shore dives you'll have to travel away from Waikiki (because shore diving there is poor). **O'ahu Dive Center** (263–7333) in Kailua does 2 tank intros for $90. Of their shore dive sites, try to avoid their Makapu'u site—pretty lousy.

Surf & Sea (637–9887) in Hale'iwa does intro shore dives in summer months at Sharks Cove, in winter usually at Electric Beach in Wai'anae. One tank is $75.

The Companies

Most of the dive outfits feed you little if any between dives. (Note to dive companies: The quickest way to a diver's heart is to have simple cookies between dives. Over the years we've been reviewing dive companies around the state, it's *amazing* how a $4 bucket of cookies from Costco can turn a boat full of hungry divers into raving fans.)

There are *tons* of SCUBA operators on O'ahu, and compared to the neighbor island SCUBA companies, they don't seem to put as much effort into differen-

tiating themselves from each other, especially the Waikiki operators.

Prices are higher in Waikiki, cheaper in Wai'anae and Hawai'i Kai. It's $75–$115 for a two-tank boat dive.

In Wai'anae, **Ocean Concepts** (677–7975) is one of the biggest SCUBA players on the island. Although large SCUBA operators often turn into cattle boats, these guys do an impressive job at keeping the quality up. They feed you well (but cookies after the dive would have made it better), they pace the dives well once you're in the water, and their guides are pretty good. Their boats leave from Wai'anae and Ke'ehi Lagoon near the airport. (We prefer the Wai'anae dives.) There are usually about 20 divers onboard broken into 3 groups. $100 for 2 tanks plus $20 for gear.

If you prefer 6-pack vessels, **Aaron's Dive Shop** (262–2333) out of Kailua leases various 6-pack boats operating out of multiple locations around the island, including Wai'anae. Although their shop personnel seem to slide into that arrogant dive shop attitude pretty easily, we've had good lock with their boat crews. Minimal snacks and beverages on board. Our biggest complaint is that rental gear doesn't include computers, so the dive profiles will be set by the divemaster, not your actual dive. If you have your own, bring it along and tell them you'll follow your own profile.

O'ahu Dive Center (263–7333) seems to try to appeal to divers looking for something different. Occasional night wreck dives (see ADVENTURES on page 221), scooter dives and other unusual dives are sometimes available.

Other companies include **Island Divers** (423–8222), **See in Sea** SCUBA (528–2311) **Diamond Head Divers** (732–9797), **Hawaii Watersports** (947–

8749), **Waikiki Diving Center** (922–2121) and **Dive Hawai'i** (223–4444).

Skydiving is available on the north shore at Dillingham Airport. You don't need us to tell you whether you should try this or not. It's either *yeah, cool, where do I sign?* or *yeah, right. Are you out of your mind?* Either way, it's around $175 (they may quote higher but most discount or direct you to coupons) for one of the most scenic tandem jumps available in the United States.

Having tried skydiving after I turned 18, I can say it was a rush in *every sense* of the word, and I found the event wonderful and exciting. But that was then, when I was invincible and unbreakable and *knew* that bad things only happened to other people.

Though we personally review the activities in this book, we decided to take a pass this time. Our concern isn't the companies themselves, which, though not perfect, *do* have a vested interest in trying to keep things safe, and it's undeniable that they have thousands and thousands of satisfied customers. Our problem is the trees lining the runway, especially near the east end where they land. The trade winds ripping unevenly through them creates turbulence near the ground that can—and has—caused hard landings. In an aircraft that ground turbulence might not be a big deal, you can apply power. In a parachute…it *can* be a problem. We strongly suggest that if you want to skydive here, you do so before 10 a.m. when the winds are usually much calmer. It takes about 90 min-

utes for the whole process, you'll be strapped to an instructor, and both of you will be dropped from 7,000–14,000 feet, freefalling for up to a minute. Companies to consider are **Skydive Hawai'i** (637–9700) and **Pacific Skydiving Center** (637-7472). So if you're part of the *yeah, cool* percentage, then don't worry about it. Bad things only happen to someone else. Have fun!

If you want to skydive but don't want to get too far from the comforting skirt of mother earth, consider *indoor* skydiving. This is where you don a special suit and pounce onto a column of air rising at over 100 MPH through a wire screen. That's fast enough to float on. You maneuver by altering your shape and moving your limbs. It's an absolute hoot! The air chamber is well-padded and you'll be in with there with a guide. **Skydive Hawai'i** (637–9700) has one of these at Dillingham. You'll get some instruction then you and 4 other customers enter the air chamber. It's $60 for your 3 minutes of skydiving and there's a 225-pound weight limit.

If you've ever gazed into an aquarium and wondered what it was like to see colorful fish in their *natural* environment, complete with coral and strange ocean creatures, you've come to the right place. Hawai'i features a dazzling variety of fish. Over 600 species are found in our waters. We can't conceive of a trip to Hawai'i without snorkeling at least once. We got the reef, we got the water,

Snorkeling at Sharks Cove offers some of the best conditions on the island— when the surf's calm.

Hawaiian Reefs—*Why is it That...?*

What is that crackling sound, like bacon frying, I always hear while snorkeling or diving?
For years this baffled people. In the early days of submarines, the sound interfered with sonar operations. Finally we know the answer. It's hidden snapping shrimp defining their territory. One variety is even responsible for all the dark cracks and channels you see in smooth lobe coral. A pair creates the channels, then "farms" algae inside.

Why are there so few shellfish in Hawai'i? It's too warm for some of the more familiar shellfish (which tend to be filter-feeders, and Hawai'i waters don't have as much stuff to filter). But Hawai'i has more shellfish than most people are aware of. They hide well under rocks and in sand. Also, people tend to collect shells (which is illegal), and that depletes the numbers.

Why do coral cuts take so long to heal? Coral contains a live animal. When you scrape coral, it leaves proteinaceous matter in your body, which takes much longer for your body to dispatch.

Why do some of the reefs appear dead? Much of the "coral" you see around O'ahu isn't the kind of coral you're used to. It's called coralline algae, which secretes calcium carbonate. It's not dead; it's *supposed* to look like that.

What is the state fish? Well, it used to be the humuhumunukunukuapua'a, but today we don't have a state fish. When the law expired, it was not renewed because the Legislature "didn't want to revisit this partisan issue." (How can a state fish be *partisan*?)

What do turtles eat? Dolphins. (Just teasing.) They primarily eat plants growing on rocks, as well as jellyfish when they are lucky enough to encounter them. Unfortunately for turtles and lucky for us, jellyfish aren't numerous here.

Is it harmful when people play with an octopus? Yes, if the octopus gets harmed while trying to get it out of its hole. Best to leave them alone.

Why does the ocean rarely smell fishy here in Hawai'i? Two reasons. We have relatively small tide changes, so the ocean doesn't strand large amounts of smelly seaweed at low tide. Also, the water is fairly sterile compared to mainland water, which owes much of its smell to algae and seaweed that thrives in the bacteria-rich runoff from industrial sources.

Why is the water so clear here? Because relatively little junk is poured into our water compared to the mainland. Also, natural currents tend to flush the water with a continuous supply of fresh, clean ocean water.

Why do my ears hurt when I dive deep, and how are scuba divers able to get over it? Because the increasing weight of the ocean is pressing on your ears the farther down you go. Divers alleviate this by equalizing their ears. Sounds high tech, but that simply means holding your nose while trying to blow out of it. This forces air into the eustachian tubes, creating equal pressures with the outside ocean. (It doesn't work if your sinuses are clogged.) Anything with air between it gets compressed. So if you know someone who gets a headache whenever they go under water...well, they must be an airhead.

and we got the fish. What more do you need?

We'll admit that we're snorkeling junkies and never tire of experiencing the water here. If you snorkel often, you can go right to our list below of recommended areas. But if you're completely or relatively inexperienced, you should read on.

For identifying ocean critters, the best books we've seen are *Shore Fishes of Hawai'i* by John Randall and *Hawaiian Reef Fish* by Casey Mahaney. They're what we use. You should see plenty of butterflyfish, wrasse, convict tang, achilles tang, parrotfish, angelfish, damselfish, Moorish idol, pufferfish, trumpetfish, moray eel, and humuhumunukunukuapua'a, or Picasso triggerfish—a beautiful but very skittish fish. (It's as if they somehow *know* how good they look in aquariums.)

We know people who have a fear of putting on a mask and snorkel. Gives 'em the willies. For them, we recommend boogie boards with clear windows on them to observe the life below.

A FEW TIPS

- Feeding the fish is generally not recommended since it introduces unnatural behavior to the reef, and it actually causes the variety of fish to dwindle since bolder species do well and soon crowd out meeker species. It has been officially banned at Hanauma Bay.
- Use *Sea Drops* or another brand of anti-fog goop. Spread it *thinly* on the inside of a dry mask, then do a quick rinse.
- Most damage to coral comes when people grab it or stand on it. Even touching the coral lightly can transfer your oils to the polyps, killing them. If your mask starts to leak or you get water in your snorkel, be careful not to stand on the coral to clear them.

Find a spot where you won't damage coral or drift into it. Fish and future snorkelers (not to mention the coral) will thank you.

- Don't use your arms much, or you will spook the fish—just gentle fin motion. Any rapid motion can cause the little critters to scatter.
- If you have a mustache and have trouble with a leaking mask, try a little Vaseline. Don't get any on the glass—it can get *really* ugly.
- We prefer using divers' fins (the kind that slip over reef shoes) so that we can walk easily into and out of the water without tearing up our feet. (If you wear socks or nylons under the shoes, they'll keep you from rubbing the tops of your toes raw.)
- Try to snorkel in calm areas. If you're in rougher water and a large wave comes and churns up the water with bubbles, put your arms in front of you to protect your head. You won't sense motion, and may get slammed into a rock before you know it.

WHERE TO SNORKEL

The BEACHES section describes the snorkeling potential of the various beaches around the island. Pay special attention to these:

North Shore during summer months (meaning April–September):

Sharks Cove—Outstanding snorkeling during calm seas but can be crowded.

Three Tables—Not as good as Sharks Cove but nice around the separate reef areas.

Waimea Bay—The south end (the end closest to Hale'iwa) is *fantastic* when calm and lightly snorkeled.

Kuilima Cove—Protected most of the time and often has an excellent fish count. Next to Turtle Bay near the northern tip of the island.

Sunset Beach—One small stretch can be nice when calm.

Turtle Beach—Usually cloudy water but often lives up to its name and has the friendliest turtles we've seen anywhere in the state—somebody *must* be feeding 'em.

Leeward Side (from Waikiki—which has lousy nearshore snorkeling—to the eastern tip):

Ka'alawai Beach—The nearest place to Waikiki where you can snorkel decent waters.

Hanauma Bay—Legendary. Described in detail on page 63.

Kahala Beach—Not as dramatic but nice life on a small scale.

Wai'anae Coast:

Papaoneone Beach—During calm (usually summer) months, turtles are often plentiful.

Ko Olina—Protected manmade lagoons have good snorkeling near the openings to the open ocean.

As for **snorkeling gear**, it can be rented just about anywhere. If you're going to snorkel more than once, it's nice to rent it for the week and keep it in your car so you can head to the water any time your little heart desires. If you want to buy your own, the cheapest prices will be at the Wal-Mart/Sam's Superblock outside of Waikiki on Keeaumoku. Also consider Costco if you're a member.

SNORKEL BOAT TOURS

These can be fun, though many of the boats moor close enough to Waikiki Beach to be influenced by its poor visibility. See OCEAN TOURS for more.

If you're hesitant about trying SCUBA, consider SNUBA. That's where you swim below a raft with an air tank and a 20-foot hose, regulator in mouth and an instructor by your side. Anyone 8 or older can SNUBA.

Hanauma Bay Dive Tours (256–8956) has SNUBA in fish-rich Hanauma Bay for $87. (Kids are $65.) They'll pick you up in Waikiki and pay to get you in the park. They're off on weekends, holidays and Tuesdays. This is the best place to SNUBA.

Out at Ko'olina on the Wai'anae coast, **Ko Olina Ocean Adventures** (306–0322) does this in the most protected water you'll find—one of the Ko Olina lagoons. (Water in the protected part is cloudy, but it's clearer near the lagoon opening.) It's $65 for 30-40 minutes underwater. (They also have this off a boat for $99.) They also have a version for 4–7-year olds called **SNUBA DOO** in the lagoon for $50. It's like SNUBA, but you stay on the surface. Think of it as a powered snorkel.

You won't *Run Silent, Run Deep.* You won't hear the sound of sonar pinging away in the background. And it's rare that anyone shoots torpedoes at you. But if you want to see the undersea world and *refuse* to get wet, *dis is da buggah.* **Atlantis Submarine** (973–9811) operates two subs offshore, leaving by boat from the pier at the Hilton

Hawaiian Village. Although they also have subs on Maui and the Big Island, we thought their Oʻahu tour was the best because it visits sunken ships, a plane and some artificial reefs. In fact, their dive site, which goes deeper than 100 feet, is a popular SCUBA site, so if you go in the morning, you might see SCUBA divers out your porthole, climbing over the shipwrecks.

This is the opposite of an aquarium—this world belongs to the fish, and *you* are the oddity. It's $90 (usually cheaper after noon) for the 64-passenger sub (slightly larger windows and seats), $65 for the 48-passenger sub. This 40-minute ride is a kick. Kids like it, adults like it, and even certified divers like us enjoy it. Claustrophobics will probably be too busy staring through the windows to be nervous. Photographers will want to use fast (at least 400 speed) film and turn *off* the flash. Wear a bright red shirt, and watch what happens to its color on the way down.

Make *sure* you validate your parking slip, or the parking fee might be nearly as much as the sub ride.

Now that's a window view!

Waves 101

Waves are mesmerizing to watch, and people can spend countless hours gazing at them. But most people don't realize that what they are seeing is the shock wave of an event that occurred far over the horizon.

Ocean swells are created by winds, usually hundreds or even thousands of miles away from us, that blow in the same direction long and hard enough to push the surface of the water away from what's beneath, forming ripples, then chop, then swells. These swells can travel quite efficiently over vast distances, carrying the spent energy of those localized winds with them. Think of the swell as a type of rolling battery, having been charged by winds from another part of the globe. South swells usually come from New Zealand storms; north or west swells often come from Alaska or Japan.

Near the shoreline, an ocean swell becomes a wave when it starts to feel the bottom, slowing it down. The surface water slows later than the deeper water, and the swell essentially gets ahead of itself, forming a wave. What kind of wave it will be depends on many factors, the most important being the slope of the ocean bottom. Gradually sloping bottoms like what you'll find at Waikiki form spilling waves that crumble—perfect for beginner surfers. Nearly all the energy is used up horizontally, pushing you forward. Ground that becomes shallow suddenly, like a reef ledge, form breaking waves called tubes or barrels—much lusted after by the big boys and girls. Lots of energy is directed downward in addition to the horizontal push.

The angle of the reef ledge relative to the swell is also important. If the swell hits the ledge head-on, the wave breaks everywhere at once, all across the shore—beautiful, but ultimately useless to surfers who prefer to ride more parallel to the shoreline, or down the line of a wave that's breaking over a longer period of time.

Now it might be tempting to think that the bigger the swells, the better the wave will look, but that's not the case. Each surf site has its optimal swell size. If it gets too big, the waves either break everywhere at once or break in large, irregular sections, becoming an unsurfable mess. Strong wind, either sideshore or onshore, also can close out a surf site by making it too bumpy. That's why surfers, when deciding where to surf, care about the swell direction, size and the winds. If they're hoping to surf at a prized site such as the Banzai Pipeline, the size of the swell might be perfect and winds might be light, but the direction it's coming from might be perpendicular to the ledge there, making it break all at once rather than at an angle. If the swell gets bigger, it might trigger the break at Waimea Bay (with its deeper ledge), but will close out Pipeline.

So when you see surfers gazing upon the ocean, they're looking at it from a perspective of beauty, physics and a little geometry.

What your first wave feels like...   *What it looks like.*

O'ahu is the center of surfing in the islands, some say the world. And that's as it should be. This is where it was invented, this is where it was exported from, this is where so many great surf sites are, this is where the surfing culture thrives, and this is where you'll find one of the easiest beginner surf sites the planet has to offer—right where you're staying in Waikiki. That's no exaggeration. Having lived on all the major Hawaiian islands, we can tell you that no other beach has the ideal combination of ingredients like Waikiki does. Perfectly shaped and sloped, waves at Waikiki crumble and push, spending their energy slowly. (Experts like breaking waves that curl and spend their energy faster, but those would kick your 'okole in the beginning.) Concessionaires give lessons right from the beach. It's about $35 for an hour lesson—five people max per group. You'll usually be allowed to keep the board an extra hour, but first-timers are usually so exhausted from paddling short distances (it's more tiring than it looks) that you'll probably pass on that extra hour—for now. Private lessons aren't as desirable as you may think for one reason: You'll be grateful for the rest as your fellow shredders take their turns.

Despite your preconceptions, odds are you *will* be able to ride a wave during your very first—and probably only necessary—lesson. Instructors come and go at these concessionaires, and although some of them can be pushy jerks, most are fine and it's incidental to your objective—riding your first wave. And oh, what a water god you'll feel like when you snag that first ride. The beginner boards are big and floaty, not like the small sticks you see the experts using.

Simply head to the Waikiki Beach Center in the heart of Waikiki and sign up. You don't need reservations, and classes are usually given on the hour.

Although Waikiki is the optimal choice, if the south shore is too flat (or too big) during your stay, you can also try these companies that teach elsewhere:

Hawaiian Fire (384–8855) will pick you up and take you to Kalaeloa (Barber's Point) for 2 hours of lessons for $102–$145 (depending on the number of people per instructor).

Surf and Sea (637–9887) charges $69 for 2–3 hours. You'll need to meet them at Hale'iwa on the North Shore.

Kailua Sailboards (262–2555) gives 90-minute lessons at Kailua Beach or in Waimanalo for $90.

Sunset Suzy (781–2692) charges $75 for 2-hour group lessons out of the North Shore.

Once you've had a lesson, you might want to return and rent a board to practice. Waves will seem a bit harder to catch because you don't have an instructor placing you in the perfect location and giving you a shove. Spend a few minutes on shore looking at the surf, and choose the location that seems to be breaking the way you want. As for not getting that shove off from the instructor, you'll simply have to paddle harder when you want to catch a wave. Stick with big, floaty boards. One way to cheat is to buy a pair of webbed gloves. (Speedo makes webbed gloves, and you might want to buy them on the Internet before you arrive as they're hard to find, or try Sports Authority at 596–0166 at 333 Ward Ave. near Auahi Street.) With these you don't need to paddle as many strokes because each stroke is so much more powerful. It might look a bit weird, but it'll give you an edge and it's much

less tiring. Also make *sure* you wear a rash guard or simple T-shirt, or you'll get rubbed raw from the board in two spots you *don't* want rubbed raw.

You can water ski in the ultra-protected waters of Hawai'i Kai. You should know in advance that the water there has *lots* of moon jellyfish, but they don't seem to be a problem as far as we've observed. **Hawai'i Watersports** (395–3773) does this for $49 for 20 minutes. They also have other things they can drag you on behind the boat. (If you've never water skied before, it's more tiring than it looks). Ridealongs are $10 extra. They tend to be pretty rude here.

Though they're not the only whales here, **humpbacks** are the stars of whale watching. They work in Alaska during the summer, building up fat, then vacation here from December to March or April when the females bear their young and the males sing the blues. More than 1,000 whales come to the islands each year, and the mothers and calves stay close to shore. Only the males sing, and they all sing the same song, usually with their heads pointed down. No air bubbles come out while singing, and scientists aren't sure how they do it. Humpbacks don't eat while they're here and may lose $1/3$ of their body weight during their stay in Hawai'i. (I doubt that very many *human* visitors can make that claim.) There's no question that the whale watching varies from year to year. Some years the humpbacks are boisterous and raising hell, constantly breaching, blowing and generally having a good time. Other years they seem strangely subdued, as if hung over from their Alaska trip. What's really going on is that some years O'ahu's whales visit other Hawaiian islands. Perhaps whales, too, want to avoid getting into a rut.

Few industries in Hawai'i bring as much shameless phony advertising as whale watching. Computers allow fake scenes with relative ease. (For the record, we don't use computers to doctor our photos.) Some show whales leaping so close to boats you think they're going to get swamped. Just so you know, boats are forbidden by federal law from getting closer than 100 yards. The fine for violating a whale's personal space is obscene. The whales themselves are allowed to initiate closer contact (and they're rarely fined), but in general, count on staying a football field away. That's OK, because these oversized buggas are so big that at that distance they're still incredibly impressive.

See OCEAN TOURS on page 195 for a description of the different boats. In addition, **North Shore Catamaran** (638–8279) has 2½–3 hour trips for $58 in their 40-foot sailing cat from Dec.–April. (They motor sail unless they have stiff winds.) Leave from Hale'iwa. Beverages only; bring your own food. Winter is the time of big swells on the North Shore so if you're a cookie-tosser, you may want to avoid these guys.

Star of Honolulu (983–7827) is more like a ship than a boat. Dec.–April they do 2½-hour whale watching tours for $41 with buffet lunch, $27 without

lunch. A vessel this big won't be the most responsive to whale sightings, but they'll generally go where they see the action. They also have a sorry boat called the Starlett, which is to be avoided.

Windsurfing

Windsurfing is the result of taking a surfboard and attaching a sail to it. When properly instructed, you can zip along faster than the wind. It's a first-class adrenaline charge.

During your lesson you'll actually windsurf, though tacking and jibing (changing directions by heading into or away from the wind) may elude you. In general, it's a hard sport to master at the beginning, and you should expect to fall in the water 70 or so times during your lesson. So don't be discouraged if you're not streaking like the wind gods you see around the island. (Falling's not so bad; in fact, you'll probably get real good at it.) Shorter and slimmer people seem to learn their board balance more quickly. During your lesson, don't be shy about asking your instructor to show you *exactly* what you're doing wrong.

At Kailua Beach on the windward side, **Kailua Sailboards** (262–2555) give 3-hour group lessons for $69. **Naish Hawai'i** (262–6068) charges $75 for 2 hours. Kailua has pretty consistent onshore winds, making it a good place to learn.

At Kahala Beach 15 minutes east of Waikiki in front of the **Kahala Mandarin Hotel** (739–8888), it's $35 for a half-hour lesson, but winds aren't as reliable here.

Waikiki isn't usually a very good spot to windsurf. (The wind is often weak or inconsistent.) If you want to try it there, **Prime Time Sports** (949–8952) gives 1-hour lessons off Fort DeRussy for $40.

Wear a T-shirt to keep the life jacket from rubbing you, and wear reef shoes or some kind of footwear while boarding. As for etiquette, the upwind windsurfer owns the wave, and surfers have the right-of-way over windsurfers.

KITEBOARDING

Also called kitesurfing, you may not have heard of this. It's a fairly new sport, so we're putting it here. Imagine a modified surfboard, shorter and boxier than a normal board, with fins at both ends and straps for your feet. Then let a special, controllable two-line kite drag you along. Like windsurfing, you don't have to go the direction the wind takes you—you have control. Despite what some instructors tell you when they want to sign you up, it's harder to get up on the board than windsurfing. But *oh,* what fun it is!

More fun than windsurfing once you're comfortable on the board. One way you can prepare before you get here is to buy a two-string kite and master it so that you can instinctively maneuver the kite. It's not that hard, but it helps if you can steer the kite without thinking.

Lessons are *expensive* and a bit hard to find. **Aloha Kiteboarding Academy/ KiteHIGH Kitesurfing** (637–5483) charges $249 for a 3½-hour lesson at different windward beaches. At Kailua Beach, **Kailua Sailboards** (262–2555) charges $238 for 3-hour lessons (longer and shorter lessons available).

First you need to learn how to operate the kite (which is a hoot). Next comes body dragging. Though it sounds like something they do to you if your credit card is declined, it's actually when you let the kite drag you through the ocean while you manipulate it. Then comes the good part—*riding the board*—which may or may not happen during this first lesson.

A Kailua Beach windsurf beginner stands on his board for the first time—before falling down 27 times in a row.

Don't bother bringing bait on this fishing trip—you're the bait.

Some of the activities described below are for the serious adventurer. They can be experiences of a lifetime. We are assuming that if you consider any of them that you are a person of sound judgment, capable of assessing risks. All adventures carry risks of one kind or another. Our descriptions below do not attempt to convey all risks associated with an activity. These activities are not for everyone. Good preparation is essential. In the end, it comes down to your own good judgment.

SWIMMING WITH SHARKS

One of the things that's available on Oʻahu is swimming with dolphins. But if swimming with dolphins is a little too tame for you (after all, how many people ever get eaten by mere mammals?), how about swimming with sharks? (We wanted to say something about lawyers here, but thought the better of it.) This is where you hop into a cage protruding just above the surface of the ocean. For 20 minutes you watch as sand bar sharks and possibly some Galapagos sharks circle menacingly while the crew occasionally toss bait into the water. Two, three, ten, maybe fifteen. Watching these predators just inches from you is fantastic. They're amazingly graceful and stealthy. We've SCUBA dived for years, but it wasn't until we did this simple *snorkel* trip that we were able to spend this much quality time with these animals. The cage keeps them out, and the biggest openings are covered with Plexiglas, which is appreciated when the big sharks bang into it. All in all, we thought it was an incredible adventure.

It all started with crab fishermen 3 miles off the coast of Haleʻiwa. They'd pull their traps from the sandy bottom 400 feet below and throw the remaining bait overboard. Sharks became accustomed to this buffet and started hanging around. **North Shore Shark Adventures** (228–5900) started taking people out in the early part of this century. (You know, it *still* feels funny saying that phrase now.) **Hawai'i Shark Encounters** (351–9373) also does this.

The boat ride is short, and with North Shore Shark Adventures there's no food on-board (unless you like chum—think of it as sushi without the craftsmanship). Six people per boat, two in the small cage at time, $100 per person. (Hawai'i Shark Encounter has minor snacks and puts 4 in the bigger cage so you'll end up spending a bit more time in the water, even if there are 8 people on the boat.) In all, we thought Hawai'i Shark Encounter did a slightly better job. They also charge $100 and have a hot water hose to shower with you're done.

Some people say shark cage tours are a bad idea and that it unnaturally brings sharks closer to shore. Others say it's harmless and that these types of sharks don't come near the shore and never attack beachgoers. We aren't smart enough to know which is correct; we'll just tell you what it's like and let you decide for yourself.

Consider wearing a tucked-in shirt to help keep you warm in the water, especially in the winter, and take Dramamine or the equivalent if you're prone to seasickness, since the boat will be bobbing the whole time. It'll take 2 hours from showing up at the Hale'iwa Boat Harbor to being on your way to lunch after your adventure. They go out year-round, only dissuaded if the North Shore surf is bigger than 20 feet. They claim that shark no-shows are very rare. Snorkel gear provid-

ed. And remember, this brings new meaning to the phrase, "Keep your arms and legs inside the cage at all times."

AQUARIUM DIVE

Think of this as an adventure for the less adventurous. It's as easy, controlled and safe as you'll ever get to SCUBA diving.

At **Sea Life Park** (259–7933) near the easternmost tip of the island on Hwy 72 (see page 116 for more) you can walk around in their giant aquarium with a diver's helmet attached to an air hose. They'll give you an underwater camera (which you can use to shoot your dry companion outside the glass), and for 15 minutes you'll live with the fishes. It's expensive at $68 (plus $26 to get in the park), but if you've always wanted to breathe underwater with the fish and can't bring yourself to try SCUBA or SNUBA, this is a pretty cool way to go. Those 12 and older can do it.

HAIKU STAIRS

To get to heaven, you don't need to die...just take the stairs. The Haiku Stairs, also known locally as the Stairway to Heaven, is a world-class adventure that presents some of the best views on the island. *How can a stairway be an adventure?* Well, you ain't never seen stairs quite like these before.

Wooden ladders were originally strung up this ridge during WWII to facilitate the creation of a tower anchoring part of a *mile-long* ultra-powerful radio antenna stretching across Haiku Valley. The military would use this antenna to communicate with their ships throughout the Pacific and supposedly into the Indian Ocean. (Their goal, was to have a transmitter so powerful that it could transmit to *submerged submarines in Tokyo*

Bay.) Those ladders—discarded remnants of which are still visible in places—were replaced by a wooden staircase.

Today the stairs are made from sturdy-feeling metal with two very sturdy-feeling handrails. Gloves are nice since you'll be using these railings to take some of the workload off your knees. Though the stairs make for good climbing when dry, rain can complicate things by making the railings slippery. If this happens, *take your time coming down*. A fall from these steps could be fatal.

The stairs start at 520 feet elevation and top out at 2,740 feet, a gain of 2,220 feet using 3,922 stairs. (No, we're not so anal retentive that we counted them—that number comes from the government, although someone painted some of them and counted them at 3848.) Put another way, that's 222 stories of stairs, nearly as high as both of the former World Trade Center towers *combined*. This is a good time to tell you that if you hate heights, this hike might not be for you. There are sections where the stairs are nearly vertical, and words like

intense, spooky and *'okole-squeezer* have been used to describe those stretches. After you've gone up about 10 minutes, try turning around and going down the stairs a bit (sometimes you'll want to face out, sometimes face in). If you already hate this, maybe this is as high as you want to go. The stairs are only wide enough for one person, so when you see traffic coming at you, you'll have to get intimate slipping by one another, or hop over the rail to make way.

There are five large platform landings along the way, with the first one halfway up at the 1,520-foot level. Overlooking all of Kane'ohe, the views are amazing. The elevated H-3 freeway, which was towering *above* you when you started, looks like a kid's miniature race-car set far beneath your feet. The views of the impossibly green mountains and Kane'ohe Bay will melt your heart as effectively as the stairs have been melting away pounds. Even if you decide this is as high as you want to go (after all, the summit is still another 1,200 feet of climbing), this view alone will satisfy many.

Climbing a stairway to heaven...

If you want to keep climbing, take several sips of water and get going. In all, it can take anywhere from an hour of climbing (for insane hard-core climbers) to 3 hours (for mere mortals), and coming down will be faster for most, slower for acrophobics.

There are places where the stairs traverse a knife-edge ridge as wide as a human body—and nothing else. After the second landing the remaining landing platforms come in quicker succession (and include an old cement building along the way). Once at the top (if the clouds are cooperating) you can see both sides of the island, from Waimanalo to the north part of Kane'ohe Bay in front of you, and Honolulu Airport and Pearl Harbor behind you. Winds are usually fierce up here, and clouds often rip in and out in mere moments. If you see any birds up here, they may lay the same egg three times. (You'll have to *visualize* what we mean by that.) There's some shelter up here to escape the wind. If it's cloudy at the top, at least you'll have the unique experience of literally climbing into a cloud.

Once back at the bottom you'll have wobbly legs and a wobbly grin along with the satisfaction of one very cool adventure under you belt.

Access was an awkward subject at press time. The stairway was closed way

Keep puffing, only 3,822 steps to go.

back in 1987 after some profoundly stupid vandals destroyed two sections. Now repaired, the city was preparing to reopen them as we went to press. Access would go through the Hawaii State Hospital behind Windward Community College on Keaahala Road. (See map on page 68.) They contemplated a small fee. The county was also working to open another access at the end of Kuneki Road. (See same map.) We hate to leave you hanging like this and we *despise* vague directions, but this adventure is just too juicy not to mention here, and we're taking a leap of faith that it'll be open shortly after we go to press. It was either that or don't mention it at all, and we didn't want to do that. We'll make sure our Web site (www.wizardpub.com) stays current on this. You can also call the managing director of the county parks department at 527–6634 to check on the status or register your opinion as to whether it should be open.

WA'AHILI RIDGE TO MT. OLYMPUS

Why put a ridge hike in the Adventures section? Simple. It's fairly tough (2,600 feet of climbing and 5¾ miles round trip), there are steep areas where you can slip, and there are numerous places where a wrong step could be fatal. Yup, that'll do it. But it also rewards you with a dramatic view of the windward side—from Coconut Island in Kane'ohe Bay to Bellows Beach south of Kailua—if the clouds are cooperating.

You'll start at an elevation of 1,030 feet, and your objective is at 2,486 feet. Therefore, you'll read in other places that there's about 1,500 feet of climbing. Yeah, you wish! What people seem to forget is that when a climbing-type trail undulates up and down, every downhill section on the way up to your goal means you have to gain that elevation three times. Once initially, once to regain it after a downhill, and again climbing *up* that downhill on the way back.

Right after the trailhead there's an unmarked fork; you'll take the left one. The trail is hot and windless in the beginning, and vegetation blocks all views. You'll start climbing right away, then promptly lose much of the elevation you just sweated for. Get used to it. There will be some super steep sections followed by infuriating descents.

Keep on eye out on the left for some awesome views behind you of Honolulu. If you're afraid of heights, you'll hate some of the stretches where a narrow ridge trail straddles your demise on both sides. You'll probably also dislike some of the rockface scrambles. A couple of side trails merely lead to power poles.

Unfortunately, you can't often see the summit you're striving for, so you'll start to silently threaten it. *Those clouds better not be surrounding that summit, grumble, grumble…*

The intersection of the Kolowalo Trail (which goes left; you'll go right) also should have a warning sign saying the trail is unmaintained from this point. Sure enough, it'll get a bit rougher from here (but it's impossible to miss since you stay on a ridge). Some steep climbing stretches make having a rope a good idea (for the return). You can loop it around a tree to help you down, then pull on one side at the bottom. The last part is especially steep, slippery and there's not much to grab. If it's raining, you're screwed—simple as that. Either way you may choose to slide back down on your 'okole during your return. Long pants aren't a bad idea as they'll also protect your legs from the ferns that sometimes scratch at them during the second half of the trail.

Though your legs may still be shaking, stop on your way down from Mt. Olympus to admire the view of Honolulu.

Once at the top the view truly is Olympian, though not as expansive as from the Hawaiiloa Ridge Trail. Keep heading to your right along the ridge for a better opening. Then ponder whether you want to scramble that last little saddle to the actual summit, or simply drink in the view from this part of the Ko'olaus while remembering all those downhill sections (which are now *uphill* sections) that now await.

It'll take most people at least 6 hours to complete this trip. To get to the trailhead from H-1 going west, take the King Street exit (25A), turn left under the highway onto Waialae Avenue, then turn left onto St. Louis Drive. After lots of winding, just before St. Louis ends, turn right onto Peter Street, then turn left onto Ruth Place and head into the Wa'ahila Ridge State Recreation Area. Park in the lot and look for the trailhead. See driving map on page 62. If you're coming from Waikiki, take McCully out of Waikiki, right on Kapiolani, which becomes Waialae, left on St. Louis and follow the directions above.

NIGHT SNORKEL AT HANAUMA BAY

There you are, swimming in the ocean with an inky black sky full of stars. The only source of light is your waterproof flashlight slicing through the ocean like a light saber from *Star Wars*. Your beam cuts across a school of needlefish attracted to your light, then rests on a parrotfish snoozing in its nightly made cocoon. While it's true that snorkeling at Hanauma Bay wouldn't normally be considered an adventure, doing it at night is an entirely different matter.

Here's the deal: Hanauma Bay closes at 7 p.m. nightly, except on Saturdays when they keep it open until 10 p.m. And on those Saturday nights it's sparsely used. You can rent snorkel gear and waterproof flashlights down at the beach, or bring your own. (Their lights are a bit weak. If you're thinking of buying your own light, Longs Drugs at Ala Moana often sells powerful scuba lights for around $50 that use 8 D-cell batteries. Also look at the Wal-Mart/Sam's Superblock just outside of Waikiki on Keeaumoku.)

Although some of the day-shift fish are noticeably absent, it's fun looking for them in crevices and stumbling upon their night-shift co-workers. Bring something warm to wrap up in after your snorkeling since you won't have the sun to help out. Then head to the nearest restaurant in Hawai'i Kai—you'll be starving. (We often hit Kona Brewpub in Koko Marina for their pizza after night snorkeling here.)

SWIMMING WITH DOLPHINS

Although it's not exactly a nail-biting event, we couldn't call *hanging with dolphins* anything but an adventure. And although it's marketed toward kids, when we've been there, the majority of customers were adults.

Two companies offer this—**Dolphin Quest** (739–8918) and **Sea Life Park** (259–7933)—creating two radically different experiences. We brought along our 15-year-old nephew as a "consultant," and the verdict from all of us was unanimous—Dolphin Quest is a *far* better experience.

This is an up close and personal dolphin experience. You'll even don masks to watch underwater as they swim by you. And you'll touch them to your heart's content. The only thing you won't do is get pulled through the water by them (our nephew's only complaint with Dolphin Quest since they do that at Sea Life Park). The trainers' love and affection for these animals is obvious. Dolphin Quest's dolphins live in a much nicer world than they do at Sea Life Park. Dolphin Quest is located at the Kahala Mandarin, 15 minutes east of Waikiki. The same outfit does this on the Big Island, Bermuda and Tahiti, and for most of the year it's a good idea to reserve this a month in advance.

By the light of the moon—and their underwater flashlights—snorkelers explore the alien world of Hanauma Bay at night.

For $129 adults will spend about 25 minutes in the water with these mammals. For $189 you get the same amount of water time plus a half-hour on the dock learning more about them. Kids 5–12 years old have a 2-hour program for $154—10–15 minutes with the dolphins in the water and the rest at the beach, with some stingrays and other education experiences.

Sea Life Park has two programs—a $55 short program where interaction is minimal, and a $110 program where you'll get pulled through the water by them. For what it's worth, the dolphins didn't seem as healthy or happy here. (Granted, that's a super-subjective observation and only our admittedly untrained opinion.) And the swimming pool-like enclosures were smaller. The experience didn't feel as intimate as it did at Dolphin Quest—more like being processed. And, of course, you also have

to pay an additional $25 to get into the park.

RULE YOUR OWN ISLAND

If you ever wanted to be the master of your your own island kingdom, you can either start a revolution here in Hawai'i (hey, if you plan to lower our state taxes, we may join you) or you can simply do it this way: There's an island called Mokoli'i (AKA Chinaman's Hat) that's 614 yards offshore from Kualoa Beach Park near Kane'ohe. (We were in a particularly precise mood that day, so we measured it with a golfing rangefinder—*definitely* a par 5.) Anyway, this island can be yours—just bring your mask, fins, and make sure you eat your Wheaties that day.

During the swim over we've never experienced any particularly strong currents, though we don't fully understand the tidal mechanics at this part of the bay, so it's possible it could happen. Your trip over should be *partially* protected by an offshore reef. If the seas are

It's hard to say who's mugging for the camera—the dolphin or the person.

First step to ruling your own island—find one that's uninhabited.

calm, there's a small sandy beach on the back side of the island around the left (north) point. Otherwise, just come ashore at the nearest point and scramble up the rocks. Once on your island you can wander around the bottom portion along faint trails. You'll need shoes; either water shoes or you can stuff your regular shoes in a garbage bag and hope it doesn't leak. If you want to climb to the top, the best "trail" (such as it is) begins at the shoreline going up at the part of the island closest to O'ahu, to the right of a bare dirt spot. The second part of the climb is ridiculously steep—scramble to the peak at 206 feet while holding on for dear life. Otherwise, just hang around near the lower levels and pass new laws or whatever it is that new rulers do. Your kingdom may be invaded by kayakers from Kualoa Ranch. (But remember, only those who swam here can truly be rulers.)

As a fallback, if your conquest of Chinaman's Hat isn't possible, Goat Island (see page 149) is a worthy candidate for occupation.

NIGHT SHIPWRECK DIVE

Perhaps simple SCUBA dives seem too tame for your adventurous blood. Fair enough. How about diving a shipwreck—at night? It's hard to describe the feeling of discovery that you experience when the top of a ship—even one sunk just for divers—suddenly falls across your flashlight beam cutting through the darkness. There are several wrecks doting the island (see SCUBA on page 200 for more). The biggest problem you'll have is arranging your dive. Companies usually do these when they have an advance open water class, and you can tag along with them, but you'll need to call them in advance to coordinate. **Ocean Concepts** (677-7975), **Aaron's Dive Shop** (262-2333) and **O'ahu Dive Center** (263-7333) do this dive the most.

The dive lights they use are usually not the best. We prefer bright lights—those that take 4 or 8 D-cell batteries. If they won't provide you with a good light, consider splurging and buying one to enhance the experience.

It's hard to beat this romantic table at Le Mer.

By their very nature, restaurant reviews are the most subjective part of any guidebook. Nothing strains the credibility of a guidebook more. No matter what we say, if you eat at enough restaurants here, you will eventually have a dining experience directly in conflict with what this book leads you to believe. All it takes is one person to wreck what is usually a good meal. You've probably had an experience where a friend referred you to a restaurant using reverent terms, indicating that you were about to experience dining ecstasy. And, of course, when you go there, the food is awful and the waiter is a jerk. There are many variables involved in getting a good or bad meal. Is the chef new? Was the place sold last month? Was the waitress just released from prison for mauling a customer? We

truly hope that our reviews match your experience. If they don't (or even if they do), please drop us a line. Readers help us *tremendously* in keeping tabs on the restaurants, and we read and digest (so to speak) every e-mail.

We often leave out restaurant hours of operation because they change so frequently that the information would be immediately out of date. These decisions are usually made quite capriciously in Hawai'i. If you're going to drive a long way to eat at an establishment, it's best to call first. Restaurants that stand out from the others in some way are highlighted with this ONO symbol.

In some restaurants around the island you'll see guidebook recommendation plaques, guidebook door stickers and signed guidebooks, but you won't see ours. The reason? We *never* tell them when we're there. We review everything on the island *anonymously*. We're more interested in being treated like everyone else than in copping a free meal. How could you trust our opinion if the restaurant *knew* who we were?

By their reviews, many guidebooks lead you to believe that *every* meal you eat in Hawai'i will be a feast, the best food in the free world. Frankly, that's not our style. O'ahu, like anywhere else, has ample opportunity to have lousy food served in a rotten ambiance by uncaring waiters.

There are *tons* of restaurants on O'ahu, and we could only include so many. If you have a favorite you want to recommend, send us an e-mail and we'll check it out. We love finding new places.

For each restaurant, we list the price *per person* you can expect to pay. It ranges from the least expensive entrées to the most expensive, plus a beverage and usually an appetizer. You can spend more if you try, but this is a good guideline. *The price excludes alcoholic beverages since this component of a meal can be so variable.* Obviously, everyone's ordering pattern is different, but we thought that it would be easier to compare restaurants using actual prices than if we used symbols like different numbers of dollar signs or drawings of forks or whatever to differentiate prices between restaurants.

When we give **directions** to a restaurant, *mauka side* of highway means "toward the mountain" (or away from the ocean). The shopping centers we mention are on the maps to that area.

Most restaurants don't care how you dress. A few discourage tank tops and bathing suits. Some restaurants have dress codes requiring **resort wear**, meaning covered shoes and collared shirts for men (nice shorts are *usually* OK), dressy sportswear or dresses for women. Only a few require jackets.

It's legal to bring your own alcohol to restaurants in Hawai'i, and many restaurants, especially inexpensive ones, have no objections to letting you B.Y.O.B.

Local food can be difficult to classify. Basically, local food combines Hawaiian, American, Japanese, Chinese, Filipino and several other types and is (not surprisingly) eaten mainly by locals.

Some restaurants have the annoying and presumptuous habit of including the tip in the bill automatically. Be on the alert for it, or you may double-tip. And what if you get horrible service and don't *want* to tip? Then you're left in the awkward position of making them remove it.

Dining at the resorts is expensive, but you probably aren't being gouged as much as you think because their costs are exorbitant. One resort GM we know confided that they had over $7 million in revenue for their food and beverage department one year, but only made $100,000 in profit. (And this was the first year they had ever made *any* profit on food.)

When we mention **parking**, you should assume it'll cost. Free parking is uncommon and will be mentioned when it's available.

Many of the restaurants in the Waikiki area make their entrées available to delivery services, such as Room Service in Paradise (941–3463). For around $5 (depends on where you're staying) they'll pick up your order and bring it to you, which can be *waaay* convenient.

Below are descriptions of various island foods. Not all are Hawaiian, but this might be of assistance if you encounter unfamiliar dishes.

ISLAND FISH/SEAFOOD

Ahi–Tuna; raw in sashimi or poke, also seared, blackened, baked or grilled; good in fish sandwiches. Try painting ahi steaks with mayonnaise, which *completely* burns off when BBQ'd but seals in the moisture. You end up tasting only the moist ocean steak. Generally most plentiful April through September.

Lobster–Hawaiian spiny lobster is quite good; also called "bugs" by lobster hunters. Maine lobster kept alive on the Big Island are also available.

Mahimahi–Deep ocean fish also known as a dolphinfish; served at lu'aus; very common in restaurants. Sometimes tastes fishy (especially if frozen), which can be offset in the preparation.

Marlin–Tasty when smoked, otherwise can be tough; the Pacific Blue Marlin (kajiki) is available almost year round.

Monchong–Excellent tasting deepwater fish, available year round. Usually served marinated and grilled.

Onaga–Also known as a ruby snapper; excellent eating in many preparations.

Ono–Wahoo; *awesome* eating fish and can be prepared many ways; most plentiful May through October. Ono is also the Hawaiian word for delicious.

Opah–Moonfish; excellent eating in many different preparations; generally available April through August.

'Opakapaka–Crimson snapper; great tasting fish cooked several ways. Common October through February.

'Opihi–Using a specialized knife, these must be pried off rocks at the shoreline, which can be hazardous. Best eaten raw mixed with salt.

Poke–Fresh raw fish or octopus (tako) mixed with seaweed (limu), sesame seed and other seasonings and oil.

Shutome–Swordfish; dense meat that can be cooked several ways. Most plentiful March through July.

Shrimp–Kekaha shrimp or prawns are farm-raised on Kaua'i and are excellent.

LU'AU FOODS

Chicken lu'au–Chicken cooked in coconut milk and taro leaves.

Haupia–Coconut milk custard. Tasty, but too much will give you the...*ahem*.

Hawaiian sweet potatoes–Purple inside; not as sweet as mainland sweet potatoes but very flavorful.

Kalua pig–Pig cooked in an underground oven called an imu, shredded and mixed with Hawaiian sea salt (outstanding!).

Lomi salmon–Chilled salad consisting of raw, salted salmon, tomatoes and two kinds of onions.

Pipi Kaula–Hawaiian-style beef jerky.

Poi–Steamed taro root pounded into a paste. It's a starch that will take on the taste of other foods mixed with it. Consider dipping your pipi kaula in it. (Now *that* sounds bad if you don't read it right.) Visitors are encouraged to try it at least once so they can badmouth it with authority.

OTHER ISLAND FOODS

Apple bananas–A smaller, denser, smoother texture than regular (Williams) bananas and a bit tangy.

Barbecue sticks–Teriyaki-marinated pork, chicken or beef pieces barbecued and served on bamboo sticks.

Bento–Japanese box lunch.

Breadfruit–Melon-sized starchy fruit; served baked, deep fried, steamed or boiled. Definitely an *acquired* taste.

Crackseed–Chinese-style spicy preserved fruits and seeds.

Guava–About the size of an apricot or plum. The inside is full of seeds and tart, so it is rarely eaten raw. Used primarily for juice, jelly or jam.

Hawaiian supersweet corn–The finest corn you ever had, even raw. We'll lie, cheat, steal or maim to get it fresh. Kahuku-grown corn is often available from stands around the North Shore.

Huli huli chicken–Hawaiian BBQ style.

Ka'u oranges–Big Island oranges. Usually, the uglier the orange, the better it tastes.

Kim chee–A Korean relish consisting of pickled cabbage, onions, radishes, garlic and chilies.

Kona coffee–Grown on the Kona coast of the Big Island. Smooth, mild flavor. Better than Kaua'i coffee.

Kulolo–Steamed taro pudding. (Tasty.)

Laulau–Pork, beef or fish wrapped in taro and ti leaves, then steamed. (You don't eat the ti leaf wrapping.)

Liliko'i–Passion fruit.

Loco moco–Rice, meat patty, egg and gravy. A hit with cholesterol lovers.

Lychee–A reddish, woody peel that is discarded for the sweet, white fruit inside. Be careful of the pit. Good, small seed (or chicken-tongue) lychees are so good, they should be illegal.

Macadamia nut–A large, round nut.

Malasada–Portuguese donut dipped in sugar. Best when served hot.

Manapua–Steamed or baked bun filled with meat.

Mango–Bright orange fruit with yellow pink skin. Distinct, tasty flavor.

Manju–Cookie filled with a sweet center.

Musubi–Cold steamed rice, sliced Spam rolled in black seaweed wrappers.

Papaya–Melon-like, pear-shaped fruit with yellow skin; best eaten chilled. Good at breakfast. Don't eat too much or you'll...be sticking close to home.

Plate lunch–An island favorite as an inexpensive, filling lunch. Consists of "two-scoop rice," a scoop of macaroni salad and some type of meat, either beef, chicken or fish. Sometimes called a box lunch. Great for picnics.

Portuguese sausage–Pork sausage, highly seasoned with red pepper. Tastes weird to some people.

Pupu–Appetizer, finger foods or snacks.

Saimin–Noodles cooked in either chicken, pork or fish broth. Word is peculiar to Hawai'i. Local Japanese say the dish comes from China. Local Chinese say it comes from Japan.

Sea salt–Excellent (and strong) salt distilled from seawater.

Shave ice–A block of ice is "shaved" (*never* crushed) into a ball with flavored syrup poured over the top. Best served with ice cream on the bottom. Very delicious.

Smoothie–Usually papaya, mango, frozen passion fruit and frozen banana, but almost any fruit can be used to make this milkshake-like drink. Add milk for creaminess.

Taro–Found in everything from enchiladas to breads and rolls to taro chips and fritters. Tends to color foods purple. Has lots of fluoride for your teeth.

WAIKIKI AMERICAN

Included in this category are **Pacific Rim** (sort of a fusion of American and various countries around the Pacific, including Hawaiian and Asian) and **Seafood**. This is because so many restaurants on O'ahu blend these categories together and it just doesn't make sense to try to separate them.

A special note on breakfast:

Many of the resorts in Waikiki will be happy to hose you with sickeningly overpriced breakfasts, often buffets, with the assumption that you won't want to venture too far first thing in the morning. $15–$20 breakfast buffets of mediocre food, or $8–$13 pancakes are common. Our philosophy is if you're gonna get your pockets picked in the morning, let it at least be at an oceanfront location, where the sounds of the surf might drown out the groans of fellow patrons discovering that the check isn't really a typo after all. We've tried to present you with viable options to the usual hotel fleece job.

Banyan Veranda
2365 Kalakaua Ave. • 922–3111

If you're gonna get overcharged for breakfast, this is a good place to do it. The setting is perfect—surrounding a century-old banyan tree next to the sand at Waikiki. You'll get soaked for **$23** for a semi-fixed menu of unremarkable food (good service, though). But what a great feeling this location conveys—as long as you don't look at the bill. At the Sheraton Moana Surfrider. They also have a Sunday brunch for **$39**. There's a breakfast and lunch buffet on the other side of the courtyard called the **Beachside Café** for **$20**; their dinner buffet is **$35** and changes nightly.

Beach Bar Sheraton Moana
2365 Kalakaua Ave. • 922–3111

This is the perfect beach bar location. Sure, service is scant and drinks are expensive (good mai tais, though), but the intimacy with the beach is great. Look for the corner table on the left side. Burgers and such also available. **$5–$15** for lunch. At the Sheraton Moana Surfrider Hotel next door to the Waikiki Beach Center.

Buzz's Steak & Lobster
225 Saratoga Rd. • 923–6762

ONO Buzz's has been around Waikiki since 1957. It's a bit worn-looking, but overall, they do a pretty good job. Dinner includes the small but well-considered salad bar and soup (love their vegetable beef soup when they have it), so you might be able to pass on the appetizers. Consider the Hawaiian ono steak—marinated overnight. In general they do better with steak than seafood. The ONO rating was a squeaker—it's not world class, but it's reliable at dinner, overpriced at breakfast. Good mai tais. On Saratoga Road near Kalia—park underneath. **$7–$10** for breakfast, **$8–$13** for lunch, **$18–$35** for dinner.

Cheeseburger in Paradise
2500 Kalakaua Ave. • 923–3731

A bamboo-laden restaurant with a south seas/Caribbean atmosphere named in honor of a Jimmy Buffet song (who responded by suing them). The burgers are fine—nothing special. Their best attribute is their tasty fries or the chili cheese fries. Huge salads available. Lots of decent tropical drinks. In short, an OK choice. **$9–$20** for lunch and dinner. At Kalakaua and Kealohilani. They also have a location (with parking) at the corner of Ala Moana and Kalakaua.

Cheesecake Factory
2301 Kalakaua Ave. • 924–5001

ONO A ridiculously easy restaurant to like—if you don't mind waiting. Their menu is all over the place. You can bring your Thai grandmother here and she'd love it. (We'd crawl though hot coals for the Thai lettuce wraps.) Their Italian is also good; Uncle Vito will love it. (We brought an Italian relative here, and she was impressed with the farfalle.) And the factory burrito grande is huge and *delicioso*. Plus there's seafood, exceptionally good sandwiches, steak and lots of salads. This is a chain restaurant, and we find it amazing that they can serve 1,000 dinners a night in this 14,500-square foot restaurant and keep the quality up, but they do. Oh, and the cheesecakes...three dozen that'll rock your world. Portions are very generous—consider sharing an appetizer. The atmosphere is noisy. The only hitch is that you won't be the only one trying to eat here. Waits can be unacceptably long; 30–60 minutes is common—sometimes more—and they don't accept reservations. (If you eat between lunch and dinner, you probably won't have to wait.) If you see one of the tall tables in the bar open up, grab it and hand in your beeper. **$11–$25** for lunch and dinner. In the Royal Hawaiian Shopping Center. You get two hours of parking validation at the Royal Hawaiian.

Duke's Canoe Club
2335 Kalakaua Ave. • 922–2268

ONO As legendary as its namesake here in the islands, Duke's has the sort of dreamy atmosphere that's synonymous with Waikiki, and it's one of our favorite places to eat breakfast. Some of the tables overlook a pool, some overlook the beach. Most, however, overlook his famous surf spot, since the restaurant is next to the beach. (Duke Kahanamoku was the sport's first ambassador, the guy who introduced surfing to the American mainland.) Koa wood is everywhere, and the ambiance, though a bit loud, is pleasing. As for the food, it's dependably well-prepared. Fresh fish, steak, pizzas, sandwiches and burgers. Many items have an Asian or

Pacific twist. You can eat at the restaurant tables or the barefoot bar; each has separate menus. The breakfast buffet with an omelette station, at **$10.50**, is a no-brainer to recommend. What a great way to start the day. Lunch is either a **$10.50** buffet or off the menu for **$8–$15**. Dinner is **$20–$30**. Consider the fish sautéed and herb crusted—excellent! And the cold smoked marlin makes a good appetizer. Try the huge hula pie for dessert. Reservations recommended for dinner.

Hale Koa
2055 Kalia Rd. • 955–0555

ONO The best kept secret on Waikiki Beach is this: Although Hale Koa is a military hotel restricted to active duty and retired military, a little-known loophole in the rules allows *anyone* from the beach to walk onto their property and eat at their restaurant. This means the cheap food (with no sales tax) is available to *you*. So if you're irritated at the thought of $12 burgers at other resorts lining Waikiki, head over here and pay $3. Burgers, hot dogs, chicken sandwiches and similar items at the cheapest prices around. There's one snack bar by the pool and another one deeper into the resort. Grab a bite, plop yourself onto the beach and pat yourself on the back for your ingenuity. Behind the hedge at the Hale Koa, the second to last resort on the west side of Waikiki (at the widest part of the beach). **$3–$6** for lunch and dinner.

Hanohano Room
2255 Kalakaua Ave. • 922–4422

ONO Even if the food weren't great, this would be a compelling restaurant for one reason: It has one of the grandest views in all

Waikiki. You're on the 30th floor overlooking half of Waikiki and a giant glass wall is your gateway to the scene. And the view is still jaw-dropping once the night consumes Waikiki, because the warmth of the sun is replaced by the lights of the town. The service is good, though we have experienced some snobbery from waiters. Food is seafood and steak with mostly good results. Reservations are recommended, and collared shirts are requested for men. At the Sheraton Waikiki. **$35–$60** for dinner.

Hau Tree Beach Bar
2005 Kalia Rd. • 949–4321

ONO You're at the beach and you want a little pizza and a beverage (perhaps an adult beverage). You want to eat it on the sand. This is a good place to do it. Pizzas are made by Round Table, take less than 10 minutes and are pretty good. Beverages are available in plastic to go. (See COCKTAILS IN WAIKIKI on page 56 for more on this issue.) What more could you ask for? **$8–$10** or more for lunch. They close at 6 p.m. At the Hilton Hawaiian Village at the extreme northwest end of Waikiki Beach.

Hy's Steak House
2440 Kuhio Ave. • 922–5555

ONO A wonderfully elegant steak house that serves the best steak on the island, *bar none*. They clearly use top-notch ingredients and their preparation skills are superb. The excellent steak selection is augmented by some seafood, including lobster. The staff seems happy and relaxed, not stuffy. (They wear tuxedos, but you'll be fine in collared shirts and long pants.) The glassed-in grill room is a beautiful addition to an upscale yet comfortable atmosphere with music some nights.

Overall, though the price is almost as high as Morton's, we don't feel gouged here and look forward to re-reviewing whenever we can justify the price. **$35–$55** for dinner. Reservations recommended. Valet parking only. On Kuhio Avenue near Uluniu.

Islander Coffee House
247 Lewers St. • 971–6621

ONO An old-style Waikiki breakfast house that's loud, has no view, gives somewhat brusque service, but it's reliable and reasonably priced. We gave it an ONO for the value. Huge breakfast menu consisting of the usual suspects. You can get two eggs, bacon, hash browns, biscuits and gravy for around **$6**—hard to beat—and you can order breakfast all day. Lunch is burgers, sandwiches, chicken, steak and some pasta. **$3–$8** for breakfast, **$6–$13** for lunch and dinner. On Lewers Street on the ocean side of the Don Ho Street intersection.

Kuhio Beach Grill
2552 Kalakaua Ave. • 921–5171

Let's see…Pancakes for over $11, toast is $2.25, omelettes for $12 or a breakfast buffet for $18. Must be right on the beach, right? No! Despite the name, the restaurant is essentially in a hole. You can't see diddly from here except people's legs as they're walking by. You'd be hard pressed to find a worse choice for breakfast in Waikiki given the ridiculous prices. Dinner is steak, seafood and pizzas for **$20–$40**. At the Waikiki Beach Marriott.

M's Oceanfront Restaurant
2136 Kalakaua Ave. • 971–1766

ONO OK…we lied. Forgive us. It's not *really* called M's. If we called it by its real name—*McDon-*

ald's—you'd never read this review. But these golden arches, on Kalakaua and Liliuokalani Street, are across the street from Kuhio Beach. Grab your McMuffin and coffee and take it to one of the beachside tables. Two people—**$10**—eat on the beach. Yeah, works for us. A similar option at "Royal Burger" (ahem, Burger King) exists at Kalakaua and Ohua Street.

Mai Tai Bar at The Royal Hawaiian
2259 Kalakaua Ave. • 931–8383
A good place for an afternoon cocktail since it's right next to the beach. (Oddly, their mai tais are wildly inconsistent—sometimes way too sweet, sometimes like gasoline.) Nothing's great here. Not the food (overpriced pizza and burgers), not the service and not the drinks. (Overall, we've had bad luck with their tropical drinks here, though out of a sense of duty we'll keep trying.) But what a great location to overpay. At the Royal Hawaiian Hotel, Waikiki. **$13** burgers and **$10** salads—that's the pricing scheme here.

Moose McGillycuddy's
310 Lewers St. • 923–0751
A pretty hoppin' place at night with live music and dancing upstairs. The food is ordinary pub food—nothing special. Burgers, sandwiches and lots of pupus (appetizers) at lunch, add some Mexican, chicken and beef at dinner. They have a long happy hour from 4–8 p.m. Go for the music and night life, not for the food. **$7–$10** for breakfast (unless you order their *12-egg* omelette for $19), **$7–$12** for lunch, **$7–$15** for dinner. On Lewers Street just mauka (toward the mountain) of Kalakaua.

Ocean House
2169 Kalia Rd. • 923–2277
 It's so nice when you have a restaurant with a beach-front location, good food and good service that doesn't soak you on prices. Don't get us wrong. It's not cheap, but you get your money's worth here. It's mostly seafood with some steak, and the seafood selection is impressive with portions that are more than generous. (Their awesome coconut lobster skewers make a wonderful appetizer for two.) Flavor combinations are well-chosen and commensurate with more expensive restaurants. An easy place to recommend. **$20–$35** for dinner. At the Outrigger Reef Hotel at Kalia and Beachwalk. Reservations recommended.

Ocean Terrace
2255 Kalakaua Ave. • 931–8383
A nice beachside location, but it's overpriced. The morning fruit medley is $14, and pancakes are $10.50, so it's almost tempting to go with the buffet for **$19**. Indoor tables aren't as good as the outdoor (smoking) tables, which will probably require a wait. In general, you can do better, but if you don't mind overpaying, you'll certainly like the views. **$13–$20** for breakfast, lunch is a buffet for **$18**. Dinner buffets are usually prime rib and fish for **$32**, but it changes slightly each night. À la carte also available. At the Sheraton Waikiki at 2255 Kalakaua Avenue.

Oceanarium
2490 Kalakaua Ave. • 921–6111
You decide to open a restaurant in ultra-competitive Waikiki. If you don't have a killer beachfront location, how can you stand out? Answer: Build a 3-story, 280,000 gallon saltwater aquarium, stock it with enormous stingrays, reef fish and maybe a shark or two. At noon and 1 p.m. each day you send in a scuba diver

to feed the fish. Then spread the tables around this ultimate restaurant eyecandy. The results are impossible to resist. The food's acceptable. Breakfast buffet for $15, lunch is off the menu seafood (which we felt a little guilty ordering since their friends might see through the glass), burgers, steak, chicken and salads. Dinner is a prime rib and seafood buffet for $30 or a light dinner menu. We might not have given them an ono without the fish tank, but its inclusion makes this place a winner. Service is friendly. Upstairs is a more upscale steak and seafood restaurant called **Neptune's Garden (922–1233)**, but the views at the tank's top aren't as good, and the prices upstairs are $25–$40. Oceanarium is a perfect place for breakfast and lunch, and you can usually get a table without a reservation then (but you might want to make them anyway). Dinner reservations are recommended. In the Pacific Beach Hotel on Liliuokalani near Kalakaua. If you have something special (proposing marriage, birthday, etc.), they'll lower a sign about it into the tank if you ask 'em to. **$9–$18** for lunch, **$25–$40** for dinner.

Pâtisserie
2168 Kalia Rd. • 922–4974
A place for pastries, coffee or scrambled eggs on toast for breakfast, sandwiches for lunch. It'll do in a pinch, but it's not stellar. On Beachwalk Street at Kalia, and at Ohana Waikiki Surf Hotel. **$4–$6**. Opens at 6:30 a.m.

Perry's Smorgy
250 Lewers St. • 922–8814
2380 Kuhio Ave. • 926–0184

ono All buffets all the time. The food isn't exactly gourmet, but you can't beat the price, and you can

keep eating till you're tired. On Lewers Street and Don Ho Street, and at the corner of Kuhio and Kanekapolei. (The Kuhio location has a scenic, outdoor courtyard—an unusual luxury for such a good price.) **$6** for breakfast, **$7** for lunch, **$10** for dinner.

Planet Hollywood
2115 Kalakaua Ave. • 924–7877
The food can be good here—but you can't count on it. The menu is steak, ribs, sandwiches, pasta and pizza. The L.A. lasagna is different—it's in tubes and fried. Though you probably won't return again and again, Planet Hollywood is worth a visit once just to see the endless movie eye candy that adorns the walls and ceiling. From the DeLorean used in *Back to the Future* to a statue of Rocky Balboa, the place is stuffed with memorabilia. This chain has come back from the bankruptcy abyss twice and now has fewer than a dozen U.S. restaurants—down from 95 in the late '90s. At 2115 Kalakaua near Beachwalk Street. **$10–$25** for lunch and dinner.

Rainbow Lanai
2005 Kalia Rd. • 949–4321
You won't find a quiet little nook here. They serve 400–600 breakfasts a day. If you get a good table, it'll have nice beach and ocean views. The food's so-so and overpriced. (Think about it: Can *anything* justify $9 hot dogs?) Eat here out of convenience, not desire. Breakfast buffet is **$20** (or you can spend almost that much on off-the-menu items like $14 omelettes), lunch is **$10–$25**, dinner, which is steak and seafood, is **$20–$30** or a buffet for **$30**. At the Hilton Hawaiian Village on the northwest corner of Waikiki Beach.

Shorebird Beach Broiler
2169 Kalia Rd. • 922–2887

ono The sort of place many people are looking for. Excellent location next to a beach without getting hosed on the price. Railing tables are especially good (since you can almost hang your hand onto the sand), but even tables farther back take good advantage of the view. The breakfast buffet is a bargain at $10. Dinner is steak and fish served rare...very rare...OK, raw. You cook it yourself on their enormous grill. Salad included. If you don't feel like cooking (or want to eat from the railing tables), you can order off the lunch menu at dinner, which is sandwiches, burgers, fish and chips or fish tacos. **$10** for breakfast, **$9–$15** for lunch, **$15–$20** for dinner. At the Outrigger Reef Hotel at Kalia Road and Beachwalk.

Surf Room at The Royal Hawaiian
2259 Kalakaua Ave. • 931–8383

ono Prices are high here, but the quality is first rate. Their breakfast buffet, though **$26**, actually comes pretty darned close to justifying that price (if one can ever justify a $26 breakfast). Aside from the perfect outdoor beachside location, the buffet selection is vast and the ingredients are top of the line. From the omelette station to the fresh pancake and waffle station to the three kinds of lox, huge pastry selection, fresh fruit, made-to-order smoothies, it's hard to leave disappointed—or hungry. $25 is a ton for a breakfast buffet, but if you're gonna splurge, do it here. Their off-the-menu items—like the Royal Waffle at $12.25, which should be called the Royal Screw Job—are not as compelling. Lunch is also pricey—it's hard to order a $14 burger with a straight face—but, like

breakfast, the quality is excellent and they have some steak and seafood, as well. **$15–$25** for breakfast and lunch, **$30–$55** for dinner. At the Royal Hawaiian Hotel.

Terrace Grille
2424 Kalakaua Ave. • 923–1234

It's nice to have choices. Breakfast is an overpriced buffet at $17, or you can choose from the overpriced off-the-menu items. Lunch is sandwiches and burgers, soups and salads—not *quite* as overpriced. In short, convenient if staying at the Hyatt, but not worth walking there just for this. **$9–$18** for breakfast, **$9–$15** for lunch.

Tiki's
2570 Kalakaua Ave. • 923–8454

Their trademark is the retro-Hawaiian decor—sort of a '50s look. The food's so-so; not great, not bad, but they tend to over-salt things. Fresh fish, sandwiches, pasta, fish tacos, short ribs, fish and chips and burgers at lunch. Add prime rib, steak and lobster at dinner. Some tables have nice views of the Kapahulu Ponds across the street. They have a butterscotch banana caramel bread pudding that's excellent. Decent at lunch, a touch better at dinner. **$10–$20** for lunch, **$10–$30** for dinner. At the corner of Kalakaua and Paoakalani at the Aston Waikiki Beach Resort.

Trellisses
2500 Kuhio Ave. • 921–5566

This is exactly what comes to mind when we think of a typical resort restaurant. Pricey food that's not bad, but you eat here because you don't want to venture too far. $15 breakfast buffet (fine, but not worth $15) or à la carte for close to that. In the Radisson Hotel. About

$15 for breakfast, $10–$20 for lunch, $20–$35 for dinner.

Tropics Bar & Grill
2005 Kalia Rd. • 949–4321
In the Hilton Hawaiian Village near their pier. With $7 hot dogs (which to be fair *really are* giant) and $3.25 for a small coke, why would you come here? Simple—it's right next to the beach. They also have Round Table personal pizzas and a pretty good selection of tropical drinks. Good smoothies, too. $7–$15 for lunch and dinner.

Wailana Coffee House
1860 Ala Moana Blvd. • 955–1764
A long-time landmark since 1970. Despite the reputation among locals, the food's merely average—nothing more. The breakfast selection is pretty good (check the specials for the best deal). Lunch and dinner (served any time) is a large selection of steak, seafood, burgers, soups, local dishes and salads. At Ala Moana and Kalia in north Waikiki. $5–$9 for breakfast, $7–$14 for lunch and dinner.

WAIKIKI CHINESE

Legend Seafood
2255 Kuhio Ave. • 926–8999
ONO Absolutely epic Chinese seafood and crisp service. A giant menu of common and uncommon but well-conceived Chinese dishes including stir fry, prawns in a taro basket appetizer (*highly* recommended), stuffed duck, tofu stuffed with shrimp and ham, braised whole shark's fin soup, etc. The food is fantastic and the ingredients top quality. We don't want to set the bar too high, but frankly we can't think of a better Chinese dinner we've had in the state. Lunch is

dim sum, which is also good, but if you're looking to treat yourself, go for the dinner. Tucked away in the Waikiki Trade Center on Seaside and Kuhio; park in the garage. $8–$18 for lunch, $13–$25 for dinner (more if you push it or order the shark). Same owner as the Legend in Chinatown.

WAIKIKI FRENCH

Le Mer
2199 Kalia Rd. • 923–2311
ONO One of the most expensive meals you'll find in Waikiki. Most appetizers are a wallet-choking $35. But it also has a dreamy, romantic atmosphere, excellent service and well-crafted French food with local ingredients. A great place to propose to that someone special. Reservations recommended and long sleeves or jackets for men. $50–$130, they also have a 9 course sampler that takes 3 hours and costs $125. In the Halekulani Resort. By the way, this is where the photo at the start of this chapter was taken.

WAIKIKI ITALIAN

Arancino
255 Beachwalk Ave. • 923–5557
ONO A small Italian café with a half-dozen or so pastas and some 12-inch pizzas with thin crust and more traditional Italian toppings. (Pepperoni is not on the menu—you'll have to ask for it.) The prices are reasonable for what you get, and the place is always full by 7 p.m.—often 6 p.m. They're pretty efficient at turning the tables—perhaps too efficient. But with the price vs. food and portions quotient, it's an easy recom-

mend. **$10–$20** for dinner. On Beachwalk, paid parking at the Royal Hawaiian. They also have a location at the Marriott Waikiki Beach.

Matteo's
364 Seaside • 922–5551
Although the food's reasonably good, it's certainly not in line with the prices. It's annoying to pay $30 for an entrée that's worth half that. Pastas, seafood, steak and lobster. The atmosphere is somewhat romantic, though beware that voices carry well here. Ask for a booth. Huge wine selection. At the corner of Seaside and Kuhio in the Marine Surf Hotel. Parking in the nearby garage on Kuhio. **$20–$40** for dinner.

Round Table Pizza & Sports Bar
150 Kaiulani Ave. • 944–1199
(ONO) It's part of the Round Table chain, and they have good pizza that's reliable and not horribly overpriced (for a Waikiki hotel restaurant), plus lots of beers. In the Ohana East Hotel at Kaiulani and Prince Edward. **$8–$13** for lunch and dinner.

Sergio's
2005 Kalia Rd. • 951–6900
A fine selection of pastas and meats (the latter accounting for the higher prices) with pleasing decor and nice views of the Hilton Lagoon from the back tables. The problem is the food. It *reads* well, but results are disappointing. And avoid the appetizers, which seem surprisingly bad. Vast wine list and a huge dessert selection (unusual for an Italian restaurant). In short—overpriced for what you get. In the Hilton Hawaiian Village. **$20–$45** for dinner.

Trattoria
2168 Kalia Rd. • 923–8415
This restaurant has been here since 1970 and has a vast collection of old celeb photos. The pick-your-pasta-and-sauce is a good option with choices such as Salsiccie alla Calabiese (marinara with hot sausage), pesto and five other sauces. The saltimbocca di vitello (veal with rosemary, ham and mozzarella) is good but pretty salty. Lasagna is fairly good but *very* meaty. Consider the cannelloni. The menu's well-rounded, so there's something for everyone. The restaurant layout offers lots of cubby holes, and all tables are not created equally—reservations recommended and ask for a booth. Heavily staffed but not attentive enough in the service department. **$15–$30** for dinner. Although we generally like Trattoria, we withheld our ONO, feeling it's a bit overpriced and over-hyped for what you get. Under the Edgewater Hotel across from the Halekulani and Outrigger Reef hotels.

WAIKIKI JAPANESE

Benihana of Tokyo
2005 Kalia Rd. • 955–5955
Part of the Benihana chain of teppan yaki restaurants (where the food is prepared in front of you by a knife-wielding chef). The sushi is not the best, but the cooking show is kind of fun, and the chefs are sometimes pretty engaging. It's expensive, but if you've never done teppan yaki, it's an interesting experience. Overall, the food's not bad, but not remarkable. Steak, lobster, shrimp and vegetables on a sizzling grill. At the Hilton Hawaiian Village. **$12–$20** for lunch, **$30–$50** for dinner.

Run Sushi & Ramen
2552 Kalakaua Ave. • 923–1700
Sushi's fairly cheap and...tastes fairly cheap. You sit next to a conveyer belt and grab what you like. Tempura and

other dishes for non-sushi lovers. Service is fast, even when ordering off the menu. But the quality of the ingredients doesn't seem impressive. Hey, if you're walking by, we won't dissuade you—just don't walk too far for a meal here. At 2552 Kalakaua at Ohua Street at the Waikiki Beach Marriott, ground level. **$6–$15** for lunch.

Todai Sushi & Seafood
1910 Ala Moana Blvd. • 947–1000

Part of an expanding chain of sushi bars, this is an excellent deal for sushi lovers. They have a *huge* all-you-can-eat lunch buffet for **$15** ($2 more on weekends) and a dinner buffet for **$26–$27**. Kid's prices vary by height (so tell 'em to scrunch down). We're talking 40 kinds of sushi, plus cooked items, including tempura and lobster (at dinner). And they have a great dessert bar. It might not be the best sushi on the planet, but it's good and a great value. At Ala Moana near Ena Road. Pronounced "tow die."

WAIKIKI MEXICAN

Torito's
International Mktplace • 922–4057

A good place for good Mexican comfort food. Simple but tasty tacos, burritos, enchiladas and quesadillas. Grab it to go or use a nearby table at the International Marketplace Food Court. **$5–$9**.

WAIKIKI THAI

Keoni by Keo's
2375 Kuhio Ave. • 922–9888

An odd concept: a Thai/American restaurant with two separate kitchens. Their selection is a bit overwhelming, and you can order any of the dinner items at lunch if you wish. The food is good, especially their Thai items. It's not very hot, so speak up if you like it spicy. The American items include filet mignon, lobster, burgers, pasta, chicken and ribs. With this kind of selection, if you can't find an item that's for you...you're just too darned picky. Full bar. Park at Ohana East off Kuhio for parking validation. At Kuhio and Kaiulani. **$4–$12** for breakfast, (roughly) **$10–$20** for lunch, dinner is **$15–$30** (more for the "complete dinner" selections).

Singha Thai
1910 Ala Moana Blvd. • 941–2898

Pretty impressive Thai food in a beautiful if somewhat busy atmosphere. (There's Thai dancing nightly 7–9 p.m.) The menu is a little different than most Thai restaurants and a bit more limited. They also have a decent number of non-Thai items like steak and veal shank (with an Asian twist, however). Service can be their weak point since the large restaurant capacity—80 indoors and 80 outdoors—can slow things down, and sometimes they drop the ball completely. But the food quality tends to be high, and service disasters are uncommon if not exactly rare. **$18–$38** for dinner. (Desserts are overpriced.) At the corner of Ena and Ala Moana, parking underneath.

WAIKIKI TREATS

Cold Stone Creamery
2166 Kalakaua Ave. • 923–3866
2570 Kalakaua Ave. • 923–1656

In case you're not familiar with this growing chain, they take whatever ice cream you pick, drop it on a frozen slab and mix any number of a dazzling selection of goodies into it. From boring old sprinkles to Butterfinger candy bars, peanut butter, Heath Bars—whatever works for you. They'll smash them up and mix 'em in. The price is uncomfortably high, but you *will* like the results. On Kalakaua at Paoakalani and on Kalakaua between Lewers and Beachwalk. **$3–$7**.

Leonard's
933 Kapahulu Ave. • 737–5591

(ono) The best place on the island to try malasadas (Portuguese donuts). Fresh, hot and insanely good. Get them filled if you want. (We're predictable and usually get chocolate filling.) Technically, it's just outside Waikiki, but close enough. Less than a buck each or $4 for a half dozen. Outside Waikiki on the Diamond Head side on Kapahulu and Charles. They also have a couple of red and white trucks that wander the island. If you see one their malasadas are just as good and made fresh on the trucks.

Waiola Shave Ice & Bakery
525 Kapahulu Ave. • 735–8886

(ono) Also just outside Waikiki, they're the place for shave ice. The fineness of the ice depends on the sharpness of the blade and the pressure, and this place has the finest ice we've ever seen. Frankly, we didn't know you could *make* ice this fine. Add to that the fact that they chill their syrup (keeping it from chunking), and you get an easy-to-recommend shave ice. They also have baked goods. (Check out the delicate almond flakes.) Just mauka of Waikiki on Kapahulu at Herbert. Parking also available at the church across Herbert. **$2–$4**.

HONOLULU AMERICAN

Alan Wong's
1857 King St. • 949–2526

(ono) This is one of those places about which much hype exists. It's one of the *in* places. Sometimes *in* places are good at nothing *but* hype. But not in this case. Simply put, the food's excellent. It's unclassifiable with a Pacific Rim bent. What does that mean? Items range from ginger crusted onaga (snapper), curry seafood, cioppino (one of the few disappointments), steak, an appetizer called da bag (hard to explain but effective), macadamia nut coconut crusted lamb chops (the *best* lamb we've ever had), etc. Menu changes constantly. The restaurant's small but fairly loud. When you make reservations (which you'll need—they even call you back the day before to confirm), ask for a lanai table if possible, which have nice views of Manoa Valley in the distance. If you're a chocolate lover, it's *mandatory* that you get the pricey but insanely good chocolate sampler. (Or get their homemade chocolate bars.) Alan Wong's is pricey, but the food's top notch. **$30–$50** for dinner. Come out of Waikiki on Kalakaua and turn right on King. Look for it on your right.

Bistro at Century Center
1750 Kalakaua Ave. • 943–6500

(ono) Fine dining restaurants sometimes have attitude—but not here. The atmosphere is extremely relaxing and elegant; service is impeccable. The food is outstanding, and, most surprising, portions are more than fair. Sure, it's expensive, but you don't leave feeling gouged. For appetizers consider the diver scallops or the eggplant—both fantastic. Their steak Dianne is incredible, as is the osso bucco—falling off the bone and wonderful. Lamb, duck, venison, steak and fish. This is one of the best restaurants in Honolulu and one we happily re-review as often as the budget allows. **$35–$60**. When you make reservations, ask for a table *not* near the piano—we prefer the booths. Just outside of Waikiki at Kalakaua and Kapiolani. Parking below. Collared shirts and long pants requested.

Brew Moon
1200 Ala Moana Blvd. • 593–0088
An interesting menu of Thai curries, pizzas, burgers, stir fry and salads plus lots of pupus. Beers can be good, but don't count on it. The pizzas have an ultra-thin crust (the heavy black lager beer goes well with it) and can be ordered as an appetizer for two. Overall, the food's mixed. Curries taste canned, but the stir fry is fairly good. Pizzas are fair. Service is too light. *Hey, waiter, come on over and see me sometime.* At Ward Centre. **$10–$20** for lunch, **$20–$30** for dinner.

Bubba Gump Shrimp Co.
1450 Ala Moana Blvd. • 949–4867
A chain of theme restaurants based on the 1994 movie, *Forrest Gump.* (Although you wonder if the founders actually saw the movie since few of the shrimp recipes that Bubba rattled off to Forrest are actually on the menu.) Nonetheless, it's a fun theme that works fairly well. Service can be unresponsive until you remember that you're supposed to turn the pingpong paddle over to where it says, "Stop, Forrest, Stop." (If you never saw the movie, this must sound weird.) Anyway, lots of shrimp dishes, steak, burgers, sandwiches and seafood in a campy atmosphere. Food's not great, but not bad. Beverages include lots of smoothies and tropical

drinks. **$10–$25** for lunch and dinner. In the Ala Moana Shopping Center.

Cabanas Seaside Grill
5000 Kahala Ave. • 739–8770
ONO Breathtakingly expensive. (What else would you call a $14 hot dog?) So why the ONO? Location, location, location. Dinner here is an incredibly romantic treat. Fish is their specialty, and they mostly serve small fish like moi and 'opakapaka and fillet it tableside. Oh, and those tables...they're under cabanas next to soothing Kahala Beach. Less than a dozen cabanas in all, some with more than one table, some with only one. This setting is fantastic and worth the splurge at dinner. (But not at lunch.) They also have lobster, prawns and some beef. The all-day-slow-roast pork is excellent. All items come à la carte and portions are large—often meant for two. Only ding is service—can be slow. **$15–$20** for lunch, **$25–$55** for dinner. Reservations recommended. At the Kahala Mandarin Hotel 15 minutes east of Waikiki on Kahala Avenue. It may get a bit chilly if it's breezy, so dress accordingly.

Dave & Buster's
1030 Auahi St. • 589–2215
ONO A giant, three-story restaurant with the dining room on the bottom floor, a massive game room upstairs and a bar with great views (and pretty generous happy hours) on top. The menu is a good mix of steak, ribs, pasta, fish and chips, burgers, sandwiches, fish, etc. Most items are good and portions tend to be ample. (The grilled wrap with shrimp is an exception and should be avoided.) Service is friendly but sometimes slow, and waits are common at dinner. (They don't take reservations.) **$10–$25** for lunch and

dinner. Lunch specials can bring it down a couple bucks. On Auahi between Kamakee and Ward.

Dixie Grill
404 Ward Ave. • 596–8359
99-016 Kamehameha • 485–2722

(ono) A good 'ol BBQ menu of ribs, pulled pork, beef brisket, fried okra and hush puppies. Most items are good and they have six different BBQ sauces available. (We like the Kansas City sauce best—the Texas sauce is too chili powdery.) Non-BBQ lovers can have fish, burgers and Po'Boys. The décor is a hodge-podge of eye candy, and the service is friendly to the point of being jovial at times. Their 32 oz. mai tais will keep you happy for a while. Live blues on Tuesdays. On Ward Avenue between Queen and Ala Moana. They also have a less convenient (for visitors) location way out in Aiea at 99-016 Kamehameha Hwy. **$10–$20** for lunch and dinner.

Don Ho's Island Grill
Aloha Tower Mrktplace • 528–0807
A pretty good menu of flatboard, thin crust pizzas, pastas and local-style dishes of chicken, fish and shrimp. The restaurant is on the water overlooking the industrial but nonetheless peaceful Honolulu Harbor. And it really is relaxing to see giant container ships passing by. The food is pretty good but not stellar. The seafood platter makes a good appetizer for two, though we've seen the calamari portion of it get pretty chewy. There's live entertainment most nights and a full bar. Thatched roofs add an exotic touch. **$10–$20** for lunch, **$15–$30** for dinner. A couple miles north of Waikiki at the Aloha Tower Marketplace at Ala Moana and Bishop Street. Make *sure* you have them validate.

Gordon Biersch
Aloha Tower Mrktplace • 599–4877

(ono) A well-run restaurant with a nice menu selection of fish (love the garlic and herb crusted mahi mahi), steak, pizzas (which make a nice appetizer for two), great burgers, stir fry, salads and sandwiches. They also brew their own beer here. (The Märzen is excellent.) The views overlook busy Honolulu Harbor, but they're occasionally blocked by a large ship if it parks in front. Good desserts. (Deadly carrot cake.) The lunch menu relies more on sandwiches, pizzas, pasta and stir fry. Live entertainment some nights. Not cheap, but you get your money's worth. **$10–$20** for lunch, **$10–$25** for dinner. A couple miles north of Waikiki at the Aloha Tower Marketplace at Ala Moana and Bishop Street. Make *sure* you have them validate your parking.

Hoku's
5000 Kahala Ave. • 739–8780

(ono) A positively dreamy view of Kahala Beach and the surf rolling in. This, along with an elegant atmosphere and excellent food, make it a worthy, though pricey treat if you can foot the bill. Steak and seafood with Asian-inspired flavors. Lunch is **$20–$30**. Dinner is **$35–$55**. Reservations recommended a week *or more* in advance. At the Kahala Mandarin Hotel 15 minutes east of Waikiki on Kahala Avenue. Collared shirts and long pants required.

John Dominis
43 Ahui St. • 523–0955

(ono) This is one of those restaurants that's off the radar screen of most visitors but is a local favorite. It's an awesome seafood restaurant with a fantastic view. Located at

Kaka'ako Waterfront Park overlooking Kewalo Basin (where most of Waikiki's boats are moored—see map on page 50), the views of the harbor and Waikiki beyond are wonderful at night. They have a nice selection of seafood, including lobster, an excellent oyster bar, a sushi bar and some steak. Even if you don't get one of the coveted tables near the windows, the atmosphere is relaxing and the food is great. The prices sure ain't cheap here, but it's a nice treat overall. **$35–$60** for dinner. Five minutes west of Waikiki. Take Ala Moana, left on Ward, left on Ahui. Reservations recommended.

Kua 'Aina Sandwich
1116 Auahi St. • **591–9133**
66-214 Kamehameha • **637–6067**

A well-known burger joint that makes great burgers (with 1/3 and 1/2 pound patties), nice thin fries and fairly good sandwiches (which are outshined by the burgers). The fries grow on you as you continue to gobble them up. The place can get pretty crowded. **$6–$9** for lunch and dinner. In Ward Village Shops on Auahi Street across from Ward Centre near Kamakee Street in Honolulu. Also in Hale'iwa on Kamehameha Highway across from the Hale'iwa Shopping Plaza.

Morton's Steakhouse
1450 Ala Moana Blvd. • **949–1300**

This is a chain that features *insanely* expensive steaks. Here's how it works: You spend $37 for a steak and you get...a piece of meat. Nothing else. Want veggies? They're $7 extra. Want a potato? It's about $6 extra, and they're rather rigid when it comes to toppings. We went with someone who asked for sour cream and chives and he was told that "we don't offer chives." (Six bucks

for a potato, and they won't sprinkle some measly chives on it?) Service is friendly and competent, but they seem to go for long stretches where they forget about you. Pardon us, but for this kind of money we'd like a bit more attention and perhaps even a bit of... groveling. (You know, where even if you order peanut butter on your steak, it's an *excellent choice, sir.*) **$40–$65** for dinner. In the Ala Moana Shopping Center.

Ryan's
1200 Ala Moana Blvd. • **591–9132**

Very popular with Honolulu office workers. They have 24 beers on tap, tons of good pupus (appetizers) and a menu of seafood, pasta, ribs, pizza and salads. Add to this a vast drink and spirit list and a happenin' feel, and you have a perfect pau hana (after work) place. Some items are unusual (like the excellent grilled raviolis), but a few are disappointing. Only *occasional* bad service brings 'em down. Upstairs at Ward Centre on Auahi and Ward, a few minutes drive from Waikiki. **$12–$25** for lunch and dinner. Free parking in garage.

Zippy's
601 Kapahulu Ave. • **733–3725**
1725 King St. • **973–0877**

Think of it as a local version of Denny's (but better food). Chicken, steak, burgers, pork chops, salads, fish and chili (which is enormously popular with locals—so much so that even local Taco Bells sometimes serve it). Lots of desserts and an in-house bakery. The breakfast menu is not as big, but it's adequate. Zippy's is where a lot of local families eat when they "just feel like eating out" due to its price and consistency—the reasons we gave it an ONO. It ain't fancy, but it's a good deal for the money. **$5–$10** for breakfast, **$7–$14** for lunch and dinner. Dozens of locations, including one just outside of Waikiki at 601 Kapahulu Ave. near Campbell and one at 1725 King St. near McCully.

HONOLULU CHINESE

Legend Seafood
100 N. Beretania St. • 532–1868

(ONO) We love their Waikiki location and don't want to sound like an advertisement for them, but they have the best dim sum on O'ahu, hands down. Servers push different carts around with all kinds of selections, a few of them cooked in front of you, but most are hot from the kitchen. The variety is fantastic. Don't be afraid to ask questions, though the response might be in broken English. This is an eating adventure, and at the end you will have dined on a range of dishes you can't remember. Take your time and don't get hung up on a single cart. Entrées are so cheap that if you don't like one, leave it alone and order from the next cart. It's big and noisy inside and nearly every customer will be local—this is *not* a tourist trap. **$6–$15** for lunch and dinner. At River and Beretania Street. If they're too busy, the **New Empress** (521–5055) upstairs is a reasonable second option. Also, next door is **Legend Vegetarian**. Smaller and lunch only.

HONOLULU ITALIAN

Assaggio
1450 Ala Moana Blvd. • 942–1935

(ONO) Huge lunch and dinner menus, including lots of seafood, pastas, chicken and sandwiches. The ambiance is restful, if slightly dressy. Items like the fish arribatta

(which is good) and stuffed baked eggplant (also good) supplement more expected pasta items. Service is adequate, and it's not too horribly priced at lunch. Ask for a table near the fountain. Dinner also works well here. Note that the ONO is only for the Ala Moana location. We haven't been as pleased with the Kailua or Hawai'i Kai locations. At Ala Moana Shopping Center just outside of Waikiki on Ala Moana Boulevard. (Park near Macy's.) **$11–$25** for lunch, **$15–$27** for dinner. Reservations recommended.

Auntie Pasto's
1099 S. Beretania St. • 523–8855

(ONO) A popular restaurant with both locals and visitors alike. The festive atmosphere is a bit loud. (Tables farthest from the kitchen are the quietest.) The dinner menu is a nice selection of pastas, some calamari, cacciuco (a seafood stew composed of nearly every critter that lives in the ocean—it's pretty good) and eggplant. Try the red pepper calamari appetizer. They have good cavatelli (a ricotta dumpling). Desserts are mixed. The tiramisu is real creamy and the sin pie is as dense and radioactive as plutonium, though somehow somewhat bland...or at least one-dimensional. (Oh, aren't *we* getting pretentious?) But their cannolis are wonderful. Lunch is hot sandwiches and salads. Prices are very reasonable for the quality. At Pensacola and Beretania in downtown Honolulu. **$8–$10** for lunch, **$8–$18** for dinner. No reservations accepted.

Buca di Beppo
1030 Auahi St. • 591–0800

(ONO) This is part of a national chain of "immigrant southern Italian" cooking, and they have one particularly noteworthy attribute—*portions*. Dinner entrées are simply monster-sized. (Lunch is more normal.) If there are only two of you, you can almost certainly share an entrée. For instance, order a plate of pasta and a gigantic mountain becomes your meal. Chicken cacciatore? They use a whole chicken, and with all the ingredients it comes to 7 *pounds*. Meatballs? Expect 'em to be baseball-sized. It's pretty hard to leave this place hungry. For the pizza, consider the spicy arrabbiata—very good with an ultra-thin crust. Try the rum and espresso-soaked tiramisu—a killer! One piece will feed 2 or 3 people. Service is very friendly. When they seat you, they'll often walk you through the kitchen to show you where your next meal is coming from, and you can even eat at the table *inside* the kitchen if you reserve in advance and you're so inclined. This place seats over 400 in a dozen or so rooms. It can be loud, and weekends are a zoo—only eat here during the week. **$7–$11** for lunch, **$10–$20** for dinner. Auahi St. inland of Ala Moana Boulevard between Ward Avenue and Kamakee in Ward Entertainment Center. Reservations recommended.

Palomino Euro Bistro
66 Queen St. • 528–2400

A well-known island restaurant with a well-deserved reputation for quality and atmosphere. It's round, so some tables will have nice views of Honolulu Harbor across the street, and it's expensively appointed inside. Service is generally good but sometimes stretched a bit too thin, causing disappointing delays. But the food…excellent. Try the lobster raviolis—it's hard to believe you'll get filled up with only two raviolis but you will. Same with the pumpkin raviolis. (Consider having them go easy on the onions.) Pasta, prime rib, steak frites, lobster, pizzas, strombolis. We classified them under Italian, but their menu declares that it's "regional American food," whatever that means. The Molten Chocolate Tower is a deadly way to end the meal, or go with the tiramisu. They have a large and particularly well-chosen wine list and a good selection of ports for after dinner, including vintage ports. **$10–$20** for lunch, **$16–$35** (more for lobster) for dinner. A couple miles west of Waikiki—come down Ala Moana, until it becomes Nimitz. After Aloha Tower Marketplace look for Bethel Street. Turn right and pull into the garage for the valet parking. Reservations recommended.

Phillip Paolo's
500 Ala Moana Blvd. • 585–8142
Pasta, Italian sandwiches, 8-inch pizzas for lunch, add steak and seafood for dinner. Quality isn't much to speak of, and their bartending skills are comparable to what you'd expect at a Tibetan monastery. In short, you can do better. In Restaurant Row at Ala Moana and Punchbowl. **$7–$15** for lunch, **$15–$40** for dinner. They also have a dinner buffet for **$17**.

HONOLULU LOCAL

I Love Country Café
451 Piikoi St. • 596–8108
4211 Waialae Ave. • 735–6965

A giant selection of plate lunches, stir fry, burgers, sandwiches, salads, wraps and more. This small, O'ahu chain is wildly popular with locals (you may be the only visitor in here). Low prices, good food for the money, some relatively healthy recipes for many entrées and big portions. What's not to love? **$4–$8** for breakfast, **$6–$9** for lunch and dinner. At

451 Piikoi St. near Kona St. in Honolulu near the far side of Ala Moana Shopping Center. A long walk from Waikiki or a short drive. Also at Kahala Mall (east of Waikiki off H-1).

Kaka'ako Kitchen
1200 Ala Moana Blvd. • 596–7488

(ono) Very popular with locals. A huge menu of local and American items like teriyaki chicken, tempura fish, sandwiches, stir fry, ahi wraps, burgers, salads and a lot more. Reasonable prices for the quality. Their coconut mochi is a wonderful and dense-as-lead dessert, and their pumpkin bread is outrageously pumpkiny. (Is that a word?) Even if you don't eat your meal here, the desserts (to go) are great. On the Auahi Street side of Ward Centre near Kamakee. **$6–$9** for breakfast, **$7–$10** for lunch and dinner.

Sam Choy's Breakfast, Lunch & Crab
580 N. Nimitz • 545–7979

(ono) Everyone who lives in Hawai'i knows who Sam Choy is—he's da *beeg* bugga wit da *beeg* portions. Of his two O'ahu restaurants, this one, in an industrial section of Honolulu, is the better deal. Sometimes consistency is a problem (like undercooked fish), but the recipes are usually excellent and Sam is incredibly creative. (You ought to see what he does with the lowly *tater tot*.) Moi saimin (a giant bowl with noodles, shrimp, teriyaki beef, char sui, egg, spinach, kamaboko and crab) is a good example of a Sam Choy excess with delicious results. The herb-crusted fish is excellent. There's lobster, surf and turf, burgers, ahi salad and more. Portions are usually huge, meaning that prices are fairly reasonable for what you get. Dinner is more geared to fish, crab and lobster, plus some steak and pasta. The restaurant is

pretty big (you know it's big when you have a full-sized boat inside and it doesn't crowd anybody). They brew their own beer here; try a sampler to see which one you like. Their weekend brunches for **$15** are recommended. **$6–$13** for breakfast (love the fisherman's breakfast platter), **$8–$18** for lunch, **$20–$35** for dinner. At 580 N. Nimitz Highway which is about a mile north (Ewa) of the Punchbowl intersection.

Willows
901 Hausten St. • 952–9200

(ono) Old-time O'ahu visitors may be familiar with Willows. It goes back to 1944, when Waikiki was a sleepy, fairly unknown place that had few dining options. The natural springs on the property were incorporated into a beautiful pool. In the '90s it closed and later reopened under different management. Today its pond and waterfall have been cement-lined, and the menu is mostly buffet. But if you're looking to slip (just slightly) out of Waikiki and want a fairly good buffet with local-style flavors such as lau lau, kalua pig, curries and teri chicken, the Willows still works pretty well. The atmosphere is relaxing and peaceful. It's tucked away in a residential neighborhood. From Ala Wai Boulevard take McCully, right on Kapiolani, left on Hausten. **$16** for the lunch buffet (more on weekends), **$26** for dinner. They also have a per-plate menu (kind of hard to explain) in their Rainbow Room.

HONOLULU MEXICAN

Compadres
1200 Ala Moana Blvd. • 591–8307

(ono) A giant menu of standard and unusual Mexican items. There's almost certainly something for everyone. For instance, if you're tired of simple nachos for an appetizer, try their Thai quesadillas—fantastic and certainly unusual. Overall, items are pretty pricey here, but the quality is generally top-notch, and their tequila selection is admirable. (Pretty decent and potent mai tais, too.) Service is usually good, but occasionally inept. In Ward Centre. **$12–$25** for lunch and dinner.

HONOLULU THAI

Payao
500 Ala Moana Blvd. • 521–3511
Disappointing Thai food served by an uncaring staff. Hmm, makes it hard to justify driving to Restaurant Row at Ala Moana and Punchbowl streets. It's also uncharacteristically unkempt for a Thai restaurant. **$15–$15** for lunch, **$10–$20** for dinner.

HONOLULU TREATS

Honolulu Chocolate Company
1200 Ala Moana Blvd. • 591–2997
Expensive but well-made chocolates, truffles, pralines and other candy treats. Try a peanut butter praline. **$3–$6**. In Ward Centre at Ala Moana Boulevard and Kamakee. Parking is accessed from Auahi Street.

EAST OF HONOLULU DINING

Once you leave Honolulu and Waikiki behind, heading toward the sunrise, there are quite a few dining choices before you get to Kailua. We have almost as many categories as restaurants reviewed in this area, so we'll mention their category in the description.

Antonio's New York Pizzeria
4210 Waialae Ave. • 737–3333
Italian—N.Y.-style pizzas, Philly cheesesteaks, hoagies and pastas. Their motto is "made by Italians from N.Y.," and the N.Y. attitude certainly shows. The pizza's just OK; fairly good crust, but the pizza tends to be a bit wet. They also have a spicy sauce (a little Tabasco mixed in). Consider the sandwiches and grab 'em to go. On Waialae Avenue near Hunakai next to the Shell station, south of Waikiki, under the H-1 freeway. (Traffic noises are ever-present.) BYOB, and be careful of the tables—they have tiny bases. Closed Mon. **$6–$10** for lunch and dinner.

Bua Khao Thai
Koko Marina Center • 395–2501
Thai—A wonderfully relaxing location next to a marina in Hawai'i Kai, the all-glass wall takes good advantage of the waterfront. Food is good, not too oily. There's no separate lunch menu, so it'll seem pricey then. Your bill depends on how many items you share. They do a good job with curries and fish, and the ingredients seem to be of good quality. **$15–$25** for lunch and dinner. In Koko Marina Center off Hwy 72, Hawai'i Kai.

Bubbie's Ice Cream
Koko Marina Center • 396–8722
1010 University Ave. • 949–8984
Treats—Locally made ice cream, plus an unusually good selection of ice cream-related items like the wonderful hand-dipped mochis (you gotta get one) and cookie ice cream sandwiches. Flavors like *dark dark chocolate chocolate chip* are delicious, and prices are more reasonable than many gourmet ice cream places. They sell by weight (.55 per oz.), starting with a keiki-sized 2 oz.,

going all the way up to a whole bucket. **$2–$4**. In Koko Marina Center off Hwy 72, Hawai'i Kai. They also have a location closer to Waikiki at 1010 University Ave. (Take McCully, right on King; left on University, it's near Coyne Street.)

Cha Cha Cha Salsaria
Hawaii Kai Towne Ctr. • 395-7797

ONO **Mexican**—Good Mexican food in a small, funky atmosphere. The jerk chicken burrito (don't worry, it tastes better than it sounds) is excellent and has an unexpected hint of cinnamon. Flavors are fantastic, if not exactly authentic. Only six tables inside and a few outdoors. In the Hawai'i Kai Towne Center next to Costco. Take Hwy 72 to Keahole Street. **$6–$10** for lunch and dinner.

Chef's Table
333 Keahole St. • 394-2433

ONO **German**—Excellent German food in a calm, restful atmosphere. Purists will note that the food's more Austrian/Bavarian than traditional German from the north. (Just so you know, we weren't sophisticated enough to figure that out for ourselves; we took a German friend here who straightened us out.) The weinerschnitzel and jaegerschnitzel are both fantastic. They also do a good job with fish and steak and usually have lots of specials. Not surprisingly, the food tends to be fairly heavy and will leave you full for many hours. Service is professional yet chummy. In Hawai'i Kai. H-1 east to Hwy 72. Left on Keahole. It's in the Hawai'i Kai Towne Center. **$20–$25** for dinner. Reservations strongly recommended.

Dave's Ice Cream
41-1537 Hwy. 72 • 259-0356

Treat—Pretty good locally made ice cream. Love the pumpkin flavor. They also have changing local flavors like mango, haupia, lychee and sweet potato. In Waimanalo Town Center on Hwy 72 in Waimanalo. **$2–$5**. They also have other locations, including the International Marketplace food court in Waikiki at 2330 Kalakaua Ave.

Gourmet Express
Kahala Mall • 732-7700

If you're around Kahala Mall and are looking for a fairly quick bite, this food court eatery has healthier food than others, and it tastes good. Lots of wraps, pastas, salads vegetarian items and smoothies for **$6–$9**. In Kahala Mall a couple miles south of Waikiki off H-1—take the Waialae Ave exit and park at the mall entrance near Star Market.

Kona Brewing Co.
7192 Kalanianaole Hwy. • 394-5662

ONO **Italian**—We have a lot of affection for the original Kona Brewpub in Kailua-Kona on the Big Island. While we have to admit this one isn't as good as the Kona location, it's still good enough to merit an ONO, with some caveats. Pizza and beer; that's why you come here. The beer is brewed on the Big Island, and most of it is very good. (They even brew their own ginger ale.) The pizza comes with a variety of sauces. We like the cajun for its spiciness. The Kau Pesto pizza is a nice combination of pesto-based sauce, artichoke hearts, chicken and sun-dried tomatoes, but it doesn't have the level of flavor you might expect, and other combinations, like the Greek, are also a bit light on the flavor. Some of the tables have nice views overlooking the waters of Hawai'i Kai. The problem can be the service—sometimes insanely fumbling. If you catch 'em when they're wired tight, you'll like the experience. In the Koko Marina Center, Hawai'i Kai. **$10–$18** for lunch and dinner.

Korean Hibiscus BBQ
Aina Haina Shop. Ctr. • 373–1120

(ono) **Korean**—A Korean take-out restaurant. (No tables.) Pretty good food and lots of it for around $7. Quick and easy. In the Aina Haina Shopping Center several miles east of Waikiki on Hwy 72 (which is what H-1 becomes).

Loco Moco Drive Inn
Koko Marina Center • 396–7878

Local—First of all, it's not a drive-in. This place is designed to appeal to locals, and visitors might not find the flavors appealing. Oddly for a local-style restaurant, portions on many items are small. (The teri beef sandwich has so little meat, it could almost be classified as homeopathic.) If you're hungry after snorkeling, consider a plate lunch here—the selection is vast. Otherwise, forget it. In Koko Marina Center. **$5–$10**.

Paradise Café
7192 Kalanianaole Hwy. • 394–1170

American—What do you say when there's a local sandwich shop *next door* to a **Subway** sandwich? We'd love to root for the little guy, but you're actually better off at Subway. Sandwiches are better there, and the service is not so inept. In Koko Marina Center. **$7–$10**.

Roy's
6600 Kalanianaole Hwy. • 396–7697

(ono) **American**—Roy's is a hugely successful local chain that got its start at this location. The owner, Roy Yamaguchi, seems to have a knack for combining flavors. It's impossible to classify the menu. They

call it Hawaiian fusion cuisine. We're talking dishes like Asian pesto snapper, imu-baked oysters, sashimi, misoyaki pot roast, mac nut-encrusted mahi mahi, etc. Their fish is nearly always great. Ironically, though they're next to Keahole Street, they don't serve Keahole lobster from the Big Island as many other O'ahu restaurants do. The lobster folks on the Big Island told us that because Roy's is so far from the airport, the beasties would get too "stressed"— and therefore, tough—from the long drive. (Traffic does the same to us.) Portions aren't huge, but the quality of the food is superb. Their chocolate soufflé, which takes 30 minutes to prepare, is deadly—get it with ice cream to actually *counter* the richness. Service is good, though sometimes a bit hurried. (We call it the Roy rush.) If that's the case, simply take control and ask them to slow the pace. They will. The kitchen is exposed, and it can be a bit noisy. Views are of the ocean across the street. In all, Roy's rarely disappoints. At the Hawai'i Kai Towne Center on Hwy 72 and Keahole Street in Hawai'i Kai. **$25–$50** for dinner. Reservations recommended.

Scoop's Ice Cream
Aina Haina Shop. Ctr. • 373–5786

Treats—Like taking a trip to Maui. They carry Maui-made Roselani ice cream and Maui-made baked goods, and they assemble some pretty good ice cream sandwiches. Nice folks, average ice cream. In Aina Haina Shopping Center on Hwy 72. **$1–$3**.

(The) Shack
Hawai'i Kai Shop. Ctr. • 396–1919
95-221 Kipapa, Mililani • 627–1561
1051 Keolu Dr., Kailua • 261–1191
American—A very popular pau hana (after work) stopping place with locals.

It's mostly a sports bar with a large menu of burgers, sandwiches, salads, appetizers and lots of fried items. The different locations vary considerably with the Kailua location the weakest. The Hawai'i Kai location (in Hawai'i Kai Shopping Center up Keahole *past* the Hawai'i Kai Towne Center) is very attractive and has nice views of the waters of Hawai'i Kai. Locals may be dismayed that we didn't give it an ONO; they like it because it's a good place to unwind after a work. But visitors rarely need unwinding after a day or two here. **$7–$10**, plus whatever beer you have. Call for the directions to the Kailua or Mililani locations.

Swiss Haus
5730 Kalanianaole Hwy. • 377-5447
Swiss—We'd love to give an ONO to this place, but the entrées vary too much in their success. It's pretty hit or miss. (**Chef's Table** is better.) Lots of veal along with shrimp, steak, scallops and chicken prepared in a Swiss fashion. (Meaning *on the heavy side*.) All meals come à la carte, or you can add soup, salad and coffee for $3. Service can be unacceptably slow. Between Waikiki and the eastern tip of the island at in the Niu Valley Shopping Center on Hwy 72. **$20–$35** for dinner.

3660 on the Rise
3660 Waialae Ave. • 737-1177
American—Well-known among island residents for their dependably good food. There's no view here, but the service and food make it fairly compelling. Steak and seafood *sound* so ordinary, but the complexity of their recipes and their success at combining flavors usually makes for a very good meal. Many dishes have an Asian twist. Impressive but pretty pricey wine list. **$25–$45** for dinner; reservations

recommended. Ten minutes east of Waikiki. Take McCully or Kapahulu out of Waikiki, right on Kapiolani, which becomes Waialae. It's at 3660 Waialae Ave. Our only quibble is that the acoustics seem to lend themselves to conversations spilling across the tables more than at most places.

KAILUA DINING

Agnes' Portuguese Bake Shop
46 Hoolai St. • 262-5367
Treats—A great place for coffee and baked goods in the morning, or pick up a pie or fresh bread for later. This place is beloved by local windward residents. Especially noteworthy are the coconut macaroons and the apple turnovers and, although they don't make these here, their chocolate-covered sunflower seeds are painfully addictive. I'm jonesin' for 'em just writing about it. Agnes' has lots of coffees, teas, espressos, etc, as well as Internet access. It's spotless inside, tucked away and hard to find. In Kailua at 46 Hoolai St at Kihapai Street. Near the intersection of Kailua Road and Oneawa (these are main roads), Hoolai is the side street just west (mauka) of Oneawa. **$3–$5**.

Amina Pizzeria
3018 Hahani St. • 263-8201
Italian—French bread pizzas, lasagna, calzone, pizzas, pasta and sandwiches. (A large sign says STROMBOLI, but they never seem to have it—maybe they just got a good deal on the sign.) Food is on the bland side, and what flavors do exist seem…wrong. At the corner of Kailua and Hahani at 3018 Hahani St. in Kailua. It's small and hot inside. **$6–$15** for lunch and dinner.

Boots & Kimo's Homestyle Kitchen
119 Hekili St. • 263–7929

ONO **American**—Small, packed and loud. This place is popular with locals, and there's often a wait, especially on weekends. We could almost have classified them as local food. Their specialty is awesome macadamia nut pancakes with a marvelous creamy mac sauce. Definitely try them. Lots of omelettes, so-so hash browns and local dishes. Love their strawberry waffles—they marinate the strawberries in something wonderful. Breakfast until 2 p.m.; lunch items also served during typical lunch hours. In Kailua on Hekili between Hahani and Hamakua. **$8–$12** for breakfast.

Buzz's Original Steak House
413 Kawailoa Rd. • 261–4661

ONO **American**—Across the street from Kailua Beach Park, its location doesn't take advantage of the potential views. Though it gets fairly crowded and noisy, it has a genuine island atmosphere. Lunch is burgers, fish burgers, chicken sandwich (which needs a bigger portion—we didn't know chickens came that small) and lots of salads. Dinner is steak and seafood. The steak and lobster combo is pretty good. Love the Cajun style fish and the Chinese-style fish. *When they have it*, the stuffed ahi is amazing. They make pretty good sashimi, too. The artichoke appetizer *can* be awesome but it's also quite variable. Their "legendary mai tais" are *very* strong—like gasoline—something to remember if you're driving back to Waikiki. To improve the service, turn over the wooden paddle menu when you're ready to order. **$9–$13** for lunch, **$15–$30** for dinner. Reservations recommended. Go early or go late. Prime time is pretty hectic. No tank tops allowed after 5 p.m. No credit cards. Buzz's does disappoint on occasion, but overall rates an ONO.

Chocolate Sushi
1020 Keolu Dr. • 263–7878

ONO **Treats**—Ya gotta give 'em credit for an original concept—a chocolate and sushi shop. If anything, the sushi's even prettier than the chocolate. Perfectly presented and of good quality, though they seem to stress the homemade chocolate more, so we put it under treats. Although pretty limited in selection and certainly not cheap, it's good chocolate and worth a stop. Near this shop is **Round Table Pizza** and the chocolate goes nicely after one of their pizzas. In Enchanted Lake Shopping Center at 1020 Keolu Dr., Kailua. **$3–$10**.

Deb's Old School Soul Food
130 Kailua Rd. • 262–3327

ONO **American**—An excellent place to grab some down home comfort food. Pulled pork, fried okra, ribs, hush puppies, BBQ beans, etc. Nearly everything is tasty. In Kailua Beach Center on Kailua Road near Kalaheo Road. Items are around $2.50 and there are a few indoor and outdoor tables. **$5–$10** for dinner. Closed Tuesdays.

Island Snow (Kailua)
130 Kailua Rd. • 263–6339

Treats—Good shave ice, though they can be overgenerous with the syrup. Get ice cream on the bottom. This is convenient after a hard day beachgoing at Kailua or Lanikai Beach. At Kailua Beach Center on Kailua Road near Kalaheo; walkable from Kailua Beach Park. **$2–$3**.

K & K BBQ Inn
130 Kailua Rd. • 262–2272

Local—It's a hole in the wall with a

disheveled look and the food quality varies considerably, but the selection is huge and they are within walking distance to Kailua Beach Park. Local foods such as chicken katsu, teri steak, sweet and sour spare ribs, saimin and other noodle dishes, plus burgers, fish sandwiches, etc. In short—no great food to be had, but it's convenient to Kailua beachgoers. Nothing more. In Kailua Beach Center on Kailua Road near Kalaheo Road. $3–$6 for lunch.

Los Garcia's
14 Oneawa St. • 261–0306
Mexican—Huge menu of traditional and non-traditional Mexican items, including fajitas, steak and seafood plus vegetarian items and a full bar. Service is lightning fast. The flavors don't work for us, but they have an unusually loyal customer base who no doubt think we're full of beans. At 14 Oneawa near Kailua Road in Kailua. $8–$20 for lunch and dinner.

Lucy's Grill n' Bar
33 Aulike St. • 230–8188
ONO American—Definitely one of Kailua's better restaurants. The menu is fish, pizza, steak, ribs and duck. They call it Hawai'i regional cuisine. We've liked just about everything we've tried here—the Mongolian BBQ ribs, whole crispy moi (a fish), kalua pig pizza (a great appetizer for two or three), prawns, etc. And the desserts have all been winners. (Love the lemon bars.) Hmm, I guess they simply know how to cook. One ding is that we've occasionally gotten entrées that weren't all the way hot. It can get noisy inside, so consider an outdoor table. Reservations recommended. In Kailua at 33 Aulike Street. From the Kailua Road/Kuulei Road intersection, go toward the ocean on Kuulei and turn left on Aulike. Park in the garage. $20–$30 for dinner.

Maui Tacos
539 Kailua Rd., Kailua • 261–4155
95-221 Kipapa, Mililani • 623–9405
ONO Mexican—This small, local chain is a good place to go for tacos and burritos. It's not overly expensive (though it ain't exactly cheap), portions are large, and they're totally flexible when concocting items. Don't neglect the sauces to the right to spice things up the way you like them. In Kailua Village Shops at Kailua and Hahani in Kailua, and Mililani Shopping Center in Mililani off Kamehameha Highway (99). $4–$8.

Pepper's Place
600 Kailua Rd. • 262–3337
ONO American—Good sandwiches and Philly cheesesteaks. Try the sausage sandwich—they chop it up and mix cheese, pepper and onions in it. *Excellent!* Hot dogs and baked potatoes also. They are kind of slow, but you can call ahead. $5–$8. In Kailua Shopping Center in Kailua on Kailua Rd. near Hahani St.

Pinky's Pupu Bar & Grill
970 N. Kalaheo Ave. • 254–6255
ONO American—They usually do it right here, plain and simple. A vast appetizer menu along with a dinner menu. The local sampler for two is a great way to go. Kalua pig, beer can chicken and seared fish, along with local sides. (They'll substitute other sides if you like.) This will stuff two people for around $30. Other combos, plus ribs, stir fry, pasta, steak and a lot more. Most drinks and beers come in giant, 18-ounce schooners, so a single mai tai can do a lot of damage. Chocolate lovers will think they've died and gone to heaven with their Mauna Kea cake. Many of the tables have relaxing views of Kawainui Canal. (Look

for ducks.) This place is wildly popular with nearby residents—almost exclusively their clientele—and if we have a complaint, it's that they tend to rush you a bit in their zeal to keep the tables turning. Simply resist them. No reservations, so arrive early if you don't want to wait. **$10–$20** for dinner. Across from the Aikahi Shopping Center where Mokapu Boulevard, Kane'ohe Bay Drive and N. Kalaheo Avenue converge near the north end of Kailua Beach.

Saeng's Thai Food
315 Hahani St. • 263–9727

Thai—If you're in Kailua and looking for excellent Thai food...you're outta luck. The food's not exactly good, the service is not exactly good—the restaurant's not exactly good. Guess that about covers it. But if you're craving Thai in Kailua, it's not exactly bad (and it's better than another Kailua Thai restaurant, **Champa Thai**). Nice vegetarian selection. **$10–$25** for lunch and dinner. At 315 Hahani St. at Kailua Street in Kailua.

Teddy's Burgers
539 Kailua Rd. • 262–0820

American—A retro burger joint in the Kailua Village Shops, Kailua. Burgers aren't bad and their fries are pretty good, but overall, it's kind of pricey. Nothing to get too excited about. **$6–$10** for lunch and dinner.

KANE'OHE DINING

Boston Pizza
45-568 Kamehameha • 235–7756
29 Hoolai Rd. • 263–7757

Italian—An O'ahu chain. Pretty good reputation, but frankly, the pizza is fairly average. Their motto is "size does matter," and you have a choice of a 19-inch pizza...or a slice. Crusts are thin in the middle, thick on the edges. Flavors are simple—gourmet, it's not. In Kailua at 29 Hoolai St., which is just mauka (toward the mountain) of where Kailua Road meets Oneawa Street. Also in Kane'ohe at 45-568 Kamehameha Highway (83), mauka side. Only a few tables at most locations; most people take out. **$5–$10**.

Chao Phya Thai
45-480 Kaneohe Bay Dr. • 235–3555

ONO **Thai**—Sometimes you just want inexpensive Thai food fairly quickly. If that's your goal, you could do worse than Chao Phya. (Now *there's* a tough name to pronounce.) Fairly wide selection, and you get it quick. Portions are good and the price is right. Avoid the Thai tea—too sweet. **$8–$15** for lunch and dinner. BYOB. In Windward City Shopping Mall, Kamehameha Highway (83) and Kane'ohe Bay Drive, Kane'ohe.

Hale'iwa Joe's Seafood Grill
46-336 Haiku Rd. • 247–6671

ONO **American**—Located in a lush garden setting at Haiku Gardens, it's nice to do a pre-meal stroll in the garden and pond area if you arrive before sunset. In fact, we *strongly* recommend getting there for an early dinner (they open at 5:30 p.m.) since the view of the Ko'olau Mountains is so exquisite in the afternoon. (Plus, the garden setting might bring flying bugs later in the evening.) We like the tables near the railing the best. The food is generally very good. Try the wonderful Thai calamari for an appetizer. Dinner is steak and seafood, plus ribs, pork chops (excellent) and sometimes lobster. The décor includes lots of attractive koa wood. Service can be slow at times, and they don't take reservations. **$20–$30**

for dinner. From Hwy 830 (Kamehameha Hwy) turn toward the mountain onto Haiku Road near the Windward Mall. You'll see it on the left a while after Haiku Rd. crosses Hwy 83.

Times Coffee Shop
46-077 Kamehameha • 247–2200
153 Hamakua Dr., Kailua • 262–0300

ono **American**—Popular with locals due to the cheap prices, clean environment and reasonable food. Typical breakfast menu, plus some local items. (You gotta try the blueberry pancakes with their homemade raspberry syrup—*ono!*) Lots of burgers, sandwiches and local items at lunch. It's often crowded on weekends, and service can be too casual at times, but it's always a good deal here. **$4–$8** for breakfast and lunch. We prefer the Kane'ohe location at 46-077 Kamehameha Hwy (830). Their Kailua location is horrible and should be avoided.

BETWEEN KANE'OHE & KAHUKU

Once you drive north of Kane'ohe on Hwy 83, your options dwindle until you get to Hale'iwa 40 miles away. Here we've listed the restaurants *in the order that you'll see them*, not in alphabetical order.

Your first opportunity after Kane'ohe is a disappointment. **Crouching Lion Inn (237–8511)** is that place that everyone knows you're supposed to stop at. This is considered the place to have lunch on the windward side. Unfortunately, we've noticed a pattern here in Hawai'i. Once large numbers of tour buses start lining up at a restaurant, as they do here, energy seems to go toward processing the numbers—not working toward excellence. So it is in this case. The food's bland, unre-

markable and overpriced—period. The view's kind of pretty, overlooking the ocean if you can ignore the highway traffic and the thick powerlines. Lunch is sandwiches, burgers, seafood, chicken and some veggie items. The Salad bar is certainly not worth $9 by itself. Dinner is steak and seafood. This place is a well-known institution on O'ahu, and some residents will be shocked at our harsh review. But we suspect it's only those who haven't eaten here in a while, especially at lunch. **$10–$15** for lunch, **$15–$20** for dinner. On Hwy 83 in Ka'a'awa on the windward side.

Ahi's Punalu'u Restaurant (237–8474) is a prominent restaurant in Punalu'u that is very avoidable. The food tastes like the place looks inside. 'Nuff said.

In Hau'ula, **Shrimp Express (232–2079)** is the kind of place we really wanted to like, but didn't. It's in a converted KFC building in an area that could use more dining options. But the prices are high and the food unremarkable. They offer a half dozen shrimp (raised on Kaua'i), chili and pineapple-based desserts. But it's $11 for shrimp scampi and a banana split (albeit served in a half pineapple) is $8. Also burgers, some fish and some pastas. Service tends to be *sloooow*. On the mauka side of highway in Hau'ula at 54-296 Kamehameha Hwy. **$10–$15**.

Once you get to La'ie, your options expand a bit. There's a large shopping center with a Foodland called the La'ie Shopping Center at Anemoke Street (the stoplight) on Hwy 83. Your best bet is **La'ie Chop Suey (293–8022)**. **ono** They are fast, efficient, friendly and priced right.

Oh, and the food's good, too. An endless, sprawling menu confronts you, but at lunch most opt for either the pre-chosen lunch plate or the dinner plate (available at lunch—spring for that one). We're talking either $5 or $6 for a large portion. If you want to go off the menu, there's almost certainly something for everyone. Look at the Dr. Schlacter's Special if you like veggies. Off-the-menu prices will cost you from **$6–$15**. No alcohol. (La'ie is a strict Mormon town.)

Your best treat in La'ie is **Angel's Ice Cream** (293–8260). Forget the ice cream—it's plain ol' Dryers. And the cookies are surprisingly tasteless. It's the shave ice that stands out. Nice and finely shaved with plenty of syrup. Make sure you have them put ice cream on the bottom—it gives you an objective worth digging for. **$2–$4**.

Also in that center is a **Subway**, **Domino's Pizza**, **L&L Drive-In** (a local drive-in chain that's not bad) and the **Foodland** has a deli with sandwiches under **$5** and hot, whole rotisserie chickens for **$6**. They also have a bakery with so-so items. Down the highway is also a **McDonald's**.

KAHUKU SHRIMP

On the side of Hwy 83 in Kahuku, 25 miles north of Kane'ohe. The northern tip of the island has become synonymous with shrimp—shrimp trucks, shrimp shacks and shrimp farming. Oddly, only one of the shrimp sellers actually gets their shrimp from the nearby commercial shrimp ponds. (Most others get theirs from Kaua'i's shrimp farm, which produces *excellent* shrimp.)

Romy's Kahuku Shrimp Hut is ¾ mile past (toward Hale'iwa) Kahuku Town and after you've driven by their competitors. They harvest their shrimp that day, and the freshness shows. Garlic butter, shrimp cocktail, sweet and hot or fried; those are your choices. (The sweet and hot is great.) You get shrimp and rice for **$10**, and all but the cocktail shrimp are peeled. The tables can be windy, so you might want to eat in the car. This is the place we usually stop at.

Giovanni's Aloha Shrimp Truck is the most famous. It may have been an unassuming shrimp truck in the middle of nowhere at one time, but it's become so well-known and heavily visited that long lines and waits can be a real problem. Three shrimp dishes comprise the menu with the scampi the most popular. They use a delicious (and very garlicky) marinade. Though tasty, many people object to dealing with the shell and the shrimp legs (which you tear off), not to mention burning your fingers in the process. It's **$11** and includes rice and mac salad. The spicy shrimp *really, really* lives up to its name. We're surprised that they don't need a special HAZARDOUS MATERIALS permit to handle the sauce. The smoothies are pretty overpriced, though not bad. Definitely avoid the bathrooms. ('Nuff said about that.) This is our second favorite.

Amy's Kahuku Shrimp (293–8896) is where we go when we're feeling cheap. Sautéed or fried, both tend to taste fresh. They also have burgers plus fries for $3— hard to beat—plus stir fry, teri beef and bento boxes to go. Best value, though dreary surroundings. On the highway before the shrimp trucks.

The Famous Kahuku Shrimp Truck is junk. Weird-tasting shrimp and squid.

And the **Kahuku Sugar Mill Restaurant (293–2110)** is a good place to go if you want to be ignored. We suggest you reciprocate.

BETWEEN KAHUKU & HALE'IWA

You've rounded the top of the island and are on your way to Hale'iwa.

At the Turtle Bay Resort is **Palm Terrace (293–8811)**, They are overpriced, have sometimes distracted, even contemptibly vacuous service and average food. Breakfast and lunch are a buffet for $19 and $25 or a few à la carte items that will get pretty close. You're a presumed captive audience here at the Turtle Bay Resort, but for lunch and dinner, either hit Lei Lei's at the golf course, or head to Hale'iwa, 20 minutes away. You can do better than this place.

Lei Lei's Bar & Grill (293–2662) is at the golf course at Turtle Bay Resort. Only a few breakfast items (but a tasty croissant sandwich), sandwiches, burgers and salads for lunch, steak, prime rib, seafood and chicken for dinner. In all, not a bad place. (Certainly better than the other resort restaurant, Palm Terrace.) **$5–$8** for breakfast, **$9–$15** for lunch, **$18–$30** for dinner.

As you start seeing the North Shore surf sites like Sunset Beach, you'll come to **Ted's Bakery (638–8207)** They have pies and cakes by the slice. A convenient place to grab a sweet if you're at nearby Sunset Beach. **$2–$3**. Just northeast of Sunset Beach on Hwy 83 on the North Shore.

Then comes **Sunset Pizza (638–7660)**, a very famous north shore surfer hangout. They have good prices on pizza (huge slices

are $2.50 for cheese), sausage sandwiches (which are good), subs, lasagna, spaghetti and burgers. Just some outdoor tables which you should avoid. (Flies can make them annoying; consider taking your food to Sunset Beach, instead.) **$4–$6** for breakfast which is mostly breakfast tacos and pancakes, **$3–$7** for lunch and dinner. (You can spend more for fish at dinner.) 15 minutes north of Hale'iwa on Kamehameha Hwy (83) just south of Sunset Beach Park. Look for a sign saying, OHANA SURF.

Taste of Paradise Surf Grill (638–0855) is an oddity. It's a food truck with covered tables and table service (though with paper plates). Fish, shrimp, steak and some veggie items. The menu sounds bigger than it is. The food is good and reasonably priced. Great shrimp, generous portions, good service. Yeah, works for us. Only the flies distract from the otherwise great experience. No shirt, no shoes? No problem! At 59-254 Kamehameha Hwy (83) a few miles south (toward Hale'iwa) of Sunset Beach Park. Look for the giant wooden head out front. **$8–$12** for lunch and dinner.

Sharks Cove Grill (638–8300) is super convenient if you're at Sharks Cove or Three Tables. Burgers, salads sandwiches or ka-bobs and pretty good cookies. Overall, it's not bad. (Of course our judgment has been colored since we usually review this place after we've been diving or snorkeling at these two beaches, and even cat food would taste good after you've come out of the ocean.) **$7–$10**, across from Sharks Cove on Hwy 83 north of Waimea Bay.

HALE'IWA DINING

Breakers
66-250 Kamehameha • 637-9898

 American—A good menu, good food and a funky Polynesian/surfer atmosphere. An easy place to recommend. Steak, seafood, stir fry, burgers, great fish and chips and pizza (the latter is probably their weakest offering). Pupus are Asian items like spring rolls and satay, or try the roasted clams or calamari. We've never had a bad meal here. On Kamehameha Highway (83). Lunch is **$8–$15**, dinner is **$16–$27**.

Cholo's Homestyle Mexican
North Shore Marktplace • 637-3059

 Mexican—No frills, but flavorful food at reasonable prices. Most entrées have a pretty decent spicy bite to them. Typical Mexican items, plus fish tacos and burritos. Service is sometimes slow, and it's not the tidiest place on O'ahu. Take-out is available. At the North Shore Marketplace on Kamehameha Highway (83). Breakfast is **$5–$8**, **$7–$14** for lunch and dinner. (More for fajitas.) BYOB.

Hale'iwa Joe's
66-011 Kamehameha • 637-8005

 American—A nice menu of fresh fish, ½-pound burgers, coconut shrimp, Cajun fish sandwich (excellent), steak and more for lunch plus sushi, ceviche, ribs, etc., for pupus. Dinner is a bit more steak and seafood oriented. Consider the covered outdoor tables if it's not too windy. Flies might be a problem, but this is a Hale'iwa-wide problem. Service isn't the fastest in the world, but overall, this is a good restaurant. **$10–$25** for lunch, **$20–$30** for dinner. At the corner of Hale'iwa Road and Kamehameha Hwy (83) across from the harbor.

Homemade Ice Cream/Flavormania
Haleiwa Shopping Plaza • 637-9362

Treats—As the name implies, they have 2 dozen house-made flavors. It's very creamy, though the tastes are a bit on the subtle side for some flavors. They also sell Bubbie's Ice Cream, which is better. On Kamehameha Hwy across from Ace Hardware. **$2–$4**.

Jameson's By the Sea
62-540 Kamehameha • 637-4336

American—What do you say about a place that charges $7 for a grilled cheese sandwich or $10 for a cheeseburger at lunch? I guess *overpriced* will cover it. It would be one thing if they used only the best ingredients, but it tastes like frozen fish sandwiches and plain ol' albacore for the tuna melt. They also have $10–$15 salads, $10 summer rolls, etc. OK, enough already—you get the picture. At least the outdoor tables have a fairly pleasing view of Hale'iwa Harbor across the busy street. The indoor tables...don't. On the north side of the Anahulu Stream on Kamehameha Hwy (83) just north of Hale'iwa town. You can do better. **$8–$25** for lunch. Also inside is **Jameson's Fudge Works**. The fudge is the best we've had. Absolutely silky smooth. The only thing gritty is the service. They seem unnecessarily nasty here. They even refuse to take pennies, saying they'll round everything up and refuse your copper. It's about $5 for a half-pound, and it's radioactive enough to keep you buzzing all the way back to Waikiki.

Killer Tacos
66-560 Kamehameha • 637-4573

 Mexican—The perfect place for simple, very flavorful Mexican food without high prices. They season things very well here, and you can mix and match to create your own burritos or tacos. Nothing fancy, just an easy place to recommend. In Hale'iwa town on Kamehameha Highway near the traffic circle at Waialua Beach Road. **$3–$7** for lunch and early dinner.

Krunchies Hot Malasadas

Treat—Fairly poor malasadas (Portuguese donuts), usually plain or with haupia inside. Hot and cheap, but you can do better elsewhere. Tastes like they need to change the oil more often. **$1**. A truck on Kamehameha Highway (83) in Hale'iwa, probably across from Hale'iwa Shopping Plaza.

Kua 'Aina Sandwich
66-214 Kamehameha • 637–6067

ONO **American**—A winner like the Honolulu location. See review on page 239.

North Shore Chocolate Co.
66-470 Kamehameha • 637–3000

ONO **Treats**—Here's what happens when you have someone who runs a shop selling woodworks who also loves chocolate. They start making high-quality chocolates and truffles, and before you know it, the chocolate is the reason people stop by. The chocolates here are expensive but deadly and highly recommended. In Hale'iwa at the mauka (toward the mountain) end of town on Kamehameha Highway and Paalaa Road. **$3–$5**.

Pizza Bob's
Haleiwa Shopping Plaza • 637–5095

ONO **Italian**—A somewhat upscale pizza parlor with fairly reasonable prices that also has pastas, burgers, sandwiches, salads and a full bar. Indoor and outdoor tables. They use a five-cheese blend that works pretty well. Consider adding roasted cashews—it creates an interesting flavor. The crust is hard to describe—it…bites easily. (Not very descriptive, but we couldn't think of another way to put it.) Mosquitoes and flies can be a problem, like many places in Hale'iwa. Excellent beer prices. In Hale'iwa Shopping Plaza on Hwy 83 across from Wyland. **$8–$12** for lunch and dinner.

Rosie's Cantina
Haleiwa Shopping Plaza • 637–3538

Mexican—We'd like to give them an ONO, but their food is too often served cold—as in near room temperature—and we have no idea why. The food tastes fairly good, and they also have burgers, wraps and salads. Their Tuesday night taco bar for $9 is a decent way to go. And someone here has an obvious love affair with tequila. We've never seen a better selection, and they use it well in their margaritas. If you can live without the nicer surroundings and tequila, Cholo's down the street has better food. In Hale'iwa Shopping Plaza on Kamehameha (Hwy 83) in Hale'iwa. **$8–$18** for lunch and dinner.

Shave Ice in Hale'iwa

ONO **Treats**—There are three good sources of shave ice in Hale'iwa. **Matsumoto's** is the legendary source with high name recognition (they've been here since 1951), and almost next door to the left is **Aoki's**, and to the right is H. Miura. *Insanely* long lines are the norm at Matsumoto's, and we've seen times when there was a 45-minute wait there and only a handful of people at Aoki's. Frankly, Aoki's is just as good, and, unlike Matsumoto's, they partially chill their syrup (preventing the dreaded ice chunks at the bottom created by room temperature syrups). **H. Miura** stands out if you want one of their cream-based syrups. All three companies are cheap—around $2 with ice cream on the bottom. So in general, go where the line is shortest. And be careful of bees who seem to thrive on the dropped shave ice at all three locations. In Hale'iwa on Kamehameha Hwy between Hale'iwa Road and the Hale'iwa Shopping Center.

Spaghettini
66-200 Kamehameha • 637-0104
Italian—Lots of spaghettis and pizza by the slice served with couldn't-care-less service. Though the portions are pretty large for the price, flavors are on the dull side. Not insipid, but you certainly won't be fantasizing about it later that day. They get a lot of spillover from nearby Kua 'Aina Sandwiches (customers who don't want to wait in line at that more popular restaurant). The pizzas are marginally better than the pasta. But hey, you ain't paying much here. $3–$10 for lunch and (early) dinner. On Kamehameha Hwy in Hale'iwa.

CENTRAL O'AHU DINING

Jimmy's Lakeside Café/Bakery
1718 Wilikina Dr. • 621–6800
Italian—You can drive all around this area and never even know there's a giant, beautiful lake nearby—until you walk into Jimmy's and see their gorgeous view. As for the food, it's huge 18-inch N.Y.-style pizzas for around $11 plus toppings (or get it by the giant slice), lots of hot or cold sandwiches, salads and pasta. The food tends to be fairly good across the board and, since a big part of their clientele is from

nearby Schofield Barracks, they keep the prices pretty reasonable. They also have some delicious macaroons and other baked goods. If you want a beer, you can grab a draft at the bar next door and bring it over. Only down side is it can get a bit hot inside, and sometimes noises from the bar can leak in. If you're coming from the North Shore, drive past the Kemo'o Farm Center and make a U-turn. It's between McNair Gate and Macomb on Hwy 99 in Schofield. $6–$10 for lunch and dinner.

Molly's Smokehouse
23 S. Kamehameha • 621–4858
Good BBQ menu of ribs, beef brisket, catfish, hush puppies, sausage sandwich, fried okra, collard greens, etc. (Stay away from the beans, though.) Price is cheap, and the food's pretty good for the money. At non-peak times, however, things tend to suffer. At 23 Kam Hwy (80) at California Street across from *Wendy's* in Wahiawa. Very little parking—you'll have to improvise, but *don't* try to use the parking at *Jack in the Box*—they're touchy about it. $6–$12 for lunch and dinner.

WAI'ANAE DINING

Your options are pretty limited in Wai'anae because good food's really hard to find. The **JW Marriott Ihilani Resort at Ko Olina** is your best bet, but it ain't cheap. Their **Ushio-Tei (679–0079)** Japanese restaurant is a good dinner place with Japanese and some non-Japanese dishes. Monday and Friday there's a $40 buffet. Otherwise, it's $30–$55. Resort wear means nice shorts and collared shirt OK.

Also at the Marriott is the **Naupaka Terrace (679–0079)** for breakfast, lunch and dinner. A pretty good breakfast buffet, unremarkable lunch and dinner food. Not bad, not memorable.

Outside of Ko Olina, here are some that might work for you:

Aloha Aina Café (697–8808) in Wai'anae at 85-773 Farrington Hwy on the ocean side has a limited menu of chili, soup, Mexican wraps, sandwiches and taro burgers. The service can be slow; the food tends to be good and well-seasoned. $5–$7 for breakfast, lunch and dinner. Cash only.

Hello Sushi (696–3535) in Wai'anae Mall at 86-120 Farrington Hwy has *very* reasonably priced sushi. One of the best deals in Wai'anae. For instance, you can get 6 pieces of ahi maki for under $2. (And it's pretty good.) **$2–$6.**

Hannara's (696–6137) in Wai'anae at 86-078 Farrington Hwy is a local restaurant and a decent place for breakfast. American and Korean food. Their pancakes and loco moco are pretty good. **$4–$8.**

Red Baron's Pizza (697–1383) in Wai'anae at 85-915 Farrington Hwy will do in a pinch. Get anything *other* than the pizza.

At the Makaha Resort Golf Club the **Kaiona Restaurant (695–7515)** goes through good times and bad. Hope you catch 'em when they're in the zone. American food. **$5–$10** for lunch, **$10–$25** for dinner.

ISLAND NIGHTLIFE

While it's true that the neighbor islands are a bit lacking in night life, no one would ever make that comment about O'ahu. From simple lounges with a single musician playing Hawaiian music on an acoustic guitar to full-blown dinner shows to seedy strip clubs—Waikiki has something for just about everyone.

But people's taste in night life varies *tremendously*. This is a section where we feel a little vulnerable, because things change weekly in the world of night life. The Friday edition of the *Honolulu Advertiser* newspaper has an entertainment section that lists what's going on in the coming week. It's *extremely* comprehensive. Night life is one area where the free stuff (seen at news racks everywhere) can come in handy because of the ads. By the way, if you see something playing at the **Hawai'i Theatre** (528–0506) that sounds interesting, jump on it. This has got to be one of the most beautiful theaters you'll see. The restoration is incredible, and it looks like what an upscale theater must have looked like in the 1920s, which is when it was built.

There's literally no end to the number of bars and lounges in Waikiki. In addition, there are several dinner shows and lu'aus available.

DINNER SHOWS

You've got a few choices for dinner shows in Waikiki. We were impressed with the caliber of shows overall. Ironically, it's the dinner part of the dinner shows that's usually lacking, so consider eating elsewhere before or after the show.

Creations: A Polynesian Journey 931–4660

Go for the show, but not the dinner. The food is solidly mediocre, and the mai tais are little more than punch. Think of them as homeopathic. Perhaps they simply wave an empty rum bottle over the punchbowl. If you want a cocktail, get one before you come to the show. And while you're at it, eat either before or after (though you won't get as good a table if you don't eat their dinner). The show itself, however, is simply dazzling. It's high energy, high production value, very professional and ultimately compelling. Don't expect a traditional hula show. This is a pulse-pounding Polynesian spectacular. We're stunned that the same company that does the embarrassing show at the Royal Hawaiian lu'au puts on this excellent one-hour show. **$33** for cocktail and show, **$63** for the dinner and show and a laughable **$106** for the premium dinner and show. At the Sheraton Princess Kaiulani at Kalakaua and Kaiulani.

Magic of Polynesia 543–8359

We liked this show, but not for the reason it's marketed for. They tout it as a magic show, but the magic isn't the reason to see it. It's the Polynesian portion—unabashedly Vegasy—which is well-done with a high production value. Some of the visuals are stunning. About a third of the show is the actual magic and, though cool, much of it seems to be the same trick several different ways. A curtain goes up and when it comes down, the guy is gone or has switched objects. Impressive the first few times, but it stops surprising you after a while and big-box magic is a bit less impressive than close-up magic because people inherently distrust props. And there's little personality from the magician—as if he, too, is a prop. But don't let this dissuade you. Overall, the visuals, sound and Polynesian feel make it a fun show, and the magic's interesting, if not overwhelming. It's **$42** for a cocktail show. They also offer it as a dinner show combo for **$69**, but we recommend eating elsewhere first. At the Waikiki Beachcomber Hotel at 2300 Kalakaua. Reserve in advance.

One Variety Dinner Show 921–5000

This is a magic/juggling/singing/hula show. It's high-energy, with great sound and good magic. They do stunning things with birds, plus some more traditional tricks. The magic is effectively interwoven with Polynesian song and dance. The hula is not just filler; the dancers could carry a show on their own. Our only complaint is that it's not long enough. The name—One—could describe the show's duration; it's only one hour long. Like other shows, they have a dinner combination, but unlike most dinner shows, the buffet is pretty good, and the setting is less of a cattle call. Overall, an easy show to recommend. At the Marriott Waikiki Beach Resort. **$59**.

Don Ho 923–3981

A hard show to review. Don Ho is the most widely known entertainer in Hawai'i and has been entertaining with his music for many decades. He's literally an institution in Waikiki. When we've seen the show more recently, Mr. Ho *appeared* to be in a condition *seemingly* unsuitable for stage, and the audience initially looked uncomfortable. But by the end of the roughly 90-minute show, the man's innate charm won over everyone in the crowd (including us), who seemed sorry that it was over. Nobody who stayed appeared unsatisfied. In the end, while Don Ho doesn't have the slickness and energy of Society of Seven, the crowd seemed to love him more.

A fixed plate dinner (which is mediocre) is included for **$52**, or do the show and cocktail for **$32**. At the Waikiki Beachcomber Hotel at 2300 Kalakaua Ave.

Society of Seven 922–6408

The other long-time dinner show. This is a very talented group whose show is mostly imitations of singers past. Although the material feels pretty dated, it's hard not to enjoy the fast-paced, 90-minute show. And although the audience is skewed toward retired people, those of all ages seem to enjoy the performances. We strongly recommend, however, passing on the poor buffet and overpriced cocktails, and do the show by itself. While it's true that dinner customers get better seating, the dinner buffet is pretty avoidable. **$43** for the cocktail show, **$65** for the dinner show. At the Outrigger Waikiki on the Beach at 2335 Kalakaua Ave.

LU'AUS

We've all seen them in movies. People sit at a table with a mai tai in one hand and a plate of kalua pig in the other. There's always a show where a fire knife dancer twirls a torch lit at both ends and hula dancers bend and sway to the beat of the music. To be honest, that's not too far from the truth. The pig is baked in the ground all day, creating absolutely delicious results. Shows are usually exciting and fast-paced. Although lu'aus on the neighbor islands are smaller affairs, on O'ahu you'll be accompanied by 500–600 of your closest new friends. To be honest, we've found neighbor island lu'aus to be more fun because you're able to wander around more. They feel more like a party than O'ahu lu'aus. But two of the lu'aus here are pretty good. You'll just feel a bit more processed than on a neighbor island. *Most* include all-you-can-eat food and drinks (including alcohol) for a set fee. If the punch doesn't satisfy you, there's a bar where you can ask them to season it for you or make some-

thing more to your liking. Also remember the golden rule at the buffet line—the cheapest stuff comes first, so reserve enough plate real estate for the good stuff at the end.

Different lu'aus are held on different nights, and this changes often, so verify the days listed here before making plans.

Polynesian Cultural Center 293–3333

Probably the best lu'au on the island with one caveat. Yeah, they feed 500 people at a whack. But the food's the best of the bunch, and there's entertainment throughout in a very pretty and relaxing atmosphere. The layout doesn't encourage walking around much, and it's a tad cramped, but the manmade waterfalls and dinner show add much to the ambiance, and the entertainment's not at all cheesy. Depending on when your table is called, the experience might seem a little rushed, until you realize that you can keep eating and making trips to the buffet even after the show is over.

One thing to remember is that this is run by the Mormon church, so don't expect anything in your drinks other than fruit juice. If potent mai tais are your reason for taking in a lu'au, look elsewhere.

After dinner, the evening show called "Horizons," in a dedicated theater, is incredible. It has the highest production value of any lu'au show in Hawai'i. The authentic singing and dancing from several different countries and languages is fantastic, and the crisp perfection of the performers is in stark contrast to some of the bozos you'll find at another lu'au listed below. The fire knife dancing is the best you'll see anywhere and is a great way to end the show.

The only negative side is that it's a 60–90 minute drive back to Waikiki from La'ie on the windward side. Consider their bus ride for an extra $13. You should combine this lu'au with a day at the Polynesian Cultural Center (see page 109). Dinner, show and the day at PCC is **$79**, every night except Sunday.

Germaine's Lu'au 949–6626

Probably the second best, it's reasonably priced at **$53** (which includes the hour-long bus ride from Waikiki), and they do a very good job. There are around 650 people here, but you can tell that the crew is having fun. The food's pretty good and three drinks are included. (A tip—if you find the size of the mai tais too small, you can purchase a large glass for $6, and they'll fill *that* each time, instead. Also, you can always ask the bartender to add more seasoning to your mai tai.) The oceanside grounds are pretty, sandy and full of palm trees, and the shoreline has good sunsets most of the year (except the weeks around the summer solstice of June 21 when it sets over land). The interactive show's well done—not too Vegasy—and the audience participation seems to be well received. If the Polynesian Cultural Center's lu'au doesn't sound like it's for you, this is one you should choose. It's about 4 hours at the site and about 2 hours of travel. Located near Ko Olina Resort at the southwest corner of the island.

Royal Hawaiian Lu'au 931–7194

They call themselves the only lu'au "right on the beach" at Waikiki. Actually, it's not *on* the beach, but rather next to it and the view of the beach is partially blocked by various obstructions, but their view of Diamond Head glowing in the sunset is very pretty. We were surprisingly disappointed by this lu'au. It's a textbook example of a big resort that probably has no trouble finding 400 or so customers a night, so they seem to expend shamefully little effort striving for excellence. The show is terrible. The stage is too small, and the dancers just wiggle in place—they could simply have been having seizures for all we could tell. And the overall product was slipshod. We've seen more people get up and walk out than any lu'au we've ever reviewed. The food's fine—not great, not bad. But we'd hate to have this lu'au be the one that forms your opinion. **$81**, Monday and Thursday at the Royal Hawaiian.

Paradise Cove 842–5911

Our last choice. It's not that it's terrible. (It's better than the Royal Lu'au but not as conveniently located.) Their location *is* quite pretty, but the food and show are mediocre, and they keep you wandering around the grounds for quite a while before the food and show starts. Located near Ko Olina Resort at the southwest corner of the island. **$60**.

DINNER CRUISES

See Ocean Tours on page 195.

ISLAND DINING BEST BETS

Best Lu'au—Polynesian Cultural Center (no alcohol) or Germaine's (with it)
Best Chocolate Dessert—Alan Wong's
Best Free Cookies—Those at check-in at the DoubleTree Alana
Best Shave Ice (near Waikiki)—Waiola
Best Way to Dissolve Your Digestive Tract—Giovanni's Spicy Sauce
Best View for the Money—Any meal at Duke's (particularly breakfast)
Best Malasada—Warm from Leonard's
Best Breakfast on Your Way to the North Shore—Boots & Kimo
Best View of Fish While You're Eating—Oceanarium
Best Dine-In Kitchen—Buca di Beppo

(Hotels shown in this color. Condominiums shown in this color.)

Lovin' the lazy life above Waikiki Beach.

Your selection of where to stay is one of the more important decisions you'll make in planning your O'ahu vacation. To some, it's just a place to sleep and rather meaningless. To others, it's the difference between a good vacation and a bad one.

There are four main types of lodging on the island: hotels, condominiums, bed and breakfasts, and single-family homes. Most people will stay in one of the first two types. But B&Bs and single-family homes are often overlooked and can be very good values. If your group or family is large, you should strongly consider renting a house for privacy, roominess and plain ol' value. We don't review individual B&Bs, vacation homes or time-shares, but you can easily find them on the Internet.

The lion's share of visitors stay in Waikiki. There are only a few resorts, condos and hotels scattered outside this area.

Hotels are in green and **condominiums are in blue.** Hotels usually offer more services, but smaller spaces and no kitchens. Condos usually have full kitchens, but you won't get the kind of attention you would from a hotel, including daily maid service. There are exceptions, of course, and we will point them out when they come up. You can find their locations on the various maps.

All prices given are RACK rates, meaning *without any discounts*. Tour packages and travel agents can often get better rates. Most resorts offer discounts for stays of a week or more, and some will negotiate price with you. Some won't

See all Web reviews at: www.wizardpub.com

budge at all, while others told us *no one* pays RACK rates. Also, these prices are subject to taxes of over 11%.

SOLID GOLD VALUE The gold bar indicates that the property is exceptionally well priced for what you get.

A REAL GEM The gem means that this hotel or condominium offers something *particularly* special, not *necessarily* related to the price.

These are subjective reviews. If we say that rooms are small, we mean that we've been in them, and they feel small or cramped to us. If we say that maintenance is poor, we mean that the paint might be peeling, or the carpets are dingy, or it otherwise felt worn to us.

WHERE ARE THE REST?

You'll notice that some of the resorts listed here don't have full reviews. When we review a place to stay, we don't just want to list bare bones information on them. After all, you can get that kind of info on the Internet. We want to tell you what we *really* think about a place, and that takes space. Also, we wanted to include aerial photos of the resorts. After all, a picture speaks a thousand words (and a thousand words takes too long to read anyway). But in the end we only have so much space we can devote to accommodations.

We had a choice. Give you less info on *all* of them, or do detailed reviews on only a *portion* of them. Neither choice seemed palatable.

So we came up with a *third* way: List minimal info on all (including if they are GEMS or SOLID GOLD VALUES), print detailed reviews on *most* and post full reviews of all on our Web site, **www.wizardpub.com**. After all, most people use this section before they come to the islands. And with the Web (which has infinite space available), we could do more, like post larger aerial photos of the resorts with specific buildings labeled when appropriate, provide constant updates when necessary and put links to the various rental agents or hotels right in the review, allowing you to go to their sites and get more photos of the rooms. You should remember, however, that resorts post photos to lure you in, and some aren't above posting modified or overly flattering shots when they were new and sparkling. Our aerials don't lie and are designed to give you a feel for their ocean proximity (does oceanfront *really* mean oceanfront?), so you'll know what kind of view to expect from a given location within the resort. Resorts whose review is posted *only* on our Web site are identified with **WEB REVIEW**

Though most of our Web site is available to anyone, we thought that these extra reviews should only be available to our readers. So when you get to the page with the reviews, you'll have to enter the following password:

or8329

You'll only have to enter this once and from then on, you can look at all of them.

Please remember that all these reviews are *relative to each other*. This is important. Even staying at a dump right on the ocean is still a *golly gee!* experience. In other words, *Hey, you're on the ocean in Hawai'i!* So if we sound whiny or picky when critiquing a resort, it's only because their next door neighbor might be such a better experience. It doesn't mean you'll be miserable; it just means that *compared to another resort*, you can do better.

A FEW GROUND RULES

In general, we've noticed that few people pay the RACK rates we list below. Most have gobs of packages and discounts. Simply standing there and demanding a discount will usually get you one. But we had to use some kind of yardstick, and published rates were our only recourse. But if you're looking for a place to stay, with few exceptions you can expect to get discounts off their RACK rates by simply asking.

Unless otherwise noted, all resorts have room safes (for extra—usually $2–$4 per day), air conditioning, empty refrigerators, coin-op laundry facilities, daily maid service, data ports on their phones, lanais, coffee makers in the rooms, self-parking for $8–$12 per day, and local calls are $.75 or $1 a pop. Most resorts have handicap accessible rooms.

WAIKIKI

Ala Moana Hotel
(800) 367–6025 or (808) 955–4811
410 Atkinson Dr.

1152 rooms, pool, fitness room, room service, 5 restaurants, 8 shops, 10 conference rooms, business center. There are two towers—the 10-story Kona and the 30-story Waikiki. This hotel is just outside of Waikiki next door to the Ala Moana Shopping Center. Much of their customer base is business travelers and convention attendees. (The convention center is very close by.) Most rooms have two double beds. The top 7 floors are the Torch Ginger rooms, and they have larger beds available. Rooms in the cheaper Kona Tower have no lanais.

It's a pretty long walk into Waikiki and its beaches and restaurants, but it's also quicker when you're looking to hop on the freeway. In all, you need to decide if the location trade-offs are worth it. Rooms (325 sq. ft.) are $135–$215. Suites are $285–$2,300. "Supersaver" rates bring the price down.

Aloha Punawai
(866) 713–9694 or (808) 923–5211
305 Saratoga Rd.

Aloha Punawai

19 units on 3 floors (no elevator). All units have complete kitchens but no phones. Maid service is once a week (they'll change towels more often). No smoking in the building, no room safes. BBQ grills, beach mats and chairs available. Simple, clean, no frills. (They have a pretty little garden, though.) Parking is $7 but is limited. At times they give discounts up to 50%, which would definitely make it a SOLID GOLD VALUE. Studios (287 sq. ft.)

See all Web reviews at: www.wizardpub.com

are $85–$95, 1/1s (333–448 sq. ft.) are $95–$125. About 2 blocks to the beach.

Ambassador Hotel of Waikiki
(800) 923–2620 or (808) 941–7777
2040 Kuhio Ave.
WEB REVIEW

Aqua Marina Hotel
(866) 406–2782 or (808) 942–7722
1700 Ala Moana Blvd.

136 units, pool, spa. This is kind of an odd place. The upper part of this 40-story building is marketed as the Aqua. (The lowest 10 floors are marketed by the Hawai'i Polo Inn.) Though there are only 4 rooms per floor, the building is skinny and rooms are small and weirdly shaped. Not bad, just strange. Most of the rooms have nice ocean views. Kitchenettes in all the rooms. Not the cleanest resort we've reviewed in Waikiki. Weekly maid service, not daily. Local calls are free. Rooms (around 200 sq. ft.) are $129–$149. Suites are $195–$265. But discounts are the norm and you'll probably pay less. A block from the beach at the Hilton.

Aston Aloha Surf Hotel
(800) 922–7866 or (808) 923–0222
444 Kanekapolei St.
202 rooms, pool, Web TV, lanais on most rooms. The surf theme permeates

Aston Aloha Surf

the lobby here from surfboards to continuous play on the TV. This 16-floor building has fairly typical Waikiki rooms—adequate, nothing more. Continental breakfasts are free. The pool's pretty small. Only corner rooms have bathtubs—the rest have showers. It's two long blocks to the beach. Room sizes vary considerably from 220 to 370 sq. ft. for $115–$185. 1/1s (625 sq. ft.) are $190–$220.

Aston Coconut Plaza
(800) 922–7866 or (808) 923–8828
450 Lewers St.
WEB REVIEW

Aston Waikiki Beach Hotel
(800) 922–7866 or (808) 922–2511
2570 Kalakaua Ave.
644 rooms, pool, lanais on some, 3 restaurants. Two buildings—a 20-story tower and a very avoidable 8-story

Password for all Web reviews is: **or8329**

tower. This is a Jekyll and Hyde resort. The main building has a loud, '50s retro decor; it'll work for some and annoy others. But the mauka building is to be avoided at all costs. It's old, worn and depressing. It feels like the place they punish visitors that have been bad. Parking is a pricey $13 (valet only). Breakfast is free—you either eat it at the pool, or you can take it over to the beach across the street. No coffee makers for us coffee addicts. Overall, the place feels busy and loud. Rooms in the main building (225 sq. ft.) are $216–$406. Rooms in the mauka building (266 sq. ft.) are $153. These prices seem waaay high to us, hope you did better.

Aston Waikiki Beachside
(800) 922–7866 or (808) 931–2100
2452 Kalakaua Ave.

79 rooms, 2 shops. This 12-story boutique hotel right across the street from Waikiki Beach Center is small by Waikiki standards. The resort has an expensive Euro-Chinese decor and lots of antiques, producing an overall opulent feel. Despite the central location, they manage to achieve an atmosphere that seems somewhat removed from the main of Waikiki, producing a tranquil experience. Parking is $12 and is around the corner at the Waikiki Beach Tower. Rooms are small with only double and queen beds available, so they don't allow more than two people per room. Rooms with lanais come at the expense of the interior square footage, so only get a lanai if you really want one. If you want to be able to watch the torchlighting ceremony across the street at the beach from your room, pick a room on floors 3–5 facing the ocean. If you want your view to clear the crown of the large banyan tree across the street, you'll want floors 8 or above. There are 2 rooms on each floor that have no window and no lanai, but you can usually get around a 50% discount on these—a great deal given their location. No coffee makers, but continental breakfast is included with all rooms. No laundry facilities—you'll have to give it to the valet. Overall, a very nice resort with a great location; easy to recommend. Rooms (234 sq. ft.) are $195–$350. Suites are $270–$405.

A REAL GEM

Bamboo (Aqua)
(866) 406–2782 or (808) 922–7777
2425 Kuhio Ave.
93 rooms, pool, spa, sauna, BBQ. A 12-floor 1965 building that's been turned into a boutique hotel. The atmosphere is very tranquil: incense in the air, wind

See all Web reviews at: www.wizardpub.com

Bamboo (Aqua)

Breakers

chimes by the nice pool next to the massage table and Buddhas sprinkled about.

A REAL GEM

Sort of a contemporary Thai/Asian feel. They *really* like apples here, and they're always free in the lobby. No *true* room service, but you can get a continental breakfast delivered to your room. Because of the relatively small size, nothing feels too distant. Service is personalized, but some of the amenities are pricey here, but room safes are complimentary. You have signing privileges at the nearby Hyatt restaurants and spa. Some rooms are pretty small but laid out well so it's less of an issue. Overall, a very easy place to like, and it's a couple minutes walk to the beach. We wondered why they had the letters SGH at the bottom of the pool. Apparently it's the previous name of this place, and it was too expensive to remove the tiles. Rooms (210–226 sq. ft.) are $145, studios (208–342 sq. ft.) are $165–$185. Suites are $275–$750. If you're staying on a lower floor, opt for a deluxe studio view facing the pool.

Breakers
(800) 426–0494 or (808) 923–3181
250 Beachwalk
64 rooms, pool, kitchenettes, BBQ, lanais on upper floor. An old-time two-story low-rise that has lots of character. It's pretty inexpensive and has a fairly tranquil, Japanese feel and has changed very little over the years. It's in one of the denser sections of Waikiki, and the rooms are comfortably sized. Most of the staff goes back a long time. Parking is free but limited. (7 stalls, first come, first serve each day.) Local calls are 50¢. No permanent non-smoking rooms. Free coffee at the front desk. There's a Japanese tea house on the premises, and tea services take place Wed. and Fri. Hey, any place that is clean, two blocks from the beach, has kitchenettes and a slow pace has a lot going for it. Units facing the pool are best. No elevators. Rooms are $91–$100. Suites are $125–$151. (Suites aren't worth the upgrade.)

Cabana at Waikiki
(877) 902–2121 or (808) 926–5555
2551 Cartwright Rd.
WEB REVIEW

Continental Surf Hotel
(800) 991–9228 or (808) 922–2232
2426 Kuhio Ave.
143 rooms. A 22-story 1975 building renovated in 2002. No lanais here and no room safes (unusual for Waikiki). This is a very clean, very basic place to stay. No frills other than "daily yoga classes," but it's reasonably priced and there are limited views of the ocean from some

SOLID GOLD VALUE

Password for all Web reviews is: **or8329**

Continental Surf Hotel

rooms (which are on the small side), and it's only a couple of minutes walk to Waikiki Beach Center. Rooms (200–250 sq. ft.) are $69–$79.

Coral Reef Hotel (Aston)
(800) 922–7866 or (808) 922–1262
2299 Kuhio Ave.

WEB REVIEW

Diamond Head Beach Hotel (Marc)
(800) 535–0085 or (808) 922–1928
2947 Kalakaua Ave.

65 rooms, lanais on some. A 14-story tapered tower, so the higher up you go, the smaller the rooms get. If you want to see Diamond Head, you need to be above the 6th floor; otherwise, you're staring at buildings. If you're staying on

the 14th floor, you'll have to take the stairs that last story. Units are individually owned, and the rooms vary *considerably* more than most places we've reviewed. We've seen rooms that were nice and rooms that were horrible. Feeling lucky? If you're staying longer than a week, maid service is only twice a week. It's a short walk to a sandy beach, and the ocean-facing rooms have great views. Parking is $12. There are no restaurants nearby except the *very* pricey Hau Tree Lanai at the New Otani. Otherwise, it's at least a mile walk to Waikiki. We can't see paying the RACK rates that Marc charges. The hotel-type rooms (250–450 sq. ft.) are $199, 1/1s are $339–$439.

DoubleTree Alana Hotel
(800) 222–8733 or (808) 941–7275
1956 Ala Moana Blvd.

DoubleTree Alana Hotel

313 rooms, pool, fitness area, room service, valet parking, restaurant, 7 conference rooms, business center, coffee makers (with free coffee), hi-speed Internet access in renovated rooms and Wi-Fi in lobby, microwaves are extra and available upon request. A 19-story tower from 1974. This hotel is popular with business travelers and those who want convenient access to the Hawai'i Convention Center a few minutes walk away. The beach is farther—almost a 10 minute walk. The rooms are nicely

See all Web reviews at: www.wizardpub.com

appointed and reasonably sized, but the views are pretty unimpressive. Laundry is valet only, and room safes are free. Parking is $12 (valet only). Rooms (308–375 sq. ft.) are $209–$229, suites (667–1,340 sq. ft.) are $265–$2,100. Deep discounts are often obtainable, taking some of the sting out of the high RACK rates. It's not a dreamy vacation paradise, it's a convenient place for business travelers.

Ewa Hotel Waikiki
(800) 359–8639 or (808) 922–1677
2555 Cartwright Rd.

Ewa Hotel Waikiki

92 units, lanais in *some*. There's an Internet café on site. Parking is $6. A dreary 8-story 1960s-era building that has few redeeming qualities that we could find, except that all rooms (except standards) have kitchenettes, and it's one block to the beach. Coffee makers are extra and available upon request. Room size varies considerably here. Note that there are *no* non-smoking

rooms. Rooms (200–338 sq. ft.) are $80–$120, 1/1s (500 sq. ft.) are $160, 2/2s (700 sq. ft.) are $220.

Hale Koa
(800) 367–6027 or (808) 955–0555
2055 Kalia Rd.

Ilima Tower   Maile Tower

815 rooms, 2 pools and keiki pool, 4 lighted tennis courts, fitness room, 3 restaurants, 5 shops, 7 conference rooms, lu'au. **SOLID GOLD VALUE** First things first. You'll probably need to be in the military, reserve, national guard or retired military to stay here. (The eligibility requirements are vast—contact them to see if you can weasel yourself in.) This is the roomiest place in Waikiki. There are 72 acres of land, much of it a park open to the public. (One rule: No bikes allowed. We're not sure why.) There are tons of activities available here: volleyball, racketball, pool activities, video game room, etc., and they're located next to the widest part of Waikiki Beach. We can't imagine anyone staying here, paying these rates, and not being happy. Services are good here, and with their fantastic prices, you'll need to reserve rooms 6–9 months in advance. The biggest shocker for us was this: The military runs off coffee, yet this is one of the few places in Waikiki

where they don't have coffee makers in the room for your morning cup of joe. (When we asked why, they said it's because they have so many retired people in their 70s who'd just sit in the room all day if they had coffee makers. They want them out of the room, even if it is just to go to the lobby.) No room safes. (It's pretty unlikely you'd get ripped off here since it's a federal offense.) Parking is $4 and local calls are 50¢. Rooms have VCRs, and they rent movies at the PX. Cribs are free. No minimum stay, but there is a maximum—no more than 30 days. Rooms (300 sq. ft.) are $71–$181. Prices are based on your rank—the higher your rank, the more you pay, so suck it in, General.

Halekulani
(800) 367–2343 or (808) 923–2311
2199 Kalia Rd.

455 rooms, pool, fitness room, 24-hour room service, valet parking, 7 shops, 5 conference rooms, business center/hospitality suite.

A REAL GEM

Wow, where do we start? This is an awesome place. Comprising 5 buildings (the tallest is 17 floors), this is less of a tower resort than most of their neighbors. Services are unmatched here. For instance the check-in: Forget the desk, just have

the greeter take you on a tour and then to your room and give you a box of chocolates and an excellent fruit platter. They track your habits and try to anticipate your future needs. If you order coffee first thing in the morning, next time you're there, they'll already know that you want it. This is the way a resort should be run. You want it; you'll get it. Don't like your pillow? They'll get you a different kind. Want to eat at their top-of-the-line fine dining restaurant but left your nice clothes at home. What size do you wear, sir? There is no nickel and diming here. Most things other resorts charge extra for are free, such as room safes, local calls, valet parking, cribs, resort-wide entertainment. Child care service in summer and Christmas is $25 per day, and the kids literally call the shots. Parking is $10 (whether you do it or valet). Laundry is valet only. Room amenities are high, from the deep soaking tubs, DVD players and Wi-Fi. The motif is white and pale blue—designed to resemble their name: Halekulani means *house befitting heaven*. There is a whole host of attractions around Honolulu, like 'Iolani Palace and the Honolulu Symphony that you can get into for free because the Halekulani is a sponsor.

Halekulani's food services are incredible, and everything is created on the premises—pastries, chocolates, ice creams, breads—you name it. Their spa is so relaxing, you'll think they removed your bones when you weren't looking. It's hard to find much fault here. Biggest ding? Their beach is the thinnest part of Waikiki—much of it lined by a seawall. (That may change over time as the government steps up a beach replenishment program.) Oh, and there are no refrigerators or coffee makers in the rooms, if you hate greeting the world without your caf-

See all Web reviews at: www.wizardpub.com

feine fix. *For what you get*, rooms are reasonably priced. You'll be pampered here and may literally weep when you have to leave, and the resort exudes a tranquility that's hard to match in Waikiki. Rooms (519 sq. ft.) are $325–$540, suites (720–4,066 sq. ft.) are about $1 per square foot. Their royal suite (4,066 sq. ft.) comes with a personal butler, a baby grand piano, an airport limo and breakfast in your room daily for a *mere* $4,500 per night.

Hawai'i Polo Inn
(800) 669–7719 or (808) 949–0061
1696 Ala Moana Blvd.

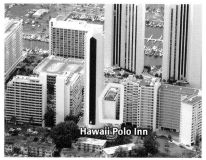
Hawaii Polo Inn

106 rooms, pool, tennis court. Such a classy-sounding name for such a dreary, institutional feel—rooms should be much cheaper than they are. They tell us that over 80% of their customers are Japanese travelers. They also have 40 rooms next door—the bottom 10 floors of the Aqua Marina. You better get a much cheaper price than their published rates to justify staying here. Rooms (350 sq. ft.) are $69–$129. A block from the beach at the Hilton.

Hawai'i Prince Hotel Waikiki
(800) 321–6248 or (808) 956–1111
100 Holomoana St.
WEB REVIEW

Hawaiian King
(800) 545–1948 or (808) 922–3894
417 Nohonani St.

Hawaiian King

67 rooms, pool, some of the coin-op laundries are in the rooms. A short building by Waikiki standards—only 6 floors built **SOLID GOLD VALUE** in 1959. They exude a 1960s feel even today, and the services are good here—very personalized. Their customer return rate is pretty high; people seem satisfied here. Each room is independently owned, so they're all different, but overall, the building is very well maintained. No room safes. No parking on site and the price varies off site. You're a few blocks from the beach. There's a BBQ available. 1/1s (588–788 sq. ft.) are $79–$149 plus cleaning fee, and they are quick to discount. The longer you stay, the more they'll discount.

Hawaiian Monarch Hotel
(800) 367–5004 or (808) 949–3911
444 Niu St.
450 rooms, pool. A 44-story tower from 1967. Well, you found it. This is the most distant hotel in Waikiki that's technically still in Waikiki. The only thing

Password for all Web reviews is: **or8329**

convenient about the location is that when you're leaving Waikiki, it's on the corner on your way out. Let's see. It's inconveniently located, the rooms are unremarkable *at best,* and it's overpriced. Hard to get happy about this one. There are no permanent non-smoking rooms and no lanais. Rooms (around 325 sq. ft.) are $120–$150. Did you get a super deal? If not, then why are you here?

Hawaiiana Hotel
(800) 367–5122 or (808) 923–3811
260 Beachwalk
WEB REVIEW

Hilton Hawaiian Village
(800) 221–2424 or (808) 949–4321
2005 Kalia Rd.
3,000+ rooms, 4 pools, 2 spas, 2 fitness rooms, 14 restaurants, 90 or so shops, 100,000 sq. ft. of conference rooms, 24-hour business center, room service, WebTV and Hi-speed Internet access from rooms, Nintendo, lanais (on most),

child care service. Where do we start? We've reviewed every resort in Hawai'i, and this is the biggest kahuna of them all. On a typical day they'll have 5,000 guests serviced by 1,800 employees, which practically qualifies it as a small town. If you're looking for a pulsating, always-moving resort, this place hums. If you're looking for peace and quiet, you've definitely come to the wrong place. Six massive towers (the tallest is 35 stories) with the Rainbow Tower being the closest to the water and the Alii Tower having the highest services. The grounds are strewn with tropical plants, flowing ponds, swimming pools, some exotic birds and lots of palm trees.

In some ways they seem to nickel and dime you here. They charge a whopping $10 per day to use the in-room hi-speed Internet access, and coffee for your maker is extra. (They make a tidy $30,000 a year just selling you coffee for that little machine.) There's no coin-op laundry. You'll have to send it out and pay extra.

The Alii Tower is the nicest tower. It's the best furnished, there are extra services there, and they throw in some extras like the above-mentioned coffee. (Alii rooms ending in -05 are particularly nice.) They have their own front desks here and in the Kalia Tower, so you can check in directly there and avoid the often-busier main lobby.

The Diamond Head Tower is our least

See all Web reviews at: www.wizardpub.com

favorite and the Lagoon Tower is completely timeshare. If you've heard horror stories about mold in the Kalia Tower, that's ancient history after their $50 million clean-up—it's a nice tower.

The beach in front of the Hilton defines the northwestern edge of Waikiki and has the calmest waters. If the prices of the restaurants here scare you off, the Hale Koa's simple food next door is considerably cheaper and, although it's a military hotel, you *can* use their restaurants.

The resort is well-known for their fireworks every Friday night. Rooms are simple and comfortable. The oceanfront category rooms on the Rainbow Tower—especially those on the Diamond Head side—have smashing views down the beach.

Rooms sizes range all over the place and cost $195–$520, suites are $500–$4,500.

Hokondo Waikiki Beachside Hotel & Hostel
(808) 923–9566 • 2556 Lemon Rd.

WEB REVIEW

Holiday Inn Waikiki
(888) 992–4545 or (808) 955–1111
1830 Ala Moana Blvd.

Holiday Inn Waikiki

199 rooms, pool, fitness room, restaurant, Nintendo. A simple, basic, reliable

15-story hotel built in the '70s. Parking is $6. Not in pristine condition but up to Holiday Inn standards. A bit pricey, however. Shoot for some kind of discount. If you're looking for a lanai, you'll need an end room or the top floor. A few minutes' walk to the beach at the Hilton. Rooms (240 sq. ft.) are $140–$180.

Holiday Surf
(877) 923–8488 or (808) 923–8488
2303 Ala Wai Blvd.

Holiday Surf

34 rooms, full kitchens, VCRs (movies available on site for rent—they *really* seem to like sci-fi), bi-weekly maid service. A 6-story building built in 1963 and right across from the Ala Wai Canal and Boulevard. (the latter can be noisy), this is a family-operated condo, and it's pretty no-frills. No room safes. You can't see the ocean, which is a pretty long walk. Studios (315 sq. ft.) are $99, 1/1s (380 sq. ft.) are $145, suites are $169–$195. Their online rates usually have a *huge* discount.

Honolulu Prince (Aston)
(800) 922–7866 or (808) 922–1616
415 Nahua St.
135 rooms, coffee makers (in most). A 10-story building from 1966. They usually discount (ask for the General Man-

Password for all Web reviews is: **or8329**

Honolulu Prince (Aston)

ager Special), making it pretty cheap. Good, because the rooms are fairly dreary and seem cheaply furnished. (At least they're pretty big, except for the standard category, which are also the only rooms that don't have lanais.) Rooms (271–340 sq. ft.) are $95–$115. 1/1s (833 sq. ft.) are $150, 2/2s (986 sq. ft.) are $180. Almost 3 blocks from the beach.

Hostelling International
(808) 926–8313
2417 Prince Edward St.

Hostelling International

12 rooms. Dorms are $23 a night (with 9 of your newfound friends in bunk beds), and studios with a bath are $54 (which isn't a good deal). No phone (other than a pay phone), no a/c, no coffee makers. Parking is $5. It's not a dump; it's a hostel. Sheets supplied, BYOT (bring your own towels). No alcohol allowed. 7 day maximum stay. DSL Internet available for extra. Bring your own padlock for the lockers. Studios require 2 person occupancy. 2 short blocks to the beach.

Hyatt Regency Waikiki
(800) 554–9288 or (808) 923–1234
2424 Kalakaua Ave.

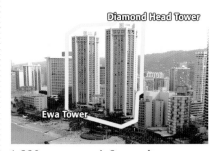

Diamond Head Tower

Ewa Tower

1,230 rooms, pool, 2 spas, fitness room, room service, 47 shops, 12 conference rooms, 6 restaurants, business center, Camp Hyatt child care (seasonal). The Hyatt is two 40-floor towers from 1976 bracketing a huge open atrium complete with a 3-story manmade waterfall. This is one of the bigger Waikiki resorts. You're right across the street from Waikiki Beach Center, but it'll take a little time to make your way through the resort to the beach. There are gobs of shops, as well as a large health spa. While the resort might not feel as Hawaiian as some of the others in Waikiki, it's a nice place to stay and the rooms are big and comfortable, if a tad stark. Room renovations were ongoing at press time, and the renovated rooms are much preferred over the older rooms. Because the buildings are octagonal, the "deluxe ocean" views might directly face the ocean, or they might be at an angle. Some of the extras can be a bit pricey—such as the "massage by the minute" at the pool ($1.25, per minute so be choosy about which limbs you want massaged). The fridge is stocked with a mini-bar—you can get an empty fridge for $7 (for the whole stay). Rates are high, but few pay the RACK rate listed below. Rooms (450 sq. ft.) are $265–$410. Suites are $800–$4,000.

See all Web reviews at: www.wizardpub.com

'Ilima Hotel
(800) 801–9366 or (808) 923–1877
445 Nohonani St.

'Ilima Hotel

99 rooms, pool, fitness room, sauna. A '60s building with 17 floors, this place has more of a family feel than similar hotels. Some **SOLID GOLD VALUE** of the items that most resorts charge for—like parking (which is limited) and local calls—are free. All rooms have full kitchens and the layouts are fairly spacious. Some have hi-speed Internet access. In short, an easy place to get comfortable. Studios (530 sq. ft.) are $129–$165, 1/1s (650 sq. ft.) are $159–$209, 2/2s (770 sq. ft.) are $230–$270. Lots of discounts available. It's 2½ blocks to the beach.

Imperial Hawai'i Resort
(800) 347–2582 or (808) 923–1827
205 Lewers St.

Imperial Hawaii Resort

250 rooms, pool, fitness room, conference room, restaurant, 4 shops, DVD players (with DVDs for rent). There are 26 floors in this 1970s building, and only floors 20 and above give you good views of the ocean. Though this is a timeshare resort, 30% of the rooms are routinely available for rent. All rooms have kitchens or kitchenettes, and the studios have pull-down Murphy beds, making good use of the space. But they don't guarantee the floor or view you'll get when you book—only the type of unit. There are *no* permanent non-smoking rooms. Parking is $15 (valet only), and local calls are free. (Sort of; you have to pay $2 per day for "free" calls and room safe.) It's clean and fairly reasonably priced given the location: The beach is only a few minutes walk away. Studios (350 sq. ft.) are $130–$140, 1/1s (450 sq. ft.) are $155–$165, 1/2s (525–575 sq. ft.) are $195–$215, 2/2s (700 sq. ft.) are $225–$235.

Island Colony
(800) 367–5004 or (808) 923–2345
2155 Kalakaua Ave.

743 rooms, pool, spa, sauna, coffee makers (in most). A 44-story 1970s tower, the place is big. The staff can be chilly here. Odd numbered upper rooms

Password for all Web reviews is: **or8329**

have the best views, but it's still pretty far from the ocean. Lanais are huge while bathrooms are small—go figure. Overall, it doesn't exude a warm, tropical feel, and it's a long walk to the beach. Rooms (308 sq. ft.) are $155–$165. Studios with kitchenettes (308 sq. ft.) are $180–$199. 1/1s (570 sq. ft.) are $199–$239.

Kai Aloha Hotel
(808) 923–6723 • 235 Saratoga Rd.

Kai Aloha Hotel

10 rooms. A 3-story (no elevator) 1950s building with no non-smoking rooms. This is a tiny, family-run resort that is simple and **SOLID GOLD VALUE** clean. The furnishings are old—perhaps the originals in some cases—but they're in good shape. You get the feeling it hasn't changed much since it was built—they even have stove-top coffee percolators in most rooms. But, hey, you ain't paying for the Haleku-lani. Parking is $27 for a 3-day pass at Ft. Derussy Park across the street; local calls are 50¢. No room safes. Studios (which have kitchenettes and two twin beds) are $65–$70, 1/1s are $76–$115 (depending on the number of people in your party). If you want less street noise, ask for a unit at the back of the building. About 2 blocks to the beach.

Kuhio Village Resort (Aqua)
(866) 406–2782 or (808) 791–7171
2463 Kuhio Ave.

WEB REVIEW

Marc Suites Waikiki
(800) 535–0085 or (808) 923–8882
412 Lewers St.

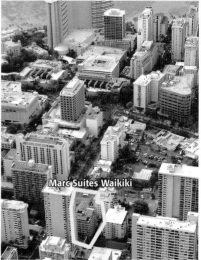

Marc Suites Waikiki

104 rooms, pool. Snotty service and dreary rooms make it hard to find any reason to stay at this 9-floor building. We couldn't think of anything we liked about it. Parking is $10 on a first-come, first-serve basis—otherwise, you'll have to scramble. Long walk to the beach. Rooms (265 sq. ft.) are $129–$149, 1/1s (420 sq. ft.) are $159–$179, and 2/2s (515 sq. ft.) are $269–$299.

Marc Waikiki Royal Suites
(800) 535–0085 or (808) 926–5641
255 Beachwalk

WEB REVIEW

Marine Surf Waikiki Hotel
(888) 456–7873 or (808) 931–2424
364 Seaside Ave.

230 rooms, pool, full kitchens, restaurant, coffee makers with free coffee daily. A 23-story tower from 1968. Each unit is individually owned, so there's variation in

See all Web reviews at: www.wizardpub.com

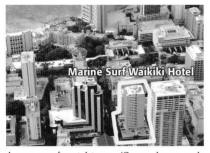

Marine Surf Waikiki Hotel

the room furnishings. (Some have only small friges, some have microwaves, etc.) Rooms are decent-sized. If you want a non-smoking room, you'll have to up-grade to Superior. There are marginal ocean views from 16th floor and above. It's a fairly long walk to the beach. Parking is $5, and local calls are 50¢. Think of it as a place to sleep, nothing more, nothing less. Rooms (450 sq. ft.) are $107–$135.

Marriott Waikiki Beach Resort
(800) 367–5370 or (808) 922–6611
2552 Kalakaua Ave.

Paoakalani Tower

Kealohilani Tower

1,310 rooms, 2 pools, fitness room, health spa, 16 conference rooms, 12 shops, PlayStations, 5 restaurants, coffee makers and free daily coffee, valet parking, room service, free cribs available, child care service in summer and winter, Wi-Fi resort-wide, business center. This is the kind of place you think of when you imagine a large, very nice Hawaiian resort.

A REAL GEM

Tropical feel, flowers everywhere. They even have a re-creation of the Halona blowhole in the lobby—wait long enough and it'll go off. There are cultural demonstrations all the time and daily hula shows. The rooms are very comfortable, nicely decorated and have large lanais. Even though it's very large, it radiates the dreamy warmth you're looking for without seeming too busy. There are two towers here—the 24-floor building is closest to the ocean, while the 33-story building is more of a walk to the beach. Parking is $12 and local calls are a hefty $1.25 (at least the room safes are free). Rooms (300–350 sq. ft.) are $320–$490. Suites are $1,500–$2,300 (which coincides with their square footages).

Miramar at Waikiki
(800) 367–2303 or (808) 922–2077
2345 Kuhio Ave.
WEB REVIEW

New Otani Kaimana Beach Hotel
(800) 356–8264 or (808) 923–1555
2863 Kalakaua Ave.
124 rooms, 2 restaurants, conference room, 2 shops, room service, valet parking, fitness room, coffee makers on request. Two buildings, 9 and 3 stories (the latter Diamond Head wing has no elevator). Their oceanfront category rooms are extremely intimate with the beach—look straight

A REAL GEM

Password for all Web reviews is: **or8329**

Ocean Resort Hotel Waikiki

Ocean Resort Hotel Waikiki
(800) 367–2317 or (808) 922–3861
175 Paoakalani Ave.

450 rooms, 2 pools, restaurant, 2 conference rooms, 2 shops, room service, Nintendo, coffee makers in some. Two 19-story 1970-ish towers. This place is a particularly good deal, especially when you consider that they *routinely* give 40%–50% off these rates simply by asking. They're a block from the beach but kind of boxed in, so views are somewhat limited—go as high as you can (10 or above). The pricier rooms (in the Pali Tower) have kitchenettes. Return guests who join the free Ohana Member club get even deeper discounts and upgrades. Clean, bright, spacious (most of them) and cheap—works for us. A no-brainer for a SOLID GOLD VALUE. Rooms (300–450 sq. ft.) are $130–$170, superior to deluxe (525–595 sq. ft.) are $180–$220, suites (550–1,100 sq. ft.) are $225–$500. The Kaua'i suite is particularly nice.

SOLID GOLD VALUE

Ohana East
(800) 462–6262 or (808) 922–5353
150 Kaiulani Ave.
445 rooms, pool, spa, fitness room, 4 restaurants, room service, 3 conference rooms, shops, Wi-Fi in the lobby, Nintendo, free room safes, 24-hour self-service business center. A 19-floor tower built in 1972 and renovated in 2004. As

down onto the sand, and since the tallest room is 9 stories up, you'll never feel completely detached. This is the reason for the GEM. It's on lovely Sans Souci Beach. Though still expensive, you won't get rooms like that for this kind of price in more centrally located Waikiki resorts. And there's the reason for the lower prices—it's a fairly long walk to the heart of Waikiki, and many will opt to drive and pay to park. But you're also away from the high energy of Waikiki. This is a smaller, quieter resort than others you'll find on the beach. Rooms aren't particularly Hawaiian in their decor, but they're simple and clean, and if you have an oceanfront room, you won't even notice the furnishings. Their services have some nice touches like a fresh pineapple welcome and an orchid with your turn-down service, and the staff is excellent. There are no permanent non-smoking rooms (but the rooms didn't have a smoky smell to us). Their Hau Tree Lanai restaurant is a great (if extremely pricey) place to have your breakfast on the beach. Parking is $12 (valet only). Rooms (202–395 sq. ft.) are $145–$335, suites (395–838 sq. ft.) are $440–$1,085. Most rooms are discounted.

See all Web reviews at: www.wizardpub.com

Ohana East

an Ohana hotel, they cater more toward families. Rooms are pretty small and tight. (City view rooms are a bit bigger and worth the extra $10.) The showers are tiny—take a deep breath, and you might force the door open). It's two blocks to the nearest beach (Waikiki Beach Center). They provide free coffee *daily* for your machine—nice touch. Rates (which few pay since they have lots of discounts) are $189–$199 (around 240 sq. ft.), kitchenettes are $199, suites are $289–$399. Overall, not a bad place if you get a discount.

Ohana Islander Waikiki
(800) 462–6262 or (808) 923–7711
270 Lewers St.

Ohana Islander Waikiki

283 rooms, pool, fitness room (free), business center, coffee maker (with free coffee), Nintendo. A 15-story tower from 1967. There are three Ohana resorts right next to each other, and this one has the best rooms of the bunch,

though they're not luxurious by any means. Small but comfortable. Ohana is sort of a cookie-cutter operation and their resorts tend to look pretty similar. Bathrooms have the typical Ohana teeny-tiny shower stalls. Kids get scratch cards to see if they get free beach balls. (Don't tell the keikis that all the cards are winners.) Parking is $10 and local calls are $1. Connecting rooms available. An acceptable place to stay. One block from the beach. Rooms (240–305 sq. ft.) are $189–$229.

Ohana Maile Sky Court
(800) 462–6262 or (808) 947–2828
2058 Kuhio Ave.
WEB REVIEW

Ohana Reef Lanai
(800) 462–6262 or (808) 923–3881
225 Saratoga Rd.

Ohana Reef Lanai

110 rooms, restaurant, Nintendo. This entire 12-story hotel is smoke-free, including the lanais. Some of the rooms have kitchenettes. Their shower stalls aren't as small as most Ohanas (but the doors are still pretty narrow), except the

Password for all Web reviews is: **or8329**

1/1s where they're still tiny. Connecting rooms available. Try to get a room above the 9th floor. Although the rooms are a bit nicer than the nearby Ohana Royal Islander, they're not $60 nicer. Rooms (300–450 sq. ft.) for $189–$249, 1/1s (500 sq. ft.) are $269. Few pay these RACK rates. One block from the beach.

Ohana Royal Islander
(800) 462–6262 or (808) 922–1961
2164 Kalia Rd.

Ohana Royal Islander

101 rooms, coffee makers (upon request), Nintendo, lanais on all (except for room 201). A small, 12-story building from 1964 with no grounds and not many extras. Rooms are adequate, nothing more. Sounds seem to carry well through the walls here. Bathrooms have the typical itsy-bitsy Ohana shower stalls. Some of the "ocean view" rooms, like those on the 8th floor, have the Pacific partially blocked by trees—try to go higher. Not overly compelling, but it's acceptable. It's a place to stay—that's it. Room square footages are widely varied from a teeny-tiny 178 to 409 sq. ft. for $129–$179, suites (580 sq. ft.) are $199–$219. Few pay these RACK rates. One block from the beach.

Ohana (Waikiki) Malia
(800) 462–6262 or (808) 923–7621
2211 Kuhio Ave.

WEB REVIEW

Ohana Waikiki Surf
(800) 462–6262 or (808) 923–7671
2200 Kuhio Ave.

Ohana Waikiki Surf

302 rooms, pool, spa, restaurant, Nintendo. A 17-story 1973 building, the resort's in decent condition, and the value is pretty good if you receive one of their easy-to-get discounts. Like other Ohana resorts, the showers are simply tiny. The pool area is nice here. Though the rooms are pretty small, overall, it's one of the better Ohanas in Waikiki. It's two long blocks to the beach. Rooms (210 sq. ft.) are $129, kitchenette (245 sq. ft.) are $149, 1/1s (375 sq. ft.) are $199.

Ohana Waikiki Surf East
(800) 462–6262 or (808) 923–7671
422 Royal Hawaiian Ave.

WEB REVIEW

See all Web reviews at: www.wizardpub.com

Ohana Waikiki Tower
(800) 462–6262 or (808) 922–6424
200 Lewers St.

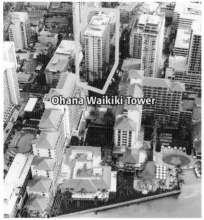

439 rooms, pool, 3 restaurants, 5 shops, conference room, business center, Nintendo, lanais on most (except 1st floor). A 21-story 1970s building that has a busy feel due to its location. Rooms are fine—not bad, not great. Bathrooms have the typical Ohana teeny-tiny shower stalls. Between the Waikiki Village and its sister property, Waikiki Tower, we'd give a marginal nod toward the Village. But Tower is a tad closer to the ocean one block away. Avoid the ultra-small rooms behind the elevators. Rooms (178–313 sq. ft.) are $149–$229.

Ohana Waikiki Village
(800) 462–6262 or (808) 923–3881
240 Lewers St.
WEB REVIEW

Ohana (Waikiki) West
(800) 462–6262 or (808) 922–5022
2330 Kuhio Ave.
663 rooms, pool, 2 restaurants, Nintendo, lanais (most rooms), poolside bar, a conference room. An 18-story tower

from 1973 that shows its age. Until they renovate it, we can't recommend it. Views improve with with height—but not much. Your best view is from the pool of the nearby Miramar's tile mosaic. Tiny showers—good for rinsing your vegetables but not much else. It's fairly centrally located—three blocks from the beach. Rooms (264 sq. ft.) are $129, kitchenettes (280 sq. ft.) are $139—worth the upgrade. Kitchenette combos are $269. These are a standard and a kitchenette with a $1 toll charge to use the connecting door. Insanely overpriced suites (340 sq. ft.) are $199–$399.

Outrigger Luana Waikiki
(800) 688–7444 or (808) 955–6000
2045 Kalakaua Ave.

217 rooms, pool, fitness room. A 16-story building from the '70s that was re-

Password for all Web reviews is: **or8329**

modeled in 2004. Although each room is individually owned, they are decorated similarly in an antique Hawaiiana theme and are nicely appointed. Rooms facing the ocean have unusually good views given the distance thanks to the tranquil park between you and the water ⅓ mile away. Best views are from the 8th floor and above. Overall, this is probably the best property in the immediate area. Studios have kitchenettes but the "lodging" units don't have microwaves or cooktops. Studios (310–325 sq. ft.) are $210–$265, 1/1s (500–700 sq. ft.) are $325–$375. These RACK rates are too high but most get discounts.

Outrigger Reef on the Beach
(800) 688–7444 or (808) 923–3111
2169 Kalia Rd.

Outrigger Reef on the Beach

858 rooms, pool, spa, fitness room, room service, valet parking, 3 restau-

rants, 14 shops, 4 conference rooms, business center, coffee makers (with free coffee), Nintendo, lanais on most, free cribs, child care service. Three buildings, the tallest is 17 stories. Overall, the resort design doesn't have a peaceful, Hawaiian feel. The pool area is a zoo. It can be insanely busy since their sister Ohana properties have pool privileges there. *Any* place in Waikiki is quieter than their pool, and their lobby area has a similar level of franticness. The timeshare salesmen in the lobby can be particularly annoying. Just look at them and mumble something that sounds like a foreign language to get them off your back. Their Shorebird Restaurant is a good place for a breakfast buffet. Child care is available for $55, but there are no off-site excursions. Parking is $13 (valet only). Rooms facing the Waikiki Shore are uncomfortably close to that building. You can practically reach over and peel the paint off their walls. The buildings were all completed at different times and they don't mesh well together. The resort has a hard-to-put-into-words annoying feel. On the up side, part of the resort borders the beach, so you won't walk far and there are lots of Hawaiian cultural demonstrations. Renovations were planned at press time. Rooms (240–384 sq. ft.) are $240–$510, suites (488–1,300 sq. ft.) are $460–$1,500.

Outrigger Waikiki on the Beach
(800) 688–7444 or (808) 923–0711
2335 Kalakaua Ave.

530 rooms, pool and spa, fitness center, room service (breakfast and dinner), 3 restaurants, 31 shops, 4 conference rooms, business center, room safes (free), Web TV in some, Nintendo. A 16-story tower right on the

A REAL GEM

See all Web reviews at: www.wizardpub.com

beach that's an easy place to like. The location is fantastic, though the building design means only a small percentage are right over the beach. They're near the center of action in Waikiki, and their restaurants—especially Duke's Canoe Club and Hula Grill—are winners. Dukes is a particularly great place for a breakfast buffet.

Services are nice here—even the check-in process is less painful than at other resorts. Other little touches indicate that customer comfort is more than a slogan here. Parking is $13 (valet only). The rooms are nicely decorated, and the deluxe oceanfront categories have separate showers and double Jacuzzi bathtubs. Connecting rooms are available. If you spring for oceanfront, avoid 3rd and 4th floors due to blockage from palm tree crowns. And some of the "ocean view" rooms get pretty marginal the farther back you go on the Diamond Head side. But overall, this is a good resort with a good attitude and a great location. There

are lots of beach activities available. Rooms (340 sq. ft.) are $290–$530. Suites are $650–$700. Lots of packages reduce these prices.

Pacific Beach Hotel
(800) 367–6060 or (808) 922–1233
2490 Kalakaua Ave.
WEB REVIEW

Pacific Monarch (Aston)
(800) 922–7866 or (808) 923–9805
2427 Kuhio Ave.

Pacific Monarch (Aston)

260 rooms, pool. A 31-floor 1979 building where the units are individually owned. Rooms are inexpensively furnished but adequate and comfortably sized. Lanais are large, and some of the views (especially from the rooftop pool) are pretty good. Definitely go for a room higher up. It's 3 short blocks to the beach. Studios (360 sq. ft.) are $150–$180, 1/1s (443 sq. ft) are $180–$220.

Park Shore Waikiki
(800) 367–2377 or (808) 923–0411
2586 Kalakaua Ave.

226 rooms, pool, 2 conference rooms, coffee makers with free daily coffee, 3 restaurants. Two towers topping out at 18 floors built in the 1970s. Near the park and near the shore, so it's aptly named. Oddly, the *deluxe* ocean view rooms are more oriented to the park,

Password for all Web reviews is: **or8329**

while the ocean view rooms face the ocean head-on. There are no laundry facilities—you'll have to send it out. Connecting rooms available. Rooms are pretty small here, and though it's next to the ocean, the RACK rates feel overpriced to us. (Discounts are the norm, though.) You're so close to the Sunset on the Beach movies shown on weekends that you can watch them from your lanai. (Though you won't be able to hear them—like being frugal on an airline and opting out of the headphones.) Their brochure photo was either taken a long time ago or is conveniently cropped—it omits the giant resort that blocks all west-facing rooms. Across the street from the beach. Rooms (200–315 sq. ft.) are $205–$245, suites are $335–$660.

Queen Kapiolani Hotel
(800) 367–2317 or (808) 922–1941
150 Kapahulu Ave.
314 rooms, pool, restaurant, Nintendo, lanais on some. A 19-story building from 1969. This was a grand hotel in its day, but it's looking a bit worn and tired. It's not seedy or dirty, just faded. The view from their pool is particularly wonderful, with an expansive vista from Diamond

Head to part of Waikiki. Rooms facing the ocean or Diamond Head are also awesome. Staff is good. A short block to the beach. Rooms (216–299 sq. ft.) are $130–220, studios with kitchenettes (344 sq. ft.) are $225–$250. 1/1s (1,022 sq. ft.) are $325–$425. Few pay the RACK rates, and return guests get bigger discounts.

Radisson (Waikiki) Prince Kuhio
(800) 333–3333 or (808) 922–0811
2500 Kuhio Ave.
WEB REVIEW

Renaissance Ilikai Waikiki Hotel
(800) 245–4524 or (808) 949–3811
1777 Ala Moana Blvd.

783 rooms, 2 pools, spa, tennis court, fitness room, room service, valet parking, 3

A REAL GEM

restaurants, shops, 28 conference rooms, business center, coffee makers with free coffee daily, free room safes. Two towers from the 1960s, the tallest is 25 stories. A very tropical,

See all Web reviews at: www.wizardpub.com

very Hawaiian feeling resort. Lots of plants, waterfalls and other Hawaiian touches. Since it's next to the Ala Wai Yacht Harbor, a nautical sense also permeates the resort. It's not on Waikiki Beach; it's a 5-minute walk along the shoreline. The rooms are nicely appointed and designed, and the resort is immaculate. The one- and two-bedroom units have complete kitchens and some others have kitchenettes. Choose either a tub or a shower (which are very large). Their Angel Chapel is a beautiful wedding chapel. Weddings are very popular here and easy to recommend.

We gave it a GEM because the ambiance is so effective, and the resort seems well integrated into its location. They have a large monkeypod tree planted by local surfing legend, Duke Kahanamoku. It's so precious to them they punched a hole through the parking garage to accommodate it. Parking is $14. Rooms in the Ilikai Tower are twice as big and have huge lanais. Rooms (300–600 sq. ft.) are $280–$390, 1/1s (600 sq. ft.) are $600, 2/2s (1,100 sq. ft.) are $800–$1,000. Don't let these RACK rates scare you off—they have *tons* of packages.

Royal Garden at Waikiki
(800) 367–5666 or (808) 943–0202
440 Olohana St.
WEB REVIEW

Royal Grove Hotel
(808) 923–7691
161 Uluniu Ave.
80 units, pool, 4 restaurants, refrigerators in some. Only 6 stories high at this 1962 building, and nothing seems to have changed since it was built—they don't even have an 800 number. (They

Royal Grove Hotel

seem proud of that.) It's cheap, no frills, no nonsense. Don't like that? Who asked you? Take a hike. No parking here; you'll have to use the Pacific Monarch across the street for $6. Maid service frequency depends on how long you stay. The longer you're there, the dirtier your room will get. Some of the rooms don't have a/c or coffee makers (both equally crucial as far as we're concerned). But it's cheap. Rooms are $45–$125, and it's only a couple minutes walk to the beach. We considered giving it a SOLID GOLD VALUE *for the price*, but couldn't bring ourselves to do it because it was just too worn.

Royal Hawaiian (Sheraton)
(866) 500–8313 or (808) 923–7311
2259 Kalakaua Ave.

Ocean Tower

Main Building

525 rooms, pool, 24-hour room service, free room safes, valet parking, dozen shops, restaurant, lu'au. There are almost 100 places to stay in Waikiki, but if pressed, we'd have to say the Royal is the pre-

A REAL GEM

mier property. Back when they built this place in 1927 there was only one other hotel—the nearby Moana. Royal's developers had their pick of where to build, and they chose this part of the beach. And no wonder—this is probably the best stretch of Waikiki—surfable waves offshore and sandy nearshore waters. (Though the water tends to be oddly cloudy here.) Also, this area is the heart of Waikiki with tons of stuff to do nearby, yet it's insulated from busy Kalakaua Avenue by the Royal Hawaiian Shopping Center. By location alone they stand apart. But it gets even better when you add the fact that it's a 6-story, low-rise building (except for the 17-story "new tower" built in 1969), and the pretty grounds have plenty of breathing room, dominated by some old, meandering trees. The result is a less bustling atmosphere than many of the nearby tower-dominated resorts.

Known locally as the **Pink Palace**, every shade of pink imaginable is represented—that's their trademark. Of the two buildings, we recommend the "historic" low-rise. Although the rooms are slightly smaller than the 350 sq. ft. tower rooms, they're more quaintly decorated in early 20th century style and feel more upscale. Since the building's old, expect some annoyances like a/c that's too loud in some. The "large luxury" category adds *a lot* of extra square footage for about $50—worth the upgrade. Suites are very roomy.

If you want your ocean views a bit more unobstructed, go with the tower rooms. They're comfortable. (Though the plumber must have been a munchkin because they mounted some of the showerheads at 5 feet.)

It can take up to 20 minutes to get your car from valet ($15 per day), so call

them way in advance or simply park yourself for $10. They have a lu'au Mon. and Thur., but it's surprisingly bad. Their Mai Tai Bar is right next to the beach, and, unlike other resorts, they have a roped off section of sand where you can *legally* drink your mai tai.

Overall, it's true that you might find crisper service at some other resorts. (Laundry is coin-op at the Sheraton next door and there are no coffee makers in the rooms.) With a location like this, they can pretty much charge what they want and they'll get it. But staff does a reasonable job. Their restaurant, the Surf Room, has a great breakfast buffet, though pricey at $23. You also have signing privileges at the Sheraton Waikiki next door.

Rates are expensive, but you can always get a discount if you ask for the "escape rate" or by becoming a Starwood member. Rooms vary in size from around 300–360 sq. ft. and are $380–$655. Suites start at $850.

Sheraton Moana Surfrider
(866) 500–8313 or (808) 922–3111
2365 Kalakaua Ave.

793 rooms, pool, 24-hour room service, 4 restaurants, 3 lounges, shops, free daily coffee for the rooms, free room safes, 10 conference rooms, Nintendo, child care (at the Sheraton Waikiki). This is one of Waikiki's most historic hotels, and the second floor has a nice display

See all Web reviews at: www.wizardpub.com

describing the legacy of this establishment. Their three buildings surround a century-old banyan tree than lends an air of timelessness to the ambiance. As an early player here in Waikiki, their location is among the best on the beach, but they seem to be relying on that fact perhaps a bit more than they should. The resort seems to be in need of a major upgrade. It feels overly worn. Nearly every room we saw had lots of stains, worn fixtures and furnishings in need of replacement—unacceptable for a resort charging these kind of prices.

The buildings are compact enough that you won't have to do much walking (except to where your car is parked behind the Princess Kaiulani). Valet parking is $15 per day, or you can pay $10 to self park. The oceanfront rooms labeled *Oceanfront Diamond* are the most recommended. The views are amazing and the sound of the ocean ever-present. *Historic Banyan Ocean* rooms are a mixed bag since they're in an older building with older fixtures, plus some labeled this way don't face the ocean head-on. Upper *Deluxe Ocean Towers* are best closer to the ocean. Avoid rooms nearest Kalakaua Avenue, especially in the Banyan Wing—traffic noises might be more than you'd expect, and the old windows there allow in lots of sound. In fact, if you're not going to spring for the admittedly overpriced oceanfront rooms, consider staying elsewhere. The Standard and City View rooms are a real disappointment.

The GEM rating refers to the grand beachside location and assumes you're in an oceanfront room. In general, if you got a good deal (or if price is no object) and you're willing to overlook some of the wear and tear the resort shows, you'll be happy with the oceanfront rooms here.

The views were so good, we chose a shot taken from one of the balconies to start this chapter. And after our stay, we left this hotel feeling delightfully relaxed—until we got credit card bill in the mail.

As a Starwood hotel, they may charge extra if you choose to check out before your original departure date.

Rates are $270–$575, Suites are $1,025 and up.

Sheraton Princess Kaiulani
(866) 500–8313 or (808) 922–5811
120 Kaiulani Ave.
WEB REVIEW

Sheraton Waikiki
(866) 500–8313 or (808) 922–4422
2255 Kalakaua Ave.

1,695 rooms, 2 pools, fitness room, 24-hour room service, 4 restaurants, 20 shops, 29 conference rooms, room safes (free), Web TV (in some), Nintendo, child care service. Although there are bigger resorts, this 31-story tower is the single biggest hotel building in all Hawai'i. It's so big you can actually get lost in the hallways, which keep going, and going and going. You can do a lot of walking at this sprawling resort, which can feel pretty busy. The oceanfront rooms *directly facing the beach* are simply glorious, looking down onto the beach and the reef, but you might want to avoid what they classify as oceanfront if they face the Royal Hawaiian. Oceanfront seems too generous for those rooms. If you're paying for cheaper views, it doesn't make much sense to pay the difference between city and mountain view. Pocket the money and splurge elsewhere.

Their kids' program is very extensive—it's $30 per day plus lunch, and they don't just jam them into a toy-filled room. They go to the zoo, aquarium, they have cooking days and plenty of other activities. (Parents can join the kids for the day for $10.) The fitness room is $8 per day or $16 for your whole stay.

One of their restaurants—the Hanohano Room—has one of the most commanding views of any Waikiki restaurant. You have charging privileges at any of the four Waikiki Sheratons. Parking is $10 ($15 for valet). The rooms are on the small side, but their location is fantastic. There are only a few resorts in Waikiki that feel this cozy with the beach.

Overall, you'll love this if you are jonesin' to be near the beach; you won't love it if you're looking for tranquility. Rooms (225–300 sq. ft.) are $290–$600, suites (1,112 or 2,224 sq. ft.) are $865–$2,450.

W Honolulu Diamond Head
(877) 946–8357 or (808) 922–1700
2885 Kalakaua Ave.

WEB REVIEW

day ($30 a week—a good deal by Waikiki standards). This resort seems geared toward families. They allow up to 5 people per room. There's even a playground next to the pool on the 6th floor, and when kids under 12 arrive, they're given a beach-related grab bag. They also lend children's books and have kids' videos for rent. If you're in Tower #2, you want a room ending in 12 or 14; otherwise, the view is totally dominated by Tower #1. Some of their category descriptions seem overly optimistic. (Ocean view? How you figga?) Rooms have fairly no-frills furnishings. There's one thing that got under our skin. They have BBQ grills available, but you'll have to bring quarters, because they're *coin-operated*. Yeah, it's minor, but it's annoying. In general, the resort is not a bad place for families, but child-free travelers might want to look elsewhere. One long block to the beach. 1/1s (600–625 sq. ft.) are $180–$260.

Waikiki Beach Tower (Aston)
(800) 922–7866 or (808) 926–6400
2470 Kalakaua Ave.
140 rooms, pool, spa, sauna, complete kitchens (with dishwashers), washer/dryers in units, lighted tennis court, 3 conference rooms. A skinny 40-story building (only 4 units per floor) built in 1984 with *giant* rooms

A REAL GEM

Waikiki Banyan (Aston)
(800) 922–7866 or (808) 922–0555
201 Ohua Ave.
876 rooms, pool, sauna, tennis court, 2 conference rooms. Two towers (37 & 38 stories tall) from 1969. Parking is $5 per

See all Web reviews at: www.wizardpub.com

that are *almost* across the street from the beach. All of the rooms above the 18th floor have tasty ocean views. (Even those below 18 are fairly good.) Services are high, and they don't nickel and dime you here. Parking is free—even *valet* is free—and so is coffee. No charge for room safes—even beach towels and beach chairs are there for you to take to the beach. (Too bad they charge you 75¢ for local calls.) This is a particularly good place for families since there's so much space in each unit. Lanais are large as well. 1/1s (accomplished via a lock-off creating about 900–1,000 sq. ft. of living area) are $485–$585. 2/2s (1,196–1,310 sq. ft.) are $570–$775. Pricey? You bet. But if you need gobs of room and want someplace expensively furnished, this is a nice place to stay. Besides, few people ever pay the full RACK rate.

Waikiki Beachcomber
(800) 622–4646 or (808) 922–4646
2300 Kalakaua Ave.
WEB REVIEW

Waikiki Circle (Aston)
(800) 922–7866 or (808) 923–1571
2464 Kalakaua Ave.
104 rooms, restaurant, Nintendo. This is

one of the smaller near-beachside resorts in Waikiki and is right across the street from Waikiki Beach Center. This 14-floor tower was built back in 1962 in the shape of a Chinese lantern. Most Waikiki resorts don't have a 13th floor because it's considered bad luck in western culture. The Asian owners here embrace the 13th floor and use feng shui to to make many of their decorating and designing decisions. Even the outside wall on the Diamond Head side—slated to be removed—was spared because their feng shui master said that it was necessary to hold in the good luck. Most of the staff has been here a long time, and repeat guests will often be remembered. The pie-shaped rooms are very small and feel even smaller than their stated square footages. But their space is used pretty efficiently, and the decor is all fish, all of the time. All rooms have two double beds. No coffee makers. If you want to minimize walking, this is the resort for you. It's a quick walk from the parking to the rooms—no vast corridors. And it's a quick walk to the beach. Located in the center of Waikiki, so restaurants are close by. Rooms (245 sq. ft.) are $165–$195.

Waikiki Gateway
(800) 247–1903 or (808) 955–3741
2070 Kalakaua Ave.
WEB REVIEW

Password for all Web reviews is: **or8329**

Waikiki Grand
(888) 336–4368 or (808) 923–1814
134 Kapahulu Ave.

176 units, pool, kitchenette, coffee makers with free daily coffee. A 10-floor building from 1963. Individually owned units all **SOLID GOLD VALUE** have different furnishings. Parking is $8, local calls are free. Free room safes *in some*. Rooms ending in 00 have a profound lack of privacy. All rooms are non-smoking; you're only allowed to smoke on the lanais. (And some rooms don't have lanais, so smokers will want to request one.) The beach is only a minute walk away. Some of the room categories seem pretty marginal—for instance, deluxe city view ain't that deluxe, and ocean views might take some fancy neck twisting. But prices are cheap, hence the SOLID GOLD VALUE. Rooms (280–478 sq. ft.) are $70–$120. Jr. Suites are $95–$150.

Waikiki Joy Hotel (Aston)
(800) 922–7866 or (808) 923–2300
320 Lewers St.

94 rooms, (small) pool, sauna, fitness room, restaurant. This place works for us. It's an 11-floor hotel from 1960 but it has a surprisingly fresh feel. Maintenance here seems to be top **A REAL GEM** notch, and service is very good. All rooms have oval Jacuzzi bathtubs and Bose stereos that are playing

when you check in. You can rent VCRS or DVD players. 1½ long blocks to the beach. Continental breakfast in the lobby is included, and there's an Internet café. A nice, clean refreshing resort that's not overly large and is in one of the relatively quieter regions of Waikiki. Parking is valet only and it's $10 per day. Rooms (225–250 sq. ft.) are $150–$185, club suites (350 sq. ft.) with kitchenettes are $205. 1/1s (550 sq. ft.) are $295. Few people pay the RACK rates here.

Waikiki Parc Hotel
(800) 422–0450 or (808) 921–7272
2233 Helumoa Rd.

297 rooms, pool, fitness room, room service, valet parking, business center, coffee makers on request, Nintendo. A 23-story tower from 1987. The resort doesn't have much of a personality.

See all Web reviews at: www.wizardpub.com

There are no grounds, furnishings are modern, it's clean and comfortable, and rooms are well-appointed. Since it's a sister property to Halekulani, you'll have signing privileges over there. Some of the lanais are standing room only, but the 8th floor rooms have giant lanais. Their "parc rooms" must be a variant of *park*, because they face the *park*ing garage. Bump up to a "mountain view" if you care at all. And deluxe ocean view means they're up high enough to peek over the Halekulani. There are no permanent non-smoking rooms. Room safes are a pricey $3.95. The fitness room overlooks the pool, so you'll be an inspiration to every lazy couch potato lounging around in the pool cabana chairs. A few minutes' walk to the beach. Rooms (327 sq. ft.) are $225–$320. That's overpriced, but easily obtained packages bring the prices way down.

Waikiki Prince Hotel
(808) 922-1544
2431 Prince Edward St.

Waikiki Prince Hotel

30 rooms, microwave. You're just looking for a place to stay. You want cheap-cheap but you don't want a dump. Here's your hotel. **SOLID GOLD VALUE** It's simple, clean and no frills. For coffee they have percolators (we didn't know they still *made* those). There are no room safes and no phones, but you can use the phone in the lobby for free local calls, and they'll take messages for you. Maid service is only every 4–5 days. Parking is $5. (Let them know

when you reserve that you'll have a car because parking's limited.) But it's only a block to the beach. Sleep here and play elsewhere. Rooms (100–300 sq. ft.) are $40–$65. Can't beat that.

Waikiki Resort Hotel
(800) 367-5116 or (808) 922-4911
130 Liliuokalani Ave.

291 rooms, pool, Nintendo, 3 shops, 5 conference rooms, 2 restaurants, 24-hour business center, room service. A 19-story **SOLID GOLD VALUE** tower from 1970. Units are fairly roomy compared to their competition and come with a simple, modern decor. There's a lot of aloha with the staff since so many have been with the resort for so long. Connecting rooms are available—not a common Waikiki trait. Price includes full breakfast for two. (And as a nice touch, if you don't use the breakfast coupons, you can accumulate them to use toward lunch or dinner.) Parking is $6. Rooms (315–384 sq. ft.) are $129–$169, suites are $360–$480. We gave them a SOLID GOLD VALUE because they have so many specials— including good Internet rates—and few people ever pay the RACK rate listed above, and it's only a couple minutes walk to Kuhio Beach Park.

Waikiki Sand Villa
(800) 247-1903 or (808) 922-4744
2375 Ala Wai Blvd.
WEB REVIEW

Waikiki Shore
(800) 367–2353 or (808) 952–4500
(800) 688–7444 or (808) 971–4500
2161 Kalia Rd.

168 rooms. A 1960s 15-story skinny building with one end touching Waikiki Beach. Nearly all units face Ft. DeRussy Park, which is good because their back is right next to the Outrigger Reef on the Beach. The higher up the better. The first set of numbers is **Castle**; the second set of numbers is for **Outrigger Resorts**, which also manage many of the rooms here. This effects things like parking ($10 to self-park through Castle; $13 to valet though Outrigger), coffee and room safes (free with Castle; extra through Outrigger), etc. All rooms have kitchens or kitchenettes, as well as washer/dryers. Castle has no pool; Outrigger lets you use their frantic pool next door. The condo units themselves are pretty nice—clean, bright and reasonably appointed. They're also roomy. Studios (400 sq. ft.) are $225–$245, 1/1s (800 sq. ft.) are $245–$350, 2/1s (1,125 sq. ft.) are $425–$460, 2/2s (1,450 sq. ft.) are $515–$650. The rooms seem pricey to us, and discounts are hard to get because the rates are set by the condo owners themselves.

Waikiki Sunset (Aston)
(800) 922–7688 or (808) 922–0511
229 Paoakalani Ave.

435 rooms, tennis court, pool, sauna, BBQs. A 38-story 1979 building. One of the nicer Astons and the rooms are comfortably sized. Staff is good and services are reasonably high. It's also a nice touch that the windows next to the beds are floor to ceiling, making maximum use of whatever view the room has. End units facing Diamond Head have great views, even on relatively low floors. (But 25 and higher are still preferred.) It's not A REAL GEM or a SOLID GOLD VALUE, but it's got some nice components of both. It's 2 blocks to the beach in a *relatively* quiet part of Waikiki. 1/1s (615 sq. ft.) are $190–$275. 2/1s (660 sq. ft.) are $355–$445.

JUST OUTSIDE OF WAIKIKI

Kahala Mandarin Oriental Hawai'i
(800) 367–2525 or (808) 739–8888
5000 Kahala Ave.
364 rooms, pool, spa, fitness room, 24-hour room service, 5 restaurants, valet parking, 9 shops, 2 conference rooms, business center, coffee makers (with free

See all Web reviews at: www.wizardpub.com

Diamond Head Tower Koko Head Tower Dolphin Lagoon Terrace

A REAL GEM

coffee), mini-bar may be emptied upon request, free room safes, *no* laundry facilities, lanais on half, child care service, hi-speed Internet access in rooms. A 10-story building plus low-rise units. Typically ranked among the world's best hotels, it's a close call as to which is the top resort on O'ahu—the Halekulani or the Kahala Mandarin. In some ways they're not comparable. First of all, the Kahala Mandarin isn't in Waikiki; it's about 15 minutes outside on ultra-protected Kahala Beach. And in the ambiance department this resort goes in a slightly different direction. The Kahala exudes a relaxed, old world luxurious feel—afternoon tea in the open-air veranda, mature gardens and grounds and clean, well-tended surroundings.

The Mandarin isn't stodgy, however. Instead of a pond filled with koi fish, theirs has dolphins and turtles cruising the waters. (See Dolphin Quest on page 219.) Some of the rooms are directly over the pond, allowing you to watch these mammals from your lanai. Others, in a low-rise building, are beachfront. Like the Halekulani, your actions are tracked so your needs might be more easily anticipated. If you order a certain wine at the restaurant, they'll remember the next night. Don't like onions? Expect all the restaurants to be aware of this dietary preference.

The rooms are spacious and nicely appointed, and the bathrooms are large with separate tubs and showers. Some rooms have pull-down Murphy beds to maximize the already-ample space. Suites are simply two somewhat different rooms connected.

All the usual beach activities are available at their often bathtub-calm beach, which won't have near the level of energy that Waikiki does.

Their spa is different than most of the others on the island—5 individual rooms create a luxury and privacy that is hard to find at other spas.

Weddings are big here; they average 3 per day and have a separate catering department dedicated to them.

If we had a ding, it's that they can be super generous with their view designations. For instance, room 912 is called "partial ocean view," but you'll see more water in your bathtub than you will out the window there.

But overall, the Kahala Mandarin conveys a dreamy tropical isolation while being a short drive to the action of Waikiki. If this is what you're looking for and you have the budget to afford it, look no further. Rooms (550 sq. ft.) are $295–$700, suites (900 sq. ft.) are $575–$4,325.

AWAY FROM WAIKIKI

Your choices of resorts is slim outside of Waikiki.

NORTH SHORE

Turtle Bay Resort
(800) 203–3650 or (808) 293–6000
57-091 Kamehameha Hwy., Kahuku

Password for all Web reviews is: **or8329**

East Cabanas 151-194
South Wing
West Cabanas 100-142
East Wing West Wing

485 rooms, 2 pools, keiki pool, 2 spas, 10 tennis courts (some lighted), fitness room, 2 golf courses, 2 restaurants, conference rooms, resort-wide Wi-Fi, valet parking, room service, health spa, child care service (during summer). This resort, built in 1972 and formerly called the **Turtle Bay Hilton**, was getting pretty long in the tooth when it was sold in the early 2000s. Its reputation had slipped, and words like "shabby" and "worn" were synonymous with it. Since then, the owners have slowly but steadily been putting money into the aging infrastructure. In other circumstances, they might have simply leveled the buildings and rebuilt them. But Hawai'is current laws would never again let them build so close to the ocean. The result is a reborn gem—albeit one with flaws. Out on a point, nearly all of its rooms have grand ocean views. And if you can swing the cost, the 43 cottages—especially the oceanfront ones—are as dreamy as any place you'll stay in Hawai'i. Some cottages have a king bed and a wet bar; others have 2 queens and no bar.

A REAL GEM

The thing that makes Turtle Bay so great is also what hurts it. It's near the northernmost tip of the island—far, far away from Waikiki. Your dining choices are limited to the on-site restaurant (which is *not* a winner), the golf course restaurant (a bit better), or you'll drive into Hale'iwa, 20 minutes away. Your night life will be almost non-existent. But that's also the charm here. Its beaches (nearby Kuilima Cove and Kawela Bay—a walk but worth it) are wonderful, the grounds are pretty, there are 2 golf courses that are never crowded on weekdays, and the pace is relaxing. This is the only place on O'ahu where you can see sunrise over the water (at least from April to September) and sunset from the same location. Because they're far from Waikiki, they have other activities (for extra) like horseback riding along the shoreline and helicopter flights from their helipad.

There's a mandatory $12 a day resort fee that will get you free local calls, newspaper, room safes, daily coffee, etc. Rooms are furnished a bit spartanly, but they're comfortable. Rates are expensive. $295–$400. Cottages are $550–$700. Suites are $500–$2,600.

KO OLINA

Out near Barbers Point at the southwestern corner of the island is the next up-and-coming resort area (if the developers are successful in drawing people out there).

JW Marriott Ihilani Resort & Spa at Ko Olina
(800) 626–4446 or (808) 679–0079
92-1001 Olani St., Kapolei
387 rooms, 6 lighted tennis courts, 3 restaurants, pool and spa, valet parking, room service, child care service, lu'au. If you're looking to stay outside of Waikiki and want luxury, this is the place. Not because of the rooms, which are

See all Web reviews at: www.wizardpub.com

nicely sized but not sumptuous, except for the well-appointed bathrooms. It's the surroundings which make it a winner. The resort oozes that laid-back, tropical feel. They are next to one of the manmade Ko Olina lagoons, and views overlooking it (the higher the better) are utterly fantastic and worth the upgrade if you can swing it. (Ocean view rooms facing north are nice but not nearly as droolable.) They have live music and a hula show at the pool every night (except Sunday or when it's raining), and it's wonderful to listen to the music drifting up to the lagoon-facing rooms. There's a meandering pond with hammerhead sharks cruising around—a nice touch—and a reef and ray adventure for kids where they get in the pond and touch the rays.

A REAL GEM

There are a few annoyances beyond the priciness. For instance, there are no ice machines. If you want ice, you call, and they'll bring it. Most people feel obligated to tip for everything, but that's an instance where you shouldn't think of yourself as cheap if you're unwilling to tip for something that you should be able to get for yourself. And it's $10 per

day to park, valet or not. (So naturally you'll tend toward using the valet and feel the same obligation to tip—and this time you should, or you may be taught a lesson by the valets.) And perhaps the ultimate example of nickel and diming is that they have mini-bars with the usual confiscatorily priced Snickers bars and sodas. If you want to use the mini-bar for your own stuff they charge you $25 to empty it or $40 to bring you an empty one. (You should at least get to keep all those goodies for that price.) Also there are no coffee makers or laundry facilities.

But overall, the resort sparkles because of its location. Rooms (640–680 sq. ft.) are $354–$549. Suites are $800–$4,500.

WAI'ANAE

Way out in Makaha near the western tip of the island there are several resorts that are rarely spoken of and largely forgotten. Makaha is light years from Waikiki, both in distance and tone. It's not a resort area; it's where many of Waikiki's workers live. You won't have tons of restaurants and activities, but you *will* have world-class sunsets and world-class beaches. See page 104 to see if this area is for you.

Hawaiian Princess
(808) 696-5892
84-1021 Lahilahi St.

120 rooms, pool, spa, tennis court, washer/dryers in the unit. A 16-story tower from 1980. First of all, it's not just a GEM, it's also a SOLID GOLD VALUE. This has the kind of beachfront location that people

A REAL GEM

Password for all Web reviews is: **or8329**

dream of. It's built right on top of Papaoneone Beach, a very picturesque and surprisingly lightly used, half-mile-long beach in Makaha. Views from all of the rooms are glorious. Some of the units here are owner-occupied, some are timeshares, but most are vacation rentals. The 1/1 units aren't spacious, but they're big enough with the living area adjacent to the lanais. (Some owners have expanded their units to include the lanais *inside*.) Corner units are 1/2s and have even better views, if that's possible. The pool is filled with saltwater. Parking and local calls are free. No room safes. Though air conditioned, it's done with a heat pump, which doesn't provide the frosty air that a regular a/c does. Some units are rented by the owners (you'll have to search the Web), and others use rental agents. The best one, listed on top, has a 7 night minimum. 1/1 (665 sq. ft.) rates through them are $105. 1/2s are $128.

Makaha Beach Cabanas
(808) 696–5892
84-965 Farrington Hwy.
162 rooms. These two 9-story buildings next door to the Hawaiian Princess

SOLID GOLD VALUE

aren't as large or well-appointed, but they're a steal, if you don't mind

renting *by the month*. The location is right on Papaoneone Beach, and the sand is straight down below your lanai. Rooms are as varied as their individual owners. Pretty small but pleasant, if their owner cares enough. The bedroom is on the ocean side; living area away from it. Many units are owner-occupied, and others are available only from the owners. The phone number above is a good rental agent with some vacation rentals available. No a/c or room safes. Parking and local calls are free. 1/1s (456 sq. ft.) are $36–$42 ($1,100–$1,250 per month). No, it ain't the Ritz, but you're living a beach-front dream for under $50 a day. Hard to beat that.

Makaha Valley Towers
(808) 696–5892
84-740 Kili Dr.
WEB REVIEW

WINDWARD SIDE

La'ie Inn
(800) 526–4562 or (808) 293–9282
55-109 Laniloa St.
WEB REVIEW

Dining Index on page 222, Where to Stay Index on page 260.

INDEX

Dining Index on page 222, Where to Stay Index on page 260.

Dining Index on page 222, Where to Stay Index on page 260.

Dining Index on page 222, Where to Stay Index on page 260.

Dining Index on page 222, Where to Stay Index on page 260.

INDEX

Dining Index on page 222, Where to Stay Index on page 260.

INDEX

Dining Index on page 222, Where to Stay Index on page 260.

Surf season 83
Surfboard fin 90
Surfing 209
Surfing houses 90
Surfing season 90
Swanzy Beach Park 144
Swimming with Dolphins 219
Swimming with Sharks 213

Tantalus Road **56,** *58*
Taxi 23
Ted's Bakery **83**
The Bus **26**
The Ponds 53
Theft 125
Three Tables 154
Thrifty **23**
Tipping 163
Tommy's Tours **64**
Twogood Kayaks **194**
Tracks 132
Trade winds 27
Tradewinds **23**
Traffic pattern 25
Train ride tour 97
Travel agent 21
Travel packages 21
Traveler's checks 43
Trike 169
Tuff 62
Tunnels 99
Turtle Bay 83, 150, 166, 189
Turtle Beach *87*, 90, 131, 156

Ulehawa Beach Park **132**
Ultralights 66, 140
Ulu-pa'u Head 75
Ulupo Heiau 72
Unnamed Beach *131*, 133
USS Arizona Memorial 103, 117
USS Bowfin Submarine *118*, 120
USS Missouri Battleship *109*, 117, 119

Valley of the Temples **75**
Vancouver, George 88
VIP 23
Volcanoes 28, 62

Wa'ahili Ridge **217**
Wahiawa 98
Wahiawa Gardens 98, 122
Wai'alae Beach Park 139
Waiale'e Beach Park 152
Wai'anae 29, 104
Wai'anae Beaches 127
Waikele Premium Outlet **43**
Waikiki 28, 45
Waikiki Aquarium 34, 111
Waikiki Beach 47
Waikiki Beach Center **53**
Waikiki Diving Center **202**
Waikiki exits 44
Waikiki Shell 55
Waikiki Trolley **26**
Wailupe Beach Park 139
Waimanalo 67
Waimanalo Bay Recreation Area 67, 141
Waimanalo Beach Park 67, 141
Waimea Bay 88
Waimea Beach Park 155
Waimea Falls Park 88
**Waimea Valley Audubon
      Center** *42*, 88, 120, *121*
Wal-Mart/Sam's Club **33, 162**
Washington Place 112
Wasps 31
Water ski 210
Waterproof fanny pack 125
Waves 101 208
Weather 27, 73
Web site for Wizard Publications 40
Wedding 26
Wellington 31
Whale watching 211
What to bring 22
Wild Bunch **163**
Wild Side Specialty Tours **197**
Windsurfing 211
Windward 123
Windward Beaches 140
Windward side 28

X-treme Parasail **199**

YO-257 ....**200**
Yokohama Bay 108, 127

Discover Hawaii's Hidden Gems

Here...

here...

and here.

Look for all our titles at your favorite bookstore.
Please visit us online for recent updates, links to cool sites, local events,
aerial photos, the latest weather and much more:

www.wizardpub.com
E-mail: aloha@wizardpub.com

WIZARD PUBLICATIONS, INC.
Believable Guides for Unbelievable Vacations™